THE PELICAN FREUD LIBRARY

Advisory Editor: Albert Dickson

VOLUME 13

THE ORIGINS OF RELIGION:

TOTEM AND TABOO,
MOSES AND MONOTHEISM
AND OTHER WORKS

Sigmund Freud

Sigmund Freud was born in 1856 in Moravia; between the ages of four and eighty-two his home was in Vienna; in 1938 Hitler's invasion of Austria forced him to seek asylum in London, where he died in the following year. His career began with several years of brilliant work on the anatomy and physiology of the nervous system. He was almost thirty when, after a period of study under Charcot in Paris, his interests first turned to psychology, and another ten years of clinical work in Vienna (at first in collaboration with Breuer, an older colleague) saw the birth of his creation, psychoanalysis. This began simply as a method of treating neurotic patients by investigating their minds, but it quickly grew into an accumulation of knowledge about the workings of the mind in general, whether sick or healthy. Freud was thus able to demonstrate the normal development of the sexual instinct in childhood and, largely on the basis of an examination of dreams, arrived at his fundamental discovery of the unconscious forces that influence our everyday thoughts and actions. Freud's life was uneventful, but his ideas have shaped not only many specialist disciplines, but the whole intellectual climate of the last half-century.

THE PELICAN FREUD LIBRARY

VOLUME 13

•

THE ORIGINS OF RELIGION:

TOTEM AND TABOO, MOSES AND MONOTHEISM AND OTHER WORKS

Sigmund Freud

•

*Translated from the German
under the general editorship of James Strachey*

*The present volume
edited by Albert Dickson*

PENGUIN BOOKS

Penguin Books Ltd, Harmondsworth, Middlesex, England
Viking Penguin Inc., 40 West 23rd Street, New York, New York 10010, U.S.A.
Penguin Books Australia Ltd, Ringwood, Victoria, Australia
'enguin Books Canada Limited, 2801 John Street, Markham, Ontario, Canada L3R 1B4
Penguin Books (N.Z.) Ltd, 182–190 Wairau Road, Auckland 10, New Zealand

The Origins of Religion:
Totem and Taboo,
Moses and Monotheism
and other works

Present English translations first published in *The Standard Edition of the Complete
Psychological Works of Sigmund Freud* by the Hogarth Press and the Institute of
Psycho-Analysis, London, as follows:

'Obsessive Actions and Religious Practices', Volume IX (1959); *Totem and
Taboo*, Volume XIII (1955); 'The Acquisition and Control of Fire', Volume
XXII (1964); *Moses and Monotheism*, Volume XXIII (1964).

'Sigmund Freud: A Sketch of his Life and Ideas' first published in *Two Short
Accounts of Psycho-Analysis* in Pelican Books 1962

This collection, *The Origins of Religion*, first published in Pelican Books 1985
Reprinted 1986

Translation and Editorial Matter copyright © The Estate of Angela
Richards and The Institute of Psycho-Analysis, 1953, 1959, 1962, 1964

Additional Editorial Matter copyright © The Estate of Angela Richards, 1985
All rights reserved

Made and printed in Great Britain by
Richard Clay (The Chaucer Press) Ltd,
Bungay, Suffolk
Filmset in Monophoto Bembo by
Northumberland Press Ltd, Gateshead

CONTENTS

VOLUME 13
THE ORIGINS OF RELIGION

CONTENTS

INTRODUCTION TO THE PELICAN
FREUD LIBRARY

The Pelican Freud Library is intended to meet the needs of the general reader by providing all Freud's major writings in translation together with an appropriate linking commentary. It is the first time that such an edition has been produced in paperback in the English language. It does not supplant *The Standard Edition of the Complete Psychological Works of Sigmund Freud*, translated from the German under the general editorship of James Strachey in collaboration with Anna Freud, assisted by Alix Strachey and Alan Tyson, editorial assistant Angela Richards (Hogarth Press, 24 volumes, 1953–74). The *Standard Edition* remains the fullest and most authoritative collection published in any language. It does, however, provide a large enough selection to meet the requirements of all but the most specialist reader – in particular it aims to cater for students of sociology, anthropology, criminology, medicine, aesthetics and education, all of them fields in which Freud's ideas have established their relevance.

The texts are reprinted unabridged, with corrections, from the *Standard Edition*. The editorial commentary – introductions, footnotes, internal cross-references, bibliographies and indexes – is also based upon the *Standard Edition*, but it has been abridged and where necessary adapted to suit the less specialized scope and purposes of the *Pelican Freud Library*. Some corrections have been made and some new material added.

Selection of Material

This is not a complete edition of Freud's psychological works – still less of his works as a whole, which included important contributions to neurology and neuropathology dating from the early part of his professional life. Of the psychological writings, virtually all the major works have been included. The arrangement is by subject-matter, so that the main contributions to any particular theme will be found in one volume. Within each volume the works are, for the main part, in chronological sequence. The aim has been to cover the whole field of Freud's observations and his theory of psychoanalysis: that is to say, in the first place, the structure and dynamics of human mental activity; secondly, psychopathology and the mechanism of mental disorder; and thirdly, the application of psychoanalytic theory to wider spheres than the disorders of individuals which Freud originally, and indeed for the greater part of his life, investigated – to the psychology of groups, to social institutions and to religion, art and literature.

In his 'Sigmund Freud: A Sketch of his Life and Ideas' (p. 11 ff. below), James Strachey includes an account of Freud's discoveries as well as defining his principal theories and tracing their development.

Writings excluded from the Edition

The works that have been excluded are: (1) The neurological writings and most of those very early works from the period before the idea of psychoanalysis had taken form. (2) Writings on the actual technique of treatment. These were written specifically for practitioners of psychoanalysis and for analysts in training and their interest is correspondingly specialized. Freud never in fact produced a complete text on psychoanalytic treatment and the papers on technique only deal with selected points of difficulty or theoretical interest. (3) Writings which cover the same ground as other major works which have been included; for example, since the *Library* includes the *Introductory Lectures on Psychoanalysis* and the *New Lectures*, it was decided to leave out several of the shorter expository works in which Freud surveys the whole subject. Similarly, because the *Interpretation of Dreams* is included, the shorter writings on this topic have been omitted. (4) Freud's private correspondence, much of which has now been published in translation.[1] This is not to imply that such letters are without interest or importance though they have not yet received full critical treatment. (5) The numerous short writings such as reviews of books, prefaces to other authors' works, obituary notices and little *pièces d'occasion* – all of which lose interest to a large extent when separated from the books or occasions to which they refer and which would often demand long editorial explanations to make them comprehensible.

All of these excluded writings (with the exception of the works on neurology and the private letters) can be found in the *Standard Edition*.

Editorial Commentary

The bibliographical information, included at the beginning of the Editor's Note or Introduction to each work, gives the title of the German (or other) original, the date and place of its first publication and the position, where applicable, of the work in Freud's *Gesammelte Werke*, the most complete edition at present available of the works in German (published by S. Fischer Verlag, Frankfurt am Main). Details of the first translation of each work into English are also included, together with the *Standard Edition* reference. Other editions are listed only if they contain significant changes. (Full details of all German editions published in Freud's lifetime and of all English editions prior to the *Standard Edition* are included in the *Standard Edition*.)

The date of original publication of each work has been added to the half-title page, with the date of composition included in square brackets wherever it is different from the former date.

Further background information is given in introductory notes and in footnotes to the text. Apart from dealing with the time and circumstances of composition, these notes aim to make it possible to follow the inception and development of

1. [See the list, p. 23 *n*. below, and the details in the Bibliography, p. 387 ff.]

important psychoanalytic concepts by means of systematic cross-references. Most of these references are to other works included in the *Pelican Freud Library*. A secondary purpose is to date additions and alterations made by Freud in successive revisions of the text and in certain cases to provide the earlier versions. No attempt has been made to do this as comprehensively as in the *Standard Edition*, but variants are given whenever they indicate a definite change of view. Square brackets are used throughout to distinguish editorial additions from Freud's text and his own footnotes.

It will be clear from this account that an overwhelming debt is due to the late James Strachey, the general editor and chief translator of the *Standard Edition*. He indeed was mainly responsible for the idea of a *Pelican Freud Library*, and for the original plan of contents. Miss Anna Freud and Mrs Alix Strachey, both now deceased, gave advice of the greatest value. The late Mr Ernst Freud and the Publications Committee of the Institute of Psycho-Analysis also helped in the preparations for this edition.

SIGMUND FREUD

A SKETCH OF HIS LIFE AND IDEAS

SIGMUND FREUD was born on 6 May 1856 in Freiberg, a small town in Moravia, which was at that time a part of Austria-Hungary. In an external sense the eighty-three years of his life were on the whole uneventful and call for no lengthy history.

He came of a middle-class Jewish family and was the eldest child of his father's second wife. His position in the family was a little unusual, for there were already two grown-up sons by his father's first wife. These were more than twenty years older than he was and one of them was already married, with a little boy; so that Freud was in fact born an uncle. This nephew played at least as important a part in his very earliest years as his own younger brothers and sisters, of whom seven were born after him.

His father was a wool-merchant and soon after Freud's birth found himself in increasing commercial difficulties. He therefore decided, when Freud was just three years old, to leave Freiberg, and a year later the whole family settled in Vienna, with the exception of the two elder half-brothers and their children, who established themselves instead in Manchester. At more than one stage in his life Freud played with the idea of joining them in England, but nothing was to come of this for nearly eighty years.

In Vienna during the whole of Freud's childhood the family lived in the most straitened conditions; but it is much to his father's credit that he gave invariable priority to the charge of Freud's education, for the boy was obviously intelligent and was a hard worker as well. The result was that he won a place in the 'Gymnasium' at the early age of nine, and for the last six of the eight years he spent at the school he was regularly top of his class. When at the age of seventeen he passed out of school his career was still undecided; his education so far had been of the most general kind, and, though he seemed in any case destined for the University, several faculties lay open to him.

Freud insisted more than once that at no time in his life did he feel 'any particular predilection for the career of a doctor. I was moved, rather,' he says, 'by a sort of curiosity, which was, however, directed more towards human concerns than towards natural objects.'[1] Elsewhere he writes: 'I have no knowledge of having had any craving in my early childhood to help suffering humanity ... In my youth I felt an overpowering need to understand something of the riddles of the world in which we live and perhaps even to contribute something to their solution.'[2] And in yet another passage in which he was discussing the sociological studies of his last years: 'My interest, after making a lifelong *détour* through the natural sciences, medicine, and psychotherapy, returned to the cultural problems which had fascinated me long before, when I was a youth scarcely old enough for thinking.'[3]

What immediately determined Freud's choice of a scientific career was, so he tells us, being present just when he was leaving school at a public reading of an extremely flowery essay on 'Nature', attributed (wrongly, it seems) to Goethe. But if it was to be science, practical considerations narrowed the choice to medicine. And it was as a medical student that Freud enrolled himself at the University in the autumn of 1873 at the age of seventeen. Even so, however, he was in no hurry to obtain a medical degree. For his first year or two he attended lectures on a variety of subjects, but gradually concentrated first on biology and then on physiology. His very first piece of research was in his third year at the University, when he was deputed by the Professor of Comparative Anatomy to investigate a detail in the anatomy of the eel, which involved the dissection of some four hundred specimens. Soon afterwards he entered the Physio-

1. [*An Autobiographical Study* (1925*d*), near the opening of the work.]
2. ['Postscript to *The Question of Lay Analysis*' (1927*a*).]
3. ['Postscript (1935) to *An Autobiographical Study*' (1935*a*).]

logical Laboratory under Brücke, and worked there happily for six years. It was no doubt from him that he acquired the main outlines of his attitude to physical science in general. During these years Freud worked chiefly on the anatomy of the central nervous system and was already beginning to produce publications. But it was becoming obvious that no livelihood which would be sufficient to meet the needs of the large family at home was to be picked up from these laboratory studies. So at last, in 1881, he decided to take his medical degree, and a year later, most unwillingly, gave up his position under Brücke and began work in the Vienna General Hospital.

What finally determined this change in his life was something more urgent than family considerations: in June 1882 he became engaged to be married, and thenceforward all his efforts were directed towards making marriage possible. His fiancée, Martha Bernays, came of a well-known Jewish family in Hamburg, and though for the moment she was living in Vienna she was very soon obliged to return to her remote North-German home. During the four years that followed, it was only for brief visits that he could have glimpses of her, and the two lovers had to content themselves with an almost daily interchange of letters. Freud now set himself to establishing a position and a reputation in the medical world. He worked in various departments of the hospital, but soon came to concentrate on neuroanatomy and neuropathology. During this period, too, he published the first inquiry into the possible medical uses of cocaine; and it was this that suggested to Koller the drug's employment as a local anaesthetic. He soon formed two immediate plans: one of these was to obtain an appointment as *Privatdozent*, a post not unlike that of a university lecturer in England, the other was to gain a travelling bursary which would enable him to spend some time in Paris, where the reigning figure was the great Charcot. Both of these aims, if they were realized, would, he felt, bring him real advantages, and in 1885, after a hard struggle, he achieved them both.

The months which Freud spent under Charcot at the Salpêtrière (the famous Paris hospital for nervous diseases) brought another change in the course of his life and this time a revolutionary one. So far his work had been concerned entirely with physical science and he was still carrying out histological studies on the brain while he was in Paris. Charcot's interests were at that period concentrated mainly on hysteria and hypnotism. In the world from which Freud came these subjects were regarded as barely respectable, but he became absorbed in them, and, though Charcot himself looked at them purely as branches of neuropathology, for Freud they meant the first beginnings of the investigation of the mind.

On his return to Vienna in the spring of 1886 Freud set up in private practice as a consultant in nervous diseases, and his long-delayed marriage followed soon afterwards. He did not, however, at once abandon all his neuropathological work: for several more years he studied in particular the cerebral palsies of children, on which he became a leading authority. At this period, too, he produced an important monograph on aphasia. But he was becoming more and more engaged in the treatment of the neuroses. After experimenting in vain with electro-therapy, he turned to hypnotic suggestion, and in 1888 visited Nancy to learn the technique used with such apparent success there by Liébeault and Bernheim. This still proved unsatisfactory and he was driven to yet another line of approach. He knew that a friend of his, Dr Josef Breuer, a Vienna consultant considerably his senior, had some ten years earlier cured a girl suffering from hysteria by a quite new procedure. He now persuaded Breuer to take up the method once more, and he himself applied it to several fresh cases with promising results. The method was based on the assumption that hysteria was the product of a psychical trauma which had been forgotten by the patient; and the treatment consisted in inducing her in a hypnotic state to recall the forgotten trauma to the accompaniment of appropriate emotions. Before very long Freud began to make changes both in the procedure and in the underlying theory; this led eventually to a breach with Breuer, and to the ultimate development by Freud of the whole system of ideas to which he soon gave the name of psychoanalysis.

From this moment onwards – from 1895, perhaps – to the very end of his life, the whole of Freud's intellectual existence revolved around this development, its far-reaching implications, and its theoretical and practical repercussions. It would, of course, be impossible to give in a few sentences any consecutive account of Freud's discoveries and ideas, but an attempt will be made presently to indicate in a disconnected fashion some of the main changes he has brought about in our habits of thought. Meanwhile we may continue to follow the course of his external life.

His domestic existence in Vienna was essentially devoid of episode: his home and his consulting rooms were in the same house from 1891 till his departure for London forty-seven years later. His happy marriage and his growing family – three sons and three daughters – provided a solid counterweight to the difficulties which, to begin with at least, surrounded his professional career. It was not only the nature of his discoveries that created prejudice against him in medical circles; just as great, perhaps, was the effect of the intense anti-semitic feeling which dominated the official world of Vienna: his appointment to a university professorship was constantly held back by political influence.

One particular feature of these early years calls for mention on account of its consequences. This was Freud's friendship with Wilhelm Fliess, a brilliant but unbalanced Berlin physician, who specialized in the ear and throat, but whose wider interests extended over human biology and the effects of periodic phenomena in vital processes. For fifteen years, from 1887 to 1902, Freud corresponded with him regularly, reported the development of his ideas, forwarded him long drafts outlining his future writings, and, most important of all, sent him an essay of some forty thousand words which has been given the name of a 'Project for a Scientific Psychology'. This essay was composed in 1895, at what might be described as the watershed of Freud's career, when he was reluctantly moving from physiology to psychology; it is an attempt to state the facts of psychology in purely neurological terms. This paper and all the rest of Freud's communications to Fliess have, by a lucky chance, survived: they throw a fascinating light on the development of Freud's ideas and show how much of the later findings of psychoanalysis were already present in his mind at this early stage.

Apart from his relations with Fliess, Freud had little outside support to begin with. He gradually gathered a few pupils round him in Vienna, but it was only after some ten years, in about 1906, that a change was inaugurated by the adhesion of a number of Swiss psychiatrists to his views. Chief among these were Bleuler, the head of the Zurich mental hospital, and his assistant Jung. This proved to be the beginning of the first spread of psychoanalysis. An international meeting of psychoanalysts gathered at Salzburg in 1908, and in 1909 Freud and Jung were invited to give a number of lectures in the United States. Freud's writings began to be translated into many languages, and groups of practising analysts sprang up all over the world. But the progress of psychoanalysis was not without its set-backs: the currents which its subject-matter stirred up in the mind ran too deep for its easy acceptance. In 1911 one of Freud's prominent Viennese supporters, Alfred Adler, broke away from him, and two or three years later Jung's differences from Freud led to their separation. Almost immediately after this came the First World War and an interruption of the international spread of psychoanalysis. Soon afterwards, too, came the gravest personal tragedies – the death of a daughter and of a favourite grandchild, and the onset of the malignant illness which was to pursue him relentlessly for the last sixteen years of his life. None of these troubles, however, brought any interruption to the development of Freud's observations and inferences. The structure of his ideas continued to expand and to find ever wider applications – particularly in the sociological field. By now he had become generally recognized as a figure of world celebrity, and no honour pleased him more than his election in 1936, the year of his eightieth birthday, as a Corresponding Member of the Royal Society. It was no doubt this fame, supported by the efforts of influential admirers, including, it is said, President

Roosevelt, that protected him from the worst excesses of the National Socialists when Hitler invaded Austria in 1938, though they seized and destroyed his publications. Freud's departure from Vienna was nevertheless essential, and in June of that year, accompanied by some of his family, he made the journey to London, and it was there, a year later, on 23 September 1939, that he died.

It has become a journalistic cliché to speak of Freud as one of the revolutionary founders of modern thought and to couple his name with that of Einstein. Most people would however find it almost as hard to summarize the changes introduced by the one as by the other.

Freud's discoveries may be grouped under three headings – an instrument of research, the findings produced by the instrument, and the theoretical hypotheses inferred from the findings – though the three groups were of course mutually interrelated. Behind all of Freud's work, however, we should posit his belief in the universal validity of the law of determinism. As regards physical phenomena this belief was perhaps derived from his experience in Brücke's laboratory and so, ultimately, from the school of Helmholtz; but Freud extended the belief uncompromisingly to the field of mental phenomena, and here he may have been influenced by his teacher, the psychiatrist Meynert, and indirectly by the philosophy of Herbart.

First and foremost, Freud was the discoverer of the first instrument for the scientific examination of the human mind. Creative writers of genius had had fragmentary insight into mental processes, but no systematic method of investigation existed before Freud. It was only gradually that he perfected the instrument, since it was only gradually that the difficulties in the way of such an investigation became apparent. The forgotten trauma in Breuer's explanation of hysteria provided the earliest problem and perhaps the most fundamental of all, for it showed conclusively that there were active parts of the mind not immediately open to inspection either by an onlooker or by the subject himself. These parts of the mind were described by

Freud, without regard for metaphysical or terminological disputes, as the unconscious. Their existence was equally demonstrated by the fact of post-hypnotic suggestion, where a person in a fully waking state performs an action which had been suggested to him some time earlier, though he had totally forgotten the suggestion itself. No examination of the mind could thus be considered complete unless it included this unconscious part of it in its scope. How was this to be accomplished? The obvious answer seemed to be: by means of hypnotic suggestion; and this was the instrument used by Breuer and, to begin with, by Freud. But it soon turned out to be an imperfect one, acting irregularly and uncertainly and sometimes not at all. Little by little, accordingly, Freud abandoned the use of suggestion and replaced it by an entirely fresh instrument, which was later known as 'free association'. He adopted the unheard-of plan of simply asking the person whose mind he was investigating to say whatever came into his head. This crucial decision led at once to the most startling results; even in this primitive form Freud's instrument produced fresh insight. For, though things went along swimmingly for a while, sooner or later the flow of associations dried up: the subject would not or could not think of anything more to say. There thus came to light the fact of 'resistance', of a force, separate from the subject's conscious will, which was refusing to collaborate with the investigation. Here was one basis for a very fundamental piece of theory, for a hypothesis of the mind as something dynamic, as consisting in a number of mental forces, some conscious and some unconscious, operating now in harmony now in opposition with one another.

Though these phenomena eventually turned out to be of universal occurrence, they were first observed and studied in neurotic patients, and the earlier years of Freud's work were largely concerned with discovering means by which the 'resistance' of these patients could be overcome and what lay behind it could be brought to light. The solution was only made possible by an extraordinary piece of self-observation on Freud's part – what we should now describe as his self-analysis.

We are fortunate in having a contemporary first-hand description of this event in his letters to Fliess which have already been mentioned. This analysis enabled him to discover the nature of the unconscious processes at work in the mind and to understand why there is such a strong resistance to their becoming conscious; it enabled him to devise techniques for overcoming or evading the resistance in his patients; and, most important of all, it enabled him to realize the very great difference between the mode of functioning of these unconscious processes and that of our familiar conscious ones. A word may be said on each of these three points, for in fact they constitute the core of Freud's contributions to our knowledge of the mind.

The unconscious contents of the mind were found to consist wholly in the activity of conative trends – desires or wishes – which derive their energy directly from the primary physical instincts. They function quite regardless of any consideration other than that of obtaining immediate satisfaction, and are thus liable to be out of step with those more conscious elements in the mind which are concerned with adaptation to reality and the avoidance of external dangers. Since, moreover, these primitive trends are to a great extent of a sexual or of a destructive nature, they are bound to come in conflict with the more social and civilized mental forces. Investigations along this path were what led Freud to his discoveries of the long-disguised secrets of the sexual life of children and of the Oedipus complex.

In the second place, his self-analysis led him to an inquiry into the nature of dreams. These turned out to be, like neurotic symptoms, the product of a conflict and a compromise between the primary unconscious impulses and the secondary conscious ones. By analysing them into their elements it was therefore possible to infer their hidden unconscious contents; and, since dreams are common phenomena of almost universal occurrence, their interpretation turned out to be one of the most useful technical contrivances for penetrating the resistances of neurotic patients.

Finally, the painstaking examination of dreams enabled Freud to classify the remarkable differences between what he termed the primary and secondary processes of thought, between events in the unconscious and conscious regions of the mind. In the unconscious, it was found, there is no sort of organization or coordination: each separate impulse seeks satisfaction independently of all the rest; they proceed uninfluenced by one another; contradictions are completely inoperative, and the most opposite impulses flourish side by side. So, too, in the unconscious, associations of ideas proceed along lines without any regard to logic: similarities are treated as identities, negatives are equated with positives. Again, the objects to which the conative trends are attached in the unconscious are extraordinarily changeable – one may be replaced by another along a whole chain of associations that have no rational basis. Freud perceived that the intrusion into conscious thinking of mechanisms that belong properly to the primary process accounts for the oddity not only of dreams but of many other normal and pathological mental events.

It is not much of an exaggeration to say that all the later part of Freud's work lay in an immense extension and elaboration of these early ideas. They were applied to an elucidation of the mechanisms not only of the psychoneuroses and psychoses but also of such normal processes as slips of the tongue, making jokes, artistic creation, political institutions, and religions; they played a part in throwing fresh light on many applied sciences – archaeology, anthropology, criminology, education; they also served to account for the effectiveness of psychoanalytic therapy. Lastly, too, Freud erected on the basis of these elementary observations a theoretical superstructure, what he named a 'metapsychology', of more general concepts. These, however, fascinating as many people will find them, he always insisted were in the nature of provisional hypotheses. Quite late in his life, indeed, influenced by the ambiguity of the term 'unconscious' and its many conflicting uses, he proposed a new structural account of the mind in which the uncoordinated instinctual trends were called the 'id', the organized realistic part the 'ego', and the critical and moralizing function the 'super-ego' – a new account which has certainly made for a clarification of many issues.

This, then, will have given the reader an outline of the external events of Freud's life and some notion of the scope of his discoveries. Is it legitimate to ask for more? to try to penetrate a little further and to inquire what sort of person Freud was? Possibly not. But human curiosity about great men is insatiable, and if it is not gratified with true accounts it will inevitably clutch at mythological ones. In two of Freud's early books (*The Interpretation of Dreams* and *The Psychopathology of Everyday Life*) the presentation of his thesis had forced on him the necessity of bringing up an unusual amount of personal material. Nevertheless, or perhaps for that very reason, he intensely objected to any intrusion into his private life, and he was correspondingly the subject of a wealth of myths. According to the first and most naïve rumours, for instance, he was an abandoned profligate, devoted to the corruption of public morals. Later fantasies have tended in the opposite direction: he has been represented as a harsh moralist, a ruthless disciplinarian, an autocrat, egocentric and unsmiling, and an essentially unhappy man. To anyone who was acquainted with him, even slightly, both these pictures must seem equally preposterous. The second of them was no doubt partly derived from a knowledge of his physical sufferings during his last years; but partly too it may have been due to the unfortunate impression produced by some of his most widespread portraits. He disliked being photographed, at least by professional photographers, and his features on occasion expressed the fact; artists too seem always to have been overwhelmed by the necessity for representing the inventor of psychoanalysis as a ferocious and terrifying figure. Fortunately, however, alternative versions exist of a more amiable and truer kind – snapshots, for instance, taken on a holiday or with his children, such as will be found in his eldest son's memoir of his father (*Glory Reflected*, by Martin Freud [1957]). In many ways, indeed, this delightful and amusing book serves to redress the balance from more official biographies, invaluable as they are, and reveals something of Freud as he was in ordinary life. Some of these portraits show us that in his earlier days he had well-filled features, but in later life, at any rate after the First World War and even before his illness, this was no longer so, and his features, as well as his whole figure (which was of medium height), were chiefly remarkable for the impression they gave of tense energy and alert observation. He was serious but kindly and considerate in his more formal manners, but in other circumstances could be an entertaining talker with a pleasantly ironical sense of humour. It was easy to discover his devoted fondness for his family and to recognize a man who would inspire affection. He had many miscellaneous interests – he was fond of travelling abroad, of country holidays, of mountain walks – and there were other, more engrossing subjects, art, archaeology, literature. Freud was a very well read man in many languages, not only in German. He read English and French fluently, besides having a fair knowledge of Spanish and Italian. It must be remembered, too, that though the later phases of his education were chiefly scientific (it is true that at the University he studied philosophy for a short time) at school he had learnt the classics and never lost his affection for them. We happen to have a letter written by him at the age of seventeen to a school friend.[1] In it he describes his varying success in the different papers of his school-leaving examination: in Latin a passage from Virgil, and in Greek thirty-three lines from, of all things, *Oedipus Rex*.

In short, we might regard Freud as what in England we should consider the best kind of product of a Victorian up-bringing. His tastes in literature and art would obviously differ from ours, his views on ethics, though decidedly liberal, would not belong to the post-Freudian age. But we should see in him a man who lived a life of full emotion and of much suffering without embitterment. Complete honesty and directness were qualities that stood out in him, and so too did his intellectual

1. [Emil Fluss. The letter is included in the volume of Freud's correspondence (1960a).]

readiness to take in and consider any fact, however new or extraordinary, that was presented to him. It was perhaps an inevitable corollary and extension of these qualities, combined with a general benevolence which a surface misanthropy failed to disguise, that led to some features of a surprising kind. In spite of his subtlety of mind he was essentially unsophisticated, and there were sometimes unexpected lapses in his critical faculty – a failure, for instance, to perceive an untrustworthy authority in some subject that was off his own beat such as Egyptology or philology, and, strangest of all in someone whose powers of perception had to be experienced to be believed, an occasional blindness to defects in his acquaintances. But though it may flatter our vanity to declare that Freud was a human being of a kind like our own, that satisfaction can easily be carried too far. There must in fact have been something very extraordinary in the man who was first able to recognize a whole field of mental facts which had hitherto been excluded from normal conscious-ness, the man who first interpreted dreams, who first accepted the facts of infantile sexuality, who first made the distinction between the primary and secondary processes of thinking – the man who first made the unconscious mind real to us.

JAMES STRACHEY

[Those in search of further information will find it in the three-volume biography of Freud by Ernest Jones, an abridged version of which was published in Pelican in 1964 (reissued 1974), in the important volume of Freud's letters edited by his son and daughter-in-law, Ernst and Lucie Freud (1960a), in several further volumes of his correspondence, with Wilhelm Fliess (1950a), Karl Abraham (1965a), C. G. Jung (1974a), Oskar Pfister (1963a), Lou Andreas-Salomé (1966a), Edoardo Weiss (1970a) and Arnold Zweig (1968a), and above all in the many volumes of Freud's own works.]

CHRONOLOGICAL TABLE

This table traces very roughly some of the main turning-points in Freud's intellectual development and opinions. A few of the chief events in his external life are also included in it.

1856. 6 May. Birth at Freiberg in Moravia.

1860. Family settles in Vienna.

1865. Enters Gymnasium (secondary school).

1873. Enters Vienna University as medical student.

1876–82. Works under Brücke at the Institute of Physiology in Vienna.

1877. First publications: papers on anatomy and physiology.

1881. Graduates as Doctor of Medicine.

1882. Engagement to Martha Bernays.

1882–5. Works in Vienna General Hospital, concentrating on cerebral anatomy: numerous publications.

1884–7. Researches into the clinical uses of cocaine.

1885. Appointed *Privatdozent* (University Lecturer) in Neuropathology.

1885 (October)–1886 (February). Studies under Charcot at the Salpêtrière (hospital for nervous diseases) in Paris. Interest first turns to hysteria and hypnosis.

1886. Marriage to Martha Bernays. Sets up private practice in nervous diseases in Vienna.

1886–93. Continues work on neurology, especially on the cerebral palsies of children at the Kassowitz Institute in Vienna, with numerous publications. Gradual shift of interest from neurology to psychopathology.

1887. Birth of eldest child (Mathilde).

1887–1902. Friendship and correspondence with Wilhelm Fliess in Berlin. Freud's letters to him during this period, published posthumously in 1950, throw much light on the development of his views.

1887. Begins the use of hypnotic suggestion in his practice.

c. 1888. Begins to follow Breuer in using hypnosis for cathartic treatment of hysteria. Gradually drops hypnosis and substitutes free association.

1889. Visits Bernheim at Nancy to study his suggestion technique.

1889. Birth of eldest son (Martin).

1891. Monograph on Aphasia.
    Birth of second son (Oliver).

1892. Birth of youngest son (Ernst).

1893. Publication of Breuer and Freud 'Preliminary Communication': exposition of trauma theory of hysteria and of cathartic treatment.
Birth of second daughter (Sophie).

1893–8. Researches and short papers on hysteria, obsessions, and anxiety.

1895. Jointly with Breuer, *Studies on Hysteria*: case histories and description by Freud of his technique, including first account of transference.

1893–6. Gradual divergence of views between Freud and Breuer. Freud introduces concepts of defence and repression and of neurosis being a result of a conflict between the ego and the libido.

1895. *Project for a Scientific Psychology*: included in Freud's letters to Fliess and first published in 1950. An abortive attempt to state psychology in neurological terms; but foreshadows much of Freud's later theories.
Birth of youngest child (Anna).

1896. Introduces the term 'psychoanalysis'.
Death of father (aged eighty).

1897. Freud's self-analysis, leading to the abandonment of the trauma theory and the recognition of infantile sexuality and the Oedipus complex.

1900. *The Interpretation of Dreams*, with final chapter giving first full account of Freud's dynamic view of mental processes, of the unconscious, and of the dominance of the 'pleasure principle'.

1901. *The Psychopathology of Everyday Life.* This, together with the book on dreams, made it plain that Freud's theories applied not only to pathological states but also to normal mental life.

1902. Appointed Professor Extraordinarius.

1905. *Three Essays on the Theory of Sexuality*: tracing for the first time the course of development of the sexual instinct in human beings from infancy to maturity.

c. 1906. Jung becomes an adherent of psychoanalysis.

1908. First international meeting of psychoanalysts (at Salzburg).

1909. Freud and Jung invited to the USA to lecture.
Case history of the first analysis of a child (Little Hans, aged five): confirming inferences previously made from adult analyses, especially as to infantile sexuality and the Oedipus and castration complexes.

c. 1910. First emergence of the theory of 'narcissism'.

1911–15. Papers on the technique of psychoanalysis.

1911. Secession of Adler.
Application of psychoanalytic theories to a psychotic case: the autobiography of Dr Schreber.

1912–13. *Totem and Taboo*: application of psychoanalysis to anthropological material.

1914. Secession of Jung.
'On the History of the Psycho-Analytic Movement'. Includes a polemical section on Adler and Jung.

Writes his last major case history, of the 'Wolf Man' (not published till 1918).

1915. Writes a series of twelve 'metapsychological' papers on basic theoretical questions, of which only five have survived.

1915–17. *Introductory Lectures*: giving an extensive general account of the state of Freud's views up to the time of the First World War.

1919. Application of the theory of narcissism to the war neuroses.

1920. Death of second daughter.

Beyond the Pleasure Principle: the first explicit introduction of the concept of the 'compulsion to repeat' and of the theory of the 'death instinct'.

1921. *Group Psychology*. Beginnings of a systematic analytic study of the ego.

1923. *The Ego and the Id*. Largely revised account of the structure and functioning of the mind with the division into an id, an ego, and a super-ego.

1923. First onset of cancer.

1925. Revised views on the sexual development of women.

1926. *Inhibitions, Symptoms, and Anxiety*. Revised views on the problem of anxiety.

1927. *The Future of an Illusion*. A discussion of religion: the first of a number of sociological works to which Freud devoted most of his remaining years.

1930. *Civilization and its Discontents*. This includes Freud's first extensive study of the destructive instinct (regarded as a manifestation of the 'death instinct').

Freud awarded the Goethe Prize by the City of Frankfurt.

Death of mother (aged ninety-five).

1933. Hitler seizes power in Germany: Freud's books publicly burned in Berlin.

1934–8. *Moses and Monotheism*: the last of Freud's works to appear during his lifetime.

1936. Eightieth birthday. Election as Corresponding Member of Royal Society.

1938. Hitler's invasion of Austria. Freud leaves Vienna for London. *An Outline of Psycho-Analysis*. A final, unfinished, but profound exposition of psychoanalysis.

1939. 23 September. Death in London.

JAMES STRACHEY

OBSESSIVE ACTIONS AND
RELIGIOUS PRACTICES
(1907)

ZWANGSHANDLUNGEN UND RELIGIONSÜBUNGEN

(A) GERMAN EDITIONS:

1907   *Zeitschrift für Religionspsychologie*, **1** (1) [April], 4–12.
1909   *S.K.S.N.*, **2**, 122–31. (1912, 2nd ed.; 1921, 3rd ed.)
1941   *Gesammelte Werke*, **7**, 129–39.

(B) ENGLISH TRANSLATIONS:
'Obsessive Acts and Religious Practices'

1924   *Collected Papers*, **2**, 25–35. (Tr. R. C. McWatters.)
1959   *Standard Edition*, **9**, 115–27. (Modified version of the 1924 translation.)

The present edition is a reprint of the *Standard Edition* version, with some editorial changes.

This paper was written in February 1907, for the first issue of a periodical directed by Bresler and Vorbrodt. It was Freud's introductory incursion into the psychology of religion, and formed a definite step towards his much extended treatment of the subject five years later in *Totem and Taboo* (1912–13); see p. 43 ff. below. But besides this the paper is of great interest as being Freud's first discussion of obsessional neurosis since the Breuer period some ten years earlier. He here gives a sketch of the mechanism of obsessional symptoms which he was to elaborate in the case history of the 'Rat Man' (1909*d*), *P.F.L.*, **9**, 31 ff., whose treatment, however, he had not begun when he wrote the present work.

Of the many mental disorders that Freud dealt with in his

writings throughout his working life, obsessional neurosis is probably the one that he discussed most frequently. Apart from the two works mentioned above, the following writings also consider various aspects of the subject: 'Character and Anal Erotism' (1908*b*), *P.F.L.*, **7**, 205; 'The Disposition to Obsessional Neurosis' (1913*i*), ibid., **10**, 129; Lecture 17 of the *Introductory Lectures* (1916–17), ibid., **1**, 296 ff.; 'On Transformations of Instinct' (1917*c*), ibid., **7**, 293; Section VI of the 'Wolf Man' case history (1918*b*), ibid., **9**, 296 ff.; and in Chapters V and VI of *Inhibitions, Symptoms and Anxiety* (1926*d*), ibid., **10**, 266 ff. and 274 ff. In the latter work, Freud concludes: 'Obsessional neurosis is unquestionably the most interesting and repaying subject of analytic research. But as a problem it has not yet been mastered' (p. 267).

OBSESSIVE ACTIONS AND
RELIGIOUS PRACTICES

I AM certainly not the first person to have been struck by the resemblance between what are called obsessive actions in sufferers from nervous affections and the observances by means of which believers give expression to their piety. The term 'ceremonial', which has been applied to some of these obsessive actions, is evidence of this. The resemblance, however, seems to me to be more than a superficial one, so that an insight into the origin of neurotic ceremonial may embolden us to draw inferences by analogy about the psychological processes of religious life.

People who carry out obsessive actions or ceremonials belong to the same class as those who suffer from obsessive thinking, obsessive ideas, obsessive impulses and the like. Taken together, these form a particular clinical entity, to which the name of 'obsessional neurosis' ['*Zwangsneurose*'] is customarily applied.[1] But one should not attempt to deduce the character of the illness from its name; for, strictly speaking, other kinds of morbid mental phenomena have an equal claim to possessing what are spoken of as 'obsessional' characteristics. In place of a definition we must for the time being be content with obtaining a detailed knowledge of these states, since we have not yet been able to arrive at a criterion of obsessional neuroses; it probably lies very

1. See Löwenfeld (1904). [According to that author (ibid., 8) the term '*Zwangsvorstellung*' ('obsessional idea' or simply 'obsession') was introduced by Krafft-Ebing in 1867. The concept (and the term) 'obsessional neurosis' originated (on the same authority, ibid., 296 and 487) from Freud himself. His first published use of it was in his first paper on anxiety neurosis (1895*b*), *P.F.L.*, **10**, 42 and *n*. 1.]

deep, although we seem to sense its presence everywhere in the manifestations of the illness.

Neurotic ceremonials consist in making small adjustments to particular everyday actions, small additions or restrictions or arrangements, which have always to be carried out in the same, or in a methodically varied, manner. These activities give the impression of being mere formalities, and they seem quite meaningless to us. Nor do they appear otherwise to the patient himself; yet he is incapable of giving them up, for any deviation from the ceremonial is visited by intolerable anxiety, which obliges him at once to make his omission good. Just as trivial as the ceremonial actions themselves are the occasions and activities which are embellished, encumbered and in any case prolonged by the ceremonial – for instance, dressing and undressing, going to bed or satisfying bodily needs. The performance of a ceremonial can be described by replacing it, as it were, by a series of unwritten laws. For instance, to take the case of the bed ceremonial: the chair must stand in a particular place beside the bed; the clothes must lie upon it folded in a particular order; the blanket must be tucked in at the bottom and the sheet smoothed out; the pillows must be arranged in such and such a manner, and the subject's own body must lie in a precisely defined position. Only after all this may he go to sleep. Thus in slight cases the ceremonial seems to be no more than an exaggeration of an orderly procedure that is customary and justifiable; but the special conscientiousness with which it is carried out and the anxiety which follows upon its neglect stamp the ceremonial as a 'sacred act'. Any interruption of it is for the most part badly tolerated, and the presence of other people during its performance is almost always ruled out.

Any activities whatever may become obsessive actions in the wider sense of the term if they are elaborated by small additions or given a rhythmic character by means of pauses and repetitions. We shall not expect to find a sharp distinction between 'ceremonials' and 'obsessive actions'. As a rule obsessive actions have grown out of ceremonials. Besides these two, prohibitions and hindrances (abulias) make up the content of the disorder; these, in fact, only continue the work of the obsessive actions, inasmuch as some things are completely forbidden to the patient and others only allowed subject to his following a prescribed ceremonial.

It is remarkable that both compulsions and prohibitions (having to do something and having *not* to do something) apply in the first instance only to the subject's solitary activities and for a long time leave his social behaviour unaffected. Sufferers from this illness are consequently able to treat their affliction as a private matter and keep it concealed for many years. And, indeed, many more people suffer from these forms of obsessional neurosis than doctors hear of. For many sufferers, too, concealment is made easier from the fact that they are quite well able to fulfil their social duties during a part of the day, once they have devoted a number of hours to their secret doings, hidden from view like Mélusine.[1]

It is easy to see where the resemblances lie between neurotic ceremonials and the sacred acts of religious ritual: in the qualms of conscience brought on by their neglect, in their complete isolation from all other actions (shown in the prohibition against interruption) and in the conscientiousness with which they are carried out in every detail. But the differences are equally obvious, and a few of them are so glaring that they make the comparison a sacrilege: the greater individual variability of [neurotic] ceremonial actions in contrast to the stereotyped character of rituals (prayer, turning to the East, etc.), their private nature as opposed to the public and communal character of religious observances, above all, however, the fact that, while the minutiae of religious ceremonial are full of significance and have a symbolic meaning, those of neurotics seem foolish and senseless. In this respect an obsessional neurosis presents a travesty, half comic and half tragic, of a private religion. But it is precisely this sharpest difference between neurotic and religious ceremonial which disappears when, with the help of the psychoanalytic technique of investigation, one penetrates

1. [A beautiful woman in mediaeval legend, who led a secret existence as a water-nymph.]

to the true meaning of obsessive actions.[1] In the course of such an investigation the appearance which obsessive actions afford of being foolish and senseless is completely effaced, and the reason for their having that appearance is explained. It is found that the obsessive actions are perfectly significant in every detail, that they serve important interests of the personality and that they give expression to experiences that are still operative and to thoughts that are cathected with affect. They do this in two ways, either by direct or by symbolic representation; and they are consequently to be interpreted either historically or symbolically.

I must give a few examples to illustrate my point. Those who are familiar with the findings of psychoanalytic investigation into the psychoneuroses will not be surprised to learn that what is being represented in obsessive actions or in ceremonials is derived from the most intimate, and for the most part from the sexual, experiences of the patient.

(a) A girl whom I was able to observe was under a compulsion to rinse round her wash-basin several times after washing. The significance of this ceremonial action lay in the proverbial saying: 'Don't throw away dirty water till you have clean.' Her action was intended to give a warning to her sister, of whom she was very fond, and to restrain her from getting divorced from her unsatisfactory husband until she had established a relationship with a better man.

(b) A woman who was living apart from her husband was subject to a compulsion, whenever she ate anything, to leave what was the best of it behind: for example, she would only take the outside of a piece of roast meat. This renunciation was explained by the date of its origin. It appeared on the day after she had refused marital relations with her husband – that is to say, after she had given up what was the best.

1. See the collection of my shorter papers on the theory of the neuroses published in 1906. [*Sammlung kleiner Schriften zur Neurosenlehre*, Vienna, 1906. – The volume contains fourteen papers published between 1893 and 1906, three of which are included in the present series: Freud (1893*a*), *P.F.L.*, **3**, 51; (1895*b*), ibid., **10**, 31; and (1906*a*), ibid., **10**, 67.]

(*c*) The same patient could only sit on one particular chair and could only get up from it with difficulty. In regard to certain details of her married life, the chair symbolized her husband, to whom she remained faithful. She found an explanation of her compulsion in this sentence: 'It is so hard to part from anything (a husband, a chair) upon which one has once settled.'

(*d*) Over a period of time she used to repeat an especially noticeable and senseless obsessive action. She would run out of her room into another room in the middle of which there was a table. She would straighten the table-cloth on it in a particular manner and ring for the housemaid. The latter had to come up to the table, and the patient would then dismiss her on some indifferent errand. In the attempts to explain this compulsion, it occurred to her that at one place on the table-cloth there was a stain, and that she always arranged the cloth in such a way that the housemaid was bound to see the stain. The whole scene proved to be a reproduction of an experience in her married life which had later on given her thoughts a problem to solve. On the wedding-night her husband had met with a not unusual mishap. He found himself impotent, and 'many times in the course of the night he came hurrying from his room into hers' to try once more whether he could succeed. In the morning he said he would feel ashamed in front of the hotel housemaid who made the beds, and he took a bottle of red ink and poured its contents over the sheet; but he did it so clumsily that the red stain came in a place that was very unsuitable for his purpose. With her obsessive action, therefore, she was representing the wedding-night. 'Bed and board'[1] between them make up marriage.

(*e*) Another compulsion which she started – of writing down the number of every bank-note before parting with it – had also to be interpreted historically. At a time when she was still intending to leave her husband if she could find another more trustworthy man, she allowed herself to receive advances from a man whom she met at a watering-place, but she was in doubt

1. [In German '*Tisch und Bett*' ('table and bed'). Cf. the phrase for a legal separation: '*separatio a mensa et toro*' ('separation from table and bed').]

as to whether his intentions were serious. One day, being short of small change, she asked him to change a five-kronen piece for her. He did so, pocketed the large coin and declared with a gallant air that he would never part with it, since it had passed through her hands. At their later meetings she was frequently tempted to challenge him to show her the five-kronen piece, as though she wanted to convince herself that she could believe in his intentions. But she refrained, for the good reason that it is impossible to distinguish between coins of the same value. Thus her doubt remained unresolved; and it left her with the compulsion to write down the number of each bank-note, by which it *can* be distinguished from all others of the same value.[1]

These few examples, selected from the great number I have met with, are merely intended to illustrate my assertion that in obsessive actions everything has its meaning and can be interpreted. The same is true of ceremonials in the strict sense, only that the evidence for this would require a more circumstantial presentation. I am quite aware of how far our explanations of obsessive actions are apparently taking us from the sphere of religious thought.

It is one of the conditions of the illness that the person who is obeying a compulsion carries it out without understanding its meaning – or at any rate its chief meaning. It is only thanks to the efforts of psychoanalytic treatment that he becomes conscious of the meaning of his obsessive action and, with it, of the motives that are impelling him to it. We express this important fact by saying that the obsessive action serves to express *unconscious* motives and ideas. In this, we seem to find a further departure from religious practices; but we must remember that as a rule the ordinary pious individual, too, performs a ceremonial without concerning himself with its significance, although priests and scientific investigators may be familiar with the – mostly symbolic – meaning of the ritual. In all believers, however, the motives which impel them to religious

1. [Freud discussed this case again, with reference to the obsessive action described in (*d*) above, at considerable length in Lecture 17 of his *Introductory Lectures* (1916–17), *P.F.L.*, **1**, 300–3.]

practices are unknown to them or are represented in consciousness by others which are advanced in their place.

Analysis of obsessive actions has already given us some sort of an insight into their causes and into the chain of motives which bring them into effect. We may say that the sufferer from compulsions and prohibitions behaves as if he were dominated by a sense of guilt, of which, however, he knows nothing, so that we must call it an unconscious sense of guilt, in spite of the apparent contradiction in terms.[1] This sense of guilt has its source in certain early mental events, but it is constantly being revived by renewed temptations which arise whenever there is a contemporary provocation. Moreover, it occasions a lurking sense of expectant anxiety, an expectation of misfortune, which is linked, through the idea of punishment, with the internal perception of the temptation. When the ceremonial is first being constructed, the patient is still conscious that he must do this or that lest some ill should befall, and as a rule the nature of the ill that is to be expected is still known to his consciousness. But what is already hidden from him is the connection – which is always demonstrable – between the occasion on which this expectant anxiety arises and the danger which it conjures up. Thus a ceremonial starts as an *action for defence* or *insurance*, a *protective measure*.

The sense of guilt of obsessional neurotics finds its counterpart in the protestations of pious people that they know that at heart they are miserable sinners; and the pious observances (such as prayers, invocations, etc.,) with which such people preface every daily act, and in especial every unusual undertaking, seem to have the value of defensive or protective measures.

A deeper insight into the mechanism of obsessional neurosis

1. [The German word used here for 'sense of guilt' is '*Schuldbewusstsein*', literally 'consciousness of guilt'. – This seems to be the earliest explicit appearance of the 'unconscious sense of guilt' which was to play such an important part in Freud's later writings – e.g. Chapter V of *The Ego and the Id* (1923b), P.F.L., **11**. 391 ff.; in 'The Economic Problem of Masochism' (1924c), ibid., **11**, 420 ff., Freud made a distinction between unconscious guilt and moral masochism. See also Chapters VII and VIII of *Civilization and its Discontents* (1930a), ibid., **12**.]

is gained if we take into account the primary fact which lies at the bottom of it. This is always *the repression of an instinctual impulse*[1] (a component of the sexual instinct) which was present in the subject's constitution and which was allowed to find expression for a while during his childhood but later succumbed to suppression. In the course of the repression of this instinct a special *conscientiousness* is created which is directed against the instinct's aims; but this psychical reaction-formation feels insecure and constantly threatened by the instinct which is lurking in the unconscious. The influence of the repressed instinct is felt as a temptation, and during the process of repression itself anxiety is generated, which gains control over the future in the form of *expectant* anxiety. The process of repression which leads to obsessional neurosis must be considered as one which is only partly successful and which increasingly threatens to fail. It may thus be compared to an unending conflict; fresh psychical efforts are continually required to counterbalance the forward pressure of the instinct.[2] Thus the ceremonial and obsessive actions arise partly as a defence against the temptation and partly as a protection against the ill which is expected. Against the temptation the protective measures seem soon to become inadequate; then the prohibitions come into play, with the purpose of keeping at a distance situations that give rise to temptation. Prohibitions take the place of obsessive actions, it will be seen, just as a phobia is designed to avert a hysterical attack. Again, a ceremonial represents the sum of the conditions subject to which something that is not yet absolutely forbidden is permitted, just as the Church's marriage ceremony signifies for the believer a sanctioning of sexual enjoyment which would otherwise be sinful. A further characteristic of obsessional neurosis, as of all similar affections, is that its manifestations (its symptoms,

1. ['*Triebregung.*' This appears to be Freud's first published use of what was to be one of his most used terms.]

2. [This passage foreshadows the concept of 'anticathexis', which is developed at length in Section IV of the paper on 'The Unconscious' (1915*e*), *P.F.L.*, **11**, 183 ff.]

including the obsessive actions) fulfil the condition of being a compromise between the warring forces of the mind. They thus always reproduce something of the pleasure which they are designed to prevent; they serve the repressed instinct no less than the agencies which are repressing it. As the illness progresses, indeed, actions which were originally mostly concerned with maintaining the defence come to approximate more and more to the proscribed actions through which the instinct was able to find expression in childhood.

Some features of this state of affairs may be seen in the sphere of religious life as well. The formation of a religion, too, seems to be based on the suppression, the renunciation, of certain instinctual impulses. These impulses, however, are not, as in the neuroses, exclusively components of the sexual instinct; they are self-seeking, socially harmful instincts, though, even so, they are usually without a sexual component. A sense of guilt following upon continual temptation and an expectant anxiety in the form of fear of divine punishment have, after all, been familiar to us in the field of religion longer than in that of neurosis. Perhaps because of the admixture of sexual components, perhaps because of some general characteristics of the instincts, the suppression of instinct proves to be an inadequate and interminable process in religious life also. Indeed, complete backslidings into sin are more common among pious people than among neurotics and these give rise to a new form of religious activity, namely acts of penance, which have their counterpart in obsessional neurosis.

We have noted as a curious and derogatory characteristic of obsessional neurosis that its ceremonials are concerned with the small actions of daily life and are expressed in foolish regulations and restrictions in connection with them. We cannot understand this remarkable feature of the clinical picture until we have realized that the mechanism of psychical *displacement*, which was first discovered by me in the construction of dreams,[1] dominates the mental processes of obsessional

1. See *The Interpretation of Dreams* (1900a), Chapter VI, Section B [*P.F.L.*, 4, 414 ff.].

neurosis. It is already clear from the few examples of obsessive actions given above that their symbolism and the detail of their execution are brought about by a displacement from the actual, important thing on to a small one which takes its place – for instance, from a husband on to a chair.[1] It is this tendency to displacement which progressively changes the clinical picture and eventually succeeds in turning what is apparently the most trivial matter into something of the utmost importance and urgency. It cannot be denied that in the religious field as well there is a similar tendency to a displacement of psychical values, and in the same direction, so that the petty ceremonials of religious practice gradually become the essential thing and push aside the underlying thoughts. That is why religions are subject to reforms which work retroactively and aim at a re-establishment of the original balance of values.

The character of compromise which obsessive actions possess in their capacity as neurotic symptoms is the character least easily detected in corresponding religious observances. Yet here, too, one is reminded of this feature of neuroses when one remembers how commonly all the acts which religion forbids – the expressions of the instincts it has suppressed – are committed precisely in the name of, and ostensibly for the sake of, religion.

In view of these similarities and analogies one might venture to regard obsessional neurosis as a pathological counterpart of the formation of a religion, and to describe that neurosis as an individual religiosity and religion as a universal obsessional neurosis. The most essential similarity would reside in the underlying renunciation of the activation of instincts that are constitutionally present; and the chief difference would lie in the nature of those instincts, which in the neurosis are exclusively sexual in their origin, while in religion they spring from egoistic sources.

A progressive renunciation of constitutional instincts, whose activation might afford the ego primary pleasure, appears

1. [Freud often described this mechanism; see, for instance, the 'Rat Man' analysis (1909*d*), *P.F.L.*, **9**, 121, where further references are given.]

to be one of the foundations of the development of human civilization.[1] Some part of this instinctual repression is effected by its religions, in that they require the individual to sacrifice his instinctual pleasure to the Deity: 'Vengeance is mine, saith the Lord.' In the development of the ancient religions one seems to discern that many things which mankind had renounced as 'iniquities' had been surrendered to the Deity and were still permitted in his name, so that the handing over to him of bad and socially harmful instincts was the means by which man freed himself from their domination. For this reason, it is surely no accident that all the attributes of man, along with the misdeeds that follow from them, were to an unlimited amount ascribed to the ancient gods. Nor is it a contradiction of this that nevertheless man was not permitted to justify his own iniquities by appealing to divine example.

VIENNA, *February 1907*

---

1. [This idea was expanded by Freud in the paper on 'civilized' sexual morality (1908*d*), *P.F.L.*, **12**, 38 ff.]

TOTEM AND TABOO

Some Points of Agreement between
the Mental Lives of Savages and Neurotics

(1913 [1912–13])

EDITOR'S NOTE

TOTEM UND TABU

(A) GERMAN EDITIONS:

1912 Parts I–II, *Imago*, **1** (1), 17–33; (3), 213–27; (4), 301–33.
      (Under the title 'Über einige Übereinstimmungen im
      Seelenleben der Wilden und der Neurotiker' ['Some
      Points of Agreement between the Mental Lives of
      Savages and Neurotics'].)

1913 Parts III–IV, *Imago*, **2** (1), 1–21; (4), 357–408. (Same
      title.)

1913 Under title *Totem und Tabu*, Leipzig and Vienna: Heller.
      (1920, 2nd ed., Leipzig, Vienna and Zurich: Inter-
      nationaler Psychoanalytischer Verlag; 1922, 3rd ed.;
      1934, 5th ed.)

1924 *Gesammelte Schriften*, **10**, 3–194.

1940 *Gesammelte Werke*, **9**, 1–205.

'Vorrede zur hebräischen Ausgabe von
Totem und Tabu'

1934 *Gesammelte Schriften*, **12**, 385.

1948 *Gesammelte Werke*, **14**, 569.

(B) ENGLISH TRANSLATIONS:
Totem and Taboo

1918 New York: Moffat, Yard. (1919, London: Routledge.)
      (Tr. A. A. Brill.)

1938 London and New York: Penguin Books.
      (Same translator.)

1950 London: Routledge and Kegan Paul. (Including 'Preface
      to the Hebrew Translation'.) (Tr. James Strachey.)

1953   *Standard Edition*, **13**, xv, 1–161. (Slightly corrected version of the 1950 translation.)

The present edition is a reprint of the *Standard Edition* version, with some editorial modifications.

In his Preface Freud tells us that his first stimulus for writing these essays came from the works of Wundt and Jung. Actually, of course, his interest in social anthropology went back much further. In the Fliess correspondence (1950*a*), apart from general allusions to his long-standing devotion to the study of archaeology and prehistory, there are a number of specific references to anthropological topics and to the light which psychoanalysis throws upon them. For instance, in Draft N (31 May 1897) in discussing the 'horror of incest' he touched upon the relation between the growth of civilization and the suppression of the instincts – a subject to which he returned in his paper on '"Civilized" Sexual Ethics' (1908*d*), *P.F.L.*, **12**, and, much later, in *Civilization and its Discontents* (1930*a*), ibid. Again, in Letter 78 (12 December 1897) he writes: 'Can you imagine what "endopsychic myths" are? They are the latest offspring of my mental labours. The dim inner perception of one's own psychical apparatus stimulates illusions of thought, which are naturally projected outwards and characteristically into the future and the world beyond. Immortality, retribution, life after death, are all reflections of our inner psyche ... psychomythology.' And, in Letter 144 (4 July 1901): 'Have you read that the English have excavated an old palace in Crete (Knossos) which they declare is the authentic labyrinth of Minos? Zeus seems originally to have been a bull. It seems, too, that our own old God, before the sublimation instigated by the Persians took place, was also worshipped as a bull. That provides food for all sorts of thoughts which it is not yet time to set down on paper.' Lastly it is worth mentioning a short passage in a footnote to the first edition of *The Interpretation of Dreams* (1900*a*), *P.F.L.*, **4**, 310 *n*. 1, which adumbrates the derivation of the monarchy from the social position of the father of the family.

But the major elements of Freud's contribution to social anthropology made their first appearance in this work, and more especially in the fourth essay, which contains his hypothesis of the primal horde and the killing of the primal father and elaborates his theory tracing from them the origins of almost the whole of later social and cultural institutions. Freud himself had a very high opinion of this last essay both as regards its content and its form. He told his present translator, probably in 1921, that he regarded it as his best-written work. Indeed, the whole book remained a favourite all his life and he constantly recurred to it. Freud's own opinion was shared by Thomas Mann, who wrote in 1929: 'If I should be asked which one of Sigmund Freud's courageous and revolutionary contributions has made the strongest impression on me, and which of his literary works first occurs to me when his name is mentioned, I should answer without hesitation: *Totem and Taboo* ... It is without doubt the one of Freud's productions which has the greatest artistic merit; both in conception and literary form, it is a literary masterpiece allied to, and comparable with, the greatest examples of literary essays.'

About the actual composition of these essays we have a good deal of information, details of which will be found in the second volume of Jones's biography of Freud (1955). He had begun his preparations for the work, and in particular his reading of a large amount of literature on the subject, as early as in 1910. The title 'Totem and Taboo' was evidently already in his mind in August 1911, though he did not finally adopt it till the essays were collected in volume form. The first essay was finished in mid-January 1912. It was published in *Imago* in the following March, and was shortly afterwards reprinted, with some small omissions, in the Vienna weekly journal *Pan* (11 and 18 April 1912) and in the Vienna daily paper *Neues Wiener Journal* (18 April). The second essay was given before the Vienna Psycho-Analytical Society on 15 May 1912 in a talk which lasted for three hours. The third and fourth essays were given before the Vienna Society on 15 January and 4 June 1913 respectively.

Totem and Taboo was translated into seven languages besides English during Freud's lifetime. The special preface which he wrote for the Hebrew translation is included in this volume.

PREFACE

THE four essays that follow were originally published (under a heading which serves as the present book's sub-title) in the first two volumes of *Imago*, a periodical issued under my direction. They represent a first attempt on my part at applying the point of view and the findings of psychoanalysis to some unsolved problems of social psychology [*Völkerpsychologie*]. Thus they offer a methodological contrast on the one hand to Wilhelm Wundt's extensive work, which applies the hypotheses and working methods of *non*-analytic psychology to the same purposes, and on the other hand to the writings of the Zurich school of psychoanalysis, which endeavour, on the contrary, to solve the problems of individual psychology with the help of material derived from social psychology. (Cf. Jung, 1912 and 1913.) I readily confess that it was from these two sources that I received the first stimulus for my own essays.

I am fully conscious of the deficiencies of these studies. I need not mention those which are necessarily characteristic of pioneering work; but others require a word of explanation. The four essays collected in these pages aim at arousing the interest of a fairly wide circle of educated readers, but they cannot in fact be understood and appreciated except by those few who are no longer strangers to the essential nature of psychoanalysis. They seek to bridge the gap between students of such subjects as social anthropology, philology and folklore on the one hand, and psychoanalysts on the other. Yet they cannot offer to either side what each lacks – to the former an adequate initiation into the new psychological technique or to the latter a sufficient grasp of the material that awaits treatment. They must therefore rest content with attracting the attention of the two parties and with encouraging a belief that occasional co-operation between them could not fail to be of benefit to research.

It will be found that the two principal themes from which the title of this little book is derived – totems and taboos – have not received the same treatment. The analysis of taboos is put forward as an assured and exhaustive attempt at the solution of the problem. The investigation of totemism does no more than declare that 'here is what psychoanalysis can at the moment contribute towards elucidating the problem of the totem'. The difference is related to the fact that taboos still exist among us. Though expressed in a negative form and directed towards another subject-matter, they do not differ in their psychological nature from Kant's 'categorical imperative', which operates in a compulsive fashion and rejects any conscious motives. Totemism, on the contrary, is something alien to our contemporary feelings – a religio-social institution which has been long abandoned as an actuality and replaced by newer forms. It has left only the slightest traces behind it in the religions, manners and customs of the civilized peoples of to-day and has been subject to far-reaching modifications even among the races over which it still holds sway. The social and technical advances in human history have affected taboos far less than the totem.

An attempt is made in this volume to deduce the original meaning of totemism from the vestiges remaining of it in childhood – from the hints of it which emerge in the course of the growth of our own children. The close connection between totems and taboos carries us a step further along the path towards the hypothesis presented in these pages; and if in the end that hypothesis bears a highly improbable appearance, that need be no argument against the possibility of its approximating more or less closely to the reality which it is so hard to reconstruct.

ROME, *September 1913*

PREFACE TO THE
HEBREW TRANSLATION[1]

No reader of [the Hebrew version of] this book will find it easy to put himself in the emotional position of an author who is ignorant of the language of holy writ, who is completely estranged from the religion of his fathers – as well as from every other religion – and who cannot take a share in nationalist ideals, but who has yet never repudiated his people, who feels that he is in his essential nature a Jew and who has no desire to alter that nature. If the question were put to him: 'Since you have abandoned all these common characteristics of your countrymen, what is there left to you that is Jewish?' he would reply: 'A very great deal, and probably its very essence.' He could not now express that essence clearly in words; but some day, no doubt, it will become accessible to the scientific mind.

Thus it is an experience of a quite special kind for such an author when a book of his is translated into the Hebrew language and put into the hands of readers for whom that historic idiom is a living tongue: a book, moreover, which deals with the origin of religion and morality, though it adopts no Jewish standpoint and makes no exceptions in favour of Jewry. The author hopes, however, that he will be at one with his readers in the conviction that unprejudiced science cannot remain a stranger to the spirit of the new Jewry.

VIENNA, *December 1930*

1. [This preface was first published in German in *Gesammelte Schriften*, **12**, 385 (1934). The Hebrew translation was published in Jerusalem by Kirjeith Zefer in 1939.]

TOTEM AND TABOO

I

THE HORROR OF INCEST

PREHISTORIC man, in the various stages of his development, is known to us through the inanimate monuments and implements which he has left behind, through the information about his art, his religion and his attitude towards life which has come to us either directly or by way of tradition handed down in legends, myths and fairy tales, and through the relics of his mode of thought which survive in our own manners and customs. But apart from this, in a certain sense he is still our contemporary. There are men still living who, as we believe, stand very near to primitive man, far nearer than we do, and whom we therefore regard as his direct heirs and representatives. Such is our view of those whom we describe as savages or half-savages; and their mental life must have a peculiar interest for us if we are right in seeing in it a well-preserved picture of an early stage of our own development.

If that supposition is correct, a comparison between the psychology of primitive peoples, as it is taught by social anthropology, and the psychology of neurotics, as it has been revealed by psychoanalysis, will be bound to show numerous points of agreement and will throw new light upon familiar facts in both sciences.

For external as well as for internal reasons, I shall select as the basis of this comparison the tribes which have been described by anthropologists as the most backward and miserable of savages, the aborigines of Australia, the youngest continent, in whose fauna, too, we can still observe much that is archaic and that has perished elsewhere.

The Australian aborigines are regarded as a distinct race, showing neither physical nor linguistic relationship with their nearest neighbours, the Melanesian, Polynesian and Malayan peoples. They do not build houses or permanent shelters; they do not cultivate the soil; they keep no domesticated animals except the dog; they are not even acquainted with the art of making pottery. They live entirely upon the flesh of all kinds of animals which they hunt, and upon roots which they dig. Kings or chiefs are unknown among them; communal affairs are decided by a council of elders. It is highly doubtful whether any religion, in the shape of a worship of higher beings, can be attributed to them. The tribes in the interior of the continent, who have to struggle against the hardest conditions of existence as a result of the scarcity of water, appear to be more primitive in all respects than those living near the coast.

We should certainly not expect that the sexual life of these poor naked cannibals would be moral in our sense or that their sexual instincts would be subjected to any great degree of restriction. Yet we find that they set before themselves with the most scrupulous care and the most painful severity the aim of avoiding incestuous sexual relations. Indeed, their whole social organization seems to serve that purpose or to have been brought into relation with its attainment.

Among the Australians the place of all the religious and social institutions which they lack is taken by the system of 'totemism'. Australian tribes fall into smaller divisions, or clans, each of which is named after its totem. What is a totem? It is as a rule an animal (whether edible and harmless or dangerous and feared) and more rarely a plant or a natural phenomenon (such as rain or water), which stands in a peculiar relation to the whole clan. In the first place, the totem is the common ancestor of the clan; at the same time it is their guardian spirit and helper, which sends them oracles and, if dangerous to others, recognizes and spares its own children. Conversely, the clansmen are under a sacred obligation (subject to automatic sanctions) not to kill or destroy their totem and to avoid eating its flesh (or deriving benefit from it in other ways). The totemic character is inherent, not in some individual animal or entity, but in all the individuals of a given class. From time to time festivals are celebrated at which the clansmen represent or imitate the motions and attributes of their totem in ceremonial dances.

The totem may be inherited either through the female or through the male line. It is possible that originally the former method of descent prevailed everywhere and was only subsequently replaced by the latter. An Australian's relation to his totem is the basis of all his social obligations: it overrides on the one hand his tribal membership and on the other hand his blood relationships.[1]

The totem is not attached to one particular place. The clansmen are distributed in different localities and live peacefully side by side with members of other totem clans.[2]

★

1. 'The Totem bond is stronger than the bond of blood or family in the modern sense.' (Frazer, 1910, **1**, 53.)

2. This highly condensed summary of the totemic system must necessarily be subject to further comments and qualifications. The word 'totem' was first introduced in 1791 (in the form 'totam') from the North American Indians by an Englishman, J. Long. The subject itself has gradually attracted great scientific interest and has produced a copious literature, from which I may select as works of capital importance J. G. Frazer's four-volume *Totemism and Exogamy* (1910) and the writings of Andrew Lang, e.g. *The Secret of the Totem* (1905). The merit of having been the first to recognize the importance of totemism for human prehistory lies with a Scotsman, John Ferguson McLennan (1869–70). Totemic institutions were, or still are, to be observed in operation, not only among the Australians, but also among the North American Indians, among the peoples of Oceania, in the East Indies and in a large part of Africa. It may also be inferred from certain vestigial remains, for which it is otherwise hard to account, that totemism existed at one time among the Aryan and Semitic aboriginal races of Europe and Asia. Many investigators are therefore inclined to regard it as a necessary phase of human development which has been passed through universally.

How did prehistoric men come to adopt totems? How, that is, did they come to make the fact of their being descended from one animal or another

And now we come at last to the characteristic of the totemic system which has attracted the interest of psychoanalysts. In almost every place where we find totems we also find *a law against persons of the same totem having sexual relations with one another and consequently against their marrying*. This, then, is 'exogamy', an institution related to totemism.

Strictly enforced as it is, this prohibition is a remarkable one. There is nothing in the concept or attributes of the totem which I have so far mentioned to lead us to anticipate it; so that it is hard to understand how it has become involved in the totemic system. We cannot, therefore, feel surprised that some investigators actually suppose that exogamy had originally – in the earliest times and in its true meaning – nothing to do with totemism, but became attached to it (without there being any underlying connection) at some time when marriage restrictions became necessary. However this may be, the bond between totemism and exogamy exists and is clearly a very firm one.

Some further considerations will make the significance of this prohibition clearer:

(*a*) The violation of the prohibition is not left to what might

---

the basis of their social obligations and, as we shall see presently, of their sexual restrictions? There are numerous theories on the subject – of which Wundt (1906 [264 ff.]) has given an epitome for German readers – but no agreement. It is my intention to devote a special study before long to the problem of totemism, in which I shall attempt to solve it by the help of a psychoanalytic line of approach. (See the fourth essay in this work.)

Not only, however, is the *theory* of totemism a matter of dispute; the facts themselves are scarcely capable of being expressed in general terms as I have tried to do in the text above. There is scarcely a statement which does not call for exceptions or contradictions. But it must not be forgotten that even the most primitive and conservative races are in some sense *ancient* races and have a long past history behind them during which their original conditions of life have been subject to much development and distortion. So it comes about that in those races in which totemism exists to-day, we may find it in various stages of decay and disintegration or in the process of transition to other social and religious institutions, or again in a stationary condition which may differ greatly from the original one. The difficulty in this last case is to decide whether we should regard the present state of things as a true picture of the significant features of the past or as a secondary distortion of them.

be called the 'automatic' punishment of the guilty parties, as in the case of other totem prohibitions, such as that against killing the totem animal. It is avenged in the most energetic fashion by the whole clan, as though it were a question of averting some danger that threatened the whole community or some guilt that was pressing upon it. A few sentences from Frazer (1910, I, 54) will show how severely such misdeeds are treated by savages who are otherwise far from being moral by our standards:

'In Australia the regular penalty for sexual intercourse with a person of a forbidden clan is death. It matters not whether the woman be of the same local group or has been captured in war from another tribe; a man of the wrong clan who uses her as his wife is hunted down and killed by his clansmen, and so is the woman; though in some cases, if they succeed in eluding capture for a certain time, the offence may be condoned. In the Ta-ta-thi tribe, New South Wales, in the rare cases which occur, the man is killed but the woman is only beaten or speared, or both, till she is nearly dead; the reason given for not actually killing her being that she was probably coerced. Even in casual amours the clan prohibitions are strictly observed; any violations of these prohibitions "are regarded with the utmost abhorrence and are punished by death".' [Quoted from Cameron (1885, 351).]

(b) Since the same severe punishment is inflicted in the case of passing love-affairs which have not resulted in any children, it seems unlikely that the reasons for the prohibition are of a practical nature.

(c) Since totems are hereditary and not changed by marriage, it is easy to follow the consequences of the prohibition. Where, for instance, descent is through the female line, if a man of the Kangaroo totem marries a woman of the Emu totem, all the children, both boys and girls, belong to the Emu clan. The totem regulation will therefore make it impossible for a son of this marriage to have incestuous intercourse with his mother or sisters, who are Emus like himself.[1]

(d) But a little more reflection will show that exogamy linked

_____

1. On the other hand, at all events so far as this prohibition is concerned,

with the totem effects more (and therefore *aims* at more) than the prevention of incest with a man's mother and sisters. It makes sexual intercourse impossible for a man with all the women of his own clan (that is to say with a number of women who are not his blood-relatives) by treating them all as though they *were* his blood-relatives. It is difficult at first sight to see the psychological justification for this very extensive restriction, which goes far beyond anything comparable among civilized peoples. It may be gathered from this, however, that the part played by the totem as common ancestor is taken very seriously. All those who are descended from the same totem are blood-relations. They form a single family, and within that family even the most distant degree of kinship is regarded as an absolute hindrance to sexual intercourse.

We see, then, that these savages have an unusually great horror of incest, or are sensitive on the subject to an unusual degree, and that they combine this with a peculiarity which remains obscure to us – of replacing real blood-relationship by totem kinship. This latter contrast must not, however, be too much exaggerated, and we must remember that the totem prohibitions include that against real incest as a special case.

The riddle of how it came about that the real family was replaced by the totem clan must perhaps remain unsolved till the nature of the totem itself can be explained. At the same time, it is to be observed that if there were a certain degree of freedom of sexual intercourse outside marriage, blood-relationship, and consequently the prevention of incest, would become so uncertain that the prohibition would stand in need of a wider basis. It is therefore worth remarking that Australian customs permit

---

the father, who is a Kangaroo, is free to commit incest with his daughters, who are Emus. If the totem descended through the *male* line, however, the Kangaroo father would be prohibited from incest with his daughters (since all his children would be Kangaroos), whereas the son would be free to commit incest with his mother. These implications of totem prohibitions suggest that descent through the female line is older than that through the male, since there are grounds for thinking that totem prohibitions were principally directed against the incestuous desires of the son.

the occurrence, in certain social situations and during certain festivals, of breaches in a man's exclusive conjugal rights over a woman.

Linguistic usage in these Australian tribes[1] exhibits a peculiarity which is no doubt relevant here. For the terms used by them to express the various degrees of kinship do not denote a relation between two individuals but between an individual and a group. This is what L. H. Morgan [1877] named the 'classificatory' system of relationship. Thus a man uses the term 'father' not only for his actual procreator but also for all the other men whom his mother might have married according to tribal law and who therefore might have procreated him; he uses the term 'mother' not only for the woman who actually bore him but also for all the other women who might have borne him without transgressing the tribal law; he uses the terms 'brother' and 'sister' not only for the children of his actual parents but also for the children of all those persons who stand in the relation of parents to him in the classificatory sense; and so on. Thus the kinship terms which two Australians apply to each other do not necessarily indicate any consanguinity, as ours would do: they represent social rather than physical relationships. Something approaching the classificatory system is to be found among us when, for instance, children are encouraged to refer to all their parents' friends as 'Uncle' or 'Aunt', or when we speak in a metaphorical sense of 'brothers in Apollo' or 'sisters in Christ'.

Though this use of words strikes us as so puzzling, it is easily explained if we look on it as a survival of the marriage institution which the Rev. L. Fison has called 'group marriage' and which consists in a certain number of men exercising conjugal rights over a certain number of women. The children of such a group marriage would then justly regard one another as brothers and sisters (though they were not all born of the same mother) and would regard all the men in the group as their fathers.

Though some authors, such as Westermarck (1901), have disputed the conclusions which others have drawn from the existence of the classificatory system of relationship, those who

1. As well as in most other totemic communities.

have the closest acquaintance with the Australian natives are agreed in regarding that system as a survival from the days of group marriage. Indeed, according to Spencer and Gillen (1899 [64]), a certain form of group marriage exists to this day in the Urabunna and Dieri tribes. Group marriage thus preceded individual marriage among these peoples, and after its disappearance left definite traces behind both in language and customs.

But when once we have put group marriage in the place of individual marriage, the apparently excessive degree of avoidance of incest which we have come across among the same peoples becomes intelligible. Totemic exogamy, the prohibition of sexual intercourse between members of the same clan, appears to have been the appropriate means for preventing group incest; it thus became established and persisted long after its *raison d'être* had ceased.

It may seem that we have thus discovered the motives that led the Australian natives to set up their marriage restrictions; but we have now to learn that the actual state of affairs reveals a far greater, and at first sight a bewildering, complexity. For there are few races in Australia in which the totem barrier is the sole prohibition. Most of them are organized in such a way as to fall into two divisions, known as marriage-classes or 'phratries'. Each of these phratries is exogamous and comprises a number of totem clans. As a rule each phratry is further subdivided into two 'sub-phratries', the whole tribe being thus divided into four, with the sub-phratries intermediate between the phratries and the totem clans.

The following diagram represents the typical organization of an Australian tribe and corresponds to the actual situation in a very large number of cases:

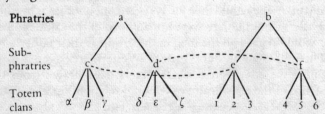

Here the twelve totem clans are divided into four sub-phratries and two phratries. All the divisions are exogamous.[1] Sub-phratries c and e form an exogamous unit; and so also do sub-phratries d and f. The result (and therefore the purpose) of these arrangements cannot be doubted: they bring about a still further restriction on the choice of marriage and on sexual liberty. Let us suppose that each clan contains an equal number of members. Then, if only the twelve totem clans existed, each member of a clan would have his choice among $\frac{11}{12}$ of all the women in the tribe. The existence of the two phratries reduces his choice to $\frac{6}{12}$ or $\frac{1}{2}$, for then a man of totem α can only marry a woman of totems 1 to 6. With the introduction of the four sub-phratries his choice is still further reduced to $\frac{3}{12}$ or $\frac{1}{4}$, for in that case a man of totem α is restricted in his choice of a wife to a woman of totems 4, 5 or 6.

The historical relation between the marriage-classes (of which in some tribes there are as many as eight) and the totem clans is completely obscure. It is merely evident that these arrangements are directed towards the same aim as totemic exogamy and pursue it still further. While, however, totemic exogamy gives one the impression of being a sacred ordinance of unknown origin – in short, of being a custom – the complicated institution of the marriage-classes, with their subdivisions and the regulations attaching to them, look more like the result of deliberate legislation, which may perhaps have taken up the task of preventing incest afresh because the influence of the totem was waning. And, while the totemic system is, as we know, the basis of all the other social obligations and moral restrictions of the tribe, the significance of the phratries seems in general not to extend beyond the regulation of marriage choice which is its aim.

The system of marriage-classes in its furthest developments bears witness to an endeavour to go beyond the prevention of natural and group incest and to forbid marriage between still more distant groups of relatives. In this it resembles the Catholic Church, which extended the ancient prohibition against mar-

1. The number of totems is chosen arbitrarily.

riage between brothers and sisters to marriage between cousins and even to marriage between those who were merely spiritual relatives [godfathers, godmothers and godchildren]. (Cf. Lang, 1910–11 [87].)

It would be little to our purpose if we were to follow in detail the extraordinarily involved and obscure discussions on the origin and significance of the marriage-classes and on their relation to the totem. For our purpose it is enough to draw attention to the great care which is devoted by the Australians, as well as by other savage peoples, to the prevention of incest.[1] It must be admitted that these savages are even more sensitive on the subject of incest than we are. They are probably liable to a greater temptation to it and for that reason stand in need of fuller protection.

But the horror of incest shown by these peoples is not satisfied by the erection of the institutions which I have described and which seem to be directed principally against group incest. We must add to them a number of 'customs' which regulate the dealings of individuals with their near relatives in our sense of the term, customs which are enforced literally with religious strictness and the purpose of which can scarcely be doubted. These customs or customary prohibitions have been termed 'avoidances'. They extend far beyond the totemic races of Australia; but once again I must ask my readers to be content with a fragmentary extract from the copious material.

In Melanesia restrictive prohibitions of this sort govern a boy's intercourse with his mother and sisters. Thus, for instance, in Lepers' Island, one of the New Hebrides, when a boy has reached a certain age he no longer lives at home, but takes up his quarters in the 'club-house', where he now regularly eats and sleeps. It is true that he may still go to his father's house to ask for food, but if his sister is at home he must go away before eating; if no sister is there he may sit down near the door and eat. If by chance a brother and sister meet in the open, she must run away or hide. If a boy knows that certain footprints in the road are his sister's, he will not follow them, nor will she follow

1. Storfer (1911 [16]) has quite recently insisted on this point.

his. Indeed, he will not even utter her name, and will avoid the use of a common word if it forms part of her name. This avoidance begins with the puberty ceremonies and is maintained throughout life. The reserve between a son and his mother increases as the boy grows up and is much more on her side than on his. If his mother brings him food, she does not give it him but puts it down for him to take. In speaking to him she does not *tutoyer* him, but uses the more distant plural forms.[1]

Similar customs prevail in New Caledonia. If a brother and sister happen to meet on a path, the sister will throw herself into the bushes and he will pass on without turning his head.[2]

Among the natives of the Gazelle Peninsula in New Britain a sister, after her marriage, is not allowed to converse with her brother; she never utters his name, but designates him by another word.[3]

In New Mecklenburg cousins of one kind are subject to similar restrictions, as are brothers and sisters. They may not come near each other, may not shake hands and may not give each other presents; but they are allowed to speak to each other at a distance of some paces. The penalty for incest with a sister is death by hanging.[4]

In Fiji these avoidance rules are particularly strict; they affect not only blood sisters but tribal sisters as well. It must strike us as all the more puzzling to hear that these same savages practise sacred orgies, in which precisely these forbidden degrees of kinship seek sexual intercourse – puzzling, that is, unless we prefer to regard the contrast as an explanation of the prohibition.[5]

Among the Battas of Sumatra the rules of avoidance apply to all near relations. 'A Batta, for example, would think it shocking were a brother to escort his sister to an evening party. Even in the presence of others a Batta brother and sister feel embar-

1. Frazer (1910, 2, 77 f.), quoting Codrington (1891 [232]).
2. [Frazer (1910, 2, 78), quoting Lambert (1900, 114).]
3. Frazer (1910, 2, 124) [quoting Parkinson (1907, 67 f.)].
4. Frazer (1910, 2, 130 f.), quoting Peckel (1908 [467]).
5. Frazer (1910, 2, 146 ff.), quoting Fison [1885, 27 ff.].

rassed. If one of them comes into the house, the other will go away. Further, a father may never be alone in the house with his daughter, nor a mother with her son ... The Dutch missionary who reports these customs adds that he is sorry to say that from what he knows of the Battas he believes the maintenance of most of these rules to be very necessary.' These people assume as a matter of course that a solitary meeting between a man and a woman will lead to an improper intimacy between them. And since they believe that intercourse between near relations will lead to punishments and calamities of all sorts, they are right to avoid any temptation to transgress these prohibitions.[1]

Curiously enough, among the Barongo of Delagoa Bay, in South Africa, the strictest rules affect a man's relations with his sister-in-law, the wife of his wife's brother. If he meets this formidable person anywhere, he carefully avoids her. He does not eat out of the same dish with her, he speaks to her with embarrassment, does not venture into her hut and greets her in a trembling voice.[2]

A rule of avoidance with which one would have expected to meet more frequently operates among the A-kamba (or Wakamba) of British East Africa. A girl has to avoid her father between the age of puberty and the time of her marriage. If they meet in the road, she hides while he passes, and she may never go and sit near him. This holds good until the moment of her betrothal. After her marriage she does not avoid her father in any way.[3]

By far the most widespread and strictest avoidance (and the most interesting from the point of view of civilized races) is that which restricts a man's intercourse with his mother-in-law. It is quite general in Australia and also extends over Melanesia, Polynesia and the Negro races of Africa, wherever traces of totemism and the classificatory system of relationship are found and probably still further. In some of these places there are similar prohibitions against a woman having innocent inter-

1. Frazer (1910, **2**, 189) [quoting Joustra (1902, 391 f.)].
2. Frazer (1910, **2**, 388), quoting Junod [1898, 73 ff.].
3. Frazer (1910, **2**, 424) [quoting C. W. Hobley (unpublished MS.)].

course with her father-in-law; but they are far less usual and severe. In a few isolated cases both parents-in-law are subject to avoidance. Since we are less concerned with the ethnographical extent of this avoidance than with its substance and purpose, I shall once again restrict myself to quoting a few examples.

Among the Melanesians of the Banks' Islands 'these rules of avoidance are very strict and minute. A man will not come near his wife's mother and she will not come near him. If the two chance to meet in a path, the woman will step out of it and stand with her back turned till he has gone by, or perhaps, if it be more convenient, he will move out of the way. At Vanua Lava, in Port Patteson, a man would not even follow his mother-in-law along the beach until the rising tide had washed her foot-prints from the sand. Yet a man and his mother-in-law may talk to each other at a distance; but a woman will on no account mention the name of her daughter's husband, nor will he name hers.'[1]

In the Solomon Islands, after his marriage a man may neither see nor converse with his mother-in-law. If he meets her, he may not recognize her, but must make off and hide himself as fast as he can.[2]

Among the Eastern Bantu 'custom requires that a man should "be ashamed of" his wife's mother, that is to say, he must studiously shun her society. He may not enter the same hut with her, and if by chance they meet on a path, one or other turns aside, she perhaps hiding behind a bush, while he screens his face with a shield. If they cannot thus avoid each other, and the mother-in-law has nothing else to cover herself with, she will tie a wisp of grass round her head as a token of ceremonial avoidance. All correspondence between the two has to be carried on either through a third party or by shouting to each other at a distance with some barrier, such as the kraal fence, interposed between them. They may not even pronounce each other's proper name.' (Frazer, 1910, 2, 385.)

Among the Basoga, a Bantu people who live in the region of

1. Frazer (1910, 2, 76) [quoting Codrington (1891, 42 ff.)].
2. Frazer (1910, 2, 117), quoting Ribbe (1903 [140 f.]).

the sources of the Nile, a man may only speak to his mother-in-law when she is in another room and out of sight. Incidentally, these people have such a horror of incest that they punish it even when it occurs among their domestic animals. (Frazer, 1910, **2**, 461.)

While there can be no doubt as to the purpose and significance of the other avoidances between near relations, and they are universally regarded as protective measures against incest, the prohibitions affecting a man's intercourse with his mother-in-law have received another interpretation in some quarters. It was with justice regarded as incomprehensible that all these different peoples should feel such great fear of the temptation presented to a man by an elderly woman, who might have been, but in fact was not, his mother. (Crawley, 1902, 405.)

This objection was also raised against the view put forward by Fison [Fison and Howitt, 1880, 104]. He pointed out that certain systems of marriage-classes had gaps in them, as a result of which marriage between a man and his mother-in-law was not theoretically impossible. For that reason, he suggested, a special guarantee against that possibility became necessary.

Sir John Lubbock (1870 [84 f.]) traced back the attitude of a mother-in-law to her son-in-law to the institution of 'marriage by capture'. 'When the capture was a reality', he writes, 'the indignation of the parents would also be real; when it became a mere symbol, the parental anger would be symbolized also, and would be continued even after its origin was forgotten.' Crawley [1902, 406] has no difficulty in showing how insufficiently this attempted explanation covers the details of the observed facts.

Tylor [1889, 246 f.] believes that the treatment given to a son-in-law by his mother-in-law is merely a form of 'cutting' or non-recognition by the wife's family: the man is regarded as an 'outsider' until the first child is born. In the first place, however, the prohibition is not always brought to an end when this occurs. But, apart from this, it may be objected that this explanation throws no light on the fact that the prohibition centres particularly on the *mother*-in-law – that the explanation overlooks the factor of sex. Moreover, it takes no account of the attitude of religious horror expressed in the prohibition. (Crawley, 1902, 407.)

A Zulu woman, questioned as to the basis of the prohibition, gave the sensitive reply: 'It is not right that he should see the breasts which suckled his wife.'[1]

As we know, the relation between son-in-law and mother-in-law is also one of the delicate points of family organization in *civilized* communities. That relation is no longer subject to rules of avoidance in the social system of the white peoples of Europe and America; but many disputes and much unpleasantness could often be eliminated if the avoidance still existed as a custom and did not have to be re-erected by individuals. It may be regarded by some Europeans as an act of high wisdom on the part of these savage races that by their rules of avoidance they entirely precluded any contact between two persons brought into this close relationship to each other. There is scarcely room for doubt that something in the psychological relation of a mother-in-law to a son-in-law breeds hostility between them and makes it hard for them to live together. But the fact that in civilized societies mothers-in-law are such a favourite subject for jokes seems to me to suggest that the emotional relation involved includes sharply contrasted components. I believe, that is, that this relation is in fact an 'ambivalent' one, composed of conflicting affectionate and hostile impulses.

Some of those impulses are obvious enough. On the side of the mother-in-law there is reluctance to give up the possession of her daughter, distrust of the stranger to whom she is to be handed over, an impulse to retain the dominating position which she has occupied in her own house. On the man's side there is a determination not to submit any longer to someone else's will, jealousy of anyone who possessed his wife's affection before he did, and, last but not least, an unwillingness to allow anything to interfere with the illusory overvaluation bred of his sexual feelings. The figure of his mother-in-law usually causes such an interference, for she has many features which remind

1. Crawley (1902, 401), quoting Leslie (1875 [141]).

him of her daughter and yet lacks all the charms of youth, beauty and spiritual freshness which endear his wife to him.

But we are able to bring forward other motives than these, thanks to the knowledge of concealed mental impulses which we have acquired from the psychoanalytic examination of individual human beings. A woman whose psychosexual needs should find satisfaction in her marriage and her family life is often threatened with the danger of being left unsatisfied, because her marriage relation has come to a premature end and because of the uneventfulness of her emotional life. A mother, as she grows older, saves herself from this by putting herself in her children's place, by identifying herself with them; and this she does by making their emotional experiences her own. Parents are said to stay young with their children, and that is indeed one of the most precious psychological gains that parents derive from their children. Where a marriage is childless, the wife has lost one of the things which might be of most help to her in tolerating the resignation that her own marriage demands from her. A mother's sympathetic identification with her daughter can easily go so far that she herself falls in love with the man her daughter loves; and in glaring instances this may lead to severe forms of neurotic illness as a result of her violent mental struggles against this emotional situation. In any case, it very frequently happens that a mother-in-law is subject to an *impulse* to fall in love in this way, and this impulse itself or an opposing trend are added to the tumult of conflicting forces in her mind. And very often the unkind, sadistic components of her love are directed on to her son-in-law in order that the forbidden, affectionate ones may be the more severely suppressed.

A man's relation to his mother-in-law is complicated by similar impulses, though they have another source. It is regularly found that he chose his mother as the object of his love, and perhaps his sister as well, before passing on to his final choice. Because of the barrier that exists against incest, his love is deflected from the two figures on whom his affection was centred in his childhood on to an outside object that is modelled upon them. The place of his own and his sister's mother is taken by his mother-in-law. He has an impulse to fall back upon his original choice, though everything in him fights against it. His horror of incest insists that the genealogical history of his choice of an object for his love shall not be recalled. His repudiation of this impulse is also facilitated by the fact that his mother-in-law is only a contemporary figure; he has not known her all his life, so that there is no unchangeable picture of her preserved in his unconscious. A streak of irritability and malevolence that is apt to be present in the medley of his feelings leads us to suspect that she does in fact offer him a temptation to incest; and this is confirmed by the not uncommon event of a man openly falling in love with the woman who is later to be his mother-in-law before transferring his love to her daughter.

I can see nothing against the presumption that it is precisely this incestuous factor in the relation that provides savages with the motive for their rules of avoidance between son-in-law and mother-in-law. Thus the explanation which we should adopt for these strictly enforced avoidances among primitive peoples is that put forward by Fison [see p. 66], which regards them merely as a further protection against possible incest. The same explanation holds good of all other avoidances, between both blood and tribal relations. The only difference would be that in the case of blood relations the possibility of incest is an immediate one and the intention to prevent it may be conscious; in the other cases, including that of a man's relation to his mother-in-law, the possibility of incest would seem to be a temptation in phantasy set in motion through the agency of unconscious connecting links.

There has been little opportunity in the preceding pages for showing how new light can be thrown upon the facts of social psychology by the adoption of a psychoanalytic method of approach: for the horror of incest displayed by savages has long been recognized as such and stands in need of no further interpretation. All that I have been able to add to our understanding of it is to emphasize the fact that it is essentially an *infantile* feature and that it reveals a striking agreement with the mental life of neurotic patients. Psychoanalysis has taught us that a boy's earliest choice of objects for his love is incestuous and that those objects are forbidden ones – his mother and his sister.[1] We have learnt, too, the manner in which, as he grows up, he liberates himself from this incestuous attraction. A neurotic, on the other hand, invariably exhibits some degree of psychical infantilism. He has either failed to get free from the psycho-sexual conditions that prevailed in his childhood or he has returned to them – two possibilities which may be summed up as developmental inhibition and regression. Thus incestuous fixations of libido continue to play (or begin once more to play) the principal part in his unconscious mental life. We have arrived at the point of regarding a child's relation to his parents, dominated as it is by incestuous longings, as the nuclear complex of neurosis. This revelation of the importance of incest in neurosis is naturally received with universal scepticism by adults and normal people. Similar expressions of disbelief, for instance, inevitably greet the writings of Otto Rank [e.g. 1907 and 1912], which have brought more and more evidence to show the extent to which the interest of creative writers centres round the theme of incest and how the same theme, in countless variations and distortions, provides the subject-matter of poetry. We are driven to believe that this rejection is principally a product of the distaste which human beings feel for their early incestuous wishes, now overtaken by repression. It is therefore of no small importance that we are able to show that these same incestuous wishes, which are later destined to become unconscious, are still regarded by savage peoples as immediate perils against which the most severe measures of defence must be enforced.

1. [This topic was first discussed at length by Freud in the third of his *Three Essays* (1905*d*), *P.F.L.*, **7**, 148 ff.]

II

TABOO AND EMOTIONAL AMBIVALENCE

(1)

'TABOO' is a Polynesian word. It is difficult for us to find a translation for it, since the concept connoted by it is one which we no longer possess. It was still current among the ancient Romans, whose '*sacer*' was the same as the Polynesian 'taboo'. So, too, the '*ἄγος*' of the Greeks and the '*kadesh*' of the Hebrews must have had the same meaning as is expressed in 'taboo' by the Polynesians and in analogous terms by many other races in America, Africa (Madagascar) and North and Central Asia.

The meaning of 'taboo', as we see it, diverges in two contrary directions. To us it means, on the one hand, 'sacred', 'consecrated', and on the other 'uncanny', 'dangerous', 'forbidden', 'unclean'. The converse of 'taboo' in Polynesian is '*noa*', which means 'common' or 'generally accessible'. Thus 'taboo' has about it a sense of something unapproachable, and it is principally expressed in prohibitions and restrictions. Our collocation 'holy dread' would often coincide in meaning with 'taboo'.

Taboo restrictions are distinct from religious or moral prohibitions. They are not based upon any divine ordinance, but may be said to impose themselves on their own account. They differ from moral prohibitions in that they fall into no system that declares quite generally that certain abstinences must be observed and gives reasons for that necessity. Taboo prohibitions have no grounds and are of unknown origin. Though they are unintelligible to *us*, to those who are dominated by them they are taken as a matter of course.

Wundt (1906, 308) describes taboo as the oldest human

71

unwritten code of laws. It is generally supposed that taboo is older than gods and dates back to a period before any kind of religion existed.

Since we need an impartial account of taboo to submit to psychoanalytic examination, I shall now give some extracts and summaries of portions of the article 'Taboo' in the *Encyclopaedia Britannica* (1910–11*b*),[1] the author of which was Northcote W. Thomas, the anthropologist.

'Properly speaking taboo includes only (*a*) the sacred (or unclean) character of person or things, (*b*) the kind of prohibition which results from this character, and (*c*) the sanctity (or uncleanness) which results from a violation of the prohibition. The converse of taboo in Polynesia is *noa* and allied forms, which mean "general" or "common" ...

'Various classes of taboo in the wider sense may be distinguished: (i) natural or direct, the result of *mana* (mysterious power) inherent in a person or thing; (ii) communicated or indirect, equally the result of *mana*, but (*a*) acquired or (*b*) imposed by a priest, chief or other person; (iii) intermediate, where both factors are present, as in the appropriation of a wife to her husband ...' The term is also applied to other ritual restrictions, but what is better described as a 'religious interdiction' should not be referred to as taboo.

'The objects of taboo are many: (i) direct taboos aim at (*a*) the protection of important persons – chiefs, priests, etc. – and things against harm; (*b*) the safeguarding of the weak – women, children and common people generally – from the powerful *mana* (magical influence) of chiefs and priests; (*c*) the provision against the dangers incurred by handling or coming in contact with corpses, by eating certain foods, etc.; (*d*) the guarding the chief acts of life – birth, initiation, marriage and sexual functions, etc., against interference; (*e*) the securing of human beings against the wrath or power of gods and spirits;[2] (*f*) the securing of unborn infants and young children, who stand in a specially

1. This includes a bibliography of the chief literature on the subject.

2. In the present context this use of the term 'taboo' may be disregarded as not being a primary one.

sympathetic relation with one or both parents, from the consequences of certain actions, and more especially from the communication of qualities supposed to be derived from certain foods. (ii) Taboos are imposed in order to secure against thieves the property of an individual, his fields, tools, etc. ...'

The punishment for the violation of a taboo was no doubt originally left to an internal, automatic agency: the violated taboo itself took vengeance. When, at a later stage, ideas of gods and spirits arose, with whom taboo became associated, the penalty was expected to follow automatically from the divine power. In other cases, probably as a result of a further evolution of the concept, society itself took over the punishment of offenders, whose conduct had brought their fellows into danger. Thus the earliest human penal systems may be traced back to taboo.

'The violation of a taboo makes the offender himself taboo ...' Certain of the dangers brought into existence by the violation may be averted by acts of atonement and purification.

The source of taboo is attributed to a peculiar magical power which is inherent in persons and spirits and can be conveyed by them through the medium of inanimate objects. 'Persons or things which are regarded as taboo may be compared to objects charged with electricity; they are the seat of a tremendous power which is transmissible by contact, and may be liberated with destructive effect if the organisms which provoke its discharge are too weak to resist it; the result of a violation of a taboo depends partly on the strength of the magical influence inherent in the taboo object or person, partly on the strength of the opposing *mana* of the violator of the taboo. Thus, kings and chiefs are possessed of great power, and it is death for their subjects to address them directly; but a minister or other person of greater *mana* than common can approach them unharmed, and can in turn be approached by their inferiors without risk ... So too indirect taboos depend for their strength on the *mana* of him who imposes them; if it is a chief or a priest, they are more powerful than those imposed by a common person ...'

It is no doubt the transmissibility of taboo which accounts

for the attempts to throw it off by suitable purificatory ceremonies.

Taboos may be permanent or temporary. Among the former are those attaching to priests and chiefs, as well as to dead persons and anything belonging to them. Temporary taboos may be attached to certain particular states, such as menstruation and child-birth, to warriors before and after an expedition, or to special activities such as fishing and hunting. A general taboo may (like a Papal Interdict) be imposed upon a whole region and may then last for many years.

If I judge my readers' feelings aright, I think it is safe to say that in spite of all that they have now heard about taboo they still have very little idea of the meaning of the term or of what place to give it in their thoughts. This is no doubt due to the insufficiency of the information I have given them and to my having omitted to discuss the relation between taboo and superstition, the belief in spirits, and religion. On the other hand, I am afraid a more detailed account of what is known about taboo would have been even more confusing, and I can assure them that in fact the whole subject is highly obscure.

What we are concerned with, then, is a number of prohibitions to which these primitive races are subjected. Every sort of thing is forbidden; but they have no idea why, and it does not occur to them to raise the question. On the contrary, they submit to the prohibitions as though they were a matter of course and feel convinced that any violation of them will be automatically met by the direst punishment. We have trustworthy stories of how any unwitting violation of one of these prohibitions is in fact automatically punished. An innocent wrong-doer, who may, for instance, have eaten a forbidden animal, falls into a deep depression, anticipates death and then dies in real earnest. These prohibitions are mainly directed against liberty of enjoyment and against freedom of movement and communication. In some cases they have an intelligible meaning and are clearly aimed at abstinences and renunciations. But in other cases their subject-matter is quite incomprehensible; they are concerned with trivial details and seem to be of a purely ceremonial nature.

Behind all these prohibitions there seems to be something in the nature of a theory that they are necessary because certain persons and things are charged with a dangerous power, which can be transferred through contact with them, almost like an infection. The *quantity* of this dangerous attribute also plays a part. Some people or things have more of it than others and the danger is actually proportional to the difference of potential of the charges. The strangest fact seems to be that anyone who has transgressed one of these prohibitions himself acquires the characteristic of being prohibited – as though the whole of the dangerous charge had been transferred over to him. This power is attached to all *special* individuals, such as kings, priests or new-born babies, to all *exceptional* states, such as the physical states of menstruation, puberty or birth, and to all *uncanny* things, such as sickness and death and what is associated with them through their power of infection or contagion.

The word 'taboo' denotes everything, whether a person or a place or a thing or a transitory condition, which is the vehicle or source of this mysterious attribute. It also denotes the prohibitions arising from the same attribute. And, finally, it has a connotation which includes alike 'sacred' and 'above the ordinary', as well as 'dangerous', 'unclean' and 'uncanny'.

This word and the system denoted by it give expression to a group of mental attitudes and ideas which seem remote indeed from our understanding. In particular, there would seem to be no possibility of our coming into closer contact with them without examining the belief in ghosts and spirits which is characteristic of these low levels of culture.

Why, it may be asked at this point, should we concern ourselves at all with this riddle of taboo? Not only, I think, because it is worth while trying to solve *any* psychological problem for its own sake, but for other reasons as well. It may begin to dawn on us that the taboos of the savage Polynesians are after all not so remote from us as we were inclined to think at first, that the moral and conventional prohibitions by which we ourselves are governed may have some essential relationship with these primitive taboos and that an explanation of taboo might throw a light upon the obscure origin of our own 'categorical imperative'.

Accordingly, we shall be particularly interested to hear the views of so notable an investigator as Wilhelm Wundt on the subject of taboo, especially as he promises 'to trace back the concept of taboo to its earliest roots' (1906, 301).

Wundt writes of that concept that 'it comprises all of the usages in which is expressed a dread of certain objects related to cult ideas or of actions connected with them'. (Ibid., 237.) And, in another passage: 'If we understand by it [taboo], in accordance with the general meaning of the word, every prohibition (whether laid down in usage or custom or in explicitly formulated laws) against touching an object or making use of it for one's own purposes or against using certain proscribed words ...' then, he goes on, there can be no race and no level of culture which has escaped the ill-effects of taboo. [Ibid., 301.]

Wundt next proceeds to explain why it seems to him advisable to study the nature of taboo in the primitive conditions of the Australian savages rather than in the higher culture of the Polynesian peoples. [Ibid., 302.] He divides the taboo prohibitions among the Australians into three classes, according as they affect animals, human beings or other objects. The taboos on animals, which consist essentially of prohibitions against killing and eating them, constitute the nucleus of *Totemism*. [Ibid., 303.][1] The second class of taboos, those directed towards human beings, are of an entirely different kind. They are restricted in the first instance to circumstances in which the person on whom the taboo is imposed finds himself in an unusual situation. Thus young men are taboo at their initiation ceremonies, women are taboo during menstruation and immediately after giving birth; so too new-born babies, sick persons and, above all, the dead are taboo. A man's property which is in his constant use is permanently taboo to all other men: his clothing, for instance, his

1. Cf. the first and fourth essays in this work [p. 53 ff. and p. 159 ff.].

tools and weapons. Included in a man's most personal property, in Australia, is the new name which he received when he was a boy at his initiation. It is taboo and must be kept secret. The third class of taboos, which are imposed on trees, plants, houses and localities, are less stable. They appear to follow a rule that anything that is uncanny or provokes dread for any reason becomes subject to taboo. [Ibid., 304.]

The modifications shown by taboo in the richer culture of Polynesia and the Malay Archipelago are, as Wundt himself is obliged to admit, not very profound. The more marked social differences among these peoples find expression in the fact that chiefs, kings and priests exercise a specially effective taboo and are themselves subject to a taboo of the greatest force. [Ibid., 305–6.]

But, adds Wundt, the true sources of taboo lie deeper than in the interests of the privileged classes: 'they have their origin in the source of the most primitive and at the same time most lasting of human instincts – in fear of "demonic" powers.' (Ibid., 307.) 'Taboo is originally nothing other than the objectified fear of the "demonic" power which is believed to lie hidden in a tabooed object. The taboo prohibits anything that may provoke that power and commands that, if it has been injured, whether wittingly or unwittingly, the demon's vengeance must be averted.' [Ibid., 308.]

Little by little, we are told, taboo then grows into a force with a basis of its own, independent of the belief in demons. It develops into the rule of custom and tradition and finally of law. 'But the unspoken command underlying all the prohibitions of taboo, with their numberless variations according to the time and place, is originally one and one only: "Beware of the wrath of demons!"' [Loc. cit.]

Wundt informs us, then, that taboo is an expression and derivative of the belief of primitive peoples in 'demonic' power. Later, he tells us, it freed itself from this root and remained a power simply because it *was* a power – from a kind of mental conservatism. And thereafter it itself became the root of our moral precepts and of our laws. Though the first of these assertions may provoke little contradiction, I believe I shall be expressing the thoughts of many readers when I say that Wundt's explanation comes as something of a disappointment. This is surely not tracing back the concept of taboo to its sources or revealing its earliest roots. Neither fear nor demons can be regarded by psychology as 'earliest' things, impervious to any attempt at discovering their antecedents. It would be another matter if demons really existed. But we know that, like gods, they are creations of the human mind: they were made by something and out of something.

Wundt has important views on the double significance of taboo, though these are not very clearly expressed. According to him, the distinction between 'sacred' and 'unclean' did not exist in the primitive beginnings of taboo. For that very reason those concepts were at that stage without the peculiar significance which they could only acquire when they became opposed to each other. Animals, human beings or localities on which a taboo was imposed were 'demonic', not 'sacred', nor, therefore, in the sense which was later acquired, 'unclean'. It is precisely this neutral and intermediate meaning – 'demonic' or 'what may not be touched' – that is appropriately expressed by the word 'taboo', since it stresses a characteristic which remains common for all time both to what is sacred and to what is unclean: the dread of contact with it. The persistence, however, of this important common characteristic is at the same time evidence that the ground covered by the two was originally one and that it was only as a result of further influences that it became differentiated and eventually developed into opposites. [Ibid., 309.]

According to Wundt, this original characteristic of taboo – the belief in a 'demonic' power which lies hidden in an object and which, if the object is touched or used unlawfully, takes its vengeance by casting a spell over the wrong-doer – is still wholly and solely 'objectified fear'. That fear has not yet split up into the two forms into which it later develops: veneration and horror. [Ibid., 310.]

But how did this split take place? Through the transplanting, so Wundt tells us, of the taboo ordinances from the sphere of demons into the sphere of belief in gods. [Ibid., 311.] The contrast between 'sacred' and 'unclean' coincides with a succession of two stages of mythology. The earlier of these stages did not completely disappear when the second one was reached but persisted in what was regarded as an inferior and eventually a contemptible form. [Ibid., 312.] It is, he says, a general law of mythology that a stage which has been passed, for the very reason that it has been overcome and driven under by a superior stage, persists in an inferior form alongside the later one, so that the objects of its veneration turn into objects of horror. [Ibid., 313.]

The remainder of Wundt's discussion deals with the relation of the concept of taboo to purification and sacrifice.

(2)

Anyone approaching the problem of taboo from the angle of psychoanalysis, that is to say, of the investigation of the unconscious portion of the individual mind, will recognize, after a moment's reflection, that these phenomena are far from unfamiliar to him. He has come across people who have created for themselves individual taboo prohibitions of this very kind and who obey them just as strictly as savages obey the communal taboos of their tribe or society. If he were not already accustomed to describing such people as 'obsessional' patients, he would find 'taboo sickness' a most appropriate name for their condition. Having learnt so much, however, about this obsessional sickness from psychoanalytic examination – its clinical aetiology and the essence of its psychical mechanism – he can scarcely refrain from applying the knowledge he has thus acquired to the parallel sociological phenomenon.

A warning must be uttered at this point. The similarity between taboo and obsessional sickness may be no more than a matter of externals; it may apply only to the *forms* in which they are manifested and not extend to their essential character. Nature delights in making use of the same forms in the most various biological connections: as it does, for instance, in the appearance of branch-like structures both in coral and in plants, and indeed in some forms of crystal and in certain chemical precipitates. It would obviously be hasty and unprofitable to infer the existence of any internal relationship from such points of agreement as these, which merely derive from the operation of the same mechanical causes. We shall bear this warning in mind, but we need not be deterred by it from proceeding with our comparison.

The most obvious and striking point of agreement between the obsessional prohibitions of neurotics and taboos is that these prohibitions are equally lacking in motive and equally puzzling in their origin. Having made their appearance at some un-specified moment, they are forcibly maintained by an irresistible fear. No external threat of punishment is required, for there is an internal certainty, a moral conviction, that any violation will lead to intolerable disaster. The most that an obsessional patient can say on this point is that he has an undefined feeling that some particular person in his environment will be injured as a result of the violation. Nothing is known of the nature of the injury; and indeed even this wretchedly small amount of information is more often obtained in connection with the expiatory and defensive actions which we shall have to discuss later than with the prohibitions themselves.

As in the case of taboo, the principal prohibition, the nucleus of the neurosis, is against touching; and thence it is sometimes known as 'touching phobia' or '*délire du toucher*'. The prohibition does not merely apply to immediate physical contact but has an extent as wide as the metaphorical use of the phrase 'to come in contact with'. Anything that directs the patient's thoughts to the forbidden object, anything that brings him into intellectual contact with it, is just as much prohibited as direct physical contact. This same extension also occurs in the case of taboo.

The purpose of some of the prohibitions is immediately obvious. Others, on the contrary, strike us as incomprehensible, senseless and silly, and prohibitions of this latter sort are described as 'ceremonial'. This distinction, too, is found in the observances of taboo. [See pp. 74–5.]

Obsessional prohibitions are extremely liable to displacement. They extend from one object to another along whatever paths the context may provide, and this new object then becomes, to use the apt expression of one of my women patients, 'impossible' – till at last the whole world lies under an embargo of 'impossibility'. Obsessional patients behave as though the 'impossible' persons and things were carriers of a dangerous infection liable to be spread by contact on to everything in their neighbourhood. I have already [p. 75] drawn attention to the same characteristic capacity for contagion and transference in my description of taboo. We know, too, that anyone who violates a taboo by coming into contact with something that is taboo becomes taboo himself and that then no one may come into contact with *him*.

I will now put side by side two instances of the transference (or, as it is better to say, the *displacement*) of a prohibition. One of these is taken from the life of the Maoris and the other from an observation of my own on a female obsessional patient.

'A Maori chief would not blow a fire with his mouth; for his sacred breath would communicate its sanctity to the fire, which would pass it on to the pot, which would pass it on to the man who ate the meat, which was in the pot, which stood on the fire, which was breathed on by the chief; so that the eater, infected by the chief's breath conveyed through these intermediaries, would surely die.'[1]

My patient's husband purchased a household article of some kind and brought it home with him. She insisted that it should be removed or it would make the room she lived in 'impossible'. For she had heard that the article had been bought in a shop situated in, let us say, 'Smith' Street.[2] 'Smith', however, was the married name of a woman friend of hers who lived in a distant town and whom she had known in her youth under

1. Frazer (1911*b*, 136) [quoting Taylor (1870, 165)].
2. ['*Hirschengasse*' and '*Hirsch*' in the original.]

her maiden name. This friend of hers was at the moment 'impossible' or taboo. Consequently the article that had been purchased here in Vienna was as taboo as the friend herself with whom she must not come into contact.

Obsessional prohibitions involve just as extensive renunciations and restrictions in the lives of those who are subject to them as do taboo prohibitions; but some of them can be lifted if certain actions are performed. Thereafter, these actions *must* be performed: they become compulsive or obsessive acts, and there can be no doubt that they are in the nature of expiation, penance, defensive measures and purification. The commonest of these obsessive acts is washing in water ('washing mania'). Some taboo prohibitions can be replaced in just the same way; or rather their violation can be made good by a similar 'ceremonial'; and here again lustration with water is the preferred method.

Let us now summarize the points in which agreement between taboo usages and obsessional symptoms is most clearly shown: (1) the fact that the prohibitions lack any assignable motive; (2) the fact that they are maintained by an internal necessity; (3) the fact that they are easily displaceable and that there is a risk of infection from the prohibited object; and (4) the fact that they give rise to injunctions for the performances of ceremonial acts.

Now both the clinical history and the psychical mechanism of obsessional neurosis have become known to us through psychoanalysis. The clinical history of a typical case of 'touching phobia' is as follows. Right at the beginning, in very early childhood, the patient shows a strong *desire* to touch, the aim of which is of a far more specialized kind that one would have been inclined to expect. This desire is promptly met by an *external* prohibition against carrying out that particular kind of touching.[1] The prohibition is accepted, since it finds support from powerful *internal* forces,[2] and proves stronger than the

1. Both the desire and the prohibition relate to the child's touching his own genitals.
2. That is, from the child's loving relation to the authors of the prohibition.

instinct which is seeking to express itself in the touching. In consequence, however, of the child's primitive psychical constitution, the prohibition does not succeed in *abolishing* the instinct. Its only result is to *repress* the instinct (the desire to touch) and banish it into the unconscious. Both the prohibition and the instinct persist: the instinct because it has only been repressed and not abolished, and the prohibition because, if it ceased, the instinct would force its way through into consciousness and into actual operation. A situation is created which remains undealt with – a psychical fixation – and everything else follows from the continuing conflict between the prohibition and the instinct.

The principal characteristic of the psychological constellation which becomes fixed in this way is what might be described as the subject's *ambivalent*[1] attitude towards a single object, or rather towards one act in connection with that object. He is constantly wishing to perform this act (the touching), [and looks on it as his supreme enjoyment, but he must not perform it] and detests it as well.[2] The conflict between these two currents cannot be promptly settled because – there is no other way of putting it – they are localized in the subject's mind in such a manner that they cannot come up against each other. The prohibition is noisily conscious, while the persistent desire to touch is unconscious and the subject knows nothing of it. If it were not for this psychological factor, an ambivalence like this could neither last so long nor lead to such consequences.

In our clinical history of a case we have insisted that the imposition of the prohibition in very early childhood is the determining point; a similar importance attaches in the subsequent developments to the mechanism of repression at the same early age. As a result of the repression which has been enforced and which involves a loss of memory – an amnesia – the motives for the prohibition (which is conscious) remain unknown; and all attempts at disposing of it by intellectual

1. To borrow the apt term coined by Bleuler [1910].
2. [From the second edition (1920) onwards, the words in square brackets were, perhaps accidentally, omitted.]

processess must fail, since they cannot find any base of attack. The prohibition owes its strength and its obsessive character precisely to its unconscious opponent, the concealed and undiminished desire – that is to say, to an internal necessity inaccessible to conscious inspection. The ease with which the prohibition can be transferred and extended reflects a process which falls in with the unconscious desire and is greatly facilitated by the psychological conditions that prevail in the unconscious. The instinctual desire is constantly shifting in order to escape from the *impasse* and endeavours to find substitutes – substitute objects and substitute acts – in place of the prohibited ones. In consequence of this, the prohibition itself shifts about as well, and extends to any new aims which the forbidden impulse may adopt. Any fresh advance made by the repressed libido is answered by a fresh sharpening of the prohibition. The mutual inhibition of the two conflicting forces produces a need for discharge, for reducing the prevailing tension; and to this may be attributed the reason for the performance of obsessive acts. In the case of a neurosis these are clearly compromise actions: from one point of view they are evidences of remorse, efforts at expiation, and so on, while on the other hand they are at the same time substitutive acts to compensate the instinct for what has been prohibited. It is a law of neurotic illness that these obsessive acts fall more and more under the sway of the instinct and approach nearer and nearer to the activity which was originally prohibited.

Let us now make the experiment of treating taboo as though it were of the same nature as an obsessional prohibition in one of our patients. We must make it clear beforehand, however, that many of the taboo prohibitions that come under our notice are of a secondary, displaced and distorted kind, and that we shall have to be satisfied if we can throw only a little light on the most fundamental and significant taboos. Moreover, the differences between the situation of a savage and of a neurotic are no doubt of sufficient importance to make any exact agreement impossible and to prevent our carrying the comparison to the point of identity in every detail.

In the first place, then, it must be said that there is no sense in asking savages to tell us the real reason for their prohibitions – the origin of taboo. It follows from our postulates that they cannot answer since their real reason must be 'unconscious'. We can, however, reconstruct the history of taboo as follows on the model of obsessional prohibitions. Taboos, we must suppose, are prohibitions of primaeval antiquity which were at some time externally imposed upon a generation of primitive men; they must, that is to say, no doubt have been impressed on them violently by the previous generation. These prohibitions must have concerned activities towards which there was a strong inclination. They must have persisted from generation to generation, perhaps merely as a result of tradition transmitted through parental and social authority. Possibly, however, in later generations they may have become 'organized' as an inherited psychical endowment. Who can decide whether such things as 'innate ideas' exist, or whether in the present instance they have operated, either alone or in conjunction with education, to bring about the permanent fixing of taboos? But one thing would certainly follow from the persistence of the taboo, namely that the original desire to do the prohibited thing must also still persist among the tribes concerned. They must therefore have an ambivalent attitude towards their taboos. In their unconscious there is nothing they would like more than to violate them, but they are afraid to do so; they are afraid precisely because they would like to, and the fear is stronger than the desire. The desire is unconscious, however, in every individual member of the tribe just as it is in neurotics.

The most ancient and important taboo prohibitions are the two basic laws of totemism: not to kill the totem animal and to avoid sexual intercourse with members of the totem clan of the opposite sex.

These, then, must be the oldest and most powerful of human desires. We cannot hope to understand this or test our hypothesis on these two examples, so long as we are totally ignorant of the meaning and origin of the totemic system. But the wording of these two taboos and the fact of their concurrence will remind anyone acquainted with the findings of psychoanalytic investigations on individuals of something quite definite, which psychoanalysts regard as the centre-point of childhood wishes and as the nucleus of neuroses.[1]

The multiplicity of the manifestations of taboo, which have led to the attempts at classification that I have already mentioned, are reduced to a single unity by our thesis: the basis of taboo is a prohibited action, for performing which a strong inclination exists in the unconscious.

We have heard [see p. 73], though without understanding it, that anyone who does what is forbidden, that is, who violates a taboo, becomes taboo himself. How is this to be brought into line with the fact that taboo attaches not only to a person who has done what is forbidden but also to persons in particular states, to the states themselves, as well as to impersonal objects? What can the dangerous attribute be which remains the same under all these different conditions? There is only one thing it can be: the quality of exciting men's ambivalence and *tempting* them to transgress the prohibition.

Anyone who has violated a taboo becomes taboo himself because he possesses the dangerous quality of tempting others to follow his example: why should *he* be allowed to do what is forbidden to others? Thus he is truly contagious in that every example encourages imitation, and for that reason he himself must be shunned.

But a person who has not violated any taboo may yet be permanently or temporarily taboo because he is in a state which possesses the quality of arousing forbidden desires in others and of awakening a conflict of ambivalence in them. The majority of exceptional positions and exceptional states [see p. 75] are of this kind and possess this dangerous power. The king or chief arouses envy on account of his privileges: everyone, perhaps, would like to be a king. Dead men, new-born

1. Cf. my forthcoming study upon totemism, to which I have referred more than once in these pages (the fourth essay in this work) [p. 159 ff. below].

babies and women menstruating or in labour stimulate desires by their special helplessness; a man who has just reached maturity stimulates them by the promise of new enjoyment. For that reason all of these persons and all of these states are taboo, since temptation must be resisted.

Now, too, we can understand why the amounts of *mana* possessed by different persons can be subtracted from one another and can to some extent cancel one another out [see p. 73]. A king's taboo is too strong for one of his subjects because the social difference between them is too great. But a minister may without any harm serve as an intermediary between them. If we translate this from the language of taboo into that of normal psychology, it means something like this. A subject, who dreads the great temptation presented to him by contact with the king, can perhaps tolerate dealings with an official whom he does not need to envy so much and whose position may even seem attainable to him. A minister, again, can mitigate his envy of the king by reflecting on the power which he himself wields. So it comes about that smaller differences between the amounts of the tempting magical force possessed by two people are less to be feared than greater ones.

It is equally clear why it is that the violation of certain taboo prohibitions constitutes a social danger which must be punished or atoned for by *all* the members of the community if they are not all to suffer injury [see p. 73]. If we replace the unconscious desires by conscious impulses we shall see that the danger is a real one. It lies in the risk of imitation, which would quickly lead to the dissolution of the community. If the violation were not avenged by the other members they would become aware that they wanted to act in the same way as the transgressor.

We cannot be surprised at the fact that, in the restrictions of taboo, touching plays a part similar to the one which it plays in 'touching phobias', though the secret meaning of the prohibition cannot be of such a specialized nature in taboo as it is in the neurosis. Touching is the first step towards obtaining any sort of control over, or attempting to make use of, a person or object.

We have translated the contagious power inherent in taboo into the possession of some attribute likely to produce temptation or encourage imitation. This does not appear to tally with the fact that the contagious character of taboo is shown chiefly by its transmissibility on to material objects, which then themselves become carriers of taboo.

This transmissibility of taboo is a reflection of the tendency, on which we have already remarked, for the unconscious instinct in the neurosis to shift constantly along associative paths on to new objects. Our attention is thus directed to the fact that the dangerous magical force of *mana* corresponds to two powers of a more realistic sort: the power of reminding a man of his own prohibited wishes and the apparently more important one of inducing him to transgress the prohibition in obedience to those wishes. These two functions can be reduced to one, however, if we suppose that in a primitive mind the awakening of the memory of a forbidden action is naturally linked with the awakening of an impulse to put that action into effect. Thus recollection and temptation come together again. It must be admitted, too, that, in so far as the example of a man transgressing a prohibition tempts another man to do the same, disobedience to prohibitions spreads like a contagion, in just the same way as a taboo is transferred from a person to a material object and from one material object to another.

If the violation of a taboo can be made good by atonement or expiation, which involve the renunciation of some possession or some freedom, this proves that obedience to the taboo injunction meant in itself the renunciation of something desirable. Emancipation from one renunciation is made up for by the imposition of another one elsewhere. This leads us to conclude that atonement is a more fundamental factor than purification in the ceremonials of taboo.

I will now sum up the respects in which light has been

thrown on the nature of taboo by comparing it with the obsessional prohibitions of neurotics. Taboo is a primaeval prohibition forcibly imposed (by some authority) from outside, and directed against the most powerful longings to which human beings are subject. The desire to violate it persists in their unconscious; those who obey the taboo have an ambivalent attitude to what the taboo prohibits. The magical power that is attributed to taboo is based on the capacity for arousing temptation; and it acts like a contagion because examples are contagious and because the prohibited desire in the unconscious shifts from one thing to another. The fact that the violation of a taboo can be atoned for by a renunciation shows that renunciation lies at the basis of obedience to taboo.

(3)

What we now want to discover is how much value is to be attributed to the parallel we have drawn between taboo and obsessional neurosis and to the view of taboo which we have based on that parallel. Their value must clearly depend on whether the view we have put forward has any advantages over others, and whether it gives us a clearer understanding of taboo than we could otherwise reach. We may be inclined to feel that we have given sufficient evidence of the applicability of our view in what has already been said; yet we must attempt to strengthen the evidence by entering into our explanation of taboo prohibitions and usages in greater detail.

There is also another path open to us. We can start an inquiry as to whether some of the hypotheses which we have carried over from neuroses to taboo or some of the results to which that procedure has led us may not be directly verifiable in the phenomena of taboo. But we must decide what we are to look for. Our assertion that taboo originated in a primaeval prohibition imposed at one time or other by some external authority is obviously incapable of demonstration. What we shall rather endeavour to confirm, therefore, are the psychological determinants of taboo, which we have learnt to know from obsessional neurosis. How did we arrive at our knowledge of these psychological factors in the case of the neurosis? Through the analytical study of its symptoms, and particularly of obsessional acts, defensive measures and obsessional commands. We found that they showed every sign of being derived from *ambivalent* impulses, either corresponding simultaneously to *both* a wish and a counter-wish or operating predominantly on behalf of *one* of the two opposing trends. If, now, we could succeed in demonstrating that ambivalence, that is, the dominance of opposing trends, is also to be found in the observances of taboo, or if we could point to some of them which, like obsessional acts, give simultaneous expression to both currents, we should have established the psychological agreement between taboo and obsessional neurosis in what is perhaps their most important feature.

The two fundamental prohibitions of taboo are, as I have already remarked, inaccessible to our analysis owing to their connection with totemism; while certain others of its injunctions are of a secondary nature and consequently useless for our purpose. For taboo has become the ordinary method of legislation in the communities affected by it and it has come to serve social purposes which are certainly more recent than taboo itself: such, for instance, are the taboos imposed by chiefs and priests for the protection of their own property and privileges. There nevertheless remain a large group of observances on which our investigation can be made. From these I shall select the taboos attaching (*a*) to enemies, (*b*) to chiefs and (*c*) to the dead; and I shall take the material for our examination from the excellent collection included by Frazer in *Taboo and the Perils of the Soul* (1911*b*), the second part of his great work *The Golden Bough*.

(*a*) The Treatment of Enemies

We may be inclined to suppose that savage and half-savage races are guilty of uninhibited and ruthless cruelty towards their enemies. We shall be greatly interested to learn, then, that even in their case the killing of a man is governed by a number of observances which are included among the usages of taboo. These observances fall easily into four groups. They demand (1) the appeasement of the slain enemy, (2) restrictions upon the slayer, (3) acts of expiation and purification by him and (4) certain ceremonial observances. Our incomplete information on the subject does not enable us to determine with certainty how general or the reverse these usages may be among the peoples concerned; but for our purposes this is a matter of indifference. It may safely be assumed, in any case, that what we have before us are not isolated peculiarities but widespread usages.

The rites of *appeasement* performed in the island of Timor, when a warlike expedition has returned in triumph bringing the heads of the vanquished foe, are particularly remarkable, since in addition to them the leader of the expedition is submitted to severe restrictions (see below, p. 93). On the occasion of the expedition's return, sacrifices are offered to appease the souls of the men whose heads have been taken. 'The people think that some misfortune would befall the victor were such offerings omitted. Moreover, a part of the ceremony consists of a dance accompanied by a song, in which the death of the slain man is lamented and his forgiveness is entreated. "Be not angry", they say, "because your head is here with us; had we been less lucky, our heads might now have been exposed in your village. We have offered the sacrifice to appease you. Your spirit may now rest and leave us in peace. Why were you our enemy? Would it not have been better that we should remain friends? Then your blood would not have been spilt and your head would not have been cut off." '[1] The same is true of the people of Paloo, in Celebes. So, too, 'the Gallas [of East Africa] returning from war sacrifice to the jinn or guardian spirits of their slain foes before they will re-enter their own houses'.[2]

1. Frazer (1911b, 166) [quoting Gramberg (1872, 216)].
2. Frazer (loc. cit.), quoting Paulitschke (1893–6 [**2**, 50, 136]).

Other peoples have found a means for changing their former enemies after their death into guardians, friends and benefactors. This method lies in treating their severed heads with affection, as some of the savage races of Borneo boast of doing. When the Sea Dyaks of Sarawak bring home a head from a successful head-hunting expedition, for months after its arrival it is treated with the greatest consideration and addressed with all the names of endearment of which their language is capable. The most dainty morsels of food are thrust into its mouth, delicacies of all kinds and even cigars. The head is repeatedly implored to hate its former friends and to love its new hosts since it has now become one of them. It would be a great mistake to suppose that these observances, which strike us as so horrible, are performed with any intention of ridicule.[1]

In several of the savage tribes of North America observers have been struck by the mourning over enemies who have been killed and scalped. When a Choctaw had killed an enemy, he went into mourning for a month during which he was subjected to severe restrictions; and the Dacotas had similar practices. When the Osages, reports a witness, have mourned over their own dead, 'they will mourn for the foe just as if he was a friend'.[2]

Before considering the remaining classes of taboo usages in connection with enemies, we must deal with an obvious objection. It will be argued against us, with Frazer and others, that the grounds for such rites of appeasement are simple enough and have nothing to do with any such thing as 'ambivalence'. These peoples are dominated by a superstitious fear of the ghosts of the slain – a fear which was not unknown in classical antiquity and which was put upon the stage by the great English dramatist in the hallucinations of Macbeth and Richard III. All the rites of appeasement follow logically from this superstition, as well as the restrictions and acts of expiation which will be discussed presently. This view is also supported

1. Frazer (1914, I, 295), quoting Low (1848 [206]).
2. Frazer (1911b, 181), quoting Dorsey (1884 [126]).

by the fourth group of these observances, which can only be explained as attempts at driving away the ghosts of the victims that are pursuing their murderers.[1] In addition to this, the savages openly admit their fear of the ghosts of dead enemies and themselves attribute to it the taboo usages which we are discussing.

This objection is indeed an obvious one, and if it covered the whole ground we could save ourselves the trouble of any further attempt at an explanation. I shall put off dealing with it until later, and for the moment I will merely state the alternative view which is derived from the hypothesis based upon our earlier discussions of taboo. The conclusion that we must draw from all these observances is that the impulses which they express towards an enemy are not solely hostile ones. They are also manifestations of remorse, of admiration for the enemy, and of a bad conscience for having killed him. It is difficult to resist the notion that, long before a table of laws was handed down by any god, these savages were in possession of a living commandment: 'Thou shalt not kill', a violation of which would not go unpunished.

Let us now return to the other three groups of taboo observances. *Restrictions* placed upon a victorious slayer are unusually frequent and as a rule severe. In Timor (cf. the rites of appeasement described above, on p. 91) the leader of the expedition is forbidden 'to return at once to his own house. A special hut is prepared for him, in which he has to reside for two months, undergoing bodily and spiritual purification. During this time he may not go to his wife nor feed himself; the food must be put into his mouth by another person.'[2] In some Dyak tribes men returning from a successful expedition are obliged to keep to themselves for several days and abstain from various kinds of food; they may not touch iron nor have any intercourse with women. In Logea, an island in the neighbourhood of New Guinea, 'men who have killed or assisted

---

1. Frazer (1911b, 169–74). These ceremonies consist of beating on shields, shouting and screaming, making noises with musical instruments, etc.

2. Frazer (1911b, 166), quoting Müller (1857 [2, 252]).

in killing enemies shut themselves up for about a week in their houses. They must avoid all intercourse with their wives and friends, and they may not touch food with their hands. They may eat vegetable food only, which is brought to them cooked in special pots. The intention of these restrictions is to guard the men against the smell of the blood of the slain; for it is believed that if they smelt the blood they would fall ill and die. In the Toaripi or Motumotu tribe of south-eastern New Guinea a man who has killed another may not go near his wife, and may not touch food with his fingers. He is fed by others, and only with certain kinds of food. These observances last till the new moon.' (Frazer, 1911b, 167.)

I shall not attempt to give a complete catalogue of the instances quoted by Frazer of restrictions imposed upon victorious manslayers. I will only remark upon a few more such cases in which their taboo character is particularly marked or in which the restrictions are accompanied by expiation, purification and other ceremonials.

'Among the Monumbos of German New Guinea anyone who has slain a foe in war becomes thereby "unclean"' – the same term being applied to women who are menstruating or in child-bed. He 'must remain a long time in the men's club-house, while the villagers gather round him and celebrate his victory with dance and song. He may touch nobody, not even his own wife and children; if he were to touch them it is believed that they would be covered with sores. He becomes clean again by washing and using other modes of purification.' [Ibid., 169.]

'Among the Natchez of North America young braves who had taken their first scalps were obliged to observe certain rules of abstinence for six months. They might not sleep with their wives nor eat flesh; their only food was fish and hasty-pudding ... When a Choctaw had killed an enemy and taken his scalp, he went into mourning for a month, during which he might not comb his hair, and if his head itched he might not scratch it except with a little stick which he wore fastened to his wrist for the purpose.' [Ibid., 181.]

'When a Pima Indian had killed an Apache, he had to go through severe ceremonies of purification and atonement. During a sixteen-day fast he might not touch meat nor salt, nor look on a blazing fire, nor speak to a human being. He lived alone in the woods, waited on by an old woman, who brought him his scanty dole of food. He bathed often in the river and (as a sign of mourning) kept his head covered with a plaster of mud. On the seventeenth day there was a public ceremony of solemn purification of the man and his weapons. Since the Pima Indians took the taboo on killing much more seriously than their enemies and did not, like them, postpone the expiation and purification till the end of the expedition, their warlike efficiency suffered greatly from their moral strictness, or piety, if that term is preferred. Despite their extreme courage, the Americans found them unsatisfactory allies in their operations against the Apaches.' [Ibid., 182–4.]

However much the details and variations of the ceremonies of expiation and purification after the slaying of enemies might be of interest for deeper research into the subject, I shall break off at this point, since for our present purpose they have nothing more to tell us. I may perhaps suggest that the temporary or permanent isolation of professional executioners, which has persisted to the present day, may belong in this connection. The position of the public hangman in mediaeval society offers a good picture of the workings of taboo among savages.[1]

In the accepted explanation of all these observances of appeasement, restriction, expiation and purification, two principles are combined: the extension of the taboo from the slain man on to everything that has come in contact with him, and the fear of the slain man's ghost. How these two factors are to be combined with each other to explain the ceremonials, whether they are to be regarded as of equal weight, whether one is primary and the other secondary, and if so which – none of these questions receives an answer, and indeed it would be hard to find one. We, on the other hand, can lay stress on

1. Further examples of these practices will be found in Frazer (1911b, 165–90) in the section upon 'Manslayers tabooed'.

the *unity* of our view, which derives all of these observances from emotional ambivalence towards the enemy.

(b) *The Taboo upon Rulers*

The attitude of primitive peoples to their chiefs, kings and priests is governed by two basic principles which seem to be complementary rather than contradictory. A ruler 'must not only be guarded, he must also be guarded against'. (Frazer, 1911*b*, 132.) Both of these ends are secured by innumerable taboo observances. We know already why it is that rulers must be guarded against. It is because they are vehicles of the mysterious and dangerous magical power which is transmitted by contact like an electric charge and which brings death and ruin to anyone who is not protected by a similar charge. Any immediate or indirect contact with this dangerous sacred entity is therefore avoided; and, if it cannot be avoided, some ceremonial is devised to avert the dreaded consequences. The Nubas of East Africa, for instance, 'believe that they would die if they entered the house of their priestly king; however they can evade the penalty of their intrusion by baring the left shoulder and getting the king to lay his hand on it'. [Loc. cit.] Here we are met by the remarkable fact that contact with the king is a remedy and protection against the dangers provoked by contact with the king. No doubt, however, there is a contrast to be drawn between the remedial power of a touch made deliberately by the king and the danger which arises if he is touched – a contrast between a passive and an active relation to the king.

For examples of the healing power of the royal touch there is no need to resort to savages. The kings of England, in times that are not yet remote, enjoyed the power of curing scrofula, which was known accordingly as 'the King's Evil'. Queen Elizabeth I exercised this royal prerogative no less than her successors. Charles I is said to have cured a hundred patients at a stroke in 1633. But it was after the Restoration of the monarchy under his dissolute son, Charles II, that the royal cures of scrofula reached their climax. In the course of his reign he is reputed to have touched close upon a hundred thousand persons. The crowd of those in search of cure used to be so great that on one occasion six or seven of those who came to be healed were trampled to death. The sceptical William of Orange, who became King of England after the dismissal of the Stuarts, refused to lend himself to these magical practices. On the only occasion on which he was persuaded into laying his hands on a patient, he said to him: 'God give you better health and more sense.' (Frazer, 1911a, I, 368–70).

The stories which follow are evidence of the fearful effects of active contact made, even unintentionally, with a king or anything belonging to him. 'It once happened that a New Zealand chief of high rank and great sanctity had left the remains of his dinner by the wayside. A slave, a stout, hungry fellow, coming up after the chief had gone, saw the unfinished dinner, and ate it up without asking questions. Hardly had he finished when he was informed by a horror-stricken spectator that the food of which he had eaten was the chief's.' He was a strong, courageous man, but 'no sooner did he hear the fatal news than he was seized with the most extraordinary convulsions and cramp in the stomach, which never ceased till he died, about sundown the same day'.[1] 'A Maori woman having eaten of some fruit, and being afterwards told that the fruit had been taken from a tabooed place, exclaimed that the spirit of the chief, whose sanctity had been thus profaned, would kill her. This was in the afternoon, and next day by twelve o'clock she was dead.'[2] 'A Maori chief's tinder-box was once the means of killing several persons; for, having been lost by him, and found by some men who used it to light their pipes, they died of fright on learning to whom it had belonged.'[3]

It is not to be wondered at that a need was felt for isolating such dangerous persons as chiefs and priests from the rest of the community – to build a barrier round them which would make them inaccessible. It may begin to dawn on us that this

1. Frazer (1911b, 134–5), quoting a Pakeha Maori (1884 [96 f.]).
2. Frazer (loc. cit.), quoting Brown (1845 [76]).
3. Frazer (loc. cit.) [quoting Taylor (1870, 164)].

barrier, originally erected for the observance of taboo, exists to this day in the form of court ceremonial.

But perhaps the major part of this taboo upon rulers is not derived from the need for protection *against* them. The second reason for the special treatment of privileged persons – the need to provide protection *for* them against the threat of danger – has had an obvious part in creating taboos and so of giving rise to court etiquette.

The need to protect the king from every possible form of danger follows from his immense importance to his subjects, whether for weal or woe. It is his person which, strictly speaking, regulates the whole course of existence. 'The people have to thank him for the rain and sunshine which foster the fruits of the earth, for the wind which brings ships to their coasts, and even for the solid ground beneath their feet.' (Frazer, 1911*b*, 7.)

These rulers among savage peoples possess a degree of power and a capacity to confer benefits which are an attribute only of gods, and with which at later stages of civilization only the most servile of courtiers would pretend to credit them.

It must strike us as self-contradictory that persons of such unlimited power should need to be protected so carefully from the threat of danger; but that is not the only contradiction shown in the treatment of royal personages among savage peoples. For these peoples also think it necessary to keep a watch on their king to see that he makes a proper use of his powers; they feel by no means convinced of his good intentions or conscientiousness. Thus an element of distrust may be traced among the reasons for the taboo observances that surround the king. 'The idea', writes Frazer (1911*b*, 7 f.), 'that early kingdoms are despotisms in which the people exist only for the sovereign, is wholly inapplicable to the monarchies we are considering. On the contrary, the sovereign in them exists only for his subjects; his life is only valuable so long as he discharges the duties of his position by ordering the course of nature for his people's benefit. So soon as he fails to do so, the care, the devotion, the religious homage which they had hitherto lavished on him cease and are changed into hatred and contempt; he is dismissed ignominiously, and may be thankful if he escapes with his life. Worshipped as a god one day, he is killed as a criminal the next. But in this changed behaviour of the people there is nothing capricious or inconstant. On the contrary, their conduct is entirely of a piece. If their king is their god, he is or should be also their preserver; and if he will not preserve them, he must make room for another who will. So long, however, as he answers their expectations, there is no limit to the care which they take of him, and which they compel him to take of himself. A king of this sort lives hedged in by a ceremonious etiquette, a network of prohibitions and observances, of which the intention is not to contribute to his dignity, much less to his comfort, but to restrain him from conduct which, by disturbing the harmony of nature, might involve himself, his people, and the universe in one common catastrophe. Far from adding to his comfort, these observances, by trammelling his every act, annihilate his freedom and often render the very life, which it is their object to preserve, a burden and sorrow to him.'

One of the most glaring instances of a sacred ruler being fettered and paralysed in this way by taboo ceremonials is to be found in the mode of life of the Mikado of Japan in earlier centuries. An account written more than two hundred years ago reports that the Mikado 'thinks it would be very prejudicial to his dignity and holiness to touch the ground with his feet; for this reason, when he intends to go anywhere, he must be carried thither on men's shoulders. Much less will they suffer that he should expose his sacred person to the open air, and the sun is not thought worthy to shine on his head. There is such a holiness ascribed to all parts of his body that he dares to cut off neither his hair, nor his beard, nor his nails. However, lest he should grow too dirty, they may clean him in the night when he is asleep; because, they say, that which is taken from his body at that time hath been stolen from him and that such a theft doth not prejudice his holiness or dignity. In ancient times he was obliged to sit on the throne for some hours every morning, with the imperial crown on his head, but to sit altogether like a statue, without stirring either hands or feet, head or eyes, nor indeed any part of his body, because, by this means, it was thought that he could preserve peace and tranquillity in his empire; for if, unfortunately, he turned himself on one side or the other, or if he looked a good while towards any part of his dominions, it was apprehended that war, famine, fire, or some other great misfortune was near at hand to desolate the country.'[1]

Some of the taboos laid upon barbarian kings remind one vividly of the restrictions imposed upon murderers. Thus in West Africa, 'at Shark Point near Cape Pardon, in Lower Guinea, lives the priestly king Kukulu, alone in a wood. He may not touch a woman nor leave his house; indeed he may not even quit his chair, in which he is obliged to sleep sitting, for if he lay down no wind would arise and navigation would be stopped. He regulates storms, and in general maintains a wholesome and equable state of the atmosphere.' The same writer says of Loango (in the same part of the world) that the more powerful a king is, the more taboos he is bound to observe.[2] The heir to the throne is also subject to them from infancy; their number increases as he advances in life, till at the moment that he ascends the throne he is positively suffocated by them.

Our space will not allow nor does our interest require us to enter further into a description of the taboos associated with the dignity of kings and priests. I will only add that the principal part is played in them by restrictions upon freedom of movement and upon diet. Two examples of taboo ceremonials occurring in civilized communities of a far higher level of culture will serve to show, however, what a conservative effect upon ancient usages is exercised by contact with these privileged personages.

The Flamen Dialis, the high priest of Jupiter in ancient

1. Kaempfer (1727 [I, 150]), quoted by Frazer (1911b, 3 f.).
2. Frazer (1911b, 5 and 8), quoting Bastian (1874–5 [I, 287 and 355]).

Rome, was obliged to observe an extraordinary number of taboos. He 'might not ride or even touch a horse, nor see an army under arms, not wear a ring which was not broken, nor have a knot on any part of his garments; ... he might not touch wheaten flour or leavened bread; he might not touch or even name a goat, a dog, raw meat, beans, and ivy; ... his hair could be cut only by a free man and with a bronze knife, and his hair and nails when cut had to be buried under a lucky tree; ... he might not touch a dead body; ... he might not be uncovered in the open air', and so on. 'His wife, the Flaminica, had to observe nearly the same rules, and others of her own besides. She might not ascend more than three steps of the kind of staircase called Greek; at a certain festival she might not comb her hair; the leather of her shoes might not be made from a beast that had died a natural death, but only from one that had been slain or sacrificed; if she heard thunder she was tabooed till she had offered an expiatory sacrifice.' (Frazer, 1911*b*, 13 f.)

The ancient kings of Ireland were subject to a number of exceedingly strange restrictions. If these were obeyed, every kind of blessing would descend upon the country, but if they were violated, disasters of every kind would visit it. A complete list of these taboos is contained in the *Book of Rights*, the two oldest manuscript copies of which date from 1390 and 1418. The prohibitions are of the most detailed character, and refer to specific actions at specific times: the king, for instance, may not stay in a certain town on a particular day of the week; he may not cross a certain river at a particular hour of the day; he may not encamp for nine days on a certain plain, and so on. (Frazer, 1911*b*, 11 f.)

Among many savage peoples the severity of these taboo restrictions upon priestly kings has led to consequences which have been important historically and are of particular interest from our point of view. The dignity of their position ceased to be an enviable thing, and those who were offered it often took every possible means of escaping it. Thus in Cambodia, where there are kingships of Fire and Water, it is often necessary to force successors into accepting these distinctions. On Niuē or Savage Island, a coral island in the South Pacific, the monarchy actually came to an end because no one could be induced to take over the responsible and dangerous office. 'In some parts of West Africa, when the king dies, a family council is secretly held to determine his successor. He on whom the choice falls is suddenly seized, bound, and thrown into the fetish-house, where he is kept in durance till he consents to accept the crown. Sometimes the heir finds means of evading the honour which it is thought to thrust upon him; a ferocious chief has been known to go about constantly armed, resolute to resist by force any attempt to set him on the throne.'[1] Among the natives of Sierra Leone the objection to accepting the honour of kingship became so great that most tribes were obliged to choose foreigners as their kings.

Frazer (1911b, 17–25) attributes to these circumstances the fact that in the course of history there eventually came about a division of the original priestly kingship into a spiritual and a temporal power. Weighed down by the burden of their sacred office, kings became unable to exert their dominance in real affairs and these were left in the hands of inferior but practical persons, who were ready to renounce the honours of kingship. These, then, became the temporal rulers, while spiritual supremacy, deprived of any practical significance, was left to the former taboo kings. It is familiar knowledge how far this hypothesis finds confirmation in the history of old Japan.

If we take a general survey of the relations of primitive men to their rulers, we are left with an expectation that we shall have no great difficulty in advancing from a description of them to a psychoanalytic understanding of them. Those relations are of a complex kind and not free from contradictions. Rulers are allowed great privileges, which coincide exactly with the taboo prohibitions imposed on other people. They are privileged persons: they may do or enjoy precisely what

1. Frazer (1911b, 17 f.), quoting Bastian (1874–5 [1, 354 and 2, 9]).

other people are forbidden by taboo. As against this freedom, however, we find that they are restricted by other taboos from which common people are exempt. Here we have a first contrast – a contradiction, almost – the fact, that is, of the same individual being both more free and more restricted. Again, they are regarded as possessing extraordinary powers of magic, so that people are afraid of coming into contact with their persons or their property, while on the other hand the most beneficial consequences are expected from that same contact. Here there seems to be another, particularly glaring, contradiction; but, as we have already seen, it is only an apparent one. Contacts originating from the king himself are healing and protective; the dangerous contacts are those effected by common men upon the king or his belongings – probably because they may hint at aggressive impulses. Yet another contradiction, and one not so easily resolved, is to be found in the fact that the ruler is believed to exercise great authority over the forces of Nature, but that he has to be most carefully protected against the threat of danger – as though his own power, which can do so much, cannot do this. The situation is made still more difficult by the fact that the ruler cannot be trusted to make use of his immense powers in the right way, that is, for the benefit of his subjects and for his own protection. Thus people distrust him and feel justified in keeping a watch on him. The etiquette of taboos to which the king's whole life is subjected serves all these protective purposes at once: his own protection from dangers and the protection of his subjects from the dangers with which he threatens them.

It seems plausible to explain the complicated and contradictory attitude of primitive peoples to their rulers in some such way as the following. For superstitious and other reasons, a variety of different impulses find expression in relation to kings; and each of these impulses is developed to an extreme point without regard to the others. This gives rise to contradictions – by which, incidentally, a savage intellect is as little disturbed as is a highly civilized one when it comes to such matters as religion or 'loyalty'.

So far so good; but the technique of psychoanalysis allows us to go into the question further and to enter more into the details of these various impulses. If we submit the recorded facts to analysis, as though they formed part of the symptoms presented by a neurosis, our starting-point must be the excessive apprehensiveness and solicitude which is put forward as the reason for the taboo ceremonials. The occurrence of excessive solicitude of this kind is very common in neuroses, and especially in obsessional neuroses, with which our comparison is chiefly drawn. We have come to understand its origin quite clearly. It appears wherever, in addition to a predominant feeling of affection, there is also a contrary, but unconscious, current of hostility – a state of affairs which represents a typical instance of an ambivalent emotional attitude. The hostility is then shouted down, as it were, by an excessive intensification of the affection, which is expressed as solicitude and becomes compulsive, because it might otherwise be inadequate to perform its task of keeping the unconscious contrary current of feeling under repression. Every psychoanalyst knows from experience with what certainty this explanation of solicitous over-affection is found to apply even in the most unlikely circumstances – in cases, for instance, of attachments between a mother and child or between a devoted married couple. If we now apply this to the case of privileged persons, we shall realize that alongside the veneration, and indeed idolization, felt towards them, there is in the unconscious an opposing current of intense hostility; that, in fact, as we expected, we are faced by a situation of emotional ambivalence. The distrust which provides one of the unmistakable elements in kingly taboos would thus be another, more direct, expression of the same unconscious hostility. Indeed, owing to the variety of outcomes of a conflict of this kind which are reached among different peoples, we are not at a loss for examples in which the existence of this hostility is still more obviously shown. 'The savage Timmes of Sierra Leone', we learn from Frazer,[1] 'who elect their king, reserve to themselves the right of beating

1. Frazer (1911b, 18), quoting Zweifel and Moustier (1880 [28]).

him on the eve of his coronation; and they avail themselves of this constitutional privilege with such hearty goodwill that sometimes the unhappy monarch does not long survive his elevation to the throne. Hence when the leading chiefs have a spite at a man and wish to rid themselves of him, they elect him king.' Even in glaring instances like this, however, the hostility is not admitted as such, but masquerades as a ceremonial.

Another side of the attitude of primitive peoples towards their rulers recalls a procedure which is common in neuroses generally but comes into the open in what are known as delusions of persecution. The importance of one particular person is immensely exaggerated and his absolute power is magnified to the most improbable degree, in order that it may be easier to make him responsible for everything disagreeable that the patient may experience. Savages are really behaving in just the same way with their kings when they ascribe to them power over rain and sunshine, wind and weather, and then depose them or kill them because Nature disappoints their hopes of a successful hunt or a rich harvest. The model upon which paranoics base their delusions of persecution is the relation of a child to his father. A son's picture of his father is habitually clothed with excessive powers of this kind, and it is found that distrust of the father is intimately linked with admiration for him. When a paranoic turns the figure of one of his associates into a 'persecutor', he is raising him to the rank of a father: he is putting him into a position in which he can blame him for all his misfortunes. Thus this second analogy between savages and neurotics gives us a glimpse of the truth that much of a savage's attitude to his ruler is derived from a child's infantile attitude to his father.

But the strongest support for our effort to equate taboo prohibitions with neurotic symptoms is to be found in the taboo ceremonials themselves, the effect of which upon the position of royalty has already been discussed. These ceremonials unmistakably reveal their double meaning and their derivation from ambivalent impulses, as soon as we are ready to allow that the results which they bring about were intended from the first. The taboo does not only pick out the king and exalt him above all common mortals, it also makes his existence a torment and an intolerable burden and reduces him to a bondage far worse than that of his subjects. Here, then, we have an exact counterpart of the obsessional act in the neurosis, in which the suppressed impulse and the impulse that suppresses it find simultaneous and common satisfaction. The obsessional act is *ostensibly* a protection against the prohibited act; but *actually*, in our view, it is a repetition of it. The 'ostensibly' applies to the *conscious* part of the mind, and the 'actually' to the *unconscious* part. In exactly the same way, the ceremonial taboo of kings is *ostensibly* the highest honour and protection for them, while *actually* it is a punishment for their exaltation, a revenge taken on them by their subjects. The experiences of Sancho Panza (as described by Cervantes) when he was Governor of his island convinced him that this view of court ceremonial was the only one that met the case. If we could hear the views of modern kings and rulers on the subject, we might find that there were many others who agreed with him.

The question of why the emotional attitude towards rulers includes such a powerful unconscious element of hostility raises a very interesting problem, but one that lies outside the limits of the present study. I have already hinted at the fact that the child's complex of emotions towards his father – the father-complex – has a bearing on the subject, and I may add that more information on the early history of the kingship would throw a decisive light on it. Frazer (1911a) has put forward impressive reasons, though, as he himself admits, not wholly conclusive ones, for supposing that the earliest kings were foreigners who, after a brief reign, were sacrificed with solemn festivities as representatives of the deity. It is possible that the course taken by the evolution of kings may also have had an influence upon the myths of Christendom.

(c) The Taboo upon the Dead

We know that the dead are powerful rulers; but we may perhaps be surprised when we learn that they are treated as enemies.

The taboo upon the dead is – if I may revert to the simile of infection – especially virulent among most primitive peoples. It is manifested, in the first instance, in the consequences that follow contact with the dead and in the treatment of mourners.

Among the Maoris anyone who had handled a corpse or taken any part in its burial was in the highest degree unclean and was almost cut off from intercourse with his fellow-men, or, as we might put it, was boycotted. He could not enter any house, or come into contact with any person or thing without infecting them. He might not even touch food with his hands, which, owing to their uncleanness, had become quite useless. 'Food would be set for him on the ground, and he would then sit or kneel down, and, with his hands carefully held behind his back, would gnaw at it as best he could. In some cases he would be fed by another person, who with outstretched arm contrived to do it without touching the tabooed man; but the feeder was himself subjected to many severe restrictions, little less onerous than those which were imposed upon the other. In almost every populous village there lived a degraded wretch, the lowest of the low, who earned a sorry pittance by thus waiting upon the defiled.' He alone was allowed 'to associate at arm's length with one who had paid the last offices ... to the dead. And when, the dismal term of his seclusion being over, the mourner was about to mix with his fellows once more, all the dishes he had used in his seclusion were diligently smashed, and all the garments he had worn were carefully thrown away.' [Frazer, 1911b, 138 f.]

The taboo observances after bodily contact with the dead are the same over the whole of Polynesia, Melanesia and a part of Africa. Their most regular feature is the prohibition against those who have had such contact touching food themselves, and the consequent necessity for their being fed by other people. It is a remarkable fact that in Polynesia (though the report may perhaps refer only to Hawaii) priestly kings were subject to the same restriction while performing their sacred functions.[1] The case of the taboo upon the dead in Tonga offers a specially clear instance of the way in which the degree of prohibition varies according to the taboo power of the person upon whom the taboo is imposed. Thus anyone who touches a dead chief is unclean for ten months; but if he himself is a chief he is only tabooed for three, four, or five months according to the rank of the dead man; but if the dead man were the 'great divine chief', even the greatest chief would be tabooed for ten months. These savages believe firmly that anyone who violates the taboo ordinances is bound to fall ill and die; indeed they believe it so firmly that, in the opinion of an observer, 'no native ever made an experiment to prove the contrary'.[2]

Essentially the same prohibitions (though from our point of view they are more interesting) apply to those who have been in contact with the dead only in a metaphorical sense: the dead person's mourning relations, widowers and widows. The observances that we have so far mentioned may seem merely to give characteristic expression to the virulence of the taboo and its contagious power. But those which now follow give us a hint at the *reasons* for the taboo – both the ostensible ones and what we must regard as the deep-lying real ones.

'Among the Shuswap of British Columbia widows and widowers in mourning are secluded and forbidden to touch their own head or body; the cups and cooking vessels which they use may be used by no one else ... No hunter would come near such mourners, for their presence is unlucky. If their shadow were to fall on anyone, he would be taken ill at once. They employ thorn-bushes for bed and pillow ... and thorn-bushes are also laid all around their beds.'[3] This last

1. Frazer (loc. cit.) [quoting Ellis (1832–6, **4**, 388)].
2. Frazer (1911*b*, 140), quoting Mariner (1818 [**1**, 141]).
3. [Frazer (1911*b*, 142), quoting Boas (1890, 643 f.).]

measure is designed to keep the dead person's ghost at a distance. The same purpose is shown still more clearly in the usage reported from another North American tribe which provides that, after her husband's death, 'a widow would wear a breech-cloth made of dry bunch-grass for several days to prevent her husband's ghost having intercourse with her.'[1] This suggests that contact 'in a metaphorical sense' is after all understood as being bodily contact, for the dead man's ghost does not leave his relations and does not cease to 'hover' round them during the time of mourning.

'Among the Agutainos, who inhabit Palawan, one of the Philippine Islands, a widow may not leave her hut for seven or eight days after the death; and even then she may only go out at an hour when she is not likely to meet anybody, for whoever looks upon her dies a sudden death. To prevent this fatal catastrophe, the widow knocks with a wooden peg on the trees as she goes along, thus warning people of her dangerous proximity; and the very trees on which she knocks soon die.'[2] The nature of the danger feared from a widow such as this is made plain by another example. 'In the Mekeo district of British New Guinea a widower loses all his civil rights and becomes a social outcast, an object of fear and horror, shunned by all. He may not cultivate a garden, nor show himself in public, nor walk on the roads and paths. Like a wild beast he must skulk in the long grass and the bushes; and if he sees or hears anyone coming, especially a woman, he must hide behind a tree or a thicket.'[3] This last hint makes it easy to trace the origin of the dangerous character of widowers or widows to the danger of *temptation*. A man who has lost his wife must resist a desire to find a substitute for her; a widow must fight against the same wish and is moreover liable, being without a lord and master, to arouse the desires of other men. Substitutive satisfactions of such a kind run counter to the sense

1. [Frazer (1911*b*, 143), quoting Teit (1900, 332 f.).]
2. [Frazer (1911*b*, 144), quoting Blumentritt (1891, 182).]
3. [Frazer (1911*b*, 144), quoting Guis (1902, 208 f.).]

of mourning and they would inevitably kindle the ghost's wrath.[1]

One of the most puzzling, but at the same time instructive, usages in connection with mourning is the prohibition against uttering the name of the dead person. This custom is extremely widespread, it is expressed in a variety of ways and has had important consequences. It is found not only among the Australians and Polynesians (who usually show us taboo observances in the best state of preservation), but also among 'peoples so widely separated from each other as the Samoyeds of Siberia and the Todas of southern India; the Mongols of Tartary and the Tuaregs of the Sahara; the Ainos of Japan and the Akamba and Nandi of central Africa; the Tinguianes of the Philippines and the inhabitants of the Nicobar Islands, of Borneo, of Madagascar, and of Tasmania.' (Frazer, 1911b, 353.) In some of these cases the prohibition and its consequences last only during the period of mourning, in others they are permanent; but it seems invariably to diminish in strictness with the passage of time.

The avoidance of the name of a dead person is as a rule enforced with extreme severity. Thus in some South American tribes it is regarded as a deadly insult to the survivors to mention the name of a dead relative in their presence, and the punishment for it is not less than that laid down for murder. (Ibid., 352.) It is not easy at first to see why the mention of the name should be regarded with such horror; but the dangers involved have given rise to a whole number of methods of evasion which are interesting and important in various ways. Thus the Masai in East Africa resort to the device of changing the dead man's name immediately after his death; he may then be mentioned freely under his new name while all the restrictions remain attached to the old one. This seems to presuppose that

1. The patient whose 'impossibilities' I compared with taboos earlier in this paper (see p. 81 f.) told me that whenever she met anyone dressed in mourning in the street she was filled with indignation: such people, she thought, should be forbidden to go out.

the dead man's ghost does not know and will not get to know his new name. [Ibid., 354.] The Adelaide and Encounter Bay tribes of South Australia are so consistently careful that after a death everyone bearing the same name as the dead man's, or a very similar one, changes it for another. [Ibid., 355.] In some instances, as for instance among certain tribes in Victoria and in North-West America, this is carried a step further, and after a death all the dead person's relations change their names, irrespective of any similarity in their sound. [Ibid., 357.] Indeed, among the Guaycurus in Paraguay, when a death had taken place, the chief used to change the name of every member of the tribe; and 'from that moment everybody remembered his new name just as if he had borne it all his life'.[1]

Moreover, if the name of the dead man happens to be the same as that of an animal or common object, some tribes think it necessary to give these animals or objects new names, so that the use of the former names shall not recall the dead man to memory. This usage leads to a perpetual change of vocabulary, which causes much difficulty to the missionaries, especially when such changes are permanent. In the seven years which the missionary Dobrizhoffer spent among the Abipones of Paraguay, 'the native word for jaguar was changed thrice, and the words for crocodile, thorn, and the slaughter of cattle underwent similar though less varied vicissitudes'.[2] The dread of uttering a dead person's name extends, indeed, to an avoidance of the mention of anything in which the dead man played a part; and an important consequence of this process of suppression is that these peoples possess no tradition and no historical memory, so that any research into their early history is faced by the greatest difficulties. [Ibid., 362 f.] A number of these primitive races have, however, adopted compensatory usages which revive the names of dead persons after a long period of mourning by giving them to children, who are thus regarded as reincarnations of the dead. [Ibid., 364 f.]

This taboo upon names will seem less puzzling if we bear

1. Frazer (1911*b*, 357), quoting an old Spanish observer [Lozano (1733, 70)].
2. Frazer (1911*b*, 360), quoting Dobrizhoffer [1784, **2**, 301].

in mind the fact that savages regard a name as an essential part of a man's personality and as an important possession: they treat words in every sense as things. As I have pointed out elsewhere,[1] our own children do the same. They are never ready to accept a similarity between two words as having no meaning; they consistently assume that if two things are called by similar-sounding names this must imply the existence of some deep-lying point of agreement between them. Even a civilized adult may be able to infer from certain peculiarities in his own behaviour that he is not so far removed as he may have thought from attributing importance to proper names, and that his own name has become to a very remarkable extent bound up with his personality. So, too, psychoanalytic practice comes upon frequent confirmations of this in the evidence it finds of the importance of names in unconscious mental activities.[2]

As was only to be expected, obsessional neurotics behave exactly like savages in relation to names. Like other neurotics, they show a high degree of 'complexive sensitiveness'[3] in regard to uttering or hearing particular words and names; and their attitude towards their own names imposes numerous, and often serious, inhibitions upon them. One of these taboo patients of my acquaintance had adopted a rule against writing her own name, for fear that it might fall into the hands of someone who would then be in possession of a portion of her personality. She was obliged to fight with convulsive loyalty against the temptations to which her imagination subjected her, and so forbade herself 'to surrender any part of her person'. This included in the first place her name, and later extended to her handwriting, till finally she gave up writing altogether.

We shall no longer feel surprised, therefore, at savages regarding the name of a dead person as a portion of his personality and making it subject to the relevant taboo. So,

1. [Cf. *Jokes and their Relation to the Unconscious* (1905*c*), *P.F.L.*, **6**, 168 and *n*. 1.]

2. Cf. Stekel [1911] and Abraham [1911].

3. ['*Komplexempfindlichkeit*' – a term used by Jung (1906, 1909) in connection with his word-association experiments.]

too, uttering the name of a dead person is clearly a derivative of having contact with him. We may therefore turn to the wider problem of why such contact is submitted to so strict a taboo.

The most obvious explanation would point to horror roused by dead bodies and by the changes which quickly become visible in them. Some part must also be played in the matter by mourning for the dead person, since it must be a motive force in everything relating to him. But horror at the corpse clearly does not account for all the details of the taboo observances, and mourning cannot explain why the uttering of the dead man's name is an insult to his survivors. Mourning, on the contrary, tends to be preoccupied with the dead man, to dwell upon his memory and to preserve it as long as possible. Something other than mourning must be held responsible for the peculiarities of the taboo usages, something which has very different purposes in view. It is precisely the taboo upon names that gives us the clue to this unknown motive; and if the usages alone did not tell us, we should learn it from what the mourning savages say to us themselves.

For they make no disguise of the fact that they are *afraid* of the presence or of the return of the dead person's ghost; and they perform a great number of ceremonies to keep him at a distance or drive him off.[1] They feel that to utter his name is equivalent to invoking him and will quickly be followed by his presence.[2] And accordingly they do everything they can to avoid any such evocation. They disguise themselves so that the ghost shall not recognize them,[3] or they change his name or their own; they are furious with reckless strangers who by uttering the ghost's name incite him against the survivors. It is impossible to escape the conclusion that, in the words of

1. Frazer (1911*b*, 353) mentions the Tuaregs of the Sahara as an example of this explanation being given by the savages themselves.

2. Subject, perhaps, to the condition that some of his bodily remains are still in existence. (Ibid., 372.)

3. In the Nicobar Islands. (Ibid., 358.)

Wundt (1906, 49), they are victims to a fear of 'the dead man's soul which has become a demon'. Here, then, we seem to have found a confirmation of Wundt's view, which, as we have already seen (p. 77), considers that the essence of taboo is a fear of demons.

This theory is based on a supposition so extraordinary that it seems at first sight incredible: the supposition, namely, that a dearly loved relative at the moment of his death changes into a demon, from whom his survivors can expect nothing but hostility and against whose evil desires they must protect themselves by every possible means. Nevertheless, almost all the authorities are at one in attributing these views to primitive peoples. Westermarck, who, in my opinion, takes far too little notice of taboo in his book on *The Origin and Development of the Moral Ideas*, actually writes in his chapter on 'Regard for the Dead': 'Generally speaking, my collection of facts has led me to the conclusion that the dead are more commonly regarded as enemies than friends, and that Professor Jevons and Mr Grant Allen are mistaken in their assertion that, according to early beliefs, the malevolence of the dead is for the most part directed against strangers only, whereas they exercise a fatherly care over the lives and fortunes of their descendants and fellow clansmen.'[1]

In an interesting volume, Rudolf Kleinpaul (1898) has used the remnants among civilized races of the ancient belief in

---

1. Westermarck (1906–8, **2**, 532 ff.). In his footnotes and in the section of the text which follows, the author gives copious confirmatory evidence, often of an extremely pertinent sort. For instance: 'Among the Maoris the nearest and most beloved relatives were supposed to have their natures changed by death, and to become malignant, even towards those they formerly loved. [Quoting Taylor (1870, 18).] ... Australian natives believed that a deceased person is malevolent for a long time after death, and the more nearly related the more he is feared. [Quoting Fraser (1892, 80).] ... According to ideas prevalent among the Central Eskimo, the dead are at first malevolent spirits who frequently roam around the villages, causing sickness and mischief and killing men by their touch; but subsequently they are supposed to attain rest and are no longer feared. [Quoting Boas (1888, 591).]'

spirits to throw light on the relation between the living and the dead. He, too, reaches the final conclusion that the dead, filled with a lust for murder, sought to drag the living in their train. The dead slew; and the skeleton which we use to-day to picture the dead stands for the fact that they themselves were slayers. The living did not feel safe from the attacks of the dead till there was a sheet of water between them. That is why men liked to bury the dead on islands or on the farther side of the rivers; and that, in turn, is the origin of such phrases as 'Here and in the Beyond'. Later, the malignity of the dead diminished and was restricted to special categories which had a particular right to feel resentment – such as murdered men, for instance, who in the form of evil spirits went in pursuit of their murderers, or brides who had died with their desires unsatisfied. But originally, says Kleinpaul, *all* of the dead were vampires, all of them had a grudge against the living and sought to injure them and rob them of their lives. It was from corpses that the concept of evil spirits first arose.

The hypothesis that after their death those most beloved were transformed into demons clearly raises further questions. What was it that induced primitive men to attribute such a change of feeling to those who had been dear to them? Why did they make them into demons? Westermarck (1906–8, **2**, 534 f.) is of the opinion that these questions can be answered easily. 'Death is commonly regarded as the gravest of all misfortunes; hence the dead are believed to be exceedingly dissatisfied with their fate. According to primitive ideas a person only dies if he is killed – by magic if not by force – and such a death naturally tends to make the soul revengeful and illtempered. It is envious of the living and is longing for the company of its old friends; no wonder, then, that it sends them diseases to cause their death ... But the notion that the disembodied soul is on the whole a malicious being ... is also, no doubt, intimately connected with the instinctive fear of the dead, which is in its turn the outcome of the fear of death.'

The study of psychoneurotic disorders suggests a more

comprehensive explanation, which at the same time covers that put forward by Westermarck.

When a wife has lost her husband or a daughter her mother, it not infrequently happens that the survivor is overwhelmed by tormenting doubts (to which we give the name of 'obsessive self-reproaches') as to whether she may not herself have been responsible for the death of this cherished being through some act of carelessness or neglect. No amount of recollection of the care she lavished on the sufferer, no amount of objective disproof of the accusation, serves to bring the torment to an end. It may be regarded as a pathological form of mourning, and with the passage of time it gradually dies away. The psycho-analytic investigation of such cases has revealed the secret motives of the disorder. We find that in a certain sense these obsessive self-reproaches are justified, and that this is why they are proof against contradictions and protests. It is not that the mourner was really responsible for the death or was really guilty of neglect, as the self-reproaches declare to be the case. None the less there was something in her – a wish that was unconscious to herself – which would not have been dissatisfied by the occurrence of death and which might actually have brought it about if it had had the power. And after death *has* occurred, it is against this unconscious wish that the reproaches are a reaction. In almost every case where there is an intense emotional attachment to a particular person we find that behind the tender love there is a concealed hostility in the unconscious. This is the classical example, the prototype, of the ambivalence of human emotions. This ambivalence is present to a greater or less amount in the innate disposition of everyone; normally, there is not so much of it as to produce the obsessive self-reproaches we are considering. Where, however, it is copiously present in the disposition, it will manifest itself precisely in the subject's relation to those of whom he is most fond, in the place, in fact, where one would least expect to find it. It must be supposed that the presence of a particularly large amount of this original emotional ambivalence is characteristic of the disposition of obsessional neurotics – whom I have so often brought up for comparison in this discussion upon taboo.

We have now discovered a motive which can explain the idea that the souls of those who have just died are transformed into demons and the necessity felt by survivors to protect themselves by taboos against their hostility. Let us suppose that the emotional life of primitive peoples is characterized by an amount of ambivalence as great as that which we are led by the findings of psychoanalysis to attribute to obsessional patients. It then becomes easy to understand how after a painful bereavement savages should be obliged to produce a reaction against the hostility latent in their unconscious similar to that expressed as obsessive self-reproach in the case of neurotics. But this hostility, distressingly felt in the unconscious as satisfaction over the death, is differently dealt with among primitive peoples. The defence against it takes the form of displacing it on to the object of the hostility, on to the dead themselves. This defensive procedure, which is a common one both in normal and in pathological mental life, is known as a '*projection*'. The survivor thus denies that he has ever harboured any hostile feelings against the dead loved one; the soul of the dead harbours them instead and seeks to put them into action during the whole period of mourning. In spite of the successful defence which the survivor achieves by means of projection, his emotional reaction shows the characteristics of punishment and remorse, for he is the subject of fears and submits to renunciations and restrictions, though these are in part disguised as measures of protection against the hostile demon. Once again, therefore, we find that the taboo has grown up on the basis of an ambivalent emotional attitude. The taboo upon the dead arises, like the others, from the contrast between conscious pain and unconscious satisfaction over the death that has occurred. Since such is the origin of the ghost's resentment, it follows naturally that the survivors who have the most to fear will be those who were formerly its nearest and dearest.

In this respect taboo observances, like neurotic symptoms, have a double sense. On the one hand, in their restrictive character, they are expressions of mourning; but on the other hand they clearly betray – what they seek to conceal – hostility against the dead disguised as self-defence. We have already learned that certain taboos arise out of fear of temptation. The fact that a dead man is helpless is bound to act as an encouragement to the survivor to give free rein to his hostile passions, and that temptation must be countered by a prohibition.

Westermarck is right in insisting that savages draw no distinction between violent and natural death. In the view of unconscious thinking, a man who has died a natural death is a murdered man: evil wishes have killed him.[1] Anyone who investigates the origin and significance of dreams of the death of loved relatives (of parents or brothers or sisters) will be able to convince himself that dreamers, children and savages are at one in their attitude towards the dead – an attitude based upon emotional ambivalence.[2]

At the beginning of this essay [p. 78] disagreement was expressed with Wundt's opinion that the essence of taboo was a fear of demons. Yet we have now assented to an explanation that derives the taboo upon the dead from a fear of the soul of the dead person transformed into a demon. The apparent contradiction can easily be resolved. It is true that we have accepted the presence of demons, but not as something ultimate and psychologically unanalysable. We have succeeded, as it were, in getting behind the demons, for we have explained them as projections of hostile feelings harboured by the survivors against the dead.

Both of the two sets of feelings (the affectionate and the hostile), which, as we have good reason to believe, exist towards the dead person, seek to take effect at the time of the bereavement, as mourning and as satisfaction. There is bound to be a conflict between these two contrary feelings; and, since one of the two, the hostility, is wholly or for the greater part unconscious, the outcome of the conflict cannot be to subtract, as it were, the feeling with the lesser intensity from that with

1. Cf. the next essay in this volume [p. 132 f.].
2. [Cf. *The Interpretation of Dreams* (1900a), *P.F.L.*, **4**, 347 ff.]

the greater and to establish the remainder in consciousness – as occurs, for instance, when one forgives a slight that one has received from someone of whom one is fond. The process is dealt with instead by the special psychical mechanism known in psychoanalysis, as I have said, by the name of 'projection'. The hostility, of which the survivors know nothing and moreover wish to know nothing, is ejected from internal perception into the external world, and thus detached from them and pushed on to someone else. It is no longer true that they are rejoicing to be rid of the dead man; on the contrary, they are mourning for him; but, strange to say, *he* has turned into a wicked demon ready to gloat over their misfortunes and eager to kill them. It then becomes necessary for them, the survivors, to defend themselves against this evil enemy; they are relieved of pressure from within, but have only exchanged it for oppression from without.

It cannot be disputed that this process of projection, which turns a dead man into a malignant enemy, is able to find support in any real acts of hostility on his part that may be recollected and felt as a grudge against him: his severity, his love of power, his unfairness, or whatever else may form the background of even the tenderest of human relationships. But it cannot be such a simple matter as that. This factor alone cannot explain the creation of demons by projection. The faults of the dead no doubt provide a part of the explanation of the survivors' hostility; but they would not operate in this way unless the survivors had first developed hostility on their own account. The moment of death, moreover, would certainly seem to be a most inappropriate occasion for recalling any justifiable grounds of complaint that might exist. It is impossible to escape the fact that the true determining factor is invariably *unconscious* hostility. A hostile current of feeling such as this against a person's nearest and dearest relatives may remain latent during their lifetime, that is, its existence may not be betrayed to consciousness either directly or through some substitute. But when they die this is no longer possible and the conflict becomes acute. The mourning which derives from an intensification of the affectionate feelings becomes on the one hand more impatient of the latent hostility and, on the other hand, will not allow it to give rise to any sense of satisfaction. Accordingly, there follow the repression of the unconscious hostility by the method of projection and the construction of the ceremonial which gives expression to the fear of being punished by the demons. When in course of time the mourning runs its course, the conflict grows less acute, so that the taboo upon the dead is able to diminish in severity or sink into oblivion.

(4)

Having thus explained the basis of the exceedingly instructive taboo upon the dead, we must not omit to add a few remarks that may help to increase our understanding of taboo in general.

The projection of unconscious hostility on to demons in the case of the taboo upon the dead is only a single instance of a number of processes to which the greatest influence must be attributed in the shaping of the primitive mind. In the case we have been dealing with, projection served the purpose of dealing with an emotional conflict; and it is employed in the same way in a large number of psychical situations that lead to neuroses. But projection was not created for the purpose of defence; it also occurs where there is no conflict. The projection outwards of internal perceptions is a primitive mechanism, to which, for instance, our sense perceptions are subject, and which therefore normally plays a very large part in determining the form taken by our external world. Under conditions whose nature has not yet been sufficiently established, internal perceptions of emotional and thought processes can be projected outwards in the same way as sense perceptions; they are thus employed for building up the external world, though they should by rights remain part of the *internal* world. This may have some genetic connection with the fact that the function of attention was originally directed not towards the internal world but towards the stimuli that stream in from the external world, and that that function's only information upon endopsychic processes was received from feelings of pleasure and unpleasure. It was not until a language of abstract thought had been developed, that is to say, not until the sensory residues of verbal presentations had been linked to the internal processes, that the latter themselves gradually became capable of being perceived. Before that, owing to the projection outwards of internal perceptions, primitive men arrived at a picture of the external world which we, with our intensified conscious perception, have now to translate back into psychology.[1]

The projection of their own evil impulses into demons is only one portion of a system which constituted the *Weltanschauung* [view of the universe] of primitive peoples, and which we shall come to know as 'animism' in the following essay. There we shall have to investigate that system's psychological characteristics, and we shall do so once again by reference to the similar systems which we find constructed by neurotics. For the moment I will only say that the prototype of all such systems is what we have termed the 'secondary revision' of the content of dreams.[2] And we must not forget that, at and after the stage at which systems are constructed, two sets of reasons can be assigned for every psychical event that is consciously judged – one set belonging to the system and the other set real but unconscious.[3]

Wundt (1906, 129) remarks that 'among the activities attributed by myths all over the world to demons, the harmful predominate, so that in popular belief bad demons are clearly older than good ones'. It is quite possible that the whole concept of demons was derived from the important relation of the living to the dead. The ambivalence inherent in that relation was expressed in the subsequent course of human development

1. [These remarks on attention may be made clearer by reference to a passage in *The Interpretation of Dreams* (1900a), P.F.L., **4**, 729 f.]

2. [The topic of 'secondary revision' is discussed fully in Chapter VI (I) of *The Interpretation of Dreams* (1900a), P.F.L., **4**, 628 ff.]

3. [Further explained below, p. 153 f.] The projected creations of primitive men resemble the personifications constructed by creative writers; for the latter externalize in the form of separate individuals the opposing instinctual impulses struggling within them.

by the fact that, from the same root, it gave rise to two completely opposed psychical structures: on the one hand fear of demons and ghosts and on the other hand veneration of ancestors.[1] The fact that demons are always regarded as the spirits of those who have died *recently* shows better than anything the influence of mourning on the origin of the belief in demons. Mourning has a quite specific psychical task to perform: its function is to detach the survivors' memories and hopes from the dead. When this has been achieved, the pain grows less and with it the remorse and self-reproaches and consequently the fear of the demon as well. And the same spirits who to begin with were feared as demons may now expect to meet with friendlier treatment; they are revered as ancestors and appeals are made to them for help.

If we follow the changing relations between survivors and the dead through the course of ages, it becomes obvious that there has been an extraordinary diminution in ambivalence. It is now quite easy to keep down the unconscious hostility to the dead (though its existence can still be traced) without any particular expenditure of psychical energy. Where, in earlier times, satisfied hatred and pained affection fought each other, we now find that a kind of scar has been formed in the shape of piety, which declares '*de mortuis nil nisi bonum*'. It is only neurotics whose mourning for the loss of those dear to them is still troubled by obsessive self-reproaches – the secret of which is revealed by psychoanalysis as the old emotional ambivalence. We need not discuss here how this alteration came about or how much share in it is due to a constitutional modification and how much to a real improvement in family relations. But this example suggests the probability that *the*

1. In the course of psychoanalyses of neurotics who suffer (or who suffered in their childhood) from fear of ghosts, it is often possible to show without much difficulty that the ghosts are disguises for the patient's parents. Cf. in this connection a paper upon 'Sexual Ghosts' by Haeberlin (1912). Here the person concerned was not the subject's parent (who was dead) but someone else of erotic significance to him.

psychical impulses of primitive peoples were characterized by a higher amount of ambivalence than is to be found in modern civilized man. It is to be supposed that as this ambivalence diminished, taboo (a symptom of the ambivalence and a compromise between the two conflicting impulses) slowly disappeared. Neurotics, who are obliged to reproduce the struggle and the taboo resulting from it, may be said to have inherited an archaic constitution as an atavistic vestige; the need to compensate for this at the behest of civilization is what drives them to their immense expenditure of mental energy.

And here we may recall the obscure and puzzling statement by Wundt on the double meaning of the word taboo: 'sacred' and 'unclean'. (See above [p. 78].) Originally, according to him, the word did not possess these two meanings, but described 'what is demonic', 'what may not be touched', thus stressing an important characteristic common to both the extreme concepts. The persistence, however (he added), of this common characteristic was evidence that the ground covered by the two – the sacred and the unclean – was originally one and did not become differentiated until later.

Our discussions, on the contrary, lead us to the simple conclusion that the word 'taboo' had a double meaning from the very first and that it was used to designate a particular kind of ambivalence and whatever arose from it. 'Taboo' is itself an ambivalent word; and one feels on looking back that the well-attested meaning of the word should alone have made it possible to infer – what has actually been arrived at as a result of extensive researches – that the prohibitions of taboo are to be understood as consequences of an emotional ambivalence. Study of the earliest languages has taught us that there were once many such words, which expressed contrary ideas and in a sense (though not in quite the same sense as the word 'taboo') were ambivalent.[1] Slight modifications in the pronunciation of the antithetical 'primal word' made it possible subsequently

1. Cf. my review of Abel's 'Antithetical Meaning of Primal Words' [Freud, 1910e].

to give separate verbal expression to the contrary ideas which were originally combined in it.

The word 'taboo' met with a different fate. As the importance of the ambivalence denoted by it diminished, the word itself, or rather the words analogous to it, fell out of use. I hope to be able, in a later connection, to make it probable that a definite historical chain of events is concealed behind the fate of this concept: that the word was at first attached to certain quite specific human relations which were characterized by great emotional ambivalence, and that its use than spread on to other analogous relations. [See p. 204 ff.]

If I am not mistaken, the explanation of taboo also throws light on the nature and origin of *conscience*. It is possible, without any stretching of the sense of the terms, to speak of a taboo conscience or, after a taboo has been violated, of a taboo sense of guilt. Taboo conscience is probably the earliest form in which the phenomenon of conscience is met with.

For what is 'conscience'? On the evidence of language it is related to that of which one is 'most certainly conscious'. Indeed, in some languages the words for 'conscience' and 'consciousness' can scarcely be distinguished.[1]

Conscience is the internal perception of the rejection of a particular wish operating within us. The stress, however, is upon the fact that this rejection has no need to appeal to anything else for support, that it is quite 'certain of itself'. This is even clearer in the case of consciousness of guilt – the perception of the internal condemnation of an act by which we have carried out a particular wish. To put forward any reason for this would seem superfluous: anyone who has a conscience must feel within him the justification for the condemnation, must feel the self-reproach for the act that has been carried

---

1. [E.g. the French '*conscience*', which has both meanings. The German word for 'conscience' is '*Gewissen*', which contains the same root as such words as '*wissen*', 'to know', and '*bewusst*' 'conscious', as well as the word actually used for comparison in this paragraph and the next, '*gewiss*', 'certain' or 'known with certainty'.]

out. This same characteristic is to be seen in the savage's attitude towards taboo. It is a command issued by conscience; any violation of it produces a fearful sense of guilt which follows as a matter of course and of which the origin is unknown.[1]

Thus it seems probable that conscience too arose, on a basis of emotional ambivalence, from quite specific human relations to which this ambivalence was attached; and that it arose under the conditions which we have shown to apply in the case of taboo and of obsessional neurosis – namely, that one of the opposing feelings involved shall be unconscious and kept under repression by the compulsive domination of the other one. This conclusion is supported by several things we have learnt from the analysis of neuroses.

In the first place, we have found that a feature in the character of obsessional neurotics is a scrupulous conscientiousness which is a symptom reacting against the temptation lurking in their unconscious. If their illness becomes more acute, they develop a sense of guilt of the most intense degree. In fact, one may venture to say that if we cannot trace the origin of the sense of guilt in obsessional neurotics, there can be no hope of our *ever* tracing it. This task can be directly achieved in the case of individual neurotic patients, and we may rely upon reaching a similar solution by inference in the case of primitive peoples.

In the second place, we cannot help being struck by the fact that a sense of guilt has about it much of the nature of anxiety: we could describe it without any misgivings as 'dread of conscience'. But the anxiety points to unconscious sources. The psychology of the neuroses has taught us that, if wishful impulses are repressed, their libido is transformed into anxiety. And this reminds us that there is something unknown and unconscious in connection with the sense of guilt, namely the reasons for the act of repudiation. The character of anxiety

1. The sense of guilt in the case of taboos is not in the least diminished if the violation occurs unwittingly. (Cf. the instances above [p. 97].) An interesting parallel is found in Greek mythology: the guilt of Oedipus was not palliated by the fact that he incurred it without his knowledge and even against his intention.

that is inherent in the sense of guilt corresponds to this unknown factor.[1]

Since taboos are mainly expressed in prohibitions, the underlying presence of a *positive* current of desire may occur to us as something quite obvious and calling for no lengthy proofs based on the analogy of the neuroses. For, after all, there is no need to prohibit something that no one desires to do, and a thing that is forbidden with the greatest emphasis must be a thing that is desired. If we were to apply this plausible thesis to our primitive peoples, we should be led to the conclusion that some of their strongest temptations were to kill their kings and priests, to commit incest, to maltreat the dead, and so on – which seems scarcely probable. And we should be met with the most positive contradiction if we were to apply the same thesis to instances in which we ourselves seem most clearly to hear the voice of conscience. We should maintain with the most absolute certainty that we feel not the slightest temptation to violate any of these prohibitions – the commandment to 'do no murder', for instance – and that we feel nothing but horror at the notion of violating them.

If, however, we were to admit the claims thus asserted by our conscience, it would follow, on the one hand, that these prohibitions would be superfluous – both taboo and our own moral prohibitions – and, on the other hand, the fact of conscience would remain unexplained and no place would be left for the relations between conscience, taboo and neurosis. In other words, we should be back in the state of knowledge we were in before we approached the problem from the psychoanalytic angle.

Suppose, on the other hand, that we were to take into account the finding arrived at by psychoanalysis from the

1. [It is to be remarked that Freud's views on the origin and nature both of conscience and of anxiety were greatly modified in his later writings. For his later views on conscience, see Chapters VII and VIII of *Civilization and its Discontents* (1930a), *P.F.L.*, **12**; for those on anxiety, see *Inhibitions, Symptoms and Anxiety* (1926d), ibid., **10**, 227 ff., and Lecture 32 of the *New Introductory Lectures* (1933a), ibid., **2**, 113 ff., especially 117 ff.]

dreams of normal people, to the effect that we ourselves are subject, more strongly and more often that we suspect, to a temptation to kill someone and that that temptation produces psychical effects even though it remains out of sight of our consciousness. Suppose, again, that we were to recognize the compulsive observances of certain neurotics as being guarantees against an intensified impulse to murder or as being self-punishments on account of it. In that case we should have to attach still greater importance to our thesis that where there is a prohibition there must be an underlying desire. We should have to suppose that the desire to murder is actually present in the unconscious and that neither taboos nor moral prohibitions are psychologically superfluous but that on the contrary they are explained and justified by the existence of an ambivalent attitude towards the impulse to murder.

One of the characteristics of this ambivalent relation which I have repeatedly stressed as fundamental – the fact that the positive current of desire is an unconscious one – opens the way to further considerations and to further possible explanations. Psychical processes in the unconscious are not in every respect identical with those with which our conscious mind is familiar; they enjoy some remarkable liberties that are forbidden to the latter. An unconscious impulse need not have arisen at the point where it makes its appearance; it may arise from some quite other region and have applied originally to quite other persons and connections; it may have reached the place at which it attracts our attention through the mechanism of 'displacement'. Owing, moreover, to the indestructibility and insusceptibility to correction which are attributes of unconscious processes, it may have survived from very early times to which it was appropriate into later times and circumstances in which its manifestations are bound to seem strange. These are no more than hints, but if they were attentively developed their importance for our understanding of the growth of civilization would become apparent.

Before I conclude this discussion, a further point must not

be overlooked which will pave the way for later inquiries. In maintaining the essential similarity between taboo prohibitions and moral prohibitions, I have not sought to dispute the fact that there must be a psychological difference between them. The only possible reason why the prohibitions no longer take the form of taboos must be some change in the circumstances governing the ambivalence underlying them.

In our analytical examination of the problems of taboo we have hitherto allowed ourselves to be led by the points of agreement that we have been able to show between it and obsessional neurosis. But after all taboo is not a neurosis but a social institution. We are therefore faced with the task of explaining what difference there is in principle between a neurosis and a cultural creation such as taboo.

Once again I will take a single fact as my starting-point. It is feared among primitive peoples that the violation of a taboo will be followed by a punishment, as a rule by some serious illness or by death. The punishment threatens to fall on whoever was responsible for violating the taboo. In obsessional neuroses the case is different. What the patient fears if he performs some forbidden action is that a punishment will fall not on himself but on someone else. This person's identity is as a rule left unstated, but can usually be shown without difficulty by analysis to be one of those closest and most dear to the patient. Here, then, the neurotic seems to be behaving altruistically and the primitive man egoistically. Only if the violation of a taboo is not automatically avenged upon the wrong-doer does a collective feeling arise among savages that they are all threatened by the outrage; and they thereupon hasten to carry out the omitted punishment themselves. There is no difficulty in explaining the mechanism of this solidarity. What is in question is fear of an infectious example, of the temptation to imitate – that is, of the contagious character of taboo. If one person succeeds in gratifying the repressed desire, the same desire is bound to be kindled in all the other members of the community. In order to keep the temptation down, the envied transgressor must be deprived of the fruit of his enterprise; and the punishment will not infrequently give those who carry it out an opportunity of committing the same outrage under colour of an act of expiation. This is indeed one of the foundations of the human penal system and it is based, no doubt correctly, on the assumption that the prohibited impulses are present alike in the criminal and in the avenging community. In this, psychoanalysis is no more than confirming the habitual pronouncement of the pious: we are all miserable sinners.

How, then, are we to account for the unexpected nobility of mind of the neurotic, who fears nothing on his own account but everything for someone he loves? Analytical inquiry shows that this attitude is not primary. Originally, that is to say at the beginning of the illness, the threat of punishment applied, as in the case of savages, to the patient himself; he was invariably in fear for his own life; it was not until later that the mortal fear was displaced on to another and a loved person. The process is a little complicated, but we can follow it perfectly. At the root of the prohibition there is invariably a hostile impulse against someone the patient loves – a wish that that person should die. This impulse is repressed by a prohibition and the prohibition is attached to some particular act, which, by displacement, represents, it may be, a hostile act against the loved person. There is a threat of death if this act is performed. But the process goes further, and the original *wish* that the loved person may die is replaced by a *fear* that he may die. So that when the neurosis appears to be so tenderly altruistic, it is merely *compensating* for an underlying contrary attitude of brutal egoism. We may describe as 'social' the emotions which are determined by showing consideration for another person without taking him as a sexual object. The receding into the background of these social factors may be stressed as a fundamental characteristic of the neurosis, though one which is later disguised by over-compensation.

I do not propose to linger over the origin of these social impulses and their relation to the other basic human instincts but shall proceed to illustrate the second main characteristic of the neurosis by means of another example. In the forms which it assumes, taboo very closely resembles the neurotic's fear of touching, his 'touching phobia'. Now, in the case of the neurosis the prohibition invariably relates to touching of a *sexual* kind, and psychoanalysis has shown that it is in general true that the instinctual forces that are diverted and displaced in neuroses have a sexual origin. In the case of taboo the prohibited touching is obviously not to be understood in an exclusively sexual sense but in the more general sense of attacking, of getting control, and of asserting oneself. If there is a prohibition against touching a chief or anything that has been in contact with him, this means that an inhibition is to be laid on the same impulse which expresses itself on other occasions in keeping a suspicious watch upon the chief or even in ill-treating him physically before his coronation. (See above [pp. 104–5].) *Thus the fact which is characteristic of the neurosis is the preponderance of the sexual over the social instinctual elements.* The social instincts, however, are themselves derived from a combination of egoistic and erotic components into wholes of a special kind.

This single comparison between taboo and obsessional neurosis is enough to enable us to gather the nature of the relation between the different forms of neurosis and cultural institutions, and to see how it is that the study of the psychology of the neuroses is important for an understanding of the growth of civilization.

The neuroses exhibit on the one hand striking and far-reaching points of agreement with those great social institutions, art, religion and philosophy. But on the other hand they seem like distortions of them. It might be maintained that a case of hysteria is a caricature of a work of art, that an obsessional neurosis is a caricature of a religion and that a paranoic delusion is a caricature of a philosophical system. The divergence resolves itself ultimately into the fact that the neuroses are asocial structures; they endeavour to achieve by private means what is effected in society by collective effort. If we analyse the instincts at work in the neuroses, we find that the determining influence in them is exercised by instinctual forces of sexual origin; the corresponding cultural formations, on the other hand, are based upon social instincts, originating from the combination of egoistic and erotic elements. Sexual needs are not capable of uniting men in the same way as are the demands of self-preservation. Sexual satisfaction is essentially the private affair of each individual.

The asocial nature of neuroses has its genetic origin in their most fundamental purpose, which is to take flight from an unsatisfying reality into a more pleasurable world of phantasy. The real world, which is avoided in this way by neurotics, is under the sway of human society and of the institutions collectively created by it. To turn away from reality is at the same time to withdraw from the community of man.[1]

1. [Many of the points of comparison in this essay between taboo and obsessional neurosis will be found illustrated in the case history of the 'Rat Man' (1909*d*), *P.F.L.*, **9**, 31 ff. The subject of taboo was further discussed by Freud in 'The Taboo of Virginity' (1918*a*), ibid., **7**, 261 ff. – On the question of man's attitude to death, see also 'Thoughts for the Times on War and Death' (1915*b*), ibid., **12**. – The opposition between directly sexual impulses and social structures is elaborated in Chapter XII (D) of *Group Psychology* (1921*c*), ibid., **12**, 174–6.]

III

ANIMISM, MAGIC AND THE
OMNIPOTENCE OF THOUGHTS

(1)

WRITINGS that seek to apply the findings of psychoanalysis to topics in the field of the mental sciences have the inevitable defect of offering too little to readers of both classes. Such writings can only be in the nature of an instigation: they put before the specialist certain suggestions for him to take into account in his own work. This defect is bound to be extremely evident in an essay which will attempt to deal with the immense domain of what is known as 'animism'.[1]

Animism is, in its narrower sense, the doctrine of souls, and, in its wider sense, the doctrine of spiritual beings in general. The term 'animatism' has also been used to denote the theory of the living character of what appear to us to be inanimate objects [see below, p. 149], and the terms 'animalism' and 'manism' occur as well in this connection. The word 'animism', originally used to describe a particular philosophical system, seems to have been given its present meaning by Tylor.[2]

What led to the introduction of these terms was a realization of the highly remarkable view of nature and the universe adopted by the primitive races of whom we have knowledge, whether in past history or at the present time. They people

1. The necessity for a concise treatment of the material involves the omission of any elaborate bibliography. Instead, I will merely refer to the standard works of Herbert Spencer, J. G. Frazer, Andrew Lang, E. B. Tylor and Wilhelm Wundt, from which all that I have to say about animism and magic is derived. My own contribution is visible only in my selection both of material and of opinions.

2. Cf. Tylor (1891, 1, 425), Wundt (1906 [142 f. and] 173) [and Marett (1900, 171)].

the world with innumerable spiritual beings both benevolent and malignant; and these spirits and demons they regard as the causes of natural phenomena and they believe that not only animals and plants but all the inanimate objects in the world are animated by them. A third, and perhaps the most important, article of this primitive 'philosophy of nature'[1] strikes us as less strange, since, while we have retained only a very limited belief in the existence of spirits and explain natural phenomena by the agency of impersonal physical forces, we ourselves are not very far removed from this third belief. For primitive peoples believe that human individuals are inhabited by similar spirits. These souls which live in human beings can leave their habitations and migrate into other human beings; they are the vehicle of mental activities and are to a certain extent independent of their bodies. Originally souls were pictured as very similar to persons and only in the course of a long development have they lost their material characteristics and become to a high degree 'spiritualized'.[2]

Most authorities incline to the view that these ideas of a soul are the original nucleus of the animistic system, that spirits are only souls that have made themselves independent, and that the souls of animals, plants and objects were constructed on the analogy of human souls.

How did primitive men arrive at the peculiar dualistic views on which the animistic system is based? It is supposed that they did so by observing the phenomena of sleep (including dreams) and of death which so much resembles it, and by attempting to explain those states, which are of such close concern to everyone. The chief starting-point of this theorizing must have been the problem of death. What primitive man regarded as the natural thing was the indefinite prolongation of life – immortality. The idea of death was only accepted late, and with hesitancy. Even for us it is lacking in content and has no clear

1. ['*Naturphilosophie*', the pantheistic philosophy of Friedrich Schelling (1775–1854).]

2. Wundt (1906), Chapter IV, 'Die Seelenvorstellungen'.

connotation. There have been very lively but inconclusive discussions upon the part that may have been played in the formation of the basic doctrines of animism by such other observed or experienced facts as dream-pictures, shadows, mirror images, and so on.[1]

It has been regarded as perfectly natural and not in the least puzzling that primitive man should have reacted to the phenomena which aroused his speculations by forming the idea of the soul and then of extending it to objects in the external world. In discussing the fact that the same animistic ideas have emerged among the most various races and at every period, Wundt (1906, 154) declares that 'they are the necessary psychological product of a mythopoeic consciousness ... and in this sense, therefore, primitive animism must be regarded as the spiritual expression of the natural state of man, so far as it is accessible to our observation'. The justification for attributing life to inanimate objects was already stated by Hume in his *Natural History of Religion* [Section III]: 'There is an universal tendency among mankind to conceive all beings like themselves, and to transfer to every object those qualities with which they are familiarly acquainted, and of which they are intimately conscious.'[2]

Animism is a system of thought. It does not merely give an explanation of a particular phenomenon, but allows us to grasp the whole universe as a single unity from a single point of view. The human race, if we are to follow the authorities, have in the course of ages developed three such systems of thought – three great pictures of the universe: animistic (or mythological), religious and scientific. Of these, animism, the first to be created, is perhaps the one which is most consistent and exhaustive and which gives a truly complete explanation of the nature of the universe. This first human *Weltanschauung* is a *psychological* theory. It would go beyond our present purpose

1. Cf. Wundt [loc. cit.], Herbert Spencer [1893, Part I], as well as the general articles in the *Encyclopaedia Britannica* (1910–11) on 'Animism', 'Mythology', etc.

2. Quoted by Tylor (1891, I, 477).

to show how much of it still persists in modern life, either in the debased form of superstition or as the living basis of our speech, our beliefs and our philosophies.

With these three stages in mind, it may be said that animism itself is not yet a religion but contains the foundations on which religions are later built. It is obvious, too, that myths are based on animistic premises, though the details of the relation between myths and animism seem to be unexplained in some essential respects.

(2)

Our psychoanalytic approach to the subject, however, is from another side. It is not to be supposed that men were inspired to create their first system of the universe by pure speculative curiosity. The practical need for controlling the world around them must have played its part. So we are not surprised to learn that, hand in hand with the animistic system, there went a body of instructions upon how to obtain mastery over men, beasts and things – or rather, over their spirits. These instructions go by the names of 'sorcery' and 'magic'.[1] Reinach (1905–12, 2, xv) describes them as the 'strategy of animism'; I should prefer, following Hubert and Mauss (1904 [142 ff.]), to regard them as its technique.

Can the concepts of sorcery and magic be distinguished? Perhaps – if we are prepared to show a somewhat arbitrary disregard for the fluctuations of linguistic usage. Sorcery, then, is essentially the art of influencing spirits by treating them in the same way as one would treat men in like circumstances: appeasing them, making amends to them, propitiating them, intimidating them, robbing them of their power, subduing them to one's will – by the same methods that have proved effective with living men. Magic, on the other hand, is something different: fundamentally, it disregards spirits and makes use of special procedures and not of everyday psychological methods. It is easy to guess that magic is the earlier and more

1. ['*Zauberei*' and '*Magie*' in the original.]

important branch of animistic technique; for magical methods can, among others, be used in dealing with spirits,[1] and magic can be applied as well in cases where, as it seems to us, the process of spiritualizing nature has not yet been carried out.

Magic has to serve the most varied purposes – it must subject natural phenomena to the will of man, it must protect the individual from his enemies and from dangers and it must give him power to injure his enemies. But the principle on the presumption of which magical action is based – or, more properly, the principle of magic – is so striking that none of the authorities has failed to recognize it. Tylor [1891, I, 116], if we leave on one side an accompanying moral judgement, states it in its most succinct form as mistaking an ideal connection for a real one. I will illustrate this feature from two groups of magical acts.

One of the most widespread magical procedures for injuring an enemy is by making an effigy of him from any convenient material. Whether the effigy resembles him is of little account: any object can be 'made into' an effigy of him. Whatever is then done to the effigy, the same thing happens to the detested original; whatever part of the former's body is damaged, the same part of the latter's becomes diseased. The same magical technique may be employed, not only for purposes of private enmity, but also for pious ends and for giving help to gods against malignant demons. I will quote from Frazer (1911a, I, 67): 'Every night when the sun-god Ra sank down to his home in the glowing west he was assailed by hosts of demons under the leadership of the arch-fiend Apepi. All night long he fought them, and sometimes by day the powers of darkness sent up clouds even into the blue Egyptian sky to obscure his light and weaken his power. To aid the sun-god in this daily struggle, a ceremony was daily performed in his temple at Thebes. A figure of his foe Apepi, represented as a crocodile with a hideous face or a serpent with many coils, was made of wax, and on

1. If a spirit is scared away by making a noise and shouting, the action is one purely of sorcery; if compulsion is applied to it by getting hold of its name, magic has been used against it.

it the demon's name was written in green ink. Wrapt in a papyrus case, on which another likeness of Apepi had been drawn in green ink, the figure was then tied up with black hair, spat upon, hacked with a stone knife, and cast on the ground. There the priest trod on it with his left foot again and again, and then burnt it in a fire made of a certain plant or grass. When Apepi himself had thus been effectually disposed of, waxen effigies of each of his principal demons, and of their fathers, mothers and children, were made and burnt in the same way. The service, accompanied by the recitation of certain pre-scribed spells, was repeated not merely morning, noon and night, but whenever a storm was raging, or heavy rain had set in, or black clouds were stealing across the sky to hide the sun's bright disc. The fiends of darkness, clouds, and rain felt the injuries inflicted on their images as if they had been done to themselves; they passed away, at least for a time, and the beneficent sun-god shone out triumphant once more.'[1]

From the vast number of magical acts having a similar basis I will only draw attention to two more, which have played a large part among primitive peoples of every age and which persist to some degree in the myths and cults of higher stages of civilization – that is, rituals for producing rain and fertility. Rain is produced magically by imitating it or the clouds and storms which give rise to it, by 'playing at rain', one might almost say. In Japan, for instance, 'a party of Ainos will scatter water by means of sieves, while others will take a porringer, fit it up with sails and oars as if it were a boat, and then push or draw it about the village and gardens'.[2] In the same way, the fertility of the earth is magically promoted by a dramatic representation of human intercourse. Thus, to take one from a countless number of instances, 'in some parts of Java, at the season when the bloom will soon be on the rice, the husband-

---

1. It seems probable that the Biblical prohibition against making an image of any living thing originated, not from any objection to the plastic arts, but from a desire to deprive magic (which was abominated by the Hebrew religion) of one of its tools. Cf. Frazer (1911a, I, 87 n.).

2. [Frazer (1911a, I, 251), quoting Batchelor (1901, 333).]

man and his wife visit their fields by night and there engage in sexual intercourse' to encourage the fertility of the rice by their example.[1] There is a dread, however, that prohibited, incestuous sexual relations may cause a failure of the crops and make the earth sterile.[2]

Certain negative observances, that is, magical precautions, must be included in this first group. 'When a Dyak village has turned out to hunt wild pigs in the jungle, the people who stay at home may not touch oil or water with their hands during the absence of their friends; for if they did so, the hunters would all be "butter-fingered" and the prey would slip through their hands.'[3] Or again, 'while a Gilyak hunter is pursuing game in the forest, his children at home are forbidden to make drawings on wood or on sand; for they fear that if the children did so, the paths in the forest would become as perplexed as the lines in the drawings, so that the hunter might lose his way and never return.'[4]

In these last, as in so many other instances of the workings of magic, the element of distance is disregarded; in other words, telepathy is taken for granted. We shall find no difficulty, therefore, in understanding this characteristic of magic.

There can be no doubt what is to be regarded as the operative factor in all these examples. It is the *similarity* between the act performed and the result expected. For this reason Frazer describes this sort of magic as 'imitative' or 'homoeopathic'. If I wish it to rain, I have only to do something that looks like rain or is reminiscent of rain. At a later stage of civilization, instead of this rain-magic, processions will be made to a temple and prayers for rain will be addressed to the deity living in it. Finally, this religious technique will in its turn be given up and attempts will be made to produce effects in the atmosphere which will lead to rain.

*

1. Frazer (1911a, **2**, 98) [quoting Wilken (1884, 958)].
2. An echo of this is to be found in the *Oedipus Rex* of Sophocles [e.g. in the prologue and first Chorus].
3. Frazer (1911a, **1**, 120) [quoting Roth (1896, **1**, 430)].
4. Frazer (1911a, **1**, 122) [quoting Labbé (1903, 268)].

In a second group of magical acts the principle of similarity plays no part, and its place is taken by another one, the nature of which will at once become clear from the following examples.

There is another procedure by which an enemy can be injured. One gets possession of some of his hair or nails or other waste products or even a piece of his clothing, and treats them in some hostile way. It is then exactly as though one had got possession of the man himself; and he himself experiences whatever it is that has been done to the objects that originated from him. In the view of primitive man, one of the most important parts of a person is his name. So that if one knows the name of a man or of a spirit, one has obtained a certain amount of power over the owner of the name. This is the origin of the remarkable precautions and restrictions in the use of names which we have already touched upon in the essay on taboo. (See p. 110 ff.) In these examples the place of similarity is evidently taken by affinity.

The higher motives for cannibalism among primitive races have a similar origin. By incorporating parts of a person's body through the act of eating, one at the same time acquires the qualities possessed by him. This leads in certain circumstances to precautions and restrictions in regard to diet. A woman who is with child will avoid eating the flesh of certain animals for fear that any undesirable qualities they may have (cowardice, for instance) might be passed over to the child that is nourished by her. The magical power is not affected even if the connection between the two objects has already been severed or even if the contact occurred only on a single important occasion. For instance, the belief that there is a magical bond between a wound and the weapon which caused it may be traced unaltered for thousands of years. If a Melanesian can obtain possession of the bow which caused his wound, he will keep it carefully in a cool place so as to reduce the inflammation of the wound. But if the bow was left in the enemy's possession, it will undoubtedly be hung up close to the fire so that the wound may become thoroughly hot and inflamed.[1] Pliny (in his *Natural*

History, Book xxviii [Chapter 7]) tells us that 'if you have wounded a man and are sorry for it, you have only to spit on the hand that gave the wound, and the pain of the sufferer will be instantly alleviated'. [Frazer, 1911*a*, I, 201.] Francis Bacon (in his *Sylva Sylvarum* [X, § 998]) mentions that 'it is constantly received and avouched that the anointing of the weapon that maketh the wound will heal the wound itself'. English country people are said even to-day to follow this prescription, and if they cut themselves with a scythe carefully keep the instrument clean, to prevent the wound from festering. 'At Norwich in June 1902 a woman named Matilda Henry accidentally ran a nail into her foot. Without examining the wound, or even removing her stocking, she caused her daughter to grease the nail, saying that if this were done no harm would come of the hurt. A few days afterwards she died of lockjaw' – as a result of this displaced antisepsis. (Frazer, ibid., 203.)

The last group of instances exemplify what Frazer distinguishes from 'imitative' magic under the name of 'contagious' magic. What is believed to be their effective principle is no longer similarity but spatial connection, contiguity, or at least *imagined* contiguity – the recollection of it. Since, however, similarity and contiguity are the two essential principles of processes of association, it appears that the true explanation of all the folly of magical observances is the domination of the association of ideas. The aptness of Tylor's description of magic which I have already quoted [p. 136] now becomes evident: mistaking an ideal connection for a real one. Frazer (1911*a*, I, 420) has put it almost in the same words: 'Men mistook the order of their ideas for the order of nature, and hence imagined that the control which they have, or seem to have, over their thoughts, permitted them to exercise a corresponding control over things.'

We shall at first be surprised to learn that this illuminating explanation of magic has been rejected by some writers as un-

1. [Frazer (1911*a*, I, 201), quoting Codrington (1891, 310).]

satisfactory (e.g. Thomas, 1910–11*a*). On reflection, however, it will be seen that the criticism is justified. The associative theory of magic merely explains the paths along which magic proceeds; it does not explain its true essence, namely the misunderstanding which leads it to replace the laws of nature by psychological ones. Some dynamic factor is evidently missing. But whereas the critics of Frazer's theory have gone astray in their search for it, it will be easy to arrive at a satisfactory explanation of magic merely by carrying the associative theory further and deeper.

Let us consider first the simpler and more important case of imitative magic. According to Frazer (1911*a*, I, 54) it can be practised by itself, whereas contagious magic as a rule presupposes the other. It is easy to perceive the motives which lead men to practise magic: they are human wishes. All we need to suppose is that primitive man had an immense belief in the power of his wishes. The basic reason why what he sets about by magical means comes to pass is, after all, simply that he wills it. To begin with, therefore, the emphasis is only upon his wish.

Children are in an analogous psychical situation, though their motor efficiency is still undeveloped. I have elsewhere (1911*b*) put forward the hypothesis that, to begin with, they satisfy their wishes in a hallucinatory manner, that is, they create a satisfying situation by means of centrifugal excitations of their sense organs.[1] An adult primitive man has an alternative method open to him. His wishes are accompanied by a motor impulse, the will, which is later destined to alter the whole face of the earth in order to satisfy his wishes. This motor impulse is at first employed to give a representation of the satisfying situation in such a way that it becomes possible to experience the satisfaction by means of what might be described as motor hallucinations. This kind of representation of a satisfied wish is quite comparable to children's play, which succeeds their earlier purely sensory technique of satisfaction. If children and primi-

1. ['Formulations on the Two Principles of Mental Functioning' (1911*b*), *P.F.L.*, **11**, 37 and *n.* 1.]

tive men find play and imitative representation enough for them, that is not a sign of their being unassuming in our sense or of their resignedly accepting their actual impotence. It is the easily understandable result of the paramount virtue they ascribe to their wishes, of the will that is associated with those wishes and of the methods by which those wishes operate. As time goes on, the psychological accent shifts from the *motives* for the magical act on to the *measures* by which it is carried out – that is, on to the act itself. (It would perhaps be more correct to say that it is only these measures that reveal to the subject the excessive valuation which he attaches to his psychical acts.) It thus comes to appear as though it is the magical act itself which, owing to its similarity with the desired result, alone determines the occurrence of that result. There is no opportunity, at the stage of animistic thinking, for showing any objective evidence of the true state of affairs. But a possibility of doing so *does* arrive at a later time, when, though all of these procedures are still being carried out, the psychical phenomenon of doubt has begun to emerge as an expression of a tendency to repression. At that point, men will be ready to admit that conjuring up spirits has no result unless it is accompanied by faith, and that the magical power of prayer fails if there is no piety at work behind it.[1]

The fact that it has been possible to construct a system of contagious magic on associations of contiguity shows that the importance attached to wishes and to the will has been extended from them on to all those psychical acts which are subject to the will. A general overvaluation has thus come about of all mental processes – an attitude towards the world, that is, which, in view of our knowledge of the relation between reality and thought, cannot fail to strike *us* as an overvaluation of the latter. Things become less important than ideas of things: whatever is done to the latter will inevitably also occur to the former.

---

1. Cf. the King in *Hamlet* (Act III, Scene 3):

> My words fly up, my thoughts remain below:
> Words without thoughts never to heaven go.

Relations which hold between the ideas of things are assumed to hold equally between the things themselves. Since distance is of no importance in thinking – since what lies furthest apart both in time and space can without difficulty be comprehended in a single act of consciousness – so, too, the world of magic has a telepathic disregard for spatial distance and treats past situations as though they were present. In the animistic epoch the reflection of the internal world is bound to blot out the other picture of the world – the one which *we* seem to perceive.

It is further to be noticed that the two principles of association – similarity and contiguity – are both included in the more comprehensive concept of 'contact'. Association by contiguity is contact in the literal sense; association by similarity is contact in the metaphorical sense. The use of the same word for the two kinds of relation is no doubt accounted for by some identity in the psychical processes concerned which we have not yet grasped. We have here the same range of meaning of the idea of 'contact' as we found in our analysis of taboo. (Cf. p. 80.)

By way of summary, then, it may be said that the principle governing magic, the technique of the animistic mode of thinking, is the principle of the 'omnipotence of thoughts'.

(3)

I have adopted the term 'omnipotence of thoughts' from a highly intelligent man who suffered from obsessional ideas and who, after having been set right by psychoanalytic treatment, was able to give evidence of his efficiency and good sense. (Cf. Freud, 1909*d*.[1]) He had coined the phrase as an explanation of all the strange and uncanny events by which he, like others afflicted with the same illness, seemed to be pursued. If he thought of someone, he would be sure to meet that very person immediately afterwards, as though by magic. If he suddenly asked after the health of an acquaintance whom he had not seen for a long time, he would hear that he had just died, so

1. [This was the 'Rat Man'. Cf. *P.F.L.*, **9**, 113–14 and *n*. 2.]

that it would look as though a telepathic message had arrived from him. If, without any really serious intention, he swore at some stranger, he might be sure that the man would die soon afterwards, so that he would feel responsible for his death. In the course of the treatment he himself was able to tell me how the deceptive appearance arose in most of these cases, and by what contrivances he himself had helped to strengthen his own superstitious beliefs. All obsessional neurotics are super-stitious in this way, usually against their better judgement.[1]

It is in obsessional neuroses that the survival of the omnipo-tence of thoughts is most clearly visible and that the conse-quences of this primitive mode of thinking come closest to consciousness. But we must not be misled into supposing that it is a distinguishing feature of this particular neurosis, for analytic investigation reveals the same thing in the other neu-roses as well. In all of them what determines the formation of symptoms is the reality not of experience but of thought. Neurotics live in a world apart, where, as I have said elsewhere [1911b, near the end of the paper[2]], only 'neurotic currency' is legal tender; that is to say, they are only affected by what is thought with intensity and pictured with emotion, whereas agreement with external reality is a matter of no importance. What hysterics repeat in their attacks and fix by means of their symptoms are experiences which have occurred in that form only in their imagination – though it is true that in the last resort those imagined experiences go back to actual events or are based upon them. To attribute the neurotic sense of guilt to real misdeeds would show an equal misunderstanding. An obsessional neurotic may be weighed down by a sense of guilt that would be appropriate in a mass-murderer, while in fact,

1. We appear to attribute an 'uncanny' quality to impressions that seek to confirm the omnipotence of thoughts and the animistic mode of thinking in general, after we have reached a stage at which, in our *judgement*, we have abandoned such beliefs. [Cf. Freud's subsequent paper on 'The "Un-canny"' (1919h), *P.F.L.*, **14**.]

2. ['Formulations on the Two Principles of Mental Functioning', *P.F.L.*, **11**, 43.]

from his childhood onwards, he has behaved to his fellow-men as the most considerate and scrupulous member of society. Nevertheless, his sense of guilt has a justification: it is founded on the intense and frequent death-wishes against his fellows which are unconsciously at work in him. It has a justification if what we take into account are unconscious thoughts and not intentional deeds. Thus the omnipotence of thoughts, the overvaluation of mental processes as compared with reality, is seen to have unrestricted play in the emotional life of neurotic patients and in everything that derives from it. If one of them undergoes psychoanalytic treatment, which makes what is unconscious in him conscious, he will be unable to believe that thoughts are free and will constantly be afraid of expressing evil wishes, as though their expression would lead inevitably to their fulfilment. This behaviour, as well as the superstitions which he practises in ordinary life, reveals his resemblance to the savages who believe they can alter the external world by mere thinking.

The primary obsessive acts of these neurotics are of an entirely magical character. If they are not charms, they are at all events counter-charms, designed to ward off the expectations of disaster with which the neurosis usually starts. Whenever I have succeeded in penetrating the mystery, I have found that the expected disaster was death. Schopenhauer has said that the problem of death stands at the outset of every philosophy; and we have already seen [p. 133] that the origin of the belief in souls and in demons, which is the essence of animism, goes back to the impression which is made upon men by death. It is difficult to judge whether the obsessive or protective acts performed by obsessional neurotics follow the law of similarity (or, as the case may be, of contrast); for as a rule, owing to the prevailing conditions of the neurosis, they have been distorted by being displaced on to something very small, some action in itself of the greatest triviality.[1] The protective formulas

---

1. A further motive for such displacement on to a very small action will appear in what follows. [Cf. the 'Rat Man' case history (1909*d*), *P.F.L.*, **9**, 121 and *n*. 1.]

of obsessional neuroses, too, have their counterpart in the formulas of magic. It is possible, however, to describe the course of development of obsessive acts: we can show how they begin by being as remote as possible from anything sexual – magical defences against evil wishes – and how they end by being substitutes for the forbidden sexual act and the closest possible imitations of it.

If we are prepared to accept the account given above of the evolution of human views of the universe – an animistic phase followed by a religious phase and this in turn by a scientific one – it will not be difficult to follow the vicissitudes of the 'omnipotence of thoughts' through these different phases. At the animistic stage men ascribe omnipotence to *themselves*. At the religious stage they transfer it to the gods but do not seriously abandon it themselves, for they reserve the power of influencing the gods in a variety of ways according to their wishes. The scientific view of the universe no longer affords any room for human omnipotence; men have acknowledged their smallness and submitted resignedly to death and to the other necessities of nature. None the less some of the primitive belief in omnipotence still survives in men's faith in the power of the human mind, which grapples with the laws of reality.

If we trace back the development of libidinal trends as we find them in the individual from their adult forms to the first beginnings in childhood, an important distinction emerges, which I have described in my *Three Essays on the Theory of Sexuality* (1905d). Manifestations of the sexual instincts can be observed from the very first, but to begin with they are not yet directed towards any external object. The separate instinctual components of sexuality work independently of one another to obtain pleasure and find satisfaction in the subject's own body. This stage is known as that of auto-erotism and it is succeeded by one in which an object is chosen.[1]

Further study has shown that it is expedient and indeed indispensable to insert a third stage between these two, or, putting

1. [Cf. *P.F.L.*, 7, 97 ff. and 116 ff.]

146

it in another way, to divide the first stage, that of auto-erotism, into two. At this intermediate stage, the importance of which is being made more and more evident by research, the hitherto isolated sexual instincts have already come together into a single whole and have also found an object. But this object is not an external one, extraneous to the subject, but it is his own ego, which has been constituted at about this same time. Bearing in mind pathological fixations of this new stage, which become observable later, we have given it the name of 'narcissism'. The subject behaves as though he were in love with himself; his egoistic instincts and his libidinal wishes are not yet separable under our analysis.

Although we are not yet in a position to describe with sufficient accuracy the characteristics of this narcissistic stage, at which the hitherto dissociated sexual instincts come together into a single unity and cathect the ego as an object, we suspect already that this narcissistic organization is never wholly abandoned. A human being remains to some extent narcissistic even after he has found external objects for his libido. The cathexes of objects which he effects are as it were emanations of the libido that still remains in his ego and can be drawn back into it once more. The state of being in love, which is psychologically so remarkable and is the normal prototype of the psychoses, shows these emanations at their maximum compared to the level of self-love.[1]

Primitive men and neurotics, as we have seen, attach a high valuation – in our eyes an *over*-valuation – to psychical acts. This attitude may plausibly be brought into relation with narcissism and regarded as an essential component of it. It may be said that in primitive men the process of thinking is still to a great extent sexualized. This is the origin of their belief in the omnipotence of thoughts, their unshakable confidence in the possibility of controlling the world and their inaccessibility to the experiences, so easily obtainable, which could teach

1. [The whole question of narcissism was discussed at length by Freud later on in his paper 'On Narcissism: An Introduction' (1914*c*), *P.F.L.*, **11**, 59 ff.]

them man's true position in the universe. As regards neurotics, we find that on the one hand a considerable part of this primitive attitude has survived in their constitution, and on the other hand that the sexual repression that has occurred in them has brought about a further sexualization of their thinking processes. The psychological results must be the same in both cases, whether the libidinal hypercathexis of thinking is an original one or has been produced by regression: intellectual narcissism and the omnipotence of thoughts.[1]

If we may regard the existence among primitive races of the omnipotence of thoughts as evidence in favour of narcissism, we are encouraged to attempt a comparison between the phases in the development of men's view of the universe and the stages of an individual's libidinal development. The animistic phase would correspond to narcissism both chronologically and in its content; the religious phase would correspond to the stage of object-choice of which the characteristic is a child's attachment to his parents; while the scientific phase would have an exact counterpart in the stage at which an individual has reached maturity, has renounced the pleasure principle, adjusted himself to reality and turned to the external world for the object of his desires.[2]

In only a single field of our civilization has the omnipotence of thoughts been retained, and that is in the field of art. Only in art does it still happen that a man who is consumed by desires performs something resembling the accomplishment of those desires and that what he does in play produces emotional effects – thanks to artistic illusion – just as though it were something real. People speak with justice of the 'magic of art' and compare

1. 'It is almost an axiom with writers on this subject, that a sort of Solipsism, or Berkeleianism (as Professor Sully terms it as he finds it in the Child), operates in the savage to make him refuse to recognize death as a fact.' (Marett, 1900, 178.)

2. I will only briefly allude here to the fact that the original narcissism of children has a decisive influence upon our view of the development of their character and excludes the possibility of their having any primary sense of inferiority [as Adler (1910) suggested; see Part III of 'On the History of the Psycho-Analytic Movement' (Freud, 1914d), P.F.L., 15.]

artists to magicians. But the comparison is perhaps more significant than it claims to be. There can be no doubt that art did
not begin as art for art's sake. It worked originally in the service
of impulses which are for the most part extinct to-day. And
among them we may suspect the presence of many magical
purposes.[1]

(4)

Thus the first picture which man formed of the world – animism
– was a psychological one. It needed no scientific basis as yet,
since science only begins after it has been realized that the world
is unknown and that means must therefore be sought for getting
to know it. Animism came to primitive man naturally and
as a matter of course. He knew what things were like in the
world, namely just as he felt himself to be. We are thus prepared
to find that primitive man transposed the structural conditions
of his own mind[2] into the external world; and we may attempt
to reverse the process and put back into the human mind what
animism teaches as to the nature of things.

1. Cf. Reinach, 'L'art et la magie' (1905–12, I, 125–36). In Reinach's
opinion the primitive artists who left behind the carvings and paintings of
animals in the French caves, did not desire to 'please' but to 'evoke' or conjure up. He thus explains why it is that these pictures are situated in the
darkest and most inaccessible parts of the caves and that dangerous beasts
of prey do not appear among them. 'Les modernes parlent souvent, par
hyperbole, de la magie du pinceau ou du ciseau d'un grand artiste et, en
général, de la magie de l'art. Entendu au sens propre, qui est celui d'une
contrainte mystique exercée par la volonté de l'homme sur d'autres volontés
ou sur les choses, cette expression n'est plus admissible; mais nous avons vu
qu'elle était autrefois rigoureusement vraie, du moins dans l'opinion des
artistes.' (Ibid., 136.) ['In modern times people often speak metaphorically
of the magic of a great artist's brush or chisel, or more generally of the
magic of art. This expression is no longer permissible in its proper sense
of a mystical force brought to bear by the human will upon other wills
or upon objects; but, as we have seen, there was a time when it was literally
true – at least in the artists' opinion.']

2. Which he was aware of by what is known as endopsychic perception.
[That is, by the use of the outlying portions of the retina instead of the macula.
Cf. the 'Rat Man' case history (1909d), P.F.L., 9, 45 and 111.]

The technique of animism, magic, reveals in the clearest and most unmistakable way an intention to impose the laws governing mental life upon real things; in this, spirits need not as yet play any part, though spirits may be taken as objects of magical treatment. Thus the assumptions of magic are more fundamental and older than the doctrine of spirits, which forms the kernel of animism. Our psychoanalytic point of view coincides here with a theory put forward by R. R. Marett (1900), who postulates a pre-animistic stage before animism, the character of which is best indicated by the term 'animatism', the doctrine of the universality of life. Experience has little light to throw on pre-animism, since no race has yet been discovered which is without the concept of spirits. (Cf. Wundt, 1906, 171 ff.)

Whereas magic still reserves omnipotence solely for thoughts, animism hands some of it over to spirits and so prepares the way for the construction of a religion. What, we may ask, can have induced a primitive man to make this first act of renunciation? It can scarcely have been a recognition of the falseness of his premises, for he continued to practise the magical technique.

Spirits and demons, as I have shown in the last essay, are only projections of man's own emotional impulses.[1] He turns his emotional cathexes into persons, he peoples the world with them and meets his internal mental processes again outside himself – in just the same way as that intelligent paranoic, Schreber, found a reflection of the attachments and detachments of his libido in the vicissitudes of his confabulated 'rays of God'.[2]

I propose to avoid (as I have already done elsewhere[3]) entering into the general problem of the origin of the tendency to project mental processes into the outside. It is, however, safe to assume that that tendency will be intensified when projection

1. I assume that at this early narcissistic stage cathexes arising from libidinal and from other sources of excitation may still be indistinguishable from one another.

2. Cf. Schreber (1903) and Freud (1911c [Section III (4), *P.F.L.*, **9**, 218]).

3. In my paper on Schreber (Freud, 1911c [Section III, *P.F.L.*, **9**, 204 f.]).

promises to bring with it the advantage of mental relief. Such an advantage may be expected with certainty where a conflict has arisen between different impulses all of which are striving towards omnipotence – for they clearly cannot *all* become omnipotent. The pathological process in paranoia in fact makes use of the mechanism of projection in order to deal with mental conflicts of this kind. The typical case of such a conflict is one between the two members of a pair of opposites – the case of an ambivalent attitude, which we have examined in detail as it appears in someone mourning the death of a loved relative. [Cf. p. 116 ff.] This kind of case must seem particularly likely to provide a motive for the creation of projections. Here again we are in agreement with the writers who maintain that the first-born spirits were *evil* spirits, and who derive the idea of a soul from the impression made by death upon the survivors. The only difference is that *we* do not lay stress on the *intellectual* problem with which death confronts the living; in our view the force which gives the impetus to research is rather to be attributed to the *emotional* conflict into which the survivors are plunged.

Thus man's first theoretical achievement – the creation of spirits – seems to have arisen from the same source as the first moral restrictions to which he was subjected – the observances of taboo. The fact that they had the same origin need not imply, however, that they arose simultaneously. If the survivors' position in relation to the dead was really what first caused primitive man to reflect, and compelled him to hand over some of his omnipotence to the spirits and to sacrifice some of his freedom of action, then these cultural products would constitute a first acknowledgment of 'Ανάγκη [Necessity], which opposes human narcissism. Primitive man would thus be submitting to the supremacy of death with the same gesture with which he seemed to be denying it.

If we may venture to exploit our hypothesis still further, we may inquire which essential part of our psychological structure is reflected and reproduced in the projective creation of souls and spirits. It could scarcely be disputed that the primitive conception of a soul, however much it may differ from the later, purely immaterial soul, is nevertheless intrinsically the same; that is to say, it assumes that both persons and things are of a double nature and that their known attributes and modifications are distributed between their two component portions. This original 'duality', to borrow an expression from Herbert Spencer (1893), is identical with the dualism proclaimed by our current distinction between soul and body and by such ineradicable linguistic expressions of it as the use of phrases like 'beside himself' or 'coming to himself' in relation to fits of rage or fainting (ibid., 144).

When we, no less than primitive man, project something into external reality, what is happening must surely be this: we are recognizing the existence of two states – one in which something is directly given to the senses and to consciousness (that is, is *present* to them), and alongside it another, in which the same thing is *latent* but capable of re-appearing. In short, we are recognizing the co-existence of perception and memory, or, putting it more generally, the existence of *unconscious* mental processes alongside the *conscious* ones.[1] It might be said that in the last analysis the 'spirit' of persons or things comes down to their capacity to be remembered and imagined after perception of them has ceased.

It is not, of course, to be expected that either the primitive or the present-day concept of a 'soul' will be separated from that of the other portion of the personality by the same line of demarcation which our modern science draws between conscious and unconscious mental activity. The animistic soul unites properties from both sides. Its volatile and mobile quality, its power of leaving the body and of taking possession, temporarily or permanently, of another body – these are characteristics which remind us unmistakably of the nature of consciousness. But the way in which it remains concealed behind the manifest

1. Cf. my short paper on the use of the concept 'unconscious' in psychoanalysis, first published in the *Proceedings* of the Society for Psychical Research in 1912 [Freud (1912g), *P.F.L.*, **11**, 45 ff.].

personality is reminiscent of the unconscious; immutability and indestructibility are qualities which we no longer attribute to conscious but rather to unconscious processes, and we regard the latter as the true vehicle of mental activity.

I have said [p. 121 f.] that animism is a system of thought, the first complete theory of the universe, and I shall now go on to draw certain conclusions from the psychoanalytic view of such systems. Every day of our lives our experience is in a position to show us the principal characteristics of a 'system'. We have dreams during the night and we have learnt how to interpret them during the day. Dreams may, without contradicting their nature, appear confused and disconnected. But they may, on the contrary, simulate the orderly impressions of a real experience, they may make one event follow from another and make one portion of their content refer to another. Such a result can be more or less successfully achieved; but it scarcely ever succeeds so completely as to leave no absurdity, no rift in its texture, visible. When we come to submit a dream to interpretation, we find that the erratic and irregular arrangement of its constituent parts is quite unimportant from the point of view of our understanding it. The essential elements in a dream are the dream-thoughts, and these have meaning, connection and order. But their order is quite other than that remembered by us as present in the manifest dream. In the latter the connection between the dream-thoughts has been abandoned and may either remain completely lost or be replaced by the new connection exhibited in the manifest content. The elements of the dream, apart from their being condensed, are almost invariably arranged in a new order more or less independent of their earlier arrangement. Finally, it must be added that whatever the original material of the dream-thoughts has been turned into by the dream-work is then subjected to a further influence. This is what is known as 'secondary revision', and its purpose is evidently to get rid of the disconnectedness and unintelligibility produced by the dream-work and replace it by a new 'meaning'. But this new meaning, arrived at by secondary revision, is no longer the meaning of the dream-thoughts.[1]

The secondary revision of the product of the dream-work is an admirable example of the nature and pretensions of a system. There is an intellectual function in us which demands unity, connection and intelligibility from any material, whether of perception or thought, that comes within its grasp; and if, as a result of special circumstances, it is unable to establish a true connection, it does not hesitate to fabricate a false one. Systems constructed in this way are known to us not only from dreams, but also from phobias, from obsessive thinking and from delusions. The construction of systems is seen most strikingly in delusional disorders (in paranoia), where it dominates the symptomatic picture; but its occurrence in other forms of neuro-psychosis must not be overlooked. In all these cases it can be shown that a rearrangement of the psychical material has been made with a fresh aim in view; and the rearrangement may often have to be a drastic one if the outcome is to be made to appear intelligible from the point of view of the system. Thus a system is best characterized by the fact that at least two reasons can be discovered for each of its products: a reason based upon the premises of the system (a reason, then, which may be delusional) and a concealed reason, which we must judge to be the truly operative and the real one.

This may be illustrated by an example from a neurosis. In my essay on taboo I mentioned a woman patient of mine whose obsessional prohibitions showed the most perfect agreement with a Maori taboo (p. 81). This woman's neurosis was aimed at her husband and culminated in her defence against an unconscious wish that he should die. Her manifest, systematic phobia, however, related to the mention of death in general, while her husband was entirely excluded from it and was never an object of her conscious solicitude. One day she heard her husband giving instructions that his razors, which had lost their edge, were to be taken to a particular shop to be re-set. Driven by a strange uneasiness, she herself set off for the shop. After

1. [Cf. p. 121 n. 2 above.]

reconnoitring the ground, she came back and insisted that her husband should get rid of the razors for good and all, since she had discovered that next door to the shop he had named there was an undertaker's establishment: owing to the plan he had made, she said, the razors had become inextricably involved with thoughts of death. This, then, was the *systematic* reason for her prohibition. We may be quite sure that, even without her discovery of the next-door shop, the patient would have come home with a prohibition against the razors. It would have been enough if she had met a hearse on her way to the shop, or someone dressed in mourning or carrying a funeral wreath. The net of possible determinants for the prohibition was spread wide enough to catch the quarry in any event; it merely depended on her decision whether to draw it together or not. It could be shown that on other occasions she would not put the determinants into operation, and she would explain this by saying it had been 'a better day'. The *real* cause of her prohibition upon the razors was, of course, as it was easy to discover, her repugnance to attaching any pleasurable feeling to the idea that her husband might cut his throat with the newly ground razors.

In just the same way, an inhibition upon movement (an abasia or an agoraphobia) will gradually become more complete and more detailed, when once that system has succeeded in installing itself as a representative of an unconscious wish and of the defence against the wish. Whatever other unconscious phantasies and operative reminiscences may be present in the patient force their way to expression as symptoms along this same path, once it has been opened, and group themselves into an appropriate new arrangement within the framework of the inhibition upon movement. Thus it would be a vain and indeed a foolish task to attempt to understand the complexities and details of the symptoms of (for example) an agoraphobia on the basis of its underlying premises; for the whole consistency and strictness of the combination are merely *apparent*. Just as with the façades of dreams, if we look more attentively we find the most blatant inconsistency and arbitrariness in the structure of symptoms. The real reason for the details of a systematic phobia of this kind lies in concealed determinants, which need have nothing to do with an inhibition upon movement; and that, too, is why these phobias take such various and contradictory shapes in different people.

Let us now return to the animistic system with which we are dealing. The insight we have gained into *other* psychological systems enables us to conclude that with primitive man, too, 'superstition' need not be the only or the real reason for some particular custom or observance and does not excuse us from the duty of searching for its hidden motives. Under the domination of an animistic system it is inevitable that every observance and every activity shall have a systematic basis, which nowadays we describe as 'superstitious'. 'Superstition' – like 'anxiety', 'dreams' and 'demons' – is one of those provisional psychological concepts which have crumbled under the impact of psychoanalytic research. Once we have penetrated behind these constructions, which are like screens erected as defences against correct understanding, we begin to realize that the mental life and cultural level of savages have not hitherto had all the recognition they deserve.

If we take instinctual repression as a measure of the level of civilization that has been reached, we shall have to admit that even under the animistic system advances and developments took place which are unjustly despised on account of their superstitious basis. When we are told that the warriors in a savage tribe practise the greatest continence and cleanliness when they go on the war-path, the explanation is put forward that their motive is 'a fear lest the enemy should obtain the refuse of their persons, and thus be enabled to work their destruction by magic' (Frazer, 1911*b*, 157); and an analogous superstitious reason could be suggested for their continence. None the less the fact remains that they have made an instinctual renunciation; and we can understand the position better if we suppose that the savage warrior submits to these restrictions as a counter-measure because he is on the point of yielding completely to the satisfaction of cruel and hostile impulses which are as a rule prohibited to him. The same is true of the numerous cases of sexual restrictions being imposed on anyone who is engaged on difficult or responsible work (ibid., 200 f.). Though the grounds alleged for these prohibitions may belong to a magical context, yet the fundamental idea of gaining greater strength by renouncing some instinctual satisfaction remains unmistakable; and the hygienic root of the prohibition which lies alongside its magical rationalization must not be overlooked. When the men of a savage tribe go out on an expedition to hunt, to fish, to fight or to gather precious plants, their wives left at home are subjected to many oppressive restrictions, to which the savages themselves ascribe a favourable influence, operating at a distance upon the success of the expedition. But it requires very little penetration to see that this factor which operates at a distance is nothing other than the absent men's longing thoughts of home, and that behind these disguises lies a sound piece of psychological insight that the men will only do their best if they feel completely secure about the women whom they have left behind them unguarded. Sometimes they will even themselves declare, without alleging any magical reasons, that a wife's infidelity in marriage will bring to nothing the efforts of an absent husband engaged on some responsible work.

The countless taboo regulations to which the women in savage communities are subject during menstruation are said to be due to a superstitious horror of blood, and this is no doubt in fact one of their determinants. But it would be wrong to overlook the possibility that in this case the horror of blood also serves aesthetic and hygienic purposes, which are obliged in every case to cloak themselves behind magical motives.

I am under no illusion that in putting forward these attempted explanations I am laying myself open to the charge of endowing modern savages with a subtlety in their mental activities which exceeds all probability. It seems to me quite possible, however, that the same may be true of our attitude towards the psychology of those races that have remained at the animistic level as is true of our attitude towards the mental life of children, which we adults no longer understand and whose fullness and delicacy of feeling we have in consequence so greatly under-estimated.

One further group of taboo observances, which have not hitherto been accounted for, deserve mention, since they admit of an explanation which is familiar to psychoanalysts. Among many savage peoples there is a prohibition against keeping sharp weapons or cutting instruments in a house. Frazer (1911b, 238) quotes a German superstition to the effect that a knife should not be left edge upwards, for fear that God and the angels might be injured on it. May we not recognize in this taboo a premoni-tory warning against possible 'symptomatic acts' in the execu-tion of which a sharp weapon might be employed by uncon-scious evil impulses?[1]

1. [A discussion of superstition, particularly in regard to obsessional neurosis, will be found in the 'Rat Man' case history (1909d), *P.F.L.*, **9**, 109–12.]

IV

THE RETURN OF TOTEMISM
IN CHILDHOOD

THERE are no grounds for fearing that psychoanalysis, which
first discovered that psychical acts and structures are invariably
overdetermined, will be tempted to trace the origin of anything
so complicated as religion to a single source. If psychoanalysis
is compelled – and is, indeed, in duty bound – to lay all the
emphasis upon one particular source, that does not mean it
is claiming either that that source is the only one or that it
occupies first place among the numerous contributory factors.
Only when we can synthesize the findings in the different fields
of research will it become possible to arrive at the relative importance of the part played in the genesis of religion by the
mechanism discussed in these pages. Such a task lies beyond
the means as well as beyond the purposes of a psychoanalyst.

(1)

In the first of this series of essays we became acquainted with
the concept of totemism. We heard that totemism is a system
which takes the place of a religion among certain primitive
peoples of Australia, America and Africa, and provides the basis
of their social organization. As we have heard, it was a Scotsman, McLennan, who in 1869 first drew general attention to
the phenomena of totemism (which had hitherto been regarded
as mere curiosities) by giving voice to a suspicion that a large
number of customs and usages current in various societies
ancient and modern were to be explained as remnants of a
totemic age. Since that date science has fully accepted his
estimate of totemism. Let me quote, as one of the most recent
statements on the subject, a passage from Wundt's *Elemente der*

Völkerpsychologie (1912, 139): 'In the light of all these facts, the conclusion appears highly probable that at some time totemic culture everywhere paved the way for a more advanced civilization, and, thus, that it represents a transitional stage between the age of primitive men and the era of heroes and gods.' [English translation, 139.]

The purpose of the present essays obliges us to enter more deeply into the nature of totemism. For reasons which will presently become clear I will begin with an account given by Reinach, who, in 1900,[1] sketched out a '*Code du totémisme*' in twelve Articles – a catechism, as it were, of the totemic religion:

(1) Certain animals may neither be killed nor eaten, but individual members of the species are reared by human beings and cared for by them.

(2) An animal which has died an accidental death is mourned over and buried with the same honours as a member of the clan.

(3) In some instances the eating prohibition extends only to one particular part of the animal's body.

(4) When one of the animals which are usually spared has to be killed under the stress of necessity, apologies are offered to it and an attempt is made by means of various artifices and evasions to mitigate the violation of the taboo – that is to say, the murder.

(5) When the animal is made the victim of a ritual sacrifice, it is solemnly bewailed.

(6) On particular solemn occasions and at religious ceremonies the skins of certain animals are worn. Where totemism is still in force, they are the totem animals.

(7) Clans and individuals adopt the names of animals – viz. of the totem animals.

(8) Many clans make use of representations of animals on their standards and weapons; the men have pictures of animals painted or tattooed on their bodies.

(9) If the totem is a formidable or dangerous animal, it is supposed to spare members of the clan named after it.

1. Cf. Reinach (1905–12, I, 17 ff.).

(10) The totem animal protects and gives warning to members of its clan.

(11) The totem animal foretells the future to the loyal members of its clan and serves them as guide.

(12) The members of the totemic clan often believe that they are related to the totem animal by the bond of a common ancestry.

This catechism of the totemic religion can only be seen at its proper value if we take into account the fact that Reinach has included in it all the indications and traces from which the earlier existence of a totemic system can be inferred. The author's peculiar attitude to the problem is shown by his partial neglect of the essential features of totemism. As we shall see, he has relegated one of the two principal articles of the totemic catechism to the background and entirely overlooked the other.

To obtain a correct picture of the nature of totemism we must turn to another author, who has devoted a four-volume work to the subject, which combines the fullest collection of the relevant observations with the most detailed discussion of the problems they raise. We shall remain indebted to J. G. Frazer, the author of *Totemism and Exogamy* (1910), both for enjoyment and instruction, even if psychoanalytic research may lead to conclusions which differ widely from his.[1]

1. It may be as well, however, to warn the reader, in advance, of the difficulties with which any statements on the subject have to contend.

In the first place, those who collect the observations are not the same as those who examine and discuss them. The former are travellers and missionaries while the latter are students who may never have set eyes on the objects of their researches. Again, communication with savages is not an easy matter. The observers are not always acquainted with the native language but may be obliged to rely on the help of interpreters or to conduct their inquiries through the medium of pidgin-English. Savages are not communicative on the subject of the most intimate details of their cultural life and they talk openly only to those foreigners who have lived among them for many years. They often give false or misleading information for a great variety of motives. (Cf. Frazer, 1910, 1, 150 f.) It should not be forgotten that primitive races are not young races but are in fact as old as civilized races. There is no reason to suppose that, for the benefit of our information, they

'A totem,' wrote Frazer in his first essay on the subject,[1] 'is a class of material objects which a savage regards with superstitious respect, believing that there exists between him and every member of the class an intimate and altogether special relation ... The connection between a man and his totem is mutually beneficent; the totem protects the man, and the man shows his respect for the totem in various ways, by not killing it if it be an animal, and not cutting or gathering it if it be a plant. As distinguished from a fetish, a totem is never an isolated individual, but always a class of objects, generally a species of animals or of plants, more rarely a class of inanimate natural objects, very rarely a class of artificial objects ...

'Totems are of at least three kinds: (1) the clan totem, common to a whole clan, and passing by inheritance from generation to generation; (2) the sex totem, common either to all the males or to all the females of a tribe, to the exclusion in either case of the other sex; (3) the individual totem, belonging to a single individual and not passing to his descendants ...'

The last two kinds of totem do not compare in significance with the clan totem. Unless we are quite mistaken, they are late developments and of little importance for the essential nature of the totem.

'The clan totem is reverenced by a body of men and women who call themselves by the name of the totem, believe them-

---

have retained their original ideas and institutions undeveloped and undistorted. On the contrary, it is certain that there have been profound changes in every direction among primitive races, so that it is never possible to decide without hesitation how far their present-day conditions and opinions preserve the primaeval past in a petrified form and how far they are distortions and modifications of it. Hence arise the all-too-frequent disputes among the authorities as to which characteristics of a primitive civilization are to be regarded as primary and as to which are later and secondary developments. The determination of the original state of things thus invariably remains a matter of construction. Finally, it is not easy to feel one's way into primitive modes of thinking. We misunderstand primitive men just as easily as we do children, and we are always apt to interpret their actions and feelings according to our own mental constellations.

1. *Totemism*, Edinburgh, 1887, reprinted in Frazer (1910, **1**, 3 ff.).

selves to be of one blood, descendants of a common ancestor, and are bound together by common obligations to each other and by a common faith in the totem. Totemism is thus both a religious and a social system. In its religious aspect it consists of the relations of mutual respect and protection between a man and his totem; in its social aspect it consists of the relations of the clansmen to each other and to men of other clans. In the later history of totemism these two sides, the religious and the social, tend to part company; the social system sometimes survives the religious; and, on the other hand, religion sometimes bears traces of totemism in countries where the social system based on totemism has disappeared. How in the origin of totemism these two sides were related to each other it is, in our ignorance of that origin, impossible to say with certainty. But on the whole the evidence points strongly to the conclusion that the two sides were originally inseparable; that, in other words, the farther we go back, the more we should find that the clansman regards himself and his totem as beings of the same species, and the less he distinguishes between conduct towards his totem and towards his fellow-clansmen.'

In giving particulars of totemism as a religious system, Frazer begins by stating that the members of a totem clan call themselves by the name of their totem, and *commonly believe themselves to be actually descended from it*. It follows from this belief that they will not hunt the totem animal or kill or eat it and, if it is something other than an animal, they refrain from making use of it in other ways. The rules against killing or eating the totem are not the only taboos; sometimes they are forbidden to touch it, or even to look at it; in a number of cases the totem may not be spoken of by its proper name. Any violation of the taboos that protect the totem are automatically punished by severe illness or death.[1]

Specimens of the totem animal are occasionally reared by the clan and cared for in captivity.[2] A totem animal that is

1. Cf. my earlier essay on taboo [above, p. 73].
2. As is done to this day with the she-wolf in her cage beside the steps leading up to the Capitol in Rome and with the bears in their den at Berne.

found dead is mourned for and buried like a dead clansman. If it is necessary to kill a totem animal, this is done according to a prescribed ritual of apologies and ceremonies of expiation.

The clan expects to receive protection and care from its totem. If it is a dangerous animal (such as a beast of prey or a venomous snake) there is a presumption that it will do no harm to its clansmen; and if that expectation is not fulfilled the injured man is expelled from the clan. Oaths, in Frazer's opinion, were originally ordeals; thus, many tests of descent and legitimacy were submitted for decision to the totem. The totem gives help in sickness and delivers omens and warnings to its clan. The appearance of the totem in or about a house is often regarded as an omen of death; the totem has come to fetch his kinsman.[1]

In particular important circumstances the clansman seeks to emphasize his kinship with the totem by making himself resemble it externally, by dressing in the skin of the animal, by incising a picture of the totem upon his own body, and so on. This identification with the totem is carried into effect in actions and words on the ceremonial occasions of birth, initiation and burial. Various magical and religious purposes are served by dances in which all the clansmen disguise themselves as their totem and imitate its behaviour. Lastly, there are ceremonies in which the totem animal is ceremoniously killed.[2]

The social aspect of totemism is principally expressed in a severely enforced injunction and a sweeping restriction.

The members of a totem clan are brothers and sisters and are bound to help and protect one another. If a member of a clan is killed by someone outside it, the whole clan of the aggressor is responsible for the deed and the whole clan of the murdered man is at one in demanding satisfaction for the blood that has been shed. The totem bond is stronger than that of the family in our sense. The two do not coincide, since the totem is as a rule inherited through the female line, and it is

1. Like the White Lady in certain aristocratic families.
2. Frazer (1910, I, 45). See my discussion of sacrifice below [p. 193 ff.].

possible that paternal descent may originally have been left entirely out of account.

The corresponding taboo restriction prohibits members of the same totem clan from marrying or having sexual intercourse with each other. Here we have the notorious and mysterious correlate of totemism – exogamy. I have devoted the whole of the first essay in the present work to that subject, so that here I need only repeat that it originates from the intensification among savages of the horror of incest, that it would be fully explained as an assurance against incest under conditions of group marriage, and that it is primarily aimed at restraining the *younger* generation from incest and that only as a later development does it interfere with the older generation. [See above, p. 57 and footnote.]

To Frazer's account of totemism – one of the earliest in the literature of the subject – I will add a few extracts from one of the most recent ones. In his *Elemente der Völkerpsychologie*, Wundt (1912, 116 ff.) writes as follows: 'The totem animal is also usually regarded as the ancestral animal of the group in question. "Totem" is, on the one hand a group name, and, on the other, a name indicative of ancestry. In the latter connection it has also a mythological significance. These various ideas, however, interplay in numerous ways. Some of the meanings may recede, so that totems have frequently become a mere nomenclature of tribal divisions, while at other times the idea of ancestry, or, perhaps also, the cult significance, predominates ...' The concept of the totem has a decisive influence upon tribal division and tribal organization, which are subject to certain norms of custom. 'These norms, and their fixed place in the beliefs and feelings of the tribal members, are connected with the fact that originally, at all events, the totem animal was regarded, for the most part, as having not merely given its name to a group of tribal members but as having actually been its forefather ... Bound up with this is the further fact that these animal ancestors possessed a cult ... Aside from specific ceremonies and ceremonial festivals, this animal cult originally found expression primarily in the relations maintained towards the totem animal. It was not merely a particular animal that was to a certain extent held sacred, but every representative of the species. The totem members were forbidden to eat the flesh of the totem animal, or were allowed to do so only under specific conditions. A significant counter-phenomenon, not irreconcilable with this, is the fact that on certain occasions the eating of the totem flesh constituted a sort of ceremony ...'

'... The most important social aspect of this totemic tribal organization, however, consists in the fact that it involved certain norms of custom regulating the intercourse of the separate groups with one another. Of these norms, those governing marriage relations were of first importance. The tribal organization of this period was bound up with an important institution, *exogamy*, which originated in the totemic age.' [English translation, 116 f.]

If we seek to penetrate to the original nature of totemism, without regard to subsequent accretions or attenuations, we find that its essential characteristics are these: *Originally, all totems were animals, and were regarded as the ancestors of the different clans. Totems were inherited only through the female line. There was a prohibition against killing the totem* (or – which, under primitive conditions, is the same thing – against eating it). *Members of a totem clan were forbidden to practise sexual intercourse with one another.*[1]

1. The picture of totemism given by Frazer in his second work on it ('The Origin of Totemism', published in the *Fortnightly Review* in 1899) agrees with what I have written above: 'Thus, Totemism has commonly been treated as a primitive system both of religion and of society. As a system of religion it embraces the mystic union of the savage with his totem; as a system of society it comprises the relations in which men and women of the same totem stand to each other and to the members of other totemic groups. And corresponding to these two sides of the system are two rough and ready tests or canons of Totemism: first, the rule that a man may not kill or eat his totem animal or plant; and second, the rule that he may not marry or cohabit with a woman of the same totem.' [Reprinted in Frazer, 1910, I, 101.] Frazer then proceeds (thus plunging us into the middle of the controversies on totemism): 'Whether the two sides – the religious and the social – have always co-existed or are essentially independent, is a question which has been variously answered.'

We shall now, perhaps, be struck by the fact that in Reinach's *Code du totémisme* one of the two principal taboos, that of exogamy, is not mentioned at all, while the belief upon which the second one is founded, namely descent from the totem animal, is only referred to in passing. My reason, however, for selecting the account given by Reinach (a writer, incidentally, who has made very valuable contributions to the subject) was to prepare us for the differences of opinion between the authorities – differences into which we must now enter.

(2)

The more incontestable became the conclusion that totemism constitutes a regular phase in all cultures, the more urgent became the need for arriving at an understanding of it and for throwing light upon the puzzle of its essential nature. Everything connected with totemism seems to be puzzling: the decisive problems concern the origin of the idea of descent from the totem and the reasons for exogamy (or rather for the taboo upon incest of which exogamy is the expression), as well as the relation between these two institutions, totemic organization and prohibition of incest. Any satisfactory explanation should be at once a historical and a psychological one. It should tell us under what conditions this peculiar institution developed and to what psychical needs in men it has given expression.

My readers will, I am sure, be astonished to hear of the variety of angles from which attempts have been made to answer these questions, and of the wide divergences of opinion upon them put forward by the experts. Almost any generalization that could be made on the subject of totemism and exogamy seems open to question. Even the account that I have just given, derived from the book published by Frazer in 1887, is open to the criticism that it expresses the present writer's arbitrary preferences; and indeed it would be contested to-day by Frazer himself, who has repeatedly changed his opinions on the subject.[1]

1. He makes the following admirable comment upon such changes of

It is plausible to suppose that an understanding of the essential nature of totemism and exogamy would best be arrived at, if it were possible to come nearer to the origins of the two institutions. But in this connection we must bear in mind Andrew Lang's warning that even primitive peoples have not retained the original forms of those institutions nor the conditions which gave rise to them; so that we have nothing whatever but hypotheses to fall back upon as a substitute for the observations which we are without.[1] Some of the attempted explanations seem, in the judgement of a psychologist, inadequate at the very outset: they are too rational and take no account of the emotional character of the matters to be explained. Others are based on assumptions which are unconfirmed by observation. Yet others rely upon material which would be better interpreted in another way. There is generally little difficulty in refuting the various views put forward: the authorities are as usual more effective in their criticisms of one another's work than in their own productions. The conclusion upon most of the points raised must be a *non liquet*. It is not surprising, therefore, that in the most recent literature on the subject (which is for the most part passed over in the present work) an unmistakable tendency emerges to reject any general solution of totemic problems as impracticable. (See, for instance, Goldenweiser, 1910.) In the discussion of these conflicting hypotheses which follows, I have ventured to disregard their chronological sequence.

---

opinion: 'That my conclusions on these difficult questions are final, I am not so foolish as to pretend. I have changed my views repeatedly, and I am resolved to change them again with every change of the evidence, for like a chameleon the candid inquirer should shift his colours with the shifting colours of the ground he treads.' (Frazer, 1910, I, xiii.)

1. 'By the nature of the case, as the origin of totemism lies far beyond our powers of historical examination or of experiment, we must have recourse as regards this matter to conjecture.' (Lang, 1905, 27.) 'Nowhere do we see absolutely *primitive* man, and a totemic system in the making.' (Ibid., 29.)

(a) THE ORIGIN OF TOTEMISM

The question of the origin of totemism may be put in another way: how did it come about that primitive men called themselves (and their clans) after animals, plants and inanimate objects?[1]

McLennan (1865 and 1869–70), the Scot who discovered totemism and exogamy for the world of science, refrained from publishing any opinion on the origin of totemism. According to Andrew Lang (1905, 34) he was at one time inclined to think that it originated from the custom of tattooing. I propose to divide the published theories on the origin of totemism into three groups – (α) the nominalist, (β) the sociological and (γ) the psychological.

(α) *Nominalist Theories*

My accounts of these theories will justify my having brought them together under the title I have adopted.

Garcilaso de la Vega, a descendant of the Peruvian Incas, who wrote a history of his people in the seventeenth century, seems already to have attributed the origin of what he knew of totemic phenomena to the need felt by clans to distinguish themselves from one another by the use of names. (Lang, 1905, 34.) Hundreds of years later the same idea was again proposed. Keane [1899, 396][2] regards totems as 'heraldic badges' by means of which individuals, families and clans sought to distinguish themselves from one another. The same idea is expressed once more by Max-Müller (1897 [I, 201]):[3] 'A totem is a clan mark, then a clan name, then the name of the ancestor of a clan, and lastly the name of something worshipped by a clan.' Julius Pikler,[4] writing later, declares: 'Mankind required both for

1. In the first instance probably after animals only.
2. Quoted by Lang [1903, ix f.].
3. Quoted by Lang [1905, 118].
4. Pikler and Somló [1900]. These authors justly describe their attempted explanation of the origin of totemism as 'a contribution to the materialist theory of history'.

communities and for individuals a permanent name which could be fixed in writing ... Thus totemism did not arise from the religious needs of men but from their practical, everyday needs. The core of totemism, nomenclature, is a result of the primitive technique of writing. In its nature a totem is like an easily drawn pictograph. But when once savages bore the name of an animal, they went on to form the idea of kinship with it.'

In the same way, Herbert Spencer (1870 and 1893, 331–46) regards the giving of names as the decisive factor in the origin of totemism. The personal characteristics of particular individuals, he argues, prompted the idea of calling them after animals, and in that way they acquired laudatory names or nicknames which were handed on to their descendants. As a result of the vagueness and unintelligibility of primitive speech, later generations interpreted these names as evidence of descent from the actual animals. Totemism would thus be shown to be a misunderstood form of ancestor worship.

Lord Avebury (better known under his earlier name of Sir John Lubbock) gives a very similar account of the origin of totemism, though without insisting upon the element of misunderstanding. If, he says, we wish to explain animal-worship, we must not forget how often human names are borrowed from animals. The children and followers of a man who was called 'Bear' or 'Lion' naturally turned his name into a clan-name. Thence it came about that the animal itself would come to be regarded 'first with interest, then with respect and at length with a sort of awe'. [Lubbock, 1870, 171.]

What would seem to be an incontrovertible objection to this derivation of totem names from the names of individuals was brought forward by Fison.[1] He showed from conditions in Australia that the totem is invariably 'the badge of a group, not of an individual'. But even if this were not so, and the totem was originally the name of an individual, it could never – since totems are inherited through the female line – be transmitted to his children.

1. Fison and Howitt (1880, 165), quoted by Lang (1905 [141]).

Moreover, the theories which I have so far discussed are obviously inadequate. They might perhaps explain the fact that primitive peoples adopt animal names for their clans, but they could never explain the importance that has become attached to this nomenclature – namely, the totemic system. The theory belonging to this group which most deserves attention is that proposed by Andrew Lang (1903 and 1905). He, too, regards the giving of names as the heart of the problem, but he introduces two interesting psychological factors and may thus claim to have led the way towards the final solution of the enigma of totemism.

Andrew Lang regards it as initially a matter of indifference how clans obtained their animal names. It is only necessary to assume that they awoke one day to the consciousness that they bore such names and could give no account of how this had come about. *The origin of the names had been forgotten*. They would then attempt to arrive at an explanation by speculating on the subject; and, in view of their belief in the importance of names, they were bound to reach all the ideas contained in the totemic system. Primitive races (as well as modern savages and even our own children[1]) do not, like us, regard names as something indifferent and conventional, but as significant and essential. A man's name is a principal component of his personality, perhaps even a portion of his soul. The fact of a primitive man bearing the same name as an animal must lead him to assume the existence of a mysterious and significant bond between himself and that particular species of animal. What other bond could it be than one of blood relationship? Once the similarity of names had led to this conclusion, the blood taboo would immediately involve all the totemic ordinances, including exogamy. 'No more than these three things – a group animal name of unknown origin; belief in a transcendental connection between all bearers, human and bestial, of the same name; and belief in the blood superstitions – was needed to give rise to all the totemic creeds and practices, including exogamy.' (Lang, 1905, 125 f.)

1. See the discussion of taboo above, p. 110 ff.

171

Lang's explanation falls into two parts. One part of it traces the totemic system as a matter of psychological necessity from the fact of the totems having animal names – always presupposing that the origin of these names had been forgotten. The second part of his theory goes on to try to explain how the names in fact originated; as we shall see, it is of a very different character from the first part.

This second part of Lang's theory differs in no essential way from the other theories which I have called 'nominalist'. The practical necessity for differentiation compelled the various clans to adopt names, and they therefore acquiesced in the names by which each clan was called by another clan. This 'naming from without' is the special feature of Lang's construction. The fact that the names adopted in this way were borrowed from animals needs no special comment and there is no reason why they should have been regarded in primitive times as insulting or derisive. Moreover, Lang has adduced not a few instances from later historical times in which names that were originally given in derision by outsiders have been accepted and willingly adopted (e.g. *'Les Gueux'*[1], 'Whigs' and 'Tories'). The hypothesis that in the course of time the origin of these names was forgotten connects this part of Lang's theory with the other part which I have already discussed.

(β) Sociological Theories

Reinach, who has been successful in tracing survivals of the totemic system in the cults and usages of later periods but who has always attached small importance to the factor of descent from the totem, remarks confidently in one passage that in his opinion totemism is nothing more than *'une hypertrophie de l'instinct social'*. (Reinach, 1905–12, **I,** 41.) A similar view seems to run through the recent book by Durkheim (1912). The totem, he argues, is the visible representative of social religion among the races concerned: it embodies the community, which is the true object of their worship.

Other writers have sought to find a more precise basis for

1. ['The Beggars': A Dutch rebel faction in the 16th century.]

the participation of the social instincts in the formation of totemic institutions. Thus Haddon (1902 [745])[1] supposes that each primitive clan originally subsisted upon some one species of animal or plant and perhaps traded in that particular article of food and exchanged it with other clans. It would inevitably follow that this clan would be known to the others by the name of the animal which was of such importance to it. At the same time the clan would be bound to become especially familiar with the animal and develop a peculiar interest in it, though this would be founded on no psychical motive other than the most elementary and urgent of human needs, that is, on hunger.

Against this most 'rational' of all the theories of totemism it has been objected that feeding conditions of this kind are never found among primitive races and have probably never existed. Savages are omnivorous, and the more so the lower their condition. Nor is it easy to see how an exclusive diet such as this could have developed into an almost religious attitude to the totem, culminating in absolute abstention from the favourite food. [Cf. Frazer, 1910, 4, 51.]

The first of the three theories on the origin of totemism which Frazer himself has supported at different times was a psychological one, and I shall deal with it later. His second theory, with which we are here concerned, took form under the influence of a momentous publication by two men who had made researches among the natives of Central Australia.

Spencer and Gillen (1899) described a number of peculiar observances, usages and beliefs found in a group of tribes known as the Arunta nation; and Frazer agreed with their opinion that these peculiarities were to be regarded as features of a primitive condition of things and might throw light upon the original and true meaning of totemism.

The peculiarities found in the Arunta tribe (a portion of the Arunta nation) are as follows:

(1) The Arunta are divided into totem clans, but the totem is not hereditary but determined for each individual in a manner to be described presently.

1. Quoted by Frazer (1910, 4, 50).

(2) The totem clans are not exogamous; but the restrictions upon marriage are based upon a highly developed division into marriage-classes, which have no connection with the totem.

(3) The function of the totem clans lies in their performing a ceremony which has as its aim the multiplication of the edible totem object by a characteristically magical method. (This ceremony is known as *intichiuma*.)

(4) The Arunta have a peculiar theory of conception and reincarnation. They believe that there are places scattered over the country ['totem centres'] at each of which the spirits of the dead of some one totem await reincarnation and enter the body of any woman who passes by the spot. When a child is born, the mother reports at which of these places she thinks it was conceived, and the child's totem is determined accordingly. It is further believed that the spirits (both of the dead and of the reborn) are intimately associated with certain peculiar stone amulets, known as *churinga*, which are found at these same centres.

Two factors seem to have led Frazer to suppose that the observances among the Arunta constitute the oldest form of totemism. First, there was the existence of certain myths which declared that the ancestors of the Arunta regularly ate their totem and always married women of their own totem. Secondly, there was the apparent disregard of the sexual act in their theory of conception. People who had not yet discovered that conception is the result of sexual intercourse might surely be regarded as the most backward and primitive of living men.

By focusing his judgement of totemism upon the *intichiuma* ceremony, Frazer came all at once to see the totemic system in an entirely new light: as a purely practical organization for meeting the most natural of human needs. (Cf. Haddon's theory above [p. 173].)[1] The system was simply an example upon a

---

1. 'There is nothing vague or mystical about it, nothing of that metaphysical haze which some writers love to conjure up over the humble beginnings of human speculation, but which is utterly foreign to the simple, sensuous and concrete modes of thought of the savage.' (Frazer, 1910, **I**, 117.)

large scale of 'co-operative magic'. Primitive men set up what might be described as a magical producers' and consumers' union. Each totem clan undertook the business of guaranteeing the plentiful supply of one particular article of food. Where non-edible totems were concerned (such as dangerous animals, or rain, wind etc.) the duty of the totem clan lay in controlling the natural force in question and in counteracting its injurious possibilities. The achievements of each clan were to the advantage of all the rest. Since each clan might eat none, or only very little, of its own totem, it provided that valuable material for the other clans and was itself provided in exchange with what *they* produced as their social totemic duty. In the light of the insight which he thus obtained from the *intichiuma* ceremony, Frazer came to believe that the prohibition against eating one's own totem had blinded people to the more important element in the situation, namely the injunction to produce as much as possible of an edible totem to meet the needs of other people.

Frazer accepted the Arunta tradition that each totem clan had originally eaten its own totem without restriction. But it was then difficult to understand the next stage in development, at which the clansmen became content with assuring a supply of the totem for others, while themselves renouncing its enjoyment almost completely. He supposed that this restriction had arisen, not from any kind of religious deference, but perhaps from observing that animals never fed upon their own kind: to do so might imply a breach in their identification with their totem and consequently reduce their power of controlling it. Or it might be that by sparing the creatures they hoped to conciliate them. Frazer, however, makes no disguise of the difficulties involved in these explanations (1910, **1,** 121 ff.); nor does he venture to suggest by what means the custom described in the Arunta myths of marrying within the totem was transformed into exogamy.

The theory based by Frazer on the *intichiuma* ceremony stands or falls with the assertion of the primitive character of the Arunta institutions. But in face of the objections raised by

Durkheim[1] and Lang (1903 and 1905), that assertion appears untenable. On the contrary, the Arunta seem to be the most highly developed of the Australian tribes and to represent a stage of totemism in dissolution rather than its beginnings. The myths which impressed Frazer so deeply because, in contrast to the conditions that rule to-day, they lay stress upon liberty to eat the totem and to marry within the totem – these myths are easily explicable as wishful phantasies which, like the myth of a Golden Age, have been projected back into the past.

(γ) *Psychological Theories*

Frazer's first psychological theory, formed before he became acquainted with Spencer and Gillen's observations, was based on the belief in an 'external soul'.[2] The totem, according to this view, represented a safe place of refuge in which the soul could be deposited and so escape the dangers which threatened it. When a primitive man had deposited his soul in his totem he himself was invulnerable, and he naturally avoided doing any injury to the receptacle of his soul. Since, however, he did not know in which particular individual of the animal species concerned his own soul was lodged, it was reasonable for him to spare the whole species.

Frazer himself subsequently abandoned this theory that totemism was derived from a belief in souls; and, after coming to know of Spencer and Gillen's observations, adopted the sociological theory which I have already discussed. But he came to see himself that the motive from which that second theory derived totemism was too 'rational' and that it implied a social organization which was too complicated to be described as

---

1. In *L'année sociologique* (1898, 1902, 1905, etc.); see especially 'Sur le totémisme' (1902 [89 f.]).

2. See Frazer, *The Golden Bough*, first edition (1890), **2**, 332 ff. [Cf. also Frazer, 1910, **4**, 52 ff.]

primitive.[1] The magical co-operative societies now seemed to him to be the fruit rather than the seed of totemism. He sought for some simpler factor, some primitive superstition behind these structures, to which the origin of totemism might be traced back. At last he found this original factor in the Arunta's remarkable story of conception.

The Arunta, as I have already explained, eliminate the connection between the sexual act and conception. At the moment at which a woman feels she is a mother, a spirit, which has been awaiting reincarnation in the nearest totem centre where the spirits of the dead collect, has entered her body. She will bear this spirit as a child, and the child will have the same totem as all the spirits waiting at that particular centre. This theory of conception cannot explain totemism, since it presupposes the existence of totems. But let us go back a step further and suppose that originally the woman believed that the animal, plant, stone or other object, with which her imagination was occupied at the moment when she first felt she was a mother, actually made its way into her and was later born in human form. In that case the identity between a man and his totem would have a factual basis in his mother's belief and all the remaining totem ordinances (with the exception of exogamy) would follow. A man would refuse to eat this animal or plant because to do so would amount to eating himself. He would, however, have a reason for occasionally partaking of his totem in a ceremonial manner, because in that way he might strengthen his identification with the totem, which is the essence of totemism. Some observations made by Rivers [1909, 173 f.] upon the natives of the Banks' Islands[2] seemed to prove a direct identification of human beings with their totem on the basis of a similar theory of conception.

Accordingly, the ultimate source of totemism would be the

1. 'It is unlikely that a community of savages should deliberately parcel out the realm of nature into provinces, assign each province to a particular band of magicians, and bid all the bands to work their magic and weave their spells for the common good.' (Frazer, 1910, **4**, 57.)

2. Quoted by Frazer (1910, **2**, 89 ff. and **4**, 59).

savages' ignorance of the process by which men and animals reproduce their kind; and, in particular, ignorance of the part played by the male in fertilization. This ignorance must have been facilitated by the long interval between the act of fertilization and the birth of the child (or the first perception of its movements). Thus totemism would be a creation of the feminine rather than of the masculine mind: its roots would lie in 'the sick fancies of pregnant women.' 'Anything indeed that struck a woman at that mysterious moment of her life when she first knows herself to be a mother might easily be identified by her with the child in her womb. Such maternal fancies, so natural and seemingly so universal, appear to be the root of totemism.' (Frazer, 1910, 4, 63.)

The main objection to this third of Frazer's theories is the same as has already been brought against the second or sociological one. The Arunta seem to be far removed from the beginnings of totemism. Their denial of paternity does not appear to rest upon primitive ignorance; in some respects they themselves make use of descent through the father. They seem to have sacrificed paternity for the sake of some sort of speculation designed to honour the souls of their ancestors.[1] They have enlarged the myth of the impregnation of a virgin by the spirit into a general theory of conception; but that is no reason why ignorance of the conditions governing fertilization should be imputed to them any more than to the peoples of antiquity at the time of the origin of the Christian myths.

Another psychological theory of the origin of totemism has been advanced by a Dutchman, G. A. Wilken [1884, 997]. It connects totemism with the belief in the transmigration of souls. 'The animal in which the souls of the dead are thought by preference to be incarnate becomes a kinsman, an ancestor, and as such is revered.'[2] It seems more likely, however, that the belief in transmigration was derived from totemism than vice versa.

Yet another theory of totemism is held by some eminent

1. 'That belief is a philosophy far from primitive.' (Lang, 1905, 192.)
2. Quoted by Frazer (1910, 4, 45 f.).

American ethnologists, Franz Boas, C. Hill-Tout, and others. It is based upon observations on North American Indian totemic clans and maintains that the totem was originally the guardian spirit of an ancestor, who acquired it in a dream and transmitted it to his descendants. We have already heard the difficulties which stand in the way of the view that totems are inherited from single individuals [cf. p. 170]; but apart from this, the Australian evidence lends no support to the theory that totems are derived from guardian spirits. (Frazer, 1910, 4, 48 ff.)

The last of the psychological theories, that put forward by Wundt (1912, 190), is based upon two facts. 'In the first place, the original totem, and the one which continues to remain most common, is the animal; and, secondly, the earliest totem animals are identical with soul animals.' [English translation, 192.] Soul animals (such as birds, snakes, lizards and mice) are appropriate receptacles of souls which have left the body, on account of their rapid movements or flight through the air or of other qualities likely to produce surprise or alarm. Totem animals are derived from the transformations of the 'breath-soul' into animals. Thus, according to Wundt, totemism is directly connected with the belief in spirits, that is to say with animism.

(b) and (c) THE ORIGIN OF EXOGAMY AND ITS RELATION TO TOTEMISM

I have set out the different theories about totemism in some detail though even so compression has been inevitable and I fear that my account may have suffered in consequence. In what follows, however, I shall venture, for my readers' sake, to be still more condensed. The discussions on the exogamy practised by totemic peoples are, owing to the nature of the material with which they deal, particularly complicated and diffuse – one might even say confused. The purposes of the present work make it possible for me to limit myself to tracing certain of the main lines of dispute, while referring those who wish to enter into the subject more deeply to the specialized writings from which I have so frequently quoted.

The attitude taken by an author on the problems of exogamy must naturally depend to some extent on the position he has adopted towards the various theories of totemism. Some of the explanations of totemism exclude any connection with exogamy, so that the two institutions fall completely apart. Thus we find two opposing views: one which seeks to maintain the original presumption that exogamy forms an inherent part of the totemic system, and the other which denies that there is any such connection and holds that the convergence between these two features of the oldest cultures is a chance one. This latter opinion has been adopted without qualification by Frazer in his later works: 'I must request the reader to bear constantly in mind', he writes, 'that the two institutions of totemism and exogamy are fundamentally distinct in origin and nature, though they have accidentally crossed and blended in many tribes.' (Frazer, 1910, I, xii.) He gives an explicit warning that the opposite view must be a source of endless difficulties and misunderstandings.

Other writers have, on the contrary, found a means of regarding exogamy as an inevitable consequence of the basic principles of totemism. Durkheim (1898, 1902 and 1905) has put forward the view that the taboo attached to totems was bound to involve prohibition against practising sexual intercourse with a woman of the same totem. The totem is of the same blood as the man and consequently the ban upon shedding blood (in connection with defloration and menstruation) prohibits him from sexual relations with a woman belonging to his totem.[1] Andrew Lang (1905, 125), who agrees with Durkheim on this subject, believes that the prohibition against women of the same clan might operate even without any blood taboo. The general totem taboo (which, for instance, forbids a man to sit under his own totem tree) would, in Lang's opinion, have been sufficient. Incidentally, he complicates this with another explanation of exogamy (see below [p. 186]) and omits to show how the two explanations are related to each other.

---

1. See the criticisms of Durkheim's views by Frazer (1910, 4, 100 ff.).

As regards the chronological relations between the two institutions, most of the authorities agree that totemism is the older
of them and that exogamy arose later.[1]

Of the theories which seek to show that exogamy is independent of totemism I shall only draw attention to a few which
throw light on the attitude of the different authors to the
problem of incest.

McLennan (1865) ingeniously inferred the existence of exogamy from the vestiges of customs which seemed to indicate
the earlier practice of marriage by capture. He formed a
hypothesis that in the earliest times it had been a general usage
for men to obtain their wives from another group and that
marriage with a woman of their own group gradually 'came
to be considered improper because it was unusual' [ibid., 289].
He accounted for the prevalence of exogamy by supposing that
the practice of killing the majority of female children at birth
had led to a scarcity of women in primitive societies. We are
not here concerned with the question of how far these assumptions of McLennan's are supported by the actual findings. What
interests us far more is the fact that his hypotheses fail to explain
why the male members of a group should refuse themselves
access to the few remaining women of their own blood – the
fact that he entirely overlooks the problem of incest. (Frazer,
1910, 4, 71–92.)

Other students of exogamy, on the contrary, and evidently
with greater justice, have seen in exogamy an institution for
the prevention of incest.[2] When one considers the gradually
increasing complication of the Australian restrictions upon
marriage, it is impossible not to accept the opinions of Morgan
(1877), Frazer (1910, 4, 105 ff.), Howitt [1904, 143] and Baldwin
Spencer that those regulations bear (in Frazer's words) 'the
impress of deliberate design' and that they aimed at achieving
the result they have in fact achieved. 'In no other way does

1. See, for instance, Frazer (1910, 4, 75): 'The totemic clan is a totally
different social organism from the exogamous clan, and we have good
grounds for thinking that it is far older.'

2. Cf. the first essay in this work [p. 53 f. above].

it seem possible to explain in all its details a system at once so complex and so regular.' (Frazer, ibid., 106.)

It is interesting to observe that the first restrictions produced by the introduction of marriage-classes affected the sexual freedom of the *younger* generation (that is, incest between brothers and sisters and between sons and mothers) whereas incest between fathers and daughters was only prevented by a further extension of the regulations.

But the fact that exogamous sexual restrictions were imposed intentionally throws no light on the motive which led to their imposition. What is the ultimate source of the horror of incest which must be recognized as the root of exogamy? To explain it by the existence of an instinctive dislike of sexual intercourse with blood-relatives – that is to say, by an appeal to the fact that there *is* a horror of incest – is clearly unsatisfactory; for social experience shows that, in spite of this supposed instinct, incest is no uncommon event even in our present-day society, and history tells us of cases in which incestuous marriage between privileged persons was actually the rule.

Westermarck (1906–8, **2**, 368)[1] has explained the horror of incest on the ground that 'there is an innate aversion to sexual intercourse between persons living very closely together from early youth, and that, as such persons are in most cases related by blood, this feeling would naturally display itself in custom and law as a horror of intercourse between near kin'. Havelock Ellis [1914, 205 f.], though he disputed the instinctiveness of the aversion, subscribed to this explanation in the main: 'The normal failure of the pairing instinct to manifest itself in the case of brothers and sisters, or of boys and girls brought up together from infancy, is a merely negative phenomenon due to the inevitable absence in those circumstances of the conditions which evoke the pairing instinct ... Between those who have been brought up together from childhood all the sensory stimuli of vision, hearing and touch have been dulled by use, trained to the calm level of affection, and deprived of their

1. In the same chapter he replies to various objections which have been raised against his views.

potency to arouse the erethistic excitement which produces sexual tumescence.'

It seems to me very remarkable that Westermarck should consider that this innate aversion to sexual intercourse with those with whom one has been intimate in childhood is also the equivalent in psychical terms of the biological fact that in-breeding is detrimental to the species. A biological instinct of the kind suggested would scarcely have gone so far astray in its psychological expression that, instead of applying to blood-relatives (intercourse with whom might be injurious to repro-duction), it affected persons who were totally innocuous in this respect, merely because they shared a common home. I cannot resist referring, too, to Frazer's admirable criticism of Wester-marck's theory. Frazer finds it inexplicable that to-day there should be scarcely any sexual aversion to intercourse with house-mates, whereas the horror of incest, which on Wester-marck's theory is only a derivative of that aversion, should have increased so enormously. But some further comments of Frazer's go deeper, and these I shall reproduce in full, since they are in essential agreement with the arguments which I put forward in my essay on taboo:

'It is not easy to see why any deep human instinct should need to be reinforced by law. There is no law commanding men to eat and drink or forbidding them to put their hands in the fire. Men eat and drink and keep their hands out of the fire instinctively for fear of natural not legal penalties, which would be entailed by violence done to these instincts. The law only forbids men to do what their instincts incline them to do; what nature itself prohibits and punishes, it would be super-fluous for the law to prohibit and punish. Accordingly we may always safely assume that crimes forbidden by law are crimes which many men have a natural propensity to commit. If there was no such propensity there would be no such crimes, and if no such crimes were committed what need to forbid them? Instead of assuming, therefore, from the legal prohibition of incest that there is a natural aversion to incest, we ought rather to assume that there is a natural instinct in favour of it, and that if the law represses it, as it represses other natural instincts, it does so because civilized men have come to the conclusion that the satisfaction of these natural instincts is detrimental to the general interests of society.' (Frazer, 1910, 4, 97 f.)

I may add to these excellent arguments of Frazer's that the findings of psychoanalysis make the hypothesis of an innate aversion to incestuous intercourse totally untenable. They have shown, on the contrary, that the earliest sexual excitations of youthful human beings are invariably of an incestuous character and that such impulses when repressed play a part that can scarcely be over-estimated as motive forces of neuroses in later life.

Thus the view which explains the horror of incest as an innate instinct must be abandoned. Nor can anything more favourable be said of another, widely held explanation of the law against incest, according to which primitive peoples noticed at an early date the dangers with which their race was threatened by inbreeding and for that reason deliberately adopted the prohibition. There are a host of objections to this theory. (Cf. Durkheim, 1898 [33 ff.].) Not only must the prohibition against incest be older than any domestication of animals which might have enabled men to observe the effects of inbreeding upon racial characters, but even to-day the detrimental results of inbreeding are not established with certainty and cannot easily be demonstrated in man. Moreover, everything that we know of contemporary savages makes it highly improbable that their most remote ancestors were already concerned with the question of preserving their later progeny from injury. Indeed it is almost absurd to attribute to such improvident creatures motives of hygiene and eugenics to which consideration is scarcely paid in our own present-day civilization.[1]

Lastly, account must be taken of the fact that a prohibition against inbreeding, based upon practical motives of hygiene, on the ground of its tending to racial enfeeblement, seems quite inadequate to explain the profound abhorrence shown towards

1. Darwin [1875, 2, 127] writes of savages that they 'are not likely to reflect on distant evils to their progeny'.

incest in our society. As I have shown elsewhere,[1] this feeling seems to be even more active and intense among contemporary primitive peoples than among civilized ones.

It might have been expected that here again we should have before us a choice between sociological, biological and psychological explanations. (In this connection the psychological motives should perhaps be regarded as representing biological forces.) Nevertheless, at the end of our inquiry, we can only subscribe to Frazer's resigned conclusion. We are ignorant of the origin of the horror of incest and cannot even tell in what direction to look for it. None of the solutions of the enigma that have been proposed seems satisfactory.[2]

I must, however, mention one other attempt at solving it. It is of a kind quite different from any that we have so far considered, and might be described as 'historical'.

This attempt is based upon a hypothesis of Charles Darwin's upon the social state of primitive men. Darwin deduced from the habits of the higher apes that men, too, originally lived in comparatively small groups or hordes[3] within which the jealousy of the oldest and strongest male prevented sexual promiscuity. 'We may indeed conclude from what we know of the jealousy of all male quadrupeds, armed, as many of them are, with special weapons for battling with their rivals, that promiscuous intercourse in a state of nature is extremely improbable ... Therefore, if we look far enough back in the stream of time, ... judging from the social habits of man as he now exists ... the most probable view is that primaeval man aboriginally lived in small communities, each with as many wives as he could support and obtain, whom he would have jealously guarded against all other men. Or he may have lived

1. See the first essay in this work [p. 60 above].

2. 'Thus the ultimate origin of exogamy, and with it of the law of incest – since exogamy was devised to prevent incest – remains a problem nearly as dark as ever.' (Frazer, 1910, I, 165.)

3. [Here and subsequently, Freud is using the word 'horde' to denote a more or less organized group of limited size – what Atkinson (1903) terms 'the Cyclopean family'.]

with several wives by himself, like the Gorilla; for all the natives "agree that but one adult male is seen in a band; when the young male grows up, a contest takes place for mastery, and the strongest, by killing and driving out the others, establishes himself as the head of the community". (Dr Savage, in *Boston Journal of Nat Hist.*, vol. v, 1845–7, p. 423.) The younger males, being thus expelled and wandering about, would, when at last successful in finding a partner, prevent too close interbreeding within the limits of the same family.' (Darwin, 1871, **2**, 362 f.)

Atkinson (1903) seems to have been the first to realize that the practical consequence of the conditions obtaining in Darwin's primal horde must be exogamy for the young males. Each of them might, after being driven out, establish a similar horde, in which the same prohibition upon sexual intercourse would rule owing to its leader's jealousy. In course of time this would produce what grew into a conscious law: 'No sexual relations between those who share a common home.' After the establishment of totemism this regulation would assume another form and would run: 'No sexual relations within the totem.'

Andrew Lang (1905, 114 and 143) accepted this explanation of exogamy. In the same volume, however, he supports the other theory (held by Durkheim), according to which exogamy was a resultant of the totemic laws. [Cf. p. 180.] It is a little difficult to bring these two points of view into harmony: according to the first theory exogamy would have originated before totemism, while according to the second it would have been derived from it.[1]

1. 'If it be granted that exogamy existed in practice, on the lines of Mr Darwin's theory, before the totem beliefs lent to the practice a *sacred* sanction, our task is relatively easy. The first practical rule would be that of the jealous Sire, "No males to touch the females in my camp", with expulsion of adolescent sons. *In efflux of time that rule, become habitual*, would be, "No marriage within the local group". Next, let the local groups receive names, such as Emus, Crows, Opossums, Snipes, and the rule becomes, "No marriage within the local group of animal name; no Snipe to marry Snipe". But, if the primal groups were not exogamous, they would become so, as soon as totemic myths and tabus were developed out of the animal, vegetable,

(3)

Into this obscurity one single ray of light is thrown by psycho-analytic observation.

There is a great deal of resemblance between the relations of children and of primitive men towards animals. Children show no trace of the arrogance which urges adult çivilized men to draw a hard-and-fast line between their own nature and that of all other animals. Children have no scruples over allow-ing animals to rank as their full equals. Uninhibited as they are in the avowal of their bodily needs, they no doubt feel themselves more akin to animals than to their elders, who may well be a puzzle to them.

Not infrequently, however, a strange rift occurs in the excel-lent relations between children and animals. A child will suddenly begin to be frightened of some particular species of animal and to avoid touching or seeing any individual of that species. The clinical picture of an animal phobia emerges – a very common, and perhaps the earliest, form of psychoneurotic illness occurring in childhood. As a rule the phobia is attached to animals in which the child has hitherto shown a specially lively interest and it has nothing to do with any particular individual animal. There is no large choice of animals that may become objects of a phobia in the case of children living in' towns: horses, dogs, cats, less often birds, and with striking frequency very small creatures such as beetles and butterflies. The senseless and immoderate fear shown in these phobias is sometimes attached to animals only known to the child from picture books and fairy tales. On a few rare occasions it is possible to discover what has led to an unusual choice of this kind; and I have to thank Karl Abraham for telling me of a case in which the child himself explained that his fear of wasps

---

and other names of local groups.' (Lang, 1905, 143.) (The italics in the middle of this passage are mine.) In his last discussion of this subject, moreover, Lang (1911 [404]) states that he has 'abandoned the idea that exogamy is a consequence of the general totemic taboo'.

was due to their colour and stripes reminding him of tigers, which from all accounts were beasts to be feared.[1]

No detailed analytic examination has yet been made of children's animal phobias, though they would greatly repay study. This neglect has no doubt been due to the difficulty of analysing children of such a tender age. It cannot therefore be claimed that we know the general meaning of these disorders and I myself am of the opinion that this may not turn out to be of a uniform nature. But a few cases of phobias of this kind directed towards the larger animals have proved accessible to analysis and have thus yielded their secret to the investigator. It was the same in every case: where the children concerned were boys, their fear related at bottom to their father and had merely been displaced on to the animal.

Everyone with psychoanalytic experience will no doubt have come across cases of the sort and have derived the same impression from them. Yet I can quote only a few detailed publications on the subject. This paucity of literature is an accidental circumstance and it must not be supposed that our conclusions are based on a few scattered observations. I may mention, for instance, a writer who has studied the neuroses of childhood with great understanding – Dr M. Wulff, of Odessa.[2] In the course of a case history of a nine-year-old boy he reports that at the age of four the patient had suffered from a dog-phobia. 'When he saw a dog running past in the street, he would weep and call out: "Dear doggie, don't bite me! I'll be good!" By "being good" he meant "not playing on the fiddle" ' – not masturbating. (Wulff, 1912, 15.) 'The boy's dog phobia', the author explains, 'was in reality his fear of his father displaced on to dogs; for his curious exclamation "Doggie, I'll be good!" – that is, "I won't masturbate" – was directed to his father, who had forbidden him to masturbate.' Wulff adds a footnote which is in complete agreement with my views and at the same time bears witness to the frequent occurrence of such experiences: 'Phobias of this type (phobias of horses, dogs, cats, fowls

1. [Subsequently published. (Abraham, 1914, 82; English translation, 228.)]
2. [Later Dr M. Woolf of Tel-Aviv.]

and other domestic animals) are, in my opinion, at least as common in childhood as *pavor nocturnus*; and in analysis they almost invariably turn out to be a displacement on to the animals of the child's fear of one of his parents. I should not be prepared to maintain that the same mechanism applies to the widespread phobias of rats and mice.' [Ibid., 16.]

I recently published (1909b) an 'Analysis of a Phobia in a Five-Year-Old Boy', the material of which was supplied to me by the little patient's father. The boy had a phobia of horses, and as a result he refused to go out in the street. He expressed a fear that the horse would come into the room and bite him; and it turned out that this must be the punishment for a wish that the horse might fall down (that is, die). After the boy's fear of his father had been removed by reassurances, it became evident that he was struggling against wishes which had as their subject the idea of his father being absent (going away on a journey, dying). He regarded his father (as he made all too clear) as a competitor for the favours of his mother, towards whom the obscure foreshadowings of his budding sexual wishes were aimed. Thus he was situated in the typical attitude of a male child towards his parents to which we have given the name of the 'Oedipus complex' and which we regard in general as the nuclear complex of the neuroses. The new fact that we have learnt from the analysis of 'little Hans' – a fact with an important bearing upon totemism – is that in such circumstances children displace some of their feelings from their father on to an animal.

Analysis is able to trace the associative paths along which this displacement passes – both the fortuitous paths and those with a significant content. Analysis also enables us to discover the *motives* for the displacement. The hatred of his father that arises in a boy from rivalry for his mother is not able to achieve uninhibited sway over his mind; it has to contend against his old-established affection and admiration for the very same person. The child finds relief from the conflict arising out of this double-sided, this ambivalent emotional attitude towards his father by displacing his hostile and fearful feelings on to a *substitute* for his father. The displacement cannot, however, bring the conflict to an end, it cannot effect a clear-cut severance between the affectionate and the hostile feelings. On the contrary, the conflict is resumed in relation to the object on to which the displacement has been made: the ambivalence is extended to *it*. There could be no doubt that little Hans was not only *frightened* of horses; he also approached them with admiration and interest. As soon as his anxiety began to diminish, he identified himself with the dreaded creature: he began to jump about like a horse and in his turn bit his father.[1] At another stage in the resolution of his phobia he did not hesitate to identify his parents with some other large animals.[2]

It may fairly be said that in these children's phobias some of the features of totemism reappear, but reversed into their negative. We are, however, indebted to Ferenczi (1913a) for an interesting history of a single case which can only be described as an instance of *positive* totemism in a child. It is true that in the case of little Árpád (the subject of Ferenczi's report) his totemic interests did not arise in direct relation with his Oedipus complex but on the basis of its narcissistic precondition, the fear of castration. But any attentive reader of the story of little Hans will find abundant evidence that he, too, admired his father as possessing a big penis and feared him as threatening his own. The same part is played by the father alike in the Oedipus and the castration complexes – the part of a dreaded enemy to the sexual interests of childhood. The punishment which he threatens is castration, or its substitute, blinding.[3]

When little Árpád was two and a half years old, he had once, while he was on a summer holiday, tried to micturate into the fowl-house and a fowl had pecked, or pecked *at* his penis. A year later, when he was back in the same place, he himself turned into a fowl; his one interest was in the fowl-house and

1. Freud (1909b [P.F.L., 8, 213]).
2. In his giraffe phantasy [ibid., 199 ff.].
3. For the substitution of blinding for castration – a substitution that occurs, too, in the myth of Oedipus – see Reitler (1913), Ferenczi (1913b), Rank (1913) and Eder (1913).

in what went on there and he abandoned human speech in favour of cackling and crowing. At the time at which the observation was made (when he was five years old) he had recovered his speech, but his interests and his talk were entirely concerned with chickens and other kinds of poultry. They were his only toys and he only sang songs that had some mention of fowls in them. His attitude towards his totem animal was superlatively ambivalent: he showed both hatred and love to an extravagant degree. His favourite game was playing slaughtering fowls. 'The slaughtering of poultry was a regular festival for him. He would dance round the animals' bodies for hours at a time in a state of intense excitement.'[1] But afterwards he would kiss and stroke the slaughtered animal or would clean and caress the toy fowls that he had himself ill-treated.

Little Árpád himself saw to it that the meaning of his strange behaviour should not remain hidden. From time to time he translated his wishes from the totemic language into that of everyday life. 'My father's the cock', he said on one occasion, and another time: 'Now I'm small, now I'm a chicken. When I get bigger I'll be a fowl. When I'm bigger still I'll be a cock.' On another occasion he suddenly said he would like to eat some 'fricassee of mother' (on the analogy of fricassee of chicken). [Ibid., 249.] He was very generous in threatening other people with castration, just as he himself had been threatened with it for his masturbatory activities.

There was no doubt, according to Ferenczi, as to the sources of Árpád's interest in events in the poultry-yard: 'the continual sexual activity between the cock and hens, the laying of eggs and the hatching out of the young brood' gratified his sexual curiosity, the real object of which was *human* family-life. [Ibid., 250.] He showed that he had formed his own choice of sexual objects on the model of life in the hen-run, for he said one day to the neighbour's wife: 'I'll marry you and your sister and my three cousins and the cook; no, not the cook, I'll marry my mother instead.' [Ibid., 252.]

Later on we shall be able to assess the worth of this observa-

1. [Ferenczi, 1913*a* (English translation, 246).]

tion more completely. At the moment I will only emphasize two features in it which offer valuable points of agreement with totemism: the boy's complete identification with his totem animal[1] and his ambivalent emotional attitude to it. These observations justify us, in my opinion, in substituting the father for the totem animal in the formula for totemism (in the case of males). It will be observed that there is nothing new or particularly daring in this step forward. Indeed, primitive men say the very same thing themselves, and, where the totemic system is still in force to-day, they describe the totem as their common ancestor and primal father. All we have done is to take at its literal value an expression used by these people, of which the anthropologists have been able to make very little and which they have therefore been glad to keep in the background. Psychoanalysis, on the contrary, leads us to put special stress upon this same point and to take it as the starting-point of our attempt at explaining totemism.[2]

The first consequence of our substitution is most remarkable. If the totem animal is the father, then the two principal ordinances of totemism, the two taboo prohibitions which constitute its core – not to kill the totem and not to have sexual relations with a woman of the same totem – coincide in their content with the two crimes of Oedipus, who killed his father and married his mother, as well as with the two primal wishes of children, the insufficient repression or the re-awakening of which forms the nucleus of perhaps every psychoneurosis. If this equation is anything more than a misleading trick of chance, it must enable us to throw a light upon the origin of totemism in the inconceivably remote past. In other words, it would enable us to make it probable that the totemic system – like little Hans's animal phobia and little Árpád's poultry

1. This, according to Frazer (1910, 4, 5), constitutes 'the whole essence of totemism': 'totemism is an identification of a man with his totem.'

2. I have to thank Otto Rank for bringing to my notice a dog phobia in an intelligent young man. His explanation of the way in which he acquired his illness sounds markedly like the totemic theory of the Arunta which I mentioned on page 173: he thought he had heard from his father that his mother had had a severe fright from a dog during her pregnancy.

perversion – was a product of the conditions involved in the Oedipus complex. In order to pursue this possibility, we shall have, in the following pages, to study a feature of the totemic system (or, as we might say, of the totemic religion) which I have hitherto scarcely found an opportunity of mentioning.

(4)

William Robertson Smith, who died in 1894 – physicist, philologist, Bible critic and archaeologist – was a man of many-sided interests, clear-sighted and liberal-minded. In his book on the *Religion of the Semites* (first published in 1889)[1] he put forward the hypothesis that a peculiar ceremony known as the 'totem meal' had from the very first formed an integral part of the totemic system. At that time he had only a single piece of evidence in support of his theory: an account of a procedure of the kind dating from the fifth century A.D. But by an analysis of the nature of sacrifice among the ancient Semites he was able to lend his hypothesis a high degree of probability. Since sacrifice implies a divinity, it was a question of arguing back from a comparatively high phase of religious ritual to the lowest one, that is, to totemism.

I will now attempt to extract from Robertson Smith's admirable work those of his statements on the origin and meaning of the ritual of sacrifice which are of decisive interest for us. In so doing I must omit all the details, often so fascinating, and neglect all the later developments. It is quite impossible for an abstract such as this to give my readers any notion of the lucidity and convincing force of the original.

Robertson Smith [1894, 214] explains that sacrifice at the altar was the essential feature in the ritual of ancient religions. It plays the same part in all religions, so that its origin must be traced back to very general causes, operating everywhere in the same manner. Sacrifice – the sacred act *par excellence* (*sacrificium*, ἱερουργία) – originally had a somewhat different

1. [The second and revised edition, which is the one here quoted, appeared posthumously in 1894.]

meaning, however, from its later one of making an offering to the deity in order to propitiate him or gain his favour. (The non-religious usage of the word followed from this subsidiary sense of 'renunciation'. [See below, p. 212.]) It can be shown that, to begin with, sacrifice was nothing other than 'an act of fellowship between the deity and his worshippers'. [Ibid., 224.]

The materials offered for sacrifice were things that can be eaten or drunk; men sacrificed to their deity the things on which they themselves lived: flesh, cereals, fruit, wine and oil. Only in the case of flesh were there limitations and exceptions. The god shared the animal sacrifices with his worshippers, the vegetable offerings were for him alone. There is no doubt that animal sacrifices were the older and were originally the only ones. Vegetable sacrifices arose from the offering of first-fruits and were in the nature of a tribute to the lord of the earth and of the land; but animal sacrifices are more ancient than agriculture. [Ibid., 222.]

Linguistic survivals make it certain that the portion of the sacrifice allotted to the god was originally regarded as being literally his food. As the nature of gods grew progressively less material, this conception became a stumbling-block. It was avoided by assigning to the deity only the *liquid* part of the meal. Later, the use of fire, which caused the flesh of the sacrifice upon the altar to rise in smoke, afforded a method of dealing with human food more appropriate to the divine nature. [Ibid., 224, 229.] The drink-offering consisted originally of the blood of the animal victim. This was later replaced by wine. In ancient times wine was regarded as 'the blood of the grape', and it has been so described by modern poets. [Ibid., 230.]

The oldest form of sacrifice, then, older than the use of fire or the knowledge of agriculture, was the sacrifice of animals, whose flesh and blood were enjoyed in common by the god and his worshippers. It was essential that each one of the participants should have his share of the meal.

A sacrifice of this kind was a public ceremony, a festival

celebrated by the whole clan. Religion in general was an affair of the community and religious duty was a part of social obligation. Everywhere a sacrifice involves a feast and a feast cannot be celebrated without a sacrifice. The sacrificial feast was an occasion on which individuals rose joyously above their own interests and stressed the mutual dependence existing between one another and their god. [Ibid., 255.]

The ethical force of the public sacrificial meal rested upon very ancient ideas of the significance of eating and drinking together. Eating and drinking with a man was a symbol and a confirmation of fellowship and mutual social obligations. What was *directly* expressed by the sacrificial meal was only the fact that the god and his worshippers were 'commensals',[1] but every other point in their mutual relations was included in this. Customs still in force among the Arabs of the desert show that what is binding in a common meal is not a religious factor but the act of eating itself. Anyone who has eaten the smallest morsel of food with one of these Bedouin or has swallowed a mouthful of his milk need no longer fear him as an enemy but may feel secure in his protection and help. Not, however, for an unlimited time; strictly speaking, only so long as the food which has been eaten in common remains in the body. Such was the realistic view of the bond of union. It needed repetition in order to be confirmed and made permanent. [Ibid., 269–70.]

But why is this binding force attributed to eating and drinking together? In primitive societies there was only one kind of bond which was absolute and inviolable – that of kinship. The solidarity of such a fellowship was complete. 'A kin was a group of persons whose lives were so bound up together, in what must be called a physical unity, that they could be treated as parts of one common life ... In a case of homicide Arabian tribesmen do not say, "The blood of M. or N. has been spilt", naming the man; they say, "Our blood has been spilt". In Hebrew the phrase by which one claims kinship is "I am your bone and your flesh".' Thus kinship implies

1. [I.e. that they sat at one table.]

participation in a common substance. It is therefore natural that it is not merely based on the fact that a man is a part of his mother's substance, having been born of her and having been nourished by her milk, but that it can be acquired and strengthened by food which a man eats later and with which his body is renewed. If a man shared a meal with his god he was expressing a conviction that they were of one substance; and he would never share a meal with one whom he regarded as a stranger. [Ibid., 273–5.]

The sacrificial meal, then, was originally a feast of kinsmen, in accordance with the law that only kinsmen eat together. In our own society the members of a family have their meals in common; but the sacrificial meal bears no relation to the family. Kinship is an older thing than family life, and in the most primitive societies known to us the family contained members of more than one kindred. The man married a woman of another clan and the children inherited their mother's clan; so that there was no communion of kin between the man and the other members of the family. In a family of such a kind there was no common meal. To this day, savages eat apart and alone and the religious food prohibitions of totemism often make it impossible for them to eat in common with their wives and children. [Ibid., 277–8.]

Let us now turn to the sacrificial animal. As we have heard, there is no gathering of a clan without an animal sacrifice, nor – and this now becomes significant – any slaughter of an animal except upon these ceremonial occasions. While game and the milk of domestic animals might be consumed without any qualms, religious scruples made it impossible to kill a domestic animal for private purposes. [Ibid., 280, 281.] There cannot be the slightest doubt, says Robertson Smith, that the slaughter of a victim was originally among the acts which *are illegal to an individual, and can only be justified when the whole clan shares the responsibility of the deed.*[1] So far as I know, there is only one class of actions recognized by early nations to which this description applies, viz. actions which involve

1. [This sentence is italicized by Freud.]

an invasion of the sanctity of the tribal blood. In fact, a life which no single tribesman is allowed to invade, and which can be sacrificed only by the consent and common action of the kin, stands on the same footing with the life of the fellow-tribesman.' The rule that every participant at the sacrificial meal must eat a share of the flesh of the victim has the same meaning as the provision that the execution of a guilty tribesman must be carried out by the tribe as a whole. [Ibid., 284–5.] In other words, the sacrificial animal was treated as a member of the tribe; *the sacrificing community, the god and the sacrificial animal were of the same blood and members of one clan.*

Robertson Smith brings forward copious evidence for identifying the sacrificial animal with the primitive totem animal. In later antiquity there were two classes of sacrifice: one in which the victims were domestic animals of the kinds habitually used for eating, and the other extraordinary sacrifices of animals which were unclean and whose consumption was forbidden. Investigation shows that these unclean animals were sacred animals, that they were offered as sacrifices to the gods to whom they were sacred, that originally they were identical with the gods themselves, and that by means of the sacrifice the worshippers in some way laid stress upon their blood kinship with the animal and the god. [Ibid., 290–5.] But in still earlier times this distinction between ordinary and 'mystic' sacrifices disappears. Originally *all* [sacrificial] animals were sacred, their flesh was forbidden meat and might only be consumed on ceremonial occasions and with the participation of the whole clan. The slaughter of [such] an animal was equivalent to a shedding of the tribal blood and could occur subject only to the same precautions and the same insurances against incurring reproach. [Ibid., 312, 313.]

The domestication of animals and the introduction of cattle-breeding seems everywhere to have brought to an end the strict and unadulterated totemism of primaeval days.[1] But such

1. 'The inference is that the domestication to which totemism inevitably leads (when there are any animals capable of domestication) is fatal to totemism.' (Jevons, 1902, 120.)

sacred character as remained to domestic animals under what had then become 'pastoral' religion is obvious enough to allow us to infer its original totemic nature. Even in late classical times ritual prescribed in many places that the sacrificial priest must take to flight after performing the sacrifice, as though to escape retribution. The idea that slaughtering oxen was a crime must at one time have prevailed generally in Greece. At the Athenian festival of Buphonia ['ox-murder'] a regular trial was instituted after the sacrifice, and all the participants were called as witnesses. At the end of it, it was agreed that the responsibility for the murder should be placed upon the knife; and this was accordingly cast into the sea. [Smith, 1894, 304.]

In spite of the ban protecting the lives of sacred animals in their quality of fellow-clansmen, a necessity arose for killing one of them from time to time in solemn communion and for dividing its flesh and blood among the members of the clan. The compelling motive for this deed reveals the deepest meaning of the nature of sacrifice. We have heard how in later times, whenever food is eaten in common, the participation in the same substance establishes a sacred bond between those who consume it when it has entered their bodies. In ancient times this result seems only to have been effected by participation in the substance of a *sacrosanct* victim. *The holy mystery of sacrificial death 'is justified by the consideration that only in this way can the sacred cement be procured which creates or keeps alive a living bond of union between the worshippers and their god'.*[1] (Ibid., 313.)

This bond is nothing else than the life of the sacrificial animal, which resides in its flesh and in its blood and is distributed among all the participants in the sacrificial meal. A notion of this kind lies at the root of all the blood covenants by which men made compacts with each other even at a late period of history. [Loc. cit.] This completely literal way of regarding blood-kinship as identity of substance makes it easy

1. [This sentence is italicized by Freud.]

to understand the necessity for renewing it from time to time by the physical process of the sacrificial meal. [Ibid., 319.]

At this point I will interrupt my survey of Robertson Smith's line of thought and restate the gist of it in the most concise terms. With the establishment of the idea of private property sacrifice came to be looked upon as a gift to the deity, as a transference of property from men to the god. But this interpretation left unexplained all the peculiarities of the ritual of sacrifice. In the earliest times the sacrificial animal had itself been sacred and its life untouchable; it might only be killed if all the members of the clan participated in the deed and shared their guilt in the presence of the god, so that the sacred substance could be yielded up and consumed by the clansmen and thus ensure their identity with one another and with the deity. The sacrifice was a sacrament and the sacrificial animal was itself a member of the clan. It was in fact the ancient totem animal, the primitive god himself, by the killing and consuming of which the clansmen renewed and assured their likeness to the god.

From this analysis of the nature of sacrifice Robertson Smith draws the conclusion that the periodic killing and eating of the totem in times *before the worship of anthropomorphic deities* had been an important element in totemic religion. [Ibid., 295.] The ceremonial of a totem meal of this kind is, he suggests, to be found in a description of a sacrifice of comparatively late date. St Nilus records a sacrificial ritual current among the Bedouin of the Sinai Desert at the end of the fourth century A.D. The victim of the sacrifice, a camel, 'is bound upon a rude altar of stones piled together, and when the leader of the band has thrice led the worshippers round the altar in a solemn procession accompanied with chants, he inflicts the first wound ... and in all haste drinks of the blood that gushes forth. Forthwith the whole company fall on the victim with their swords, hacking off pieces of the quivering flesh and devouring them raw with such wild haste, that in the short interval between the rise of the day star[1] which marked

1. To which the sacrifice was offered.

the hour for the service to begin, and the disappearance of
its rays before the rising sun, the entire camel, body and bones,
skin, blood and entrails, is wholly devoured.' [Ibid., 338.] All
the evidence goes to show that this barbaric ritual, which bears
every sign of extreme antiquity, was no isolated instance but
was everywhere the original form taken by totemic sacrifice,
though later toned down in many different directions.

Many authorities have refused to attach importance to the
concept of the totem meal, because it was not supported by
any direct observation at the level of totemism. Robertson
Smith himself pointed to instances in which the sacramental
significance of the sacrifice seemed to be assured: for instance,
the human sacrifices of the Aztecs, and others which recall
the circumstances of the totem meal – the sacrifice of bears
by the Bear clan of the Ouataouak [Otawa] tribe in America
and the bear feast of the Aino in Japan. [Ibid., 295 *n*.] These
and similar cases have been reported in detail by Frazer in
the Fifth Part of his great work (1912, **2** [Chaps. X, XIII,
XIV]). An American Indian tribe in California, which worship
a large bird of prey (a buzzard), kill it once a year at a solemn
festival, after which it is mourned and its skin and feathers
are preserved. [Ibid., **2**, 170.] The Zuni Indians of New
Mexico behave in a similar way to their sacred turtles. [Ibid.,
2, 175.]

A feature has been observed in the *intichiuma* ceremonies
of the Central Australian tribes which agrees admirably with
Robertson Smith's conjectures. Each clan, when it is performing magic for the multiplication of its totem (which it itself
is normally prohibited from consuming), is obliged during
the ceremony to eat a small portion of its own totem before
making it accessible to the other clans. [Frazer, 1910, **1**, 110 ff.]
According to Frazer (ibid., **2**, 590) the clearest example of
a sacramental consumption of an otherwise prohibited totem
is to be found among the Bini of West Africa in connection
with their funeral ceremonies.

Accordingly, I propose that we should adopt Robertson
Smith's hypothesis that the sacramental killing and communal

eating of the totem animal, whose consumption was forbidden on all other occasions, was an important feature of totemic religion.[1]

(5)

Let us call up the spectacle of a totem meal of the kind we have been discussing, amplified by a few probable features which we have not yet been able to consider. The clan is celebrating the ceremonial occasion by the cruel slaughter of its totem animal and is devouring it raw – blood, flesh and bones. The clansmen are there, dressed in the likeness of the totem and imitating it in sound and movement, as though they are seeking to stress their identity with it. Each man is conscious that he is performing an act forbidden to the individual and justifiable only through the participation of the whole clan; nor may anyone absent himself from the killing and the meal. When the deed is done, the slaughtered animal is lamented and bewailed. The mourning is obligatory, imposed by dread of a threatened retribution. As Robertson Smith (1894, 412) remarks of an analogous occasion, its chief purpose is to disclaim responsibility for the killing.

But the mourning is followed by demonstrations of festive rejoicing: every instinct is unfettered and there is licence for every kind of gratification. Here we have easy access to an understanding of the nature of festivals in general. A festival is a permitted, or rather an obligatory, excess, a solemn breach of a prohibition. It is not that men commit the excesses because they are feeling happy as a result of some injunction they have received. It is rather that excess is of the essence of a festival; the festive feeling is produced by the liberty to do what is as a rule prohibited.

1. I am not unaware of the objections to this theory of sacrifice which have been brought forward by various writers (such as Marillier [1898, 204 ff.], Hubert and Mauss [1899, 30 ff.], etc.); but they have not diminished to any important extent the impression produced by Robertson Smith's hypothesis.

What are we to make, though, of the prelude to this festive joy – the mourning over the death of the animal? If the clansmen rejoice over the killing of the totem – a normally forbidden act – why do they mourn over it as well?

As we have seen, the clansmen acquire sanctity by consuming the totem: they reinforce their identification with it and with one another. Their festive feelings and all that follows from them might well be explained by the fact that they have taken into themselves the sacred life of which the substance of the totem is the vehicle.

Psychoanalysis has revealed that the totem animal is in reality a substitute for the father; and this tallies with the contradictory fact that, though the killing of the animal is as a rule forbidden, yet its killing is a festive occasion – with the fact that it is killed and yet mourned. The ambivalent emotional attitude, which to this day characterizes the father-complex in our children and which often persists into adult life, seems to extend to the totem animal in its capacity as substitute for the father.

If, now, we bring together the psychoanalytic translation of the totem with the fact of the totem meal and with Darwin's theories of the earliest state of human society, the possibility of a deeper understanding emerges – a glimpse of a hypothesis which may seem fantastic but which offers the advantage of establishing an unsuspected correlation between groups of phenomena that have hitherto been disconnected.

There is, of course, no place for the beginnings of totemism in Darwin's primal horde. All that we find there is a violent and jealous father who keeps all the females for himself and drives away his sons as they grow up. This earliest state of society has never been an object of observation. The most primitive kind of organization that we actually come across – and one that is in force to this day in certain tribes – consists of bands of males; these bands are composed of members with equal rights and are subject to the restrictions of the totemic system, including inheritance through the mother. Can this form of organization have developed out of the other one? and if so along what lines?

If we call the celebration of the totem meal to our help, we shall be able to find an answer. One day[1] the brothers who had been driven out came together, killed and devoured their father and so made an end of the patriarchal horde. United, they had the courage to do and succeeded in doing what would have been impossible for them individually. (Some cultural advance, perhaps, command over some new weapon, had given them a sense of superior strength.) Cannibal savages as they were, it goes without saying that they devoured their victim as well as killing him. The violent primal father had doubtless been the feared and envied model of each one of the company of brothers: and in the act of devouring him they accomplished their identification with him, and each one of them acquired a portion of his strength. The totem meal, which is perhaps mankind's earliest festival, would thus be a repetition and a commemoration of this memorable and criminal deed, which was the beginning of so many things – of social organization, of moral restrictions and of religion.[2]

1. To avoid possible misunderstanding, I must ask the reader to take into account the final sentences of the following footnote as a corrective to this description.

2. This hypothesis, which has such a monstrous air, of the tyrannical father being overwhelmed and killed by a combination of his exiled sons, was also arrived at by Atkinson (1903, 220 f.) as a direct implication of the state of affairs in Darwin's primal horde: 'The patriarch had only one enemy whom he should dread ... a youthful band of brothers living together in forced celibacy, or at most in polyandrous relation with some single female captive. A horde as yet weak in their impubescence they are, but they would, when strength was gained with time, inevitably wrench by combined attacks, renewed again and again, both wife and life from the paternal tyrant.' Atkinson, who incidentally passed his whole life in New Caledonia and had unusual opportunities for studying the natives, also pointed out that the conditions which Darwin assumed to prevail in the primal horde may easily be observed in herds of wild oxen and horses and regularly lead to the killing of the father of the herd. [Ibid., 222 f.] He further supposed that, after the father had been disposed of, the horde would be disintegrated by a bitter struggle between the victorious sons. Thus any new organization of society would be precluded: there would be 'an ever-recurring violent succession to the solitary paternal tyrant, by sons whose parricidal hands were so soon again clenched in fratricidal strife'. (Ibid., 228.) Atkinson,

In order that these latter consequences may seem plausible, leaving their premises on one side, we need only suppose that the tumultuous mob of brothers were filled with the same contradictory feelings which we can see at work in the ambivalent father-complexes of our children and of our neurotic patients. They hated their father, who presented such a formidable obstacle to their craving for power and their sexual desires; but they loved and admired him too. After they had got rid of him, had satisfied their hatred and had put into effect their wish to identify themselves with him, the affection which had all this time been pushed under was bound to make itself felt.[1] It did so in the form of remorse. A sense of guilt made its appearance, which in this instance coincided with the remorse felt by the whole group. The dead father became stronger than the living one had been – for events took the course we so often see them follow in human affairs to this day. What had up to then been prevented by his actual existence

---

who had no psychoanalytic hints to help him and who was ignorant of Robertson Smith's studies, found a less violent transition from the primal horde to the next social stage, at which numbers of males live together in a peaceable community. He believed that through the intervention of maternal love the sons – to begin with only the youngest, but later others as well – were allowed to remain with the horde, and that in return for this toleration the sons acknowledged their father's sexual privilege by renouncing all claim to their mother and sisters. [Ibid., 231 ff.]

Such is the highly remarkable theory put forward by Atkinson. In its essential feature it is in agreement with my own; but its divergence results in its failing to effect a correlation with many other issues.

The lack of precision in what I have written in the text above, its abbreviation of the time factor and its compression of the whole subject-matter, may be attributed to the reserve necessitated by the nature of the topic. It would be as foolish to aim at exactitude in such questions as it would be unfair to insist upon certainty.

1. This fresh emotional attitude must also have been assisted by the fact that the deed cannot have given complete satisfaction to those who did it. From one point of view it had been done in vain. Not one of the sons had in fact been able to put his original wish – of taking his father's place – into effect. And, as we know, failure is far more propitious for a moral reaction than satisfaction.

was thenceforward prohibited by the sons themselves, in accordance with the psychological procedure so familiar to us in psychoanalyses under the name of 'deferred obedience'.[1] They revoked their deed by forbidding the killing of the totem, the substitute for their father; and they renounced its fruits by resigning their claim to the women who had now been set free. They thus created out of their filial sense of guilt the two fundamental taboos of totemism, which for that very reason inevitably corresponded to the two repressed wishes of the Oedipus complex. Whoever contravened those taboos became guilty of the only two crimes with which primitive society concerned itself.[2]

The two taboos of totemism with which human morality has its beginning are not on a par psychologically. The first of them, the law protecting the totem animal, is founded wholly on emotional motives: the father had actually been eliminated, and in no real sense could the deed be undone. But the second rule, the prohibition of incest, has a powerful practical basis as well. Sexual desires do not unite men but divide them. Though the brothers had banded together in order to overcome their father, they were all one another's rivals in regard to the women. Each of them would have wished, like his father, to have all the women to himself. The new organization would have collapsed in a struggle of all against all, for none of them was of such over-mastering strength as to be able to take on his father's part with success. Thus the brothers had no alternative, if they were to live together, but – not, perhaps, until they had passed through many dangerous crises – to institute the law against incest, by which they all alike renounced the women whom they desired and who had been their chief motive for despatching their father. In this way they rescued the organization which had made them strong – and which

1. [An example of 'deferred obedience' is given in the analysis of 'Little Hans' (1909*b*), *P.F.L.*, **8**, 198.]

2. 'Murder and incest, or offences of a like kind against the sacred laws of blood, are in primitive society the only crimes of which the community as such takes cognizance.' (Smith, 1894, 419.)

may have been based on homosexual feelings and acts, originating perhaps during the period of their expulsion from the horde. Here, too, may perhaps have been the germ of the institution of matriarchy, described by Bachofen [1861], which was in turn replaced by the patriarchal organization of the family.

On the other hand, the claim of totemism to be regarded as a first attempt at a religion is based on the first of these two taboos – that upon taking the life of the totem animal. The animal struck the sons as a natural and obvious substitute for their father; but the treatment of it which they found imposed on themselves expressed more than the need to exhibit their remorse. They could attempt, in their relation to this surrogate father, to allay their burning sense of guilt, to bring about a kind of reconciliation with their father. The totemic system was, as it were, a covenant with their father, in which he promised them everything that a childish imagination may expect from a father – protection, care and indulgence – while on their side they undertook to respect his life, that is to say, not to repeat the deed which had brought destruction on their real father. Totemism, moreover, contained an attempt at self-justification: 'If our father had treated us in the way the totem does, we should never have felt tempted to kill him.' In this fashion totemism helped to smooth things over and to make it possible to forget the event to which it owed its origin.

Features were thus brought into existence which continued thenceforward to have a determining influence on the nature of religion. Totemic religion arose from the filial sense of guilt, in an attempt to allay that feeling and to appease the father by deferred obedience to him. All later religions are seen to be attempts at solving the same problem. They vary according to the stage of civilization at which they arise and according to the methods which they adopt; but all have the same end in view and are reactions to the same great event with which civilization began and which, since it occurred, has not allowed mankind a moment's rest.

There is another feature which was already present in totemism and which has been preserved unaltered in religion. The tension of ambivalence was evidently too great for any contrivance to be able to counteract it; or it is possible that psychological conditions in general are unfavourable to getting rid of these antithetical emotions. However that may be, we find that the ambivalence implicit in the father-complex persists in totemism and in religions generally. Totemic religion not only comprised expressions of remorse and attempts at atonement, it also served as a remembrance of the triumph over the father. Satisfaction over that triumph led to the institution of the memorial festival of the totem meal, in which the restrictions of deferred obedience no longer held. Thus it became a duty to repeat the crime of parricide again and again in the sacrifice of the totem animal, whenever, as a result of the changing conditions of life, the cherished fruit of the crime – appropriation of the paternal attributes – threatened to disappear. We shall not be surprised to find that the element of filial rebelliousness also emerges, in the *later* products of religion, often in the strangest disguises and transformations.

Hitherto we have followed the developments of the *affectionate* current of feeling towards the father, transformed into remorse, as we find them in religion and in moral ordinances (which are not sharply distinguished in totemism). But we must not overlook the fact that it was in the main with the impulses that led to parricide that the victory lay. For a long time afterwards, the social fraternal feelings, which were the basis of the whole transformation, continued to exercise a profound influence on the development of society. They found expression in the sanctification of the blood tie, in the emphasis upon the solidarity of all life within the same clan. In thus guaranteeing one another's lives, the brothers were declaring that no one of them must be treated by another as their father was treated by them all jointly. They were precluding the possibility of a repetition of their father's fate. To the religiously-based prohibition against killing the totem was now added the socially-based prohibition against fratricide. It was not until long afterwards that the prohibition ceased to be limited to members of the clan and assumed the simple form: 'Thou shalt do no murder.' The patriarchal horde was replaced in the first instance by the fraternal clan, whose existence was assured by the blood tie. Society was now based on complicity in the common crime; religion was based on the sense of guilt and the remorse attaching to it; while morality was based partly on the exigencies of this society and partly on the penance demanded by the sense of guilt.

Thus psychoanalysis, in contradiction to the more recent views of the totemic system but in agreement with the earlier ones, requires us to assume that totemism and exogamy were intimately connected and had a simultaneous origin.

(6)

A great number of powerful motives restrain me from any attempt at picturing the further development of religions from their origin in totemism to their condition to-day. I will only follow two threads whose course I can trace with especial clarity as they run through the pattern: the theme of the totemic sacrifice and the relation of son to father.[1]

Robertson Smith has shown us that the ancient totem meal recurs in the original form of sacrifice. The meaning of the act is the same: sanctification through participation in a common meal. The sense of guilt, which can only be allayed by the solidarity of all the participants, also persists. What is new is the clan deity, in whose supposed presence the sacrifice is performed, who participates in the meal as though he were a clansman, and with whom those who consume the meal become identified. How does the god come to be in a situation to which he was originally a stranger?

The answer might be that in the meantime the concept of God had emerged – from some unknown source – and

1. Cf. the discussion by C. G. Jung (1912), which is governed by views differing in certain respects from mine.

had taken control of the whole of religious life; and that, like everything else that was to survive, the totem meal had been obliged to find a point of contact with the new system. The psychoanalysis of individual human beings, however, teaches us with quite special insistence that the god of each of them is formed in the likeness of his father, that his personal relation to God depends on his relation to his father in the flesh and oscillates and changes along with that relation, and that at bottom God is nothing other than an exalted father. As in the case of totemism, psychoanalysis recommends us to have faith in the believers who call God their father, just as the totem was called the tribal ancestor. If psychoanalysis deserves any attention, then – without prejudice to any other sources or meanings of the concept of God, upon which psychoanalysis can throw no light – the paternal element in that concept must be a most important one. But in that case the father is represented twice over in the situation of primitive sacrifice: once as God and once as the totemic animal victim. And, even granting the restricted number of explanations open to psychoanalysis, one must ask whether this is possible and what sense it can have.

We know that there are a multiplicity of relations between the god and the sacred animal (the totem or the sacrificial victim). (1) Each god usually has an animal (and quite often several animals) sacred to him. (2) In the case of certain specially sacred sacrifices – 'mystic' sacrifices – the victim was precisely the animal sacred to the god (Smith, 1894 [290]). (3) The god was often worshipped in the shape of an animal (or, to look at it in another way, animals were worshipped as gods) long after the age of totemism. (4) In myths the god often transforms himself into an animal, and frequently into the animal that is sacred to him.

It therefore seems plausible to suppose that the god himself was the totem animal, and that he developed out of it at a later stage of religious feeling. But we are relieved from the necessity for further discussion by the consideration that the totem is nothing other than a surrogate of the father. Thus, while the totem may be the *first* form of father-surrogate, the god will be a later one, in which the father has regained his human shape. A new creation such as this, derived from what constitutes the root of every form of religion – a longing for the father – might occur if in the process of time some fundamental change had taken place in man's relation to the father, and perhaps, too, in his relation to animals.

Signs of the occurrence of changes of this kind may easily be seen, even if we leave on one side the beginning of a mental estrangement from animals and the disrupting of totemism owing to domestication. (See above, p. 197 f.) There was one factor in the state of affairs produced by the elimination of the father which was bound in the course of time to cause an enormous increase in the longing felt for him. Each single one of the brothers who had banded together for the purpose of killing their father was inspired by a wish to become like him and had given expression to it by incorporating parts of their father's surrogate in the totem meal. But, in consequence of the pressure exercised upon each participant by the fraternal clan as a whole, that wish could not be fulfilled. For the future no one could or might ever again attain the father's supreme power, even though that was what all of them had striven for. Thus after a long lapse of time their bitterness against their father, which had driven them to their deed, grew less, and their longing for him increased; and it became possible for an ideal to emerge which embodied the unlimited power of the primal father against whom they had once fought as well as their readiness to submit to him. As a result of decisive cultural changes, the original democratic equality that had prevailed among all the individual clansmen became untenable; and there developed at the same time an inclination, based on veneration felt for particular human individuals, to revive the ancient paternal ideal by creating gods. The notion of a man becoming a god or of a god dying strikes us to-day as shockingly presumptuous; but even in classical antiquity there was nothing revolting in it.[1] The elevation of the father who had once been murdered into a god from whom the clan claimed descent was a far more serious attempt at atonement than had been the ancient covenant with the totem.

I cannot suggest at what point in this process of development a place is to be found for the great mother-goddesses, who may perhaps in general have preceded the father-gods. It seems certain, however, that the change in attitude to the father was not restricted to the sphere of religion but that it extended in a consistent manner to that other side of human life which had been affected by the father's removal – to social organization. With the introduction of father-deities a fatherless society gradually changed into one organized on a patriarchal basis. The family was a restoration of the former primal horde and it gave back to fathers a large portion of their former rights. There were once more fathers, but the social achievements of the fraternal clan had not been abandoned; and the gulf between the new fathers of a family and the unrestricted primal father of the horde was wide enough to guarantee the continuance of the religious craving, the persistence of an unappeased longing for the father.

We see, then, that in the scene of sacrifice before the god of the clan the father *is* in fact represented twice over – as the god and as the totemic animal victim. But in our attempts at understanding this situation we must beware of interpretations which seek to translate it in a two-dimensional fashion as though it were an allegory, and which in so doing forget its historical stratification. The two-fold presence of the father corresponds to the two chronologically successive meanings of the scene. The ambivalent attitude towards the father has found a plastic expression in it, and so, too, has the victory

1. 'To us moderns, for whom the breach which divides the human and the divine has deepened into an impassable gulf, such mimicry may appear impious, but it was otherwise with the ancients. To their thinking gods and men were akin, for many families traced their descent from a divinity, and the deification of a man probably seemed as little extraordinary to them as the canonization of a saint seems to a modern Catholic.' (Frazer, 1911a, **2**, 177 f.)

of the son's affectionate emotions over his hostile ones. The scene of the father's vanquishment, of his greatest defeat, has become the stuff for the representation of his supreme triumph. The importance which is everywhere, without exception, ascribed to sacrifice lies in the fact that it offers satisfaction to the father for the outrage inflicted on him in the same act in which that deed is commemorated.

As time went on, the animal lost its sacred character and the sacrifice lost its connection with the totem feast; it became a simple offering to the deity, an act of renunciation in favour of the god. God Himself had become so far exalted above mankind that He could only be approached through an inter-mediary – the priest. At the same time divine kings made their appearance in the social structure and introduced the patriarchal system into the state. It must be confessed that the revenge taken by the deposed and restored father was a harsh one: the dominance of authority was at its climax. The subjugated sons made use of the new situation in order to unburden themselves still further of their sense of guilt. They were no longer in any way responsible for the sacrifice as it now was. It was God Himself who demanded it and regulated it. This is the phase in which we find myths showing the god himself killing the animal which is sacred to him and which is in fact himself. Here we have the most extreme denial of the great crime which was the beginning of society and of the sense of guilt. But there is a second meaning to this last picture of sacrifice which is unmistakable. It expresses satisfaction at the earlier father-surrogate having been abandoned in favour of the superior concept of God. At this point the psychoanalytic interpretation of the scene coincides approximately with the allegorical, surface translation of it, which represents the god as overcoming the animal side of his own nature.[1]

1. It is generally agreed that when, in mythologies, one generation of gods is overcome by another, what is denoted is the historical replacement of one religious system by a new one, whether as a result of foreign con-quest or of psychological development. In the latter case myth approximates

Nevertheless it would be a mistake to suppose that the hostile impulses inherent in the father-complex were completely silenced during this period of revived paternal authority. On the contrary, the first phases of the dominance of the two new father-surrogates – gods and kings – show the most energetic signs of the ambivalence that remains a characteristic of religion.

In his great work, *The Golden Bough*, Frazer [1911a, 2, Chap. XVIII] puts forward the view that the earliest kings of the Latin tribes were foreigners who played the part of a god and were solemnly executed at a particular festival. The annual sacrifice (or, as a variant, self-sacrifice) of a god seems to have been an essential element in the Semitic religions. The ceremonials of human sacrifice, performed in the most different parts of the inhabited globe, leave very little doubt that the victims met their end as representatives of the deity; and these sacrificial rites can be traced into late times, with an inanimate effigy or puppet taking the place of the living human being. The theanthropic sacrifice of the god, into which it is unfortunately impossible for me to enter here as fully as into animal sacrifice, throws a searching retrospective light upon the meaning of the older forms of sacrifice. [Smith, 1894, 410 f.] It confesses, with a frankness that could hardly be excelled, to the fact that the object of the act of sacrifice has always been the same – namely what is now worshipped as God, that is to say, the father. The problem of the relation between animal and human sacrifice thus admits of a simple solution. The original animal sacrifice was already a substitute for a human sacrifice – for the ceremonial killing of the father; so that, when the father-surrogate once more resumed its human shape, the animal sacrifice too could be changed back into a human sacrifice.

---

to what Silberer [1909] has described as 'functional phenomena'. [Cf. Freud (1900a), *P.F.L.*, 4, 645–6.] The view maintained by Jung (1912) that the god who kills the animal is a libidinal symbol implies a concept of libido other than that which has hitherto been employed and seems to me questionable from every point of view.

The memory of the first great act of sacrifice thus proved indestructible, in spite of every effort to forget it; and at the very point at which men sought to be at the farthest distance from the motives that led to it, its undistorted reproduction emerged in the form of the sacrifice of the god. I need not enlarge here upon the developments of religious thought which, in the shape of rationalizations, made this recurrence possible. Robertson Smith, who had no thought of our derivation of sacrifice from the great event in human prehistory, states that the ceremonies at the festivals in which the ancient Semites celebrated the death of a deity 'were currently interpreted as the commemoration of a mythical tragedy' [ibid., 413]. 'The mourning', he declares, 'is not a spontaneous expression of sympathy with the divine tragedy, but obligatory and enforced by fear of supernatural anger. And a chief object of the mourners is to *disclaim responsibility for the god's death*[1] – a point which has already come before us in connection with theanthropic sacrifices, such as the "ox-murder at Athens".' (Ibid., 412.) It seems most probable that these 'current interpretations' were correct and that the feelings of the celebrants were fully explained by the underlying situation.

Let us assume it to be a fact, then, that in the course of the later development of religions the two driving factors, the son's sense of guilt and the son's rebelliousness, never became extinct. Whatever attempt was made at solving the religious problem, whatever kind of reconciliation was effected between these two opposing mental forces, sooner or later broke down, under the combined influence, no doubt, of historical events, cultural changes and internal psychical modifications.

The son's efforts to put himself in the place of the father-god became ever more obvious. The introduction of agriculture increased the son's importance in the patriarchal family. He ventured upon new demonstrations of his incestuous libido, which found symbolic satisfaction in his cultivation of Mother Earth. Divine figures such as Attis, Adonis and Tammuz emerged, spirits of vegetation and at the same time youthful

1. [Italicization by Freud.]

divinities enjoying the favours of mother goddesses and committing incest with their mother in defiance of their father. But the sense of guilt, which was not allayed by these creations, found expression in myths which granted only short lives to these youthful favourites of the mother-goddesses and decreed their punishment by emasculation or by the wrath of the father in the form of an animal. Adonis was killed by a wild boar, the sacred animal of Aphrodite; Attis, beloved of Cybele, perished by castration.[1] The mourning for these gods and the rejoicings over their resurrection passed over into the ritual of another son-deity who was destined to lasting success.

When Christianity first penetrated into the ancient world it met with competition from the religion of Mithras and for a time it was doubtful which of the two deities would gain the victory. In spite of the halo of light surrounding his form, the youthful Persian god remains obscure to us. We may perhaps infer from the sculptures of Mithras slaying a bull that he represented a son who was alone in sacrificing his father and thus redeemed his brothers from their burden of complicity in the deed. There was an alternative method of allaying their guilt and this was first adopted by Christ.

---

1. Fear of castration plays an extremely large part, in the case of the youthful neurotics whom we come across, as an interference in their relations with their father. The illuminating instance reported by Ferenczi (1913a) has shown us how a little boy took as his totem the beast that had pecked at his little penis. When our [Jewish] children come to hear of ritual circumcision, they equate it with castration. The parallel in social psychology to this reaction by children has not yet been worked out, so far as I am aware. In primaeval times and in primitive races, where circumcision is so frequent, it is performed at the age of initiation into manhood and it is at that age that its significance is to be found; it was only as a secondary development that it was shifted back to the early years of life. It is of very great interest to find that among primitive peoples circumcision is combined with cutting the hair and knocking out teeth or is replaced by them, and that our children, who cannot possibly have any knowledge of this, in fact treat these two operations, in the anxiety with which they react to them, as equivalents of castration.

He sacrificed his own life and so redeemed the company of brothers from original sin.

The doctrine of original sin was of Orphic origin. It formed a part of the mysteries, and spread from them to the schools of philosophy of ancient Greece. (Reinach, 1905–12, 2, 75 ff.) Mankind, it was said, were descended from the Titans, who had killed the young Dionysus–Zagreus and had torn him to pieces. The burden of this crime weighed on them. A fragment of Anaximander relates how the unity of the world was broken by a primaeval sin,[1] and that whatever issued from it must bear the punishment. The tumultuous mobbing, the killing and the tearing in pieces by the Titans reminds us clearly enough of the totemic sacrifice described by St Nilus [ibid., 2, 93] – as, for the matter of that, do many other ancient myths, including, for instance, that of the death of Orpheus himself. Nevertheless, there is a disturbing difference in the fact of the murder having been committed on a *youthful* god.

There can be no doubt that in the Christian myth the original sin was one against God the Father. If, however, Christ redeemed mankind from the burden of original sin by the sacrifice of his own life, we are driven to conclude that the sin was a murder. The law of talion, which is so deeply rooted in human feelings, lays it down that a murder can only be expiated by the sacrifice of another life: self-sacrifice points back to blood-guilt.[2] And if this sacrifice of a life brought about atonement with God the Father, the crime to be expiated can only have been the murder of the father.

In the Christian doctrine, therefore, men were acknowledging in the most undisguised manner the guilty primaeval deed, since they found the fullest atonement for it in the sacrifice of this one son. Atonement with the father was all the more complete since the sacrifice was accompanied by a total renunciation of the women on whose account the rebellion against the father was started. But at that point the inexorable

1. 'Une sorte de péché proethnique' (Reinach, 1905–12, 2, 76).
2. We find that impulses to suicide in a neurotic turn out regularly to be self-punishments for wishes for someone else's death.

psychological law of ambivalence stepped in. The very deed in which the son offered the greatest possible atonement to the father brought him at the same time to the attainment of his wishes *against* the father. He himself became God, beside, or, more correctly, in place of, the father. A son-religion displaced the father-religion. As a sign of this substitution the ancient totem meal was revived in the form of communion, in which the company of brothers consumed the flesh and blood of the son – no longer the father – obtained sanctity thereby and identified themselves with him. Thus we can trace through the ages the identity of the totem meal with animal sacrifice, with theanthropic human sacrifice and with the Christian Eucharist, and we can recognize in all these rituals the effect of the crime by which men were so deeply weighed down but of which they must none the less feel so proud. The Christian communion, however, is essentially a fresh elimination of the father, a repetition of the guilty deed. We can see the full justice of Frazer's pronouncement that 'the Christian communion has absorbed within itself a sacrament which is doubtless far older than Christianity'.[1]

(7)

An event such as the elimination of the primal father by the company of his sons must inevitably have left ineradicable traces in the history of humanity; and the less it itself was recollected, the more numerous must have been the substitutes to which it gave rise.[2] I shall resist the temptation of pointing

1. Frazer (1912, **2**, 51). No one familiar with the literature of the subject will imagine that the derivation of Christian communion from the totem meal is an idea originating from the author of the present essay.

2. In Ariel's words from *The Tempest* [Act I, Scene 2]:

> Full fathom five thy father lies;
> Of his bones are coral made;
> Those are pearls that were his eyes:
> Nothing of him that doth fade,
> But doth suffer a sea-change
> Into something rich and strange.

out these traces in mythology, where they are not hard to find, and shall turn in another direction and take up a suggestion made by Salomon Reinach in a most instructive essay on the death of Orpheus.[1]

In the history of Greek art we come upon a situation which shows striking resemblances to the scene of the totem meal as identified by Robertson Smith, and not less profound differences from it. I have in mind the situation of the most ancient Greek tragedy. A company of individuals, named and dressed alike, surrounded a single figure, all hanging upon his words and deeds: they were the Chorus and the impersonator of the Hero. He was originally the only actor. Later, a second and third actor were added, to play as counterpart to the Hero and as characters split off from him; but the character of the Hero himself and his relation to the Chorus remained unaltered. The Hero of tragedy must suffer; to this day that remains the essence of a tragedy. He had to bear the burden of what was known as 'tragic guilt'; the basis of that guilt is not always easy to find, for in the light of our everyday life it is often no guilt at all. As a rule it lay in rebellion against some divine or human authority; and the Chorus accompanied the Hero with feelings of sympathy, sought to hold him back, to warn him and to sober him, and mourned over him when he had met with what was felt as the merited punishment for his rash undertaking.

But why had the Hero of tragedy to suffer? and what was the meaning of his 'tragic guilt'? I will cut the discussion short and give a quick reply. He had to suffer because he was the primal father, the Hero of the great primaeval tragedy which was being re-enacted with a tendentious twist; and the tragic guilt was the guilt which he had to take on himself in order to relieve the Chorus from theirs. The scene upon the stage was derived from the historical scene through a process of systematic distortion – one might even say, as the product of a refined hypocrisy. In the remote reality it had actually

1. 'La mort d'Orphée', contained in the volume which I have so often quoted (1905–12, **2**, 100 ff.).

been the members of the Chorus who caused the Hero's suffering; now, however, they exhausted themselves with sympathy and regret and it was the Hero himself who was responsible for his own sufferings. The crime which was thrown on to his shoulders, presumptuousness and rebelliousness against a great authority, was precisely the crime for which the members of the Chorus, the company of brothers, were responsible. Thus the tragic Hero became, though it might be against his will, the redeemer of the Chorus.

In Greek tragedy the special subject-matter of the performance was the sufferings of the divine goat, Dionysus, and the lamentation of the goats who were his followers and who identified themselves with him. That being so, it is easy to understand how drama, which had become extinct, was kindled into fresh life in the Middle Ages around the Passion of Christ.

At the conclusion, then, of this exceedingly condensed inquiry, I should like to insist that its outcome shows that the beginnings of religion, morals, society and art converge in the Oedipus complex. This is in complete agreement with the psychoanalytic finding that the same complex constitutes the nucleus of all neuroses, so far as our present knowledge goes. It seems to me a most surprising discovery that the problems of social psychology, too, should prove soluble on the basis of one single concrete point – man's relation to his father. It is even possible that yet another psychological problem belongs in this same connection. I have often had occasion to point out that emotional ambivalence in the proper sense of the term – that is, the simultaneous existence of love and hate towards the same object – lies at the root of many important cultural institutions. We know nothing of the origin of this ambivalence. One possible assumption is that it is a fundamental phenomenon of our emotional life. But it seems to me quite worth considering another possibility, namely that originally it formed no part of our emotional life but was acquired by the human race in connection with their father-complex,[1] precisely where the psychoanalytic examination of modern individuals still finds it revealed at its strongest.[2]

Before I bring my remarks to a close, however, I must find room to point out that, though my arguments have led to a high degree of convergence upon a single comprehensive nexus of ideas, this fact cannot blind us to the uncertainties of my premises or the difficulties involved in my conclusions. I will only mention two of the latter which may have forced themselves on the notice of a number of my readers.

No one can have failed to observe, in the first place, that I have taken as the basis of my whole position the existence of a collective mind, in which mental processes occur just as they do in the mind of an individual. In particular, I have supposed that the sense of guilt for an action has persisted for many thousands of years and has remained operative in generations which can have had no knowledge of that action. I have supposed that an emotional process, such as might have developed in generations of sons who were ill-treated by their father, has extended to new generations which were exempt from such treatment for the very reason that their father had been eliminated. It must be admitted that these are grave difficulties; and any explanation that could avoid presumptions of such a kind would seem to be preferable.

Further reflection, however, will show that I am not alone in the responsibility for this bold procedure. Without the assumption of a collective mind, which makes it possible to

1. Or, more correctly, their parental complex.
2. Since I am used to being misunderstood, I think it worth while to insist explicitly that the derivations which I have proposed in these pages do not in the least overlook the complexity of the phenomena under review. All that they claim is to have added a new factor to the sources, known or still unknown, of religion, morality and society – a factor based on a consideration of the implications of psychoanalysis. I must leave to others the task of synthesizing the explanation into a unity. It does, however, follow from the nature of the new contribution that it could not play any other than a central part in such a synthesis, even though powerful emotional resistances might have to be overcome before its great importance was recognized.

neglect the interruptions of mental acts caused by the extinction of the individual, social psychology in general cannot exist. Unless psychical processes were continued from one generation to another, if each generation were obliged to acquire its attitude to life anew, there would be no progress in this field and next to no development. This gives rise to two further questions: how much can we attribute to psychical continuity in the sequence of generations? and what are the ways and means employed by one generation in order to hand on its mental states to the next one? I shall not pretend that these problems are sufficiently explained or that direct communication and tradition – which are the first things that occur to one – are enough to account for the process. Social psychology shows very little interest, on the whole, in the manner in which the required continuity in the mental life of successive generations is established. A part of the problem seems to be met by the inheritance of psychical dispositions which, however, need to be given some sort of impetus in the life of the individual before they can be roused into actual operation. This may be the meaning of the poet's words:

> Was du ererbt von deinen Vätern hast,
> Erwirb es, um es zu besitzen.[1]

The problem would seem even more difficult if we had to admit that mental impulses could be so completely suppressed as to leave no trace whatever behind them. But that is not the case. Even the most ruthless suppression must leave room for distorted surrogate impulses and for reactions resulting from them. If so, however, we may safely assume that no generation is able to conceal any of its more important mental processes from its successor. For psychoanalysis has shown us that everyone possesses in his unconscious mental activity an apparatus which enables him to interpret other people's reactions, that is, to undo the distortions which other people have imposed on the expression of their feelings. An unconscious under-

---

1. [Goethe, *Faust*, Part I, Scene 1: 'What thou hast inherited from thy fathers, acquire it to make it thine.']

standing such as this of all the customs, ceremonies and dogmas left behind by the original relation to the father may have made it possible for later generations to take over their heritage of emotion.

Another difficulty might actually be brought forward from psychoanalytic quarters. The earliest moral precepts and restrictions in primitive society have been explained by us as reactions to a deed which gave those who performed it the concept of 'crime'. They felt remorse for the deed and decided that it should never be repeated and that its performance should bring no advantage. This creative sense of guilt still persists among us. We find it operating in an asocial manner in neurotics, and producing new moral precepts and persistent restrictions, as an atonement for crimes that have been committed and as a precaution against the committing of new ones.[1] If, however, we inquire among these neurotics to discover what were the deeds which provoked these reactions, we shall be disappointed. We find no deeds, but only impulses and emotions, set upon evil ends but held back from their achievement. What lie behind the sense of guilt of neurotics are always *psychical* realities and never *factual* ones. What characterizes neurotics is that they prefer psychical to factual reality and react just as seriously to thoughts as normal people do to realities.

May not the same have been true of primitive men? We are justified in believing that, as one of the phenomena of their narcissistic organization, they overvalued their psychical acts to an extraordinary degree.[2] Accordingly the mere hostile *impulse* against the father, the mere existence of a wishful *phantasy* of killing and devouring him, would have been enough to produce the moral reaction that created totemism and taboo. In this way we should avoid the necessity for deriving the origin of our cultural legacy, of which we justly feel so proud, from a hideous crime, revolting to all our feelings. No damage would thus be done to the causal chain stretching from the

1. Cf. the essay on taboo, the second in this work [p. 124 ff.].
2. Cf. the third essay in this work [p. 142].

beginning to the present day, for psychical reality would be strong enough to bear the weight of these consequences. To this it may be objected that an alteration in the form of society from a patriarchal horde to a fraternal clan did actually take place. This is a powerful argument, but not a conclusive one. The alteration might have been effected in a less violent fashion and none the less have been capable of determining the appearance of the moral reaction. So long as the pressure exercised by the primal father could be felt, the hostile feelings towards him were justified, and remorse on their account would have to await a later day. And if it is further argued that everything derived from the ambivalent relation to the father – taboo and the sacrificial ordinance – is characterized by the deepest seriousness and the most complete reality, this further objection carries just as little weight. For the ceremonials and inhibitions of obsessional neurotics show these same characteristics and are nevertheless derived only from psychical reality – from intentions and not from their execution. We must avoid transplanting a contempt for what is merely thought or wished from our commonplace world, with its wealth of material values, into the world of primitive men and neurotics, of which the wealth lies only within themselves.

Here we are faced by a decision which is indeed no easy one. First, however, it must be confessed that the distinction, which may seem fundamental to other people, does not in our judgement affect the heart of the matter. If wishes and impulses have the full value of facts for primitive men, it is our business to give their attitude our understanding attention instead of correcting it in accordance with our own standards. Let us, then, examine more closely the case of neurosis – comparison with which led us into our present uncertainty. It is not accurate to say that obsessional neurotics, weighed down under the burden of an excessive morality, are defending themselves only against *psychical* reality and are punishing themselves for impulses which were merely *felt*. *Historical* reality has a share in the matter as well.[1] In their childhood they had these evil impulses pure and simple, and turned them into acts so far as the impotence of childhood allowed. Each of these excessively virtuous individuals passed through an evil period in his infancy – a phase of perversion which was the forerunner and precondition of the later period of excessive morality. The analogy between primitive men and neurotics will therefore be far more fully established if we suppose that in the former instance, too, psychical reality – as to the form taken by which we are in no doubt – coincided at the beginning with factual reality: that primitive men actually *did* what all the evidence shows that they intended to do.

Nor must we let ourselves be influenced too far in our judgement of primitive men by the analogy of neurotics. There are distinctions, too, which must be borne in mind. It is no doubt true that the sharp contrast that *we* make between thinking and doing is absent in both of them. But neurotics are above all *inhibited* in their actions: with them the thought is a complete substitute for the deed. Primitive men, on the other hand, are *uninhibited*: thought passes directly into action. With them it is rather the deed that is a substitute for the thought. And that is why, without laying claim to any finality of judgement, I think that in the case before us it may safely be assumed that 'in the beginning was the Deed'.[2]

1. [The various forms of reality and truth are discussed repeatedly in Freud's later writings; see, in particular, Essay III, Part II (G) of *Moses and Monotheism* (1939a), p. 376 ff. below.]

2. ['*Im Anfang war die Tat*' (Goethe, *Faust*, Part I, Scene 3). – Freud's line of thought in this essay is carried further in Chapter X of *Group Psychology* (1921c), P.F.L., 12, later still in *The Future of an Illusion* (1927c), particularly in Chapter IV, ibid., 12, and finally in *Moses and Monotheism* (1939a), p. 379 ff. below.]

THE ACQUISITION AND CONTROL OF FIRE
OF FIRE
(1932 [1931])

EDITOR'S NOTE

ZUR GEWINNUNG DES FEUERS

(A) German Editions:

1932   *Imago*, **18** (1), 8–13.
1950   *Gesammelte Werke*, **16**, 3–9.

(B) English Translations:
'The Acquisition of Fire'

1932   *Psychoanalytic Quarterly*, **1** (2), 210–15. (Tr. E. B. Jackson.)

'The Acquisition of Power over Fire'

1932   *International Journal of Psycho-Analysis*, **13** (4), 405–10. (Tr. Joan Riviere.)
1950   *Collected Papers*, **5**, 288–94. (Revised reprint of above.)
1964   *Standard Edition*, **22**, 183–93. (Modified version, with an altered title, of the 1950 translation.)

The present edition is a reprint of the *Standard Edition* version.

This paper seems to have been written in the last month of 1931 (Jones, 1957, 177).

The connection between fire and micturition, which is the central feature of this discussion of the myth of Prometheus, had long been familiar to Freud. It provides the key to the analysis of the first dream in the case history of 'Dora' (1905*e*), *P.F.L.*, **8**, 99 ff., and it crops up again in the much later 'Wolf Man' analysis (1918*b*), ibid., **9**, 331 and *n*. 1. In both these cases the topic of enuresis is involved, and this links up with another main thread in the present paper – the close association, physiological and psychological, between the two functions of the penis (p. 234 below). This too has a long history in Freud's earlier writings, for it too is explicitly remarked on in the 'Dora' analysis (ibid., **8**, 62). Earlier still, in a letter to Fliess of 27 September 1898, Freud had declared that 'a child who regularly wets his bed up to his seventh year ..., must have experienced sexual excitation in infancy' (Freud, 1950a, Letter 97). The equivalence of enuresis and masturbation was insisted upon repeatedly at all periods: once more, for instance, in 'Dora', *P.F.L.*, **8**, 115–16; in the *Three Essays* (1905d), ibid., **7**, 107; in the paper on hysterical attacks (1909a), ibid., **10**, 101; and, much later, in 'The Dissolution of the Oedipus Complex' (1924d), ibid., **7**, 317, and the paper on the anatomical distinction between the sexes (1925j), ibid., **7**, 334.

Another connection of urethral erotism, in the field of character formation, is not mentioned in this paper, though it appears in Chapter III of *Civilization and its Discontents* (1930a), ibid., **12**, of which this paper is an expansion. The relation between urethral erotism and ambition was first pointed out explicitly in 'Character and Anal Erotism' (1908b), ibid., **7**, 215, but something very similar, its connection with feelings of grandeur and megalomania, had been discussed at two points in *The Interpretation of Dreams* (1900a), ibid., **4**, 311 and 606, in the latter of which the extinction of fire makes an incidental appearance. The connection with ambition was alluded to in passing once or twice later on, and was given a rather longer mention soon after the appearance of the present paper, in Lecture 32 of the *New Introductory Lectures* (1933a), ibid., **2**, 135.

THE ACQUISITION AND CONTROL
OF FIRE

In a footnote to my *Civilization and its Discontents*[1] I mentioned – though only incidentally – a conjecture which could be formed on the basis of psychoanalytic material, about primal man's acquisition of control over fire. I am led to take up this theme again by Albrecht Schaeffer's contradiction (1930) and by Erlenmeyer's striking reference in the preceding paper[2] to the Mongolian law against 'pissing on ashes'.[3]

For I think my hypothesis – that, in order to gain control over fire, men had to renounce the homosexually-tinged desire to put it out with a stream of urine – can be confirmed by an interpretation of the Greek myth of Prometheus, provided that we bear in mind the distortions which must be expected to occur in the transition from facts to the contents of a myth. These distortions are of the same sort as, and no worse than, those which we acknowledge every day, when we reconstruct from patients' dreams the repressed but extremely important

1. [(1930a), *P.F.L.*, **12**, 278 n. 3.]

2. [The article by Erlenmeyer (1932) was printed immediately before Freud's in the issue of *Imago* in which this first appeared, and (in an English translation) immediately after the English version of the present paper in the *International Journal of Psycho-Analysis*, **13**.]

3. This refers no doubt to hot ashes, from which fire can still be obtained, and not to ashes which are quite extinct. – The objection raised by Lorenz (1931) is based on the assumption that man's subjugation of fire only began when he discovered that he could produce it at will by some sort of manipulation. As against this, Dr J. Hárnik refers me to a remark made by Dr Richard Lasch (in Georg Buschan's compilation, *Illustrierte Völkerkunde*, 1922, **I**, 24), who writes: 'Presumably the art of *conserving* fire was understood long before that of *kindling* it; we have evidence of this in the fact that, although the present-day pygmy-like [negrito] aborigines of the Andamans possess and conserve fire, they have no indigenous method of kindling it.'

experiences of their childhood. The mechanisms employed in the distortions I have in mind are symbolic representation and turning into the opposite. I should not venture to explain *all* the features of our myth in this fashion; apart from the original set of facts, other and later occurrences may have contributed to its content. But the elements which admit of analytic interpretation are, after all, the most striking and important – viz. the manner in which Prometheus transported the fire, the character of his act (an outrage, a theft, a defrauding of the gods) and the meaning of his punishment.

The myth tells us that Prometheus the Titan, a culture-hero who was still a god[1] and who was perhaps originally himself a demiurge and a creator of men, brought fire to men, having stolen it from the gods, hidden in a hollow stick, a fennel-stalk. If we were interpreting a dream we should be inclined to regard such an object as a penis symbol, although the unusual stress laid on its hollowness might make us hesitate. But how can we bring this penis-tube into connection with the preservation of fire? There seems little chance of doing this, till we remember the procedure of reversal, of turning into the opposite, of inverting relationships, which is so common in dreams and which so often conceals their meaning from us. What a man harbours in his penis-tube is not fire. On the contrary, it is the means of *quenching* fire; it is the water of his stream of urine. This relationship between fire and water then connects up with a wealth of familiar analytic material.

Secondly, the acquisition of fire was a crime; it was accomplished by robbery or theft. This is a constant feature in all the legends about the acquiring of control over fire. It is found among the most different and widely separated peoples and not merely in the Greek myth of Prometheus the Bringer of Fire. Here, then, must be the essential content of mankind's distorted recollection. But why is the acquisition of fire inseparably connected with the idea of a crime? Who is it that was injured or defrauded by it? The Promethean myth in Hesiod gives us a straight answer; for, in another story, not

1. Heracles, at a later time, was a demi-god, and Theseus wholly human.

itself directly connected with fire, Prometheus so arranged the sacrifices to the gods as to give men the advantage over Zeus.[1] It is the gods, then, who were defrauded. We know that in myths the gods are granted the satisfaction of all the desires which human creatures have to renounce, as we have learnt from the case of incest.[2] Speaking in analytic terms, we should say that instinctual life – the id – is the god who is defrauded when the quenching of fire is renounced: in the legend, a human desire is transformed into a divine privilege. But in the legend the deity possesses nothing of the characteristics of a super-ego, he is still the representative of the paramount life of the instincts.

Transformation into the opposite is most radically present in a third feature of the legend, in the punishment of the Bringer of Fire. Prometheus was chained to a rock, and every day a vulture fed on his liver. In the fire-legends of other peoples, too, a bird plays a part, and it must have something to do with the matter; but for the moment I shall not attempt an interpretation. On the other hand, we feel on firm ground when it comes to explaining why the liver was selected as the location of the punishment. In ancient times the liver was regarded as the seat of all passions and desires; hence a punishment like that of Prometheus was the right one for a criminal driven by instinct, who had committed an offence at the prompting of evil desires. But the exact opposite is true of the Bringer of Fire: he had renounced an instinct and had shown how beneficent, and at the same time how indispensable, such a renunciation was for the purposes of civilization. And why should the legend treat a deed that was thus a benefit to

1. ['It being agreed that men should sacrifice to the gods and share the victim with them, the question arose which part of the victim should be for men and which for the gods. Prometheus was called upon to arbitrate. He killed an ox, cut it up, and separated the flesh and entrails from the bones. The latter he wrapped in fat and made, with the hide, into a bundle; the rest he enclosed in the stomach. Zeus, on being given his choice, at once snatched the inviting-looking parcel of fat, and was furious to find that he had got little but bones.' (Rose, 1928, 55, from Hesiod, *Theogonia*, 535 ff.)]

2. [Cf. 'Obsessive Actions and Religious Practices' (1907b), p. 40 above.]

civilization as a crime deserving punishment? Well, if, through all its distortions, it barely allows us to get a glimpse of the fact that the acquisition of control over fire presupposes an instinctual renunciation, at least it makes no secret of the resentment which the culture-hero could not fail to arouse in men driven by their instincts. And this is in accordance with what we know and expect. We know that a demand for a renunciation of instinct, and the enforcement of that demand, call out hostility and aggressiveness, which is only transformed into a sense of guilt in a later phase of psychical development.[1]

The obscurity of the Prometheus legend, as of other fire-myths, is increased by the fact that primitive man was bound to regard fire as something analogous to the passion of love – or, as we should say, as a symbol of the libido. The warmth that is radiated by fire calls up the same sensation that accompanies a state of sexual excitation, and the shape and movements of a flame suggest a phallus in activity. There can be no doubt about the mythological significance of flame as a phallus; we have further evidence of it in the legend of the parentage of Servius Tullius, the Roman king.[2] When we ourselves speak of the 'devouring fire' of love and of 'licking' flames – thus comparing the flame to a tongue – we have not moved so very far away from the mode of thinking of our primitive ancestors. One of the presuppositions on which we based our account of the myth of the acquisition of fire [p. 229] was, indeed, that to primal man the attempt to quench fire with his own water had the meaning of a pleasurable struggle with another phallus.

It may thus well be that, by way of this symbolic analogy, other elements, of a purely imaginative sort, have made their way into the myth and become interwoven with its historical

1. [For all of this see *Civilization and its Discontents* (1930a), particularly Chapter VII; *P.F.L.*, **12**.]

2. [His mother, Ocrisia, was a slave in the household of King Tarquin. One day she 'was offering as usual cakes and libations of wine on the royal hearth, when a flame in the shape of a male member shot out from the fire ... Ocrisia conceived by the god or spirit of the fire and in due time brought forth Servius Tullius' (Frazer, 1911a, **2**, 195).]

elements. It is difficult to resist the notion that, if the liver is the seat of passion, its significance, symbolically, is the same as that of fire itself; and that, if this is so, its being daily consumed and renewed gives an apt picture of the behaviour of the erotic desires, which, though daily satisfied, are daily revived. The bird which sates itself on the liver would then have the meaning of a penis – a meaning which is not strange to it in other connections, as we know from legends, dreams, linguistic usage and plastic representations in ancient times.[1] A short step further brings us to the phoenix, the bird which, as often as it is consumed by fire, emerges rejuvenated once more, and which probably bore the significance of a penis revivified after its collapse rather than, and earlier than, that of the sun setting in the glow of evening and afterwards rising once again.

The question may be asked whether we may attribute to the mythopoeic activity an attempt to give (in play, as it were) a disguised representation to universally familiar, though also extremely interesting, mental processes that are accompanied by physical manifestations, with no motive other than the sheer pleasure of representation. We can certainly give no decided answer to this question without having fully grasped the nature of myths; but in the two instances before us [Prometheus's liver and the phoenix], it is easy to recognize the same content and, with it, a definite purpose. Each describes the revival of libidinal desires after they have been quenched through being sated. That is to say, each brings out the indestructibility of those desires; and this emphasis is particularly appropriate as a consolation where the historical core of the myth[2] deals with a defeat of instinctual life, with a renunciation of instinct that has become necessary. It is, as it were, the second part of primal man's understandable reaction when he has suffered a blow in his instinctual life: after the punishment of the offender comes the assurance that after all at bottom he has done no damage.

1. [Cf. *The Interpretation of Dreams* (1900a), *P.F.L.*, **4**, 518 and 740.]

2. [Cf. an Editor's footnote on this in Essay III, Part II (G) of *Moses and Monotheism* (1939a), p. 379 below.]

A reversal into the opposite is unexpectedly found in another myth which in appearance has very little to do with the fire-myth. The Lernaean hydra with its countless flickering serpent's heads – one of which was immortal – was, as its name tells us, a water-dragon. Heracles, the culture-hero, fought it by cutting off its heads; but they always grew again, and it was only after he had burnt up the immortal head with fire that he overcame the monster. A water-dragon subdued by fire – that surely makes no sense. But, as in so many dreams, sense emerges if we reverse the manifest content. In that case the hydra is a brand of fire and the flickering serpent's heads are the flames; and these, in proof of their libidinal nature, once more display, like Prometheus's liver, the phenomenon of re-growth, of renewal after attempted destruction. Heracles, then, extinguishes this brand of fire with – water. (The immortal head is no doubt the phallus itself, and its destruction signifies castration.) But Heracles was also the deliverer of Prometheus and slew the bird which devoured his liver. Should we not suspect a deeper connection between the two myths? It is as though the deed of the one hero was made up for by the other. Prometheus (like the Mongolian law) had forbidden the quenching of fire; Heracles permitted it in the case in which the brand of fire threatened disaster. The second myth seems to correspond to the reaction of a later epoch of civilization to the events of the acquisition of power over fire. It looks as though this line of approach might take us quite a distance into the secrets of the myth; but admittedly we should carry a feeling of certainty with us only a short way.

In the antithesis between fire and water, which dominates the entire field of these myths, yet a third factor can be demon-strated in addition to the historical factor and the factor of symbolic phantasy. This is a physiological fact, which the poet Heine describes in the following lines:

> Was dem Menschen dient zum Seichen
> Damit schafft er Seinesgleichen.[1]

1. [Literally: 'With what serves a man for pissing he creates his like.' 'Zur Teleologie', from the *Nachlese*, 'Aus der Matratzengruft', No. XVII.]

The sexual organ of the male has two functions; and there are those to whom this association is an annoyance. It serves for the evacuation of the bladder, and it carries out the act of love which sets the craving of the genital libido at rest. The child still believes that he can unite the two functions. According to a theory of his, babies are made by the man urinating into the woman's body.[1] But the adult knows that in reality the acts are mutually incompatible – as incompatible as fire and water. When the penis is in the state of excitation which led to its comparison with a bird, and while the sensations are being experienced which suggest the warmth of fire, urination is impossible; and conversely, when the organ is serving to evacuate urine (the water of the body) all its connections with the genital function seem to be quenched. The antithesis between the two functions might lead us to say that man quenches his own fire with his own water. And primal man, who had to understand the external world by the help of his own bodily sensations and states, would surely not have failed to notice and utilize the analogies pointed out to him by the behaviour of fire.

1. [Cf. 'On the Sexual Theories of Children' (1908c), P.F.L., 7, 200 and 202.]

MOSES AND MONOTHEISM:
THREE ESSAYS
(1939 [1934-38])

EDITOR'S NOTE

DER MANN MOSES UND DIE MONOTHEISTISCHE RELIGION: DREI ABHANDLUNGEN

(A) GERMAN EDITIONS:

1939   Amsterdam: Verlag Allert de Lange.
1950   *Gesammelte Werke*, **16**, 101–246.

(B) ENGLISH TRANSLATIONS:
Moses and Monotheism

1939   London: Hogarth Press and Institute of Psycho-Analysis.
        New York: Knopf. (Tr. Katherine Jones.)
1964   *Standard Edition*, **23**, 1–137. (Tr. James Strachey.)

The present edition is a corrected reprint of the *Standard Edition* version, with some editorial changes.

The first two of the three essays that make up this work appeared originally in 1937 in *Imago*, **23** (1), 5–13 and (4), 387–419; English translations of these two appeared in the *International Journal of Psycho-Analysis*, **19** (3) (1938), 291–8, and **20** (1) (1939), 1–32. Section C of Part II of the third essay was read on the author's behalf by Anna Freud at the Paris International Psycho-Analytical Congress on 2 August 1938, and was afterwards published separately in the *Internationale Zeitschrift für Psychoanalyse und Imago*, **24** (1/2) (1939), 6–9, under the title 'Der Fortschritt in der Geistigkeit' ('The Advance in Intellectuality'). The first essay and the first three sections of the second essay were included in *Almanach 1938*, 9–43. Only a very few unimportant changes were made in these earlier publications when they were included in the complete work. These changes are noted in the present edition.

It was apparently during the summer of 1934 that Freud completed his first draft of this book, with the title: *The Man Moses, a Historical Novel* (Jones, 1957, 206). In a long letter to Arnold Zweig of 30 September 1934 (included in Freud, 1960*a*, Letter 276), he gave an account of the book, as well as of his reasons for not publishing it. These were much the same as those which he explains in the first of his prefatory notes to the third essay below (p. 295) – namely, on the one hand, doubts as to whether his argument was sufficiently well established and, on the other hand, fears of the reactions to its publication by the Roman Catholic hierarchy who were at that time dominant in the Austrian government. From the account which he then gave of the work itself, it sounds essentially the same as what we now have – even its form, in three separate sections, has remained unchanged. Nevertheless, changes must have been made in it. Freud was constantly expressing his dissatisfaction with it – in particular with the third essay. There appears to have been a general re-writing during the summer of 1936, though what we are told on the subject is far from clear (Jones, 1957, 388). At all events, the first essay was published at the beginning of the following year (1937) and the second at its end.[1] But the third essay was still held back and only finally passed for printing after Freud's arrival in England in the spring of 1938. The book was printed that autumn in Holland and the English translation was published in the following March.

What is perhaps likely to strike a reader first about *Moses and Monotheism* is a certain unorthodoxy, or even eccentricity, in its construction: three essays of greatly differing length, two prefaces, both situated at the beginning of the third essay, and a third preface situated half-way through that same essay, constant recapitulations and repetitions – such irregularities are

1. The latter was finished on 11 August 1937 (Letter 290 in Freud, 1960*a*).

unknown elsewhere in Freud's writings, and he himself points them out and apologizes for them more than once. Their explanation? Undoubtedly the circumstances of the book's composition: the long period – four years or more – during which it was being constantly revised, and the acute external difficulties of the final phase, with a succession of political disorders in Austria culminating in the Nazi occupation of Vienna and Freud's enforced migration to England. That the outcome of these influences was to be seen only in the restricted and temporary field of this single volume is very conclusively proved by the work which immediately followed this one – the *Outline of Psycho-Analysis* (1940*a*), among the most concise and well-organized of Freud's writings.

But if *Moses and Monotheism* is judged to lack something in its form of presentation, that is not to imply a criticism of the interest of its content or of the cogency of its arguments. Its historical basis is no doubt a matter for expert dispute, but the ingenuity with which the psychological developments fit in with the premises is likely to persuade the reader who is without prepossession. Those, in particular, who are familiar with the psychoanalysis of the individual will be fascinated to see the same succession of developments exhibited in an analysis of a national group. The whole work is, of course, to be regarded as a continuation of Freud's earlier studies of the origins of human social organization in *Totem and Taboo* (1912–13) and *Group Psychology* (1921*c*). A very elaborate and informative discussion of the book will be found in Chapter XIII of the third volume of Ernest Jones's biography (1957), 388–401.

A NOTE ON THE TRANSCRIPTION OF PROPER NAMES

THE occurrence in *Moses and Monotheism* of a large number of Egyptian and Hebrew names presents the translator with some special problems.

Egyptian writing does not in general record the vowels, so that the actual pronunciation of Egyptian names can only be guessed by a hazardous process of inferences. Various conventional renderings have therefore been adopted by various authorities. For instance, in discussing this question, Gardiner (1927, Appendix B) quotes four different versions of the name of the owner of a well-known tomb at Thebes: Tehutihetep, Thuthotep, Thothotpou and Dhuthotpe. Just as many varieties are to be found of the name of the 'heretic king', who figures so prominently here in Freud's argument. The choice seems to be governed a good deal by nationality. Thus, in the past, English Egyptologists were inclined to Akhnaton, the Germans preferred Echnaton, the American (Breasted) chose Ikhnaton, and the great Frenchman (Maspero) decided for Khouniatonou. Faced by these alluring alternatives, the present translator has fallen back on the humdrum version which has for many years been adopted by the *Journal of Egyptian Archaeology* and seems now to be the one becoming most generally accepted, at least in English-speaking countries: Akhenaten.[1] This same authority has been generally followed in the transcription of all other Egyptian names.

As regards Old Testament names, the answer has been simpler, and the forms found in the English Authorized Version have been employed. It must be added, however, that the unmentionable name of the Deity is here given the transcription regularly found in the works of English scholars: Yahweh.

1. See, for example, Lindon Smith, *Tombs, Temples and Ancient Art*, University of Oklahoma Press, 1956, and *The Times*, 2 April 1963, p. 14, column 5. Different versions of the name will necessarily be found where Freud quotes from other writers.

I
MOSES AN EGYPTIAN

To deprive a people of the man whom they take pride in as the greatest of their sons is not a thing to be gladly or carelessly undertaken, least of all by someone who is himself one of them. But we cannot allow any such reflection to induce us to put the truth aside in favour of what are supposed to be national interests; and, moreover, the clarification of a set of facts may be expected to bring us a gain in knowledge.

The man Moses,[1] who set the Jewish people free, who gave them their laws and founded their religion, dates from such remote times that we cannot evade a preliminary inquiry as to whether he was a historical personage or a creature of legend. If he lived, it was in the thirteenth, though it may have been in the fourteenth, century before Christ. We have no information about him except from the sacred books of the Jews and their traditions as recorded in writing. Although a decision on the question thus lacks final certainty, an overwhelming majority of historians have nevertheless pronounced in favour of the view that Moses was a real person and that the Exodus from Egypt associated with him did in fact take place. It is justly argued that the later history of the people of Israel would be incomprehensible if this premiss were not accepted. Indeed, science to-day has become altogether more circumspect and handles traditions far more indulgently than in the early days of historical criticism.

The first thing that atracts our attention about the figure of Moses is his name, which is 'Mosheh' in Hebrew. 'What is

1. [Moses is so spoken of in the Bible (cf. *Numbers*, xii, 3), and the phrase occurs repeatedly in this work. It will be recalled that the title of the German original is, literally, *The Man Moses and Monotheist Religion*.]

its origin?' we may ask, 'and what does it mean?' As we know, the account in the second chapter of *Exodus* already provides an answer. We are told there that the Egyptian princess who rescued the infant boy from exposure in the Nile gave him that name, putting forward an etymological reason: 'because I drew him out of the water'.[1] This explanation, however, is clearly inadequate. 'The Biblical interpretation of the name as "he who was drawn out of the water"', argues a writer in the *Jüdisches Lexikon*,[2] 'is popular etymology, with which, to begin with, it is impossible to harmonize the *active* form of the Hebrew word – for *"Mosheh"* can at most only mean "he who draws out".' We can support this rejection by two further arguments: in the first place, it is absurd to attribute to an Egyptian princess a derivation of the name from the Hebrew, and secondly, the water out of which the child was drawn was most probably not the water of the Nile.

On the other hand, a suspicion has long been expressed, and in many different quarters, that the name 'Moses' is derived from the Egyptian vocabulary. Instead of enumerating all the authorities who have argued in this sense, I will quote the relevant passage from a comparatively recent book, *The Dawn of Conscience* (1934), by J. H. Breasted, a writer whose *History of Egypt* (1906) is regarded as a standard work: 'It is important to notice that his name, Moses, was Egyptian. It is simply the Egyptian word "mose" meaning "child", and is an abridgement of a fuller form of such names as "Amen-mose" meaning "Amon-a-child" or "Ptah-mose" meaning "Ptah-a-child", these forms themselves being likewise abbreviations for the complete form "Amon-(has-given)-a-child" or "Ptah-(has-given)-a-child". The abbreviation "child" early became a convenient rapid form for the cumbrous full name, and the name Mose, "child", is not uncommon on the Egyptian monuments. The father of Moses without doubt prefixed to his son's name

1. [*Exodus*, ii, 10. – In this translation, all quotations from the Scriptures are given in the Authorized Version.]
2. Herlitz and Kirschner (1930), 4 (1), 303. [The contributor quoted was M. Soloweitschik.]

that of an Egyptian god like Amon or Ptah, and this divine name was gradually lost in current usage, till the boy was called "Mose". (The final *s* is an addition drawn from the Greek translation of the Old Testament. It is not in the Hebrew which has "Mosheh").'[1] I have repeated this passage word for word and I am by no means ready to share responsibility for its details. I am also rather surprised that Breasted has failed to mention precisely the analogous theophorous names which figure in the list of Egyptian kings, such as Ahmose, Thothmose and Ra-mose.

Now we should have expected that one of the many people who have recognized that 'Moses' is an Egyptian name would also have drawn the conclusion or would at least have considered the possibility that the person who bore this Egyptian name may himself have been an Egyptian. In relation to modern times we have no hesitation in drawing such conclusions, though nowadays people bear not one name but two – a family name and a personal name – and though a change of name or the adoption of a similar one in fresh circumstances is not beyond possibility. Thus we are not in the least surprised to find it confirmed that the poet Chamisso[2] was French by birth, that Napoleon Bonaparte, on the other hand, was of Italian extraction and that Benjamin Disraeli was indeed an Italian Jew, as we should expect from his name. In relation to ancient and primitive times, one would have thought that a conclusion such as this as to a person's nationality based on his name would have seemed far more reliable and in fact unimpeachable. Nevertheless, so far as I know, no historian has drawn this conclusion in the case of Moses – not even any of those who, once again like Breasted himself (1934, 354), are ready to assume that 'Moses was learned in all the wisdom of the Egyptians'.[3]

1. Breasted, 1934, 350.
2. [Adelbert von Chamisso (1781–1838), author of *Frauenliebe und -leben*, a cycle of lyrics set to music by Schumann, and *Peter Schlemihl*, the story of the man who sold his shadow.]
3. Although the suspicion that Moses was an Egyptian has been voiced

What prevented their doing so cannot be judged with certainty. Possibly their reverence for Biblical tradition was invincible. Possibly the notion that the man Moses might have been anything but a Hebrew seemed too monstrous. However that may be, it emerges that the recognition that the name of Moses is Egyptian has not been looked upon as affording decisive evidence of his origin, and that no further conclusions have been drawn from it. If the question of this great man's nationality is regarded as important, it would seem to be desirable to bring forward fresh material that would help towards answering it.

That is what my short paper aims at doing. Its claim to be given a place in the pages of *Imago* rests on the fact that the substance of what it has to contribute is an application of psychoanalysis. The argument arrived at in this way will undoubtedly only impress that minority of readers who are familiar with analytic thinking and who are able to appreciate its findings. To them, however, it will, I hope, appear significant.

In 1909 Otto Rank, who was at that time still under my influence, published, following a suggestion of mine, a book bearing the title *Der Mythus von der Geburt des Helden*.[1] It deals with the fact that 'almost all the prominent civilized nations . . . began at an early stage to glorify their heroes, legendary kings

---

often enough without reference to his name, from the earliest times up to the present. [Freud had quoted a comic anecdote to that effect in his *Introductory Lectures* (1916–17), *P.F.L.*, **1**, 195. – This footnote appeared first in the 1939 edition. It is not included in the original *Imago* version of 1937 or in the English translation of 1939. – The phrase quoted from Breasted is in fact derived from a speech by St Stephen (*Acts*, vii, 22).]

1. [*The Myth of the Birth of the Hero*.] It is far from being my intention to belittle the value of Rank's independent contributions to the work. [The quotations which follow are based on the translation by Robbins and Jelliffe, first published in 1914, to which the page references in the text also relate. Some changes have been made in the interests of greater accuracy.]

and princes, founders of religions, dynasties, empires or cities, in brief their national heroes, in a number of poetic tales and legends. The history of the birth and of the early life of these personalities came to be especially invested with phantastic features, which, in different peoples, even though widely separated by space and entirely independent of each other, present a baffling similarity and in part, indeed, a literal conformity. Many investigators have been impressed with this fact, which has long been recognized.' [P.1.] If, following Rank, we construct (by a technique a little like Galton's[1]) an 'average legend' that brings into prominence the essential features of all these stories, we arrive at the following picture:

'The hero is the child of the *most aristocratic* parents; usually the son of a king.

'His conception is preceded by difficulties, such as abstinence or prolonged barrenness or his parents having to have inter-course in secret owing to external prohibitions or obstacles. During the pregnancy, or even earlier, there is a prophecy (in the form of a dream or oracle) cautioning against his birth, usually threatening danger to his father.

'As a result of this the new-born child is condemned to death or to *exposure*, usually by the orders of *his father or of someone representing him*; as a rule he is given over to the *water* in a *casket*.

'He is afterwards rescued by animals or by *humble people* (such as shepherds) and is suckled by a *female animal* or by a *humble woman*.

'After he has grown up, he rediscovers his aristocratic parents after highly variegated experiences, *takes his revenge on his father*, on the one hand, and is *acknowledged* on the other and achieves greatness and fame.' [P. 61.]

The oldest of the historical figures to whom this myth of birth is attached is Sargon of Agade, the founder of Baby-lon (*c.* 2800 B.C.). For us in particular it will not be without

1. [Freud has in mind Galton's 'composite photographs' to which he was fond of referring. See, for instance, *The Interpretation of Dreams* (1900a), *P.F.L.*, **4**, 219–20.]

interest to quote the account of it, which is attributed to him himself:

'Sargon, the mighty King, the King of Agade am I. *My mother was a Vestal, my father I knew not*, while my father's brother dwelt in the mountains. In my city, Azupirani, which lies on the bank of the Euphrates, my mother, the Vestal, conceived me. *Secretly she bore me. She laid me in a coffer made of reeds*, closed my doorway with pitch, and *let me down into the river*, which did not drown me. The river carried me to Akki, the drawer of water. Akki, the drawer of water, lifted me out in the kindness of his heart. *Akki, the drawer of water, brought me up as his own son.* Akki, the drawer of water, made me his gardener. While I worked as a gardener, [the goddess] Ishtar grew fond of me, I became King and for forty-five years I held kingly sway.' [Pp. 12–13.]

The names most familiar to us in the series which begins with Sargon of Agade are Moses, Cyrus and Romulus. But in addition to these Rank has brought together a whole number of other heroic figures from poetry or legend, of whom the same story of their youth is told, either in its entirety or in easily recognizable fragments – including Oedipus, Karna, Paris, Telephos, Perseus, Heracles, Gilgamesh, Amphion and Zethos, and others.[1]

Rank's researches have made us acquainted with the source and purpose of this myth. I need only refer to them with some brief indications. A hero is someone who has had the courage to rebel against his father and has in the end victoriously overcome him. Our myth traces this struggle back as far as the individual's prehistory, for it represents him as being born against his father's will and rescued despite his father's evil intention. The exposure in a casket is an unmistakable symbolic representation of birth: the casket is the womb and the water is the amniotic fluid. The parent–child relationship is represented in countless dreams by pulling out of the water or

---

1. [Karna was a hero in the Sanskrit epic *Mahabharata*, Gilgamesh was a Babylonian hero and the remainder were figures in Greek mythology.]

rescuing from the water.[1] When a people's imagination attaches the myth of birth which we are discussing to an outstanding figure, it is intending in that way to recognize him as a hero and to announce that he has fulfilled the regular pattern of a hero's life. In fact, however, the source of the whole poetic fiction is what is known as a child's 'family romance', in which the son reacts to a change in his emotional relation to his parents and in particular to his father.[2] A child's earliest years are dominated by an enormous overvaluation of his father; in accordance with this a king and queen in dreams and fairy tales invariably stand for parents. Later, under the influence of rivalry and of disappointment in real life, the child begins to detach himself from his parents and to adopt a critical attitude towards his father. Thus the two families in the myth – the aristocratic one and the humble one – are both of them reflections of the child's own family as they appeared to him in successive periods of his life.

We may fairly say that these explanations make the widespread and uniform nature of myths of the birth of heroes fully intelligible. For that reason it is all the more deserving of interest that the legend of the birth and exposure of Moses occupies a special position and, indeed, in one essential respect contradicts the rest.

Let us start from the two families between which, according to the legend, the child's destiny is played out. According to the analytic interpretation, as we know, the families are one and the same and are only differentiated chronologically. In the typical form of the legend, it is the first family, the one into which the child is born, which is the aristocratic one, most often of royal rank; the second family, the one in which the child grows up, is the one that is humble or has fallen on evil days. This tallies, moreover, with the circumstances [of the 'family romance'] to which the interpretation traces the legend back. Only in the

1. [See, for instance, *The Interpretation of Dreams* (1900a), **4**, 524–7.]

2. [Cf. Freud's paper 'Family Romances' (1909c), *P.F.L.*, **7**, 217 ff. That paper was first published as part of the volume by Rank which has been quoted above.]

legend of Oedipus is this difference blurred: the child which has been exposed by one royal family is received by another royal couple. It can scarcely be by chance, one feels, that precisely in this example the original identity of the two families may be dimly perceived in the legend itself. The social contrast between the two families provides the myth – which, as we know, is designed to stress the heroic nature of a great man – with a second function which becomes of special significance when applied to historical personages. For the myth can also be employed to create a patent of nobility for the hero, to raise his social standing. To the Medes, Cyrus was a foreign conqueror; but by means of a legend of exposure he became the grandson of their king. The same applies to Romulus. If any such person existed, he must have been an adventurer of unknown origin, an upstart; the legend, however, made him offspring and heir of the royal house of Alba Longa.

With Moses things were quite different. In his case the first family, elsewhere the aristocratic one, was sufficiently modest. He was the child of Jewish Levites. But the place of the second family, elsewhere the humble one, was taken by the royal house of Egypt; the princess brought him up as her own son. This deviation from type has puzzled many people. Eduard Meyer [1906, 46 f.], and others following him, assumed that originally the legend was different. Pharaoh, according to them, had been warned by a prophetic dream[1] that a son born to his daughter would bring danger to him and his kingdom. He therefore had the child exposed in the Nile after his birth. But he was rescued by Jewish people and brought up as their child. For 'nationalist motives' (as Rank puts it[2]) the legend would then have been given the modified form in which we know it.

A moment's reflection, however, tells us that an original legend of Moses like this, one no longer deviating from the other legends, cannot have existed. For it was either of Egyptian or of Jewish origin. The first alternative is ruled out: the Egyptians had no motive for glorifying Moses, since he was

1. This is also mentioned in the account given by Flavius Josephus.
2. Rank, 1909, 80 n.

no hero to them. We are to suppose, then, that the legend was created among the Jewish people – that is to say, that it was attached in its familiar form [i.e. in the typical form of a birth-legend] to the figure of their leader. But it was totally unsuitable for that purpose, for what would be the use to a people of a legend which made their great man into a foreigner?

The legend of Moses, in the form in which we have it to-day, falls notably short of its secret intention. If Moses was not of royal birth, the legend could not stamp him as a hero; if it left him as a Jewish child, it had done nothing to raise his social standing. Only one small fragment of the entire myth remains effective: the assurance that the child had survived in the face of powerful external forces. (This feature recurs in the story of the childhood of Jesus, in which King Herod takes over the role of Pharaoh.) Thus we are in fact free to suppose that some later and clumsy adapter of the material of the legend found an opportunity for introducing into the story of his hero Moses something which resembled the classical exposure legends marking out a hero, but which, on account of the special circumstances of the case, was not applicable to Moses.

Our investigations might have had to rest content with this inconclusive and, moreover, uncertain outcome, and they might have done nothing towards answering the question of whether Moses was an Egyptian. There is, however, another and perhaps more hopeful line of approach to an assessment of the legend of exposure.

Let us return to the two families of the myth. At the level of analytic interpretation they are, as we know, identical; whereas at the level of the myth they are differentiated into an aristocratic family and a humble one. Where, however, the figure to whom the myth is attached is a historical one, there is a third level – that of reality. One of the families is the real one, in which the person in question (the great man) was actually born and grew up; the other is fictitious, fabricated by the myth in pursuit of its own intentions. As a rule the humble family is the real one and the aristocratic family the fabricated one. The situation in the case of Moses seemed somehow different. And here the new line of approach will perhaps lead to a clarification: in every instance which it has been possible to test, the first family, the one from which the child was exposed, was the invented one, and the second one, in which he was received and grew up, was the real one. If we have the courage to recognize this assertion as universally true and as applying also to the legend of Moses, then all at once we see things clearly: Moses was an Egyptian – probably an aristocrat – whom the legend was designed to turn into a Jew. And that would be our conclusion. The exposure in the water was at its correct point in the story; but, in order to fit in with the fresh purpose, its aim had to be somewhat violently twisted. From being a way of sacrificing the child, it was turned into a means of rescuing him.

The deviation of the legend of Moses from all the others of its kind can be traced back to a special feature of his history. Whereas normally a hero, in the course of his life, rises above his humble beginnings, the heroic life of the man Moses began with his stepping down from his exalted position and descending to the level of the Children of Israel.

We started on this brief inquiry in the expectation of deriving a fresh argument from it in support of the suspicion that Moses was an Egyptian. We have seen that the first argument, based on his name, failed with many people to carry conviction.[1]

---

1. Thus Eduard Meyer writes (1905, 651): 'The name "Moses" is probably Egyptian, and the name "Pinchas" in the priestly family of Shiloh ... is undoubtedly Egyptian. Of course this does not prove that these families were of Egyptian origin, but, no doubt, that they had connections with Egypt.' We may ask, to be sure, what sort of connections this is supposed to make us think of. [This paper by Meyer (1905) is a *résumé* of a very much longer one (1906) where the question of these Egyptian names is further examined (450–1). From this it appears that there were two men called 'Pinchas' ('Phinehas' in the Authorized Version) – one a grandson of Aaron (*Exodus*, vi, 25, and *Numbers*, xxv, 7) and the other a priest at Shiloh (I *Samuel*, i, 3), both of them Levites. (Cf. p. 278 below.) Shiloh was the place where the Ark was stationed before its ultimate removal to Jerusalem. (Cf. *Joshua*, xviii, 1.)]

We must be prepared to find that this new argument, based on an analysis of the legend of exposure, may have no better success. It will no doubt be objected that the circumstances of the construction and transformation of legends are, after all, too obscure to justify a conclusion such as ours and that the traditions surrounding the heroic figure of Moses – with all their confusion and contradictions and their unmistakable signs of centuries of continuous and tendentious revisions and super-impositions – are bound to baffle every effort to bring to light the kernel of historical truth that lies behind them. I do not myself share this dissenting attitude but neither am I in a position to refute it.

If no more certainty could be reached than this, why, it may be asked, have I brought this inquiry into public notice at all? I am sorry to say that even my justification for doing so cannot go beyond hints. For if one allows oneself to be carried away by the two arguments which I have put forward here, and if one sets out to take the hypothesis seriously that Moses was an aristocratic Egyptian, very interesting and far-reaching prospects are opened up. With the help of some not very remote assumptions, we shall, I believe, be able to understand the motives which led Moses in the unusual step he took and, closely related to this, to obtain a grasp of the possible basis of a number of the characteristics and peculiarities of the laws and religion which he gave to the Jewish people; and we shall even be led on to important considerations regarding the origin of monotheist religions in general. Such weighty conclusions cannot, however, be founded on psycho-logical probabilities alone. Even if one accepts the fact of Moses being an Egyptian as a first historical foothold, one would need to have at least a second firm fact in order to defend the wealth of emerging possibilities against the criticism of their being a product of the imagination and too remote from reality. Objective evidence of the period to which the life of Moses and with it the Exodus from Egypt are to be referred would perhaps have fulfilled this requirement. But this has not been obtainable, and it will therefore be better to leave unmentioned any further implications of the discovery that Moses was an Egyptian.

II
IF MOSES WAS AN EGYPTIAN . . .

In an earlier contribution to this periodical,[1] I attempted to
bring up a fresh argument in support of the hypothesis that
the man Moses, the liberator and law-giver of the Jewish
people, was not a Jew but an Egyptian. It had long been
observed that his name was derived from the Egyptian
vocabulary, though the fact had not been properly appreciated.
What I added was that the interpretation of the myth of
exposure which was linked with Moses necessarily led to the
inference that he was an Egyptian whom the needs of a people
sought to make into a Jew. I remarked at the end of my paper
that important and far-reaching implications followed from
the hypothesis that Moses was an Egyptian, but that I was not
prepared to argue publicly in favour of these implications,
since they were based only on psychological probabilities and
lacked any objective proof. The greater the importance of the
views arrived at in this way, the more strongly one feels the
need to beware of exposing them without a secure basis to the
critical assaults of the world around one – like a bronze statue
with feet of clay. Not even the most tempting probability is
a protection against error; even if all the parts of a problem
seem to fit together like the pieces of a jig-saw puzzle, one
must reflect that what is probable is not necessarily the truth
and that the truth is not always probable. And lastly, it did
not seem attractive to find oneself classed with the schoolmen
and Talmudists who delight in exhibiting their ingenuity
without regard to how remote from reality their thesis may be.

Notwithstanding these hesitations, which weigh as much
with me to-day as they did before, the outcome of my

1. *Imago*, **23** (1937). [Essay I above.]

conflicting motives is a decision to produce the present sequel to my earlier communication. But once again this is not the whole story nor the most important part of the whole story.

(1)

If, then, Moses was an Egyptian — our first yield from this hypothesis is a fresh enigma and one which it is hard to solve. If a people or a tribe[1] sets out upon a great undertaking, it is only to be expected that one of its members will take his place as their leader or will be chosen for that post. But it is not easy to guess what could induce an aristocratic Egyptian — a prince, perhaps, or a priest or high official — to put himself at the head of a crowd of immigrant foreigners at a backward level of civilization and to leave his country with them. The well-known contempt felt by the Egyptians for foreign nationals makes such a proceeding particularly unlikely. Indeed I could well believe that this has been precisely why even those historians who have recognized that the man's name was Egyptian, and who have ascribed to him all the wisdom of the Egyptians [p. 245], have been unwilling to accept the obvious possibility that Moses was an Egyptian.

This first difficulty is promptly followed by another. We must not forget that Moses was not only the political leader of the Jews settled in Egypt but was also their law-giver and educator and forced them into the service of a new religion, which to this very day is known after him as the Mosaic one. But is it so easy for one single man to create a new religion? And if anyone wishes to influence another person's religion, would he not most naturally convert him to his own? The Jewish people in Egypt were certainly not without a religion of some form or other; and if Moses, who gave them a new one, was an Egyptian, the presumption cannot be put aside that this other new religion was the Egyptian one.

There is something that stands in the way of this possibility:

1. We have no notion of what numbers were concerned in the Exodus from Egypt.

the fact of there being the most violent contrast between the Jewish religion which is attributed to Moses and the religion of Egypt. The former is a rigid monotheism on the grand scale: there is only one God, he is the sole God, omnipotent, unapproachable; his aspect is more than human eyes can tolerate, no image must be made of him, even his name may not be spoken. In the Egyptian religion there is an almost innumerable host of deities of varying dignity and origin: a few personifications of great natural forces such as heaven and earth, sun and moon, an occasional abstraction such as Ma'at (truth or justice) or a caricature such as the dwarf-like Bes; but most of them local gods, dating from the period when the country was divided into numerous provinces, with the shape of animals, as though they had not yet completed their evolution from the old totem animals, with no sharp distinctions between them, and scarcely differing in the functions allotted to them. The hymns in honour of these gods say almost the same things about all of them, and identify them with one another unhesitatingly, in a manner hopelessly confusing to us. The names of gods are combined with one another, so that one of them may almost be reduced to being an epithet of the other. Thus, in the heyday of the 'New Kingdom' the principal god of the city of Thebes was called Amen-Re'; the first part of this compound stands for the ram-headed god of the city, while Re' is the name of the falcon-headed sun-god of On [Heliopolis]. Magical and ceremonial acts, charms and amulets dominated the service of these gods as they did the daily life of the Egyptians.

Some of these differences may easily be derived from the fundamental contrast between a strict monotheism and an unrestricted polytheism. Others are evidently the result of a difference in spiritual and intellectual[1] level, since one of these religions is very close to primitive phases [of development], while the other has risen to the heights of sublime abstraction.

1. ['*Geistig*' is the word here translated 'spiritual and intellectual'. This concept becomes of great importance towards the end of this work, especially in Essay III, Part II (C). Cf. p. 358 *n*.]

It may be due to these two factors that one occasionally has an impression that the contrast between the Mosaic and the Egyptian religions is a deliberate one and has been intentionally heightened – when, for instance, one of them condemns magic and sorcery in the severest terms, while in the other they proliferate with the greatest luxuriance, or when the insatiable appetite of the Egyptians for embodying their gods in clay, stone and metal (to which our museums owe so much to-day) is confronted with the harsh prohibition against making an image of any living or imagined creature.

But there is still another contrast between the two religions which is not met by the explanations we have attempted. No other people of antiquity did so much [as the Egyptians] to deny death or took such pains to make existence in the next world possible. And accordingly Osiris, the god of the dead, the ruler of this other world, was the most popular and undisputed of all the gods of Egypt. On the other hand the ancient Jewish religion renounced immortality entirely; the possibility of existence continuing after death is nowhere and never mentioned. And this is all the more remarkable since later experiences have shown that belief in an after-life is perfectly well compatible with a monotheist religion.

It was our hope that the hypothesis that Moses was an Egyptian would turn out to be fruitful and illuminating in various directions. But the first conclusion we drew from that hypothesis – that the new religion which he gave to the Jews was his own Egyptian one – has been invalidated by our realization of the different, and indeed contradictory, character of the two religions.

(2)

Another possibility is opened to us by a remarkable event in the history of the Egyptian religion, an event which has only lately been recognized and appreciated. It remains possible that the religion which Moses gave to his Jewish people was nevertheless his own – that it was *an* Egyptian religion, though not *the* Egyptian religion.

In the glorious Eighteenth Dynasty, under which Egypt first became a world power, a young Pharaoh came to the throne in about the year 1375 B.C. To begin with he was called, like his father, Amenophis (IV), but later he changed his name and not only his name. This king set about forcing a new religion on his Egyptian subjects – a religion which ran contrary to their thousands-of-years-old traditions and to all the familiar habits of their lives. It was a strict monotheism, the first attempt of the kind, so far as we know, in the history of the world, and along with the belief in a single god religious intolerance was inevitably born, which had previously been alien to the ancient world and remained so long afterwards. The reign of Amenophis, however, lasted for only seventeen years. Very soon after his death in 1358 B.C., the new religion was swept away and the memory of the heretic king was proscribed. What little we know of him is derived from the ruins of the new royal capital which he built and dedicated to his god and from the inscriptions in the rock tombs adjacent to it. Whatever we can learn about this remarkable and, indeed, unique personality is deserving of the highest interest.[1]

Every novelty must have its preliminaries and preconditions in something earlier. The origins of Egyptian monotheism can be traced back a little way with some certainty.[2] For a considerable time, tendencies had been at work among the priesthood of the sun temple at On (Heliopolis) in the direction of developing the idea of a universal god and of emphasizing the ethical side of his nature. Ma'at, the goddess of truth, order and justice, was a daughter of the sun god Re'. During the reign of Amenophis III, the father and predecessor of the reformer, the worship of the sun god had already gained a new impetus – probably in opposition to Amun of Thebes,

1. Breasted [1906, 356] calls him 'the first individual in human history'.
2. What follows is in the main based on the accounts given by Breasted (1906 and 1934) and in the relevant sections of the *Cambridge Ancient History*, Vol. II [1924].

who had become too powerful. A very ancient name of the sun god, Aten or Atum, was brought into fresh prominence, and the young king found in this Aten religion a movement ready to hand, which he did not have to be the first to inspire but of which he could become an adherent.

The political conditions in Egypt had begun at this time to exercise a lasting influence on the Egyptian religion. As a result of the military exploits of the great conqueror, Tuthmosis III, Egypt had become a world power: the empire now included Nubia in the south, Palestine, Syria and a part of Mesopotamia in the north. This imperialism was reflected in religion as universalism and monotheism. Since the Pharaoh's responsibilities now embraced not only Egypt but Nubia and Syria as well, deity too was obliged to abandon its national limitation and, just as the Pharaoh was the sole and unrestricted ruler of the world known to the Egyptians, this must also apply to the Egyptians' new deity. Moreover, with the extension of the empire's frontiers, it was natural that Egypt would become more accessible to foreign influences; some of the royal wives were Asiatic princesses,[1] and it is possible that direct incitements to monotheism even made their way in from Syria.

Amenophis never denied his adherence to the sun cult of On. In the two Hymns to the Aten which have survived in the rock tombs and which were probably composed by him himself, he praises the sun as the creator and preserver of all living things both inside and outside Egypt with an ardour which is not repeated till many centuries later in the Psalms in honour of the Jewish god Yahweh. He was not content, however, with this astonishing anticipation of the scientific discovery of the effect of solar radiation. There is no doubt that he went a step further: that he did not worship the sun as a material object but as the symbol of a divine being whose energy was manifested in its rays.[2]

1. This may perhaps be true even of Nefertiti, the beloved wife of Amenophis.

2. 'But, however evident the Heliopolitan origin of the new state religion

We should not, however, be doing justice to the king if we regarded him merely as an adherent or promoter of an Aten religion already in existence before his time. His activity was a far more energetic intervention. He introduced something new, which for the first time converted the doctrine of a universal god into monotheism – the factor of exclusiveness. In one of his hymns he declares expressly: 'O thou sole God, beside whom there is no other!' [1] And we must not forget that in assessing the new doctrine a knowledge of its *positive* contents is not enough: its *negative* side is almost equally important – a knowledge of what it rejects. It would be a mistake, too, to suppose that the new religion was completed at a single blow and sprang to life fully armed, like Athene out of the head of Zeus. Everything suggests, rather, that in the course of the reign of Amenophis it increased little by little to ever greater clarity, consistency, harshness and intolerance. It is likely that this development came about under the influence of the violent opposition to the king's reform which arose among the priests of Amun. In the sixth year of the reign of Amenophis this antagonism had reached such a pitch that the king changed his name, of which the proscribed name of the god Amun formed a part. Instead of 'Amenophis' he now called himself 'Akhenaten'. [2] But it was not only from his own name that he expunged that of the detested god: he erased it too from every

---

might be, it was not merely sun-worship; the word Aton was employed in the place of the old word for "god" (*nuter*), and the god is clearly distinguished from the material sun.' Breasted, 1906, 360. – 'It is evident that what the king was deifying was the force by which the Sun made himself felt on earth.' Breasted, 1934, 279. – Erman (1905, 66) makes a similar judgement on a formula in honour of the god: 'These are ... words which are meant to express as abstractly as possible that it is not the heavenly body itself that is worshipped but the being which reveals itself in it.'

1. Breasted, 1906, 374 *n.*

2. [In the German editions the name is spelt 'Ikhnaton'.] I adopt here the English spelling of the name (alternatively 'Akhenaton'). The king's new

inscription – even where it occurred in the name of his father, Amenophis III. Soon after changing his name Akhenaten abandoned the Amun-dominated city of Thebes and built himself a new royal capital lower down the river, which he named Akhetaten (the horizon of the Aten). Its ruined site is now known as Tell el-'Amarna.[1]

The persecution by the king fell most harshly upon Amun, but not on him alone. Throughout the kingdom temples were closed, divine service forbidden, temple property confiscated. Indeed, the king's zeal went so far that he had the ancient monuments examined in order to have the word 'god' obliterated in them where it occurred in the plural.[2] It is not to be wondered at that these measures taken by Akhenaten provoked a mood of fanatical vindictiveness among the suppressed priesthood and unsatisfied common people, and this was able to find free expression after the king's death. The Aten religion had not become popular; it had probably remained restricted to a narrow circle surrounding the king's person. Akhenaten's end remains veiled in obscurity. We hear of a few short-lived, shadowy successors from his own family. His son-law, Tut'ankhaten, was already compelled to return to Thebes and to replace the name of the god Aten in his name by that of Amun. There followed a period of anarchy till in 1350 B.C. a general, Haremhab, succeeded in restoring order. The glorious Eighteenth Dynasty was at an end and simultaneously its conquests in Nubia and Asia were lost. During this

name has approximately the same meaning as his earlier one: 'The god is satisfied.' Cf. the German 'Gotthold' ['God is gracious'] and 'Gottfried' ['God is satisfied']. – [This footnote is translated literally from the German editions. In fact, 'Ikhnaton' was Breasted's (American) version. For all this see the 'Note on the Transcription of Proper Names', pp. 241–2 above.]

1. It was there that in 1887 the discovery – of such great historical importance – was made of the Egyptian kings' correspondence with their friends and vassals in Asia.

2. Breasted, 1906, 363.

gloomy interregnum the ancient religions of Egypt were re-established. The Aten religion was abolished, Akhenaten's royal city was destroyed and plundered and his memory proscribed as that of a criminal.

It is with a particular purpose that we shall now emphasize a few points among the negative characteristics of the Aten religion. In the first place, everything to do with myths, magic and sorcery is excluded from it.[1] In the next place, the manner in which the sun-god was represented was no longer, as in the past, by a small pyramid and a falcon,[2] but – and this seems almost prosaic – by a round disk with rays proceeding from it, which end in human hands. In spite of all the exuberant art of the Amarna period, no other representation of the sun-god – no personal image of the Aten – has been found, and it may confidently be said that none will be found.[3] Lastly, there was complete silence about the god of the dead, Osiris, and the kingdom of the dead. Neither the hymns nor the tomb inscriptions have any knowledge of what perhaps lay closest to the hearts of the Egyptians. The contrast to the popular religion cannot be more clearly demonstrated.[4]

(3)

I should now like to venture on this conclusion: if Moses was an Egyptian and if he communicated his own religion to the Jews, it must have been Akhenaten's, the Aten religion.

1. Weigall (1922, 120–1) says that Akhenaten would hear nothing of a Hell against whose terrors people might protect themselves with innumerable magical formulae: 'Akhnaton flung all these formulae into the fire. Djins, bogies, spirits, monsters, demigods, demons, and Osiris himself with all his court, were swept into the blaze and reduced to ashes.'

2. [This should perhaps read 'a pyramid or a falcon'. Cf. Breasted, 1934, 278.]

3. 'Akhnaton did not permit any graven image to be made of the Aton. The True God, said the king, had no form; and he held to this opinion throughout his life.' (Weigall, 1922, 103.)

4. 'Nothing was to be heard any more of Osiris and his kingdom.' (Erman, 1905, 70.) – 'Osiris is completely ignored. He is never mentioned in any record of Ikhnaton or in any of the tombs at Amarna.' (Breasted, 1934, 291.)

I have already compared the Jewish religion with the popular religion of Egypt and shown the opposition between them. I must now make a comparison between the Jewish and the Aten religions in the expectation of proving their original identity. This, I am aware, will present no easy task. Thanks to the vindictiveness of the priests of Amun we may perhaps know too little of the Aten religion. We only know the Mosaic religion in its final shape, as it was fixed by the Jewish priesthood some eight hundred years later in post-exilic times. If, in spite of this unfavourable state of the material, we find a few indications which favour our hypothesis, we shall be able to set a high value of them.

There would be a short path to proving our thesis that the Mosaic religion was none other than that of the Aten – namely, if we had a confession of faith, a declaration. But I fear we shall be told that this path is closed to us. The Jewish confession of faith, as is well known, runs: 'Schema Jisroel Adonai Elohenu Adonai Echod.'[1] If it is not merely by chance that the name of the Egyptian Aten (or Atum) sounds like the Hebrew word *Adonai* [lord] and the name of the Syrian deity Adonis, but if it is due to a primaeval kinship of speech and meaning, then the Jewish formula might be translated thus: 'Hear, o Israel: our god Aten (Adonai) is a sole god.' Unfortunately I am totally incompetent to answer this question, and I have been able to find but little about it in the literature of the subject.[2] But in all probability this is making things too easy for us. In any case we shall have to come back once more to the problems concerning the name of the god.

The similarities as well as the differences between the two religions are easily discernible without giving us much light.

1. ['Hear, o Israel: the Lord our God is one Lord' (*Deuteronomy*, vi, 4).]

2. Only a few passages in Weigall (1922, 12 and 19), to the effect that 'the god Atum, the aspect of Ra as the setting sun, was probably of common origin with Aton who was largely worshipped in North Syria', and that a 'foreign queen with her retinue may have therefore felt more sympathy with Heliopolis than with Thebes'. [The connection between Aten and Atum, suggested by Weigall, is not generally accepted by Egyptologists.]

Both of them were forms of a strict monotheism, and we shall be inclined *a priori* to trace back what they had in common to this fundamental characteristic. Jewish monotheism behaved in some respects even more harshly than the Egyptian: for instance in forbidding pictorial representations of any kind. The most essential difference is to be seen (apart from the gods' names) in the fact that the Jewish religion was entirely without sun-worship, in which the Egyptian one still found support. When we were making the comparison with the popular religion of Egypt, we had an impression that, apart from the fundamental contrast, a factor of *intentional* contradiction played a part in the difference between the two religions. This impression seems to be justified if now, in making the comparison, we replace the Jewish religion by the Aten religion which, as we know, was developed by Akhenaten in deliberate hostility to the popular one. We were rightly surprised to find that the Jewish religion would have nothing to do with the next world or a life after death, though a doctrine of that kind would have been compatible with the strictest monotheism. But this surprise vanishes if we turn back from the Jewish to the Aten religion and suppose that this refusal was taken over from it, since for Akhenaten it was a necessity in his fight against the popular religion, in which Osiris, the god of the dead, played a greater part, perhaps, than any god in the upper world. The agreement between the Jewish and the Aten religions on this important point is the first strong argument in favour of our thesis. We shall learn that it is not the only one.

Moses did not only give the Jews a new religion; it can be stated with equal certainty that he introduced the custom of circumcision to them. This fact is of decisive importance for our problem and has scarcely ever been considered. It is true that the Biblical account contradicts this more than once. On the one hand it traces circumcision back to the patriarchal age as a mark of a covenant between God and Abraham; on the other hand it describes in a quite particularly obscure passage how God was angry with Moses for having neglected a custom which had become holy,[1] and sought to kill him; but that his wife, a Midianite, saved her husband from God's wrath by quickly performing the operation.[2] These, however, are distortions, which should not lead us astray; later on we shall discover the reason for them. The fact remains that there is only one answer to the question of where the Jews derived the custom of circumcision from – namely, from Egypt. Herodotus, the 'father of history', tells us that the custom of circumcision had long been indigenous in Egypt,[3] and his statements are confirmed by the findings in mummies and indeed by pictures on the walls of tombs. No other people of the Eastern Mediterranean, so far as we know, practised this custom; it may safely be presumed that the Semites, Babylonians and Sumerians were uncircumcised. The Bible story itself says this is so of the inhabitants of Canaan; it is a necessary premiss to the adventure of Jacob's daughter and the prince of Shechem.[4] The possibility that the Jews acquired the custom of circumcision during their sojourn in Egypt in some way other than in connection with the religious teaching of Moses may be rejected as completely without foundation. Now, taking it as certain that circumcision was a universal popular custom in Egypt, let us for a moment adopt the ordinary hypothesis that Moses was a Jew, who sought to free his compatriots from bondage in Egypt and lead them to develop an independent and self-conscious national

1. '*Heilig.*' (Cf. p. 367.)

2. [*Genesis*, xvii, 9 ff., and *Exodus*, iv, 24 ff. Cf. the explanation of the episode on p. 284 below.]

3. [Herodotus, *History*, Book II, Chapter 104.]

4. [*Genesis*, xxxiv.] I am very well aware that in dealing so autocratically and arbitrarily with Biblical tradition – bringing it up to confirm my views when it suits me and unhesitatingly rejecting it when it contradicts me – I am exposing myself to serious methodological criticism and weakening the convincing force of my arguments. But this is the only way in which one can treat material of which one knows definitely that its trustworthiness has been severely impaired by the distorting influence of tendentious purposes. It is to be hoped that I shall find some degree of justification later on, when I come upon the track of these secret motives. Certainty is in any case unattainable and moreover it may be said that every other writer on the subject has adopted the same procedure.

existence in another country – which was what in fact happened. What sense could it have, in that case, that he should at the same time impose on them a troublesome custom which even, to some extent, made them into Egyptians and which must keep permanently alive their memory of Egypt – whereas his efforts could only be aimed in the opposite direction, towards alienating his people from the land of their bondage and overcoming their longing for the 'flesh-pots of Egypt'? No, the fact from which we started and the hypothesis which we added to it are so incompatible with each other that we may be bold enough to reach this conclusion: if Moses gave the Jews not only a new religion but also the commandment for circumcision, he was not a Jew but an Egyptian, and in that case the Mosaic religion was probably an Egyptian one and, in view of its contrast to the popular religion, the religion of the Aten, with which the later Jewish religion agrees in some remarkable respects.

I have pointed out that my hypothesis that Moses was not a Jew but an Egyptian created a fresh riddle. His course of conduct, which seemed easily intelligible in a Jew, was un-understandable in an Egyptian. If, however, we place Moses in the time of Akhenaten and suppose him in contact with that Pharaoh, the riddle vanishes and the possibility is revealed of motives which will answer all our questions. Let us start from the assumption that Moses was an aristocratic and prominent man, perhaps in fact a member of the royal house, as the legend says of him. He was undoubtedly aware of his great capacities, ambitious and energetic; he may even have played with the notion of one day being the leader of his people, of becoming the kingdom's ruler. Being close to the Pharaoh, he was a convinced adherent of the new religion, whose basic thoughts he had made his own. When the king died and the reaction set in, he saw all his hopes and prospects destroyed; if he was not prepared to abjure all the convictions that were so dear to him, Egypt had nothing more to offer him – he had lost his country. In this predicament he found an unusual solution. Akhenaten the dreamer had alienated his people and let his empire fall to pieces. The more energetic nature of Moses was more at home with the plan of founding a new kingdom, of finding a new people to whom he would present for their worship the religion which Egypt had disdained. It was, we can see, a heroic attempt to combat destiny, to compensate in two directions for the losses in which Akhenaten's catastrophe had involved him. Perhaps he was at that time Governor of the frontier province (Goshen) in which certain Semitic tribes had settled (perhaps as early as in the Hyksos period[1]). These he chose to be his new people – a historic decision.[2] He came to an agreement with them, put himself at their head and carried the Exodus through 'by strength of hand'. [*Exodus*, xiii, 3, 14 and 16.] In complete contrast to the Biblical tradition, we may presume that this Exodus took place peacefully and unpursued. The authority of Moses made this possible and at that time there was no central administration which might have interfered with it.

According to this construction of ours, the Exodus from Egypt would have occurred during the period between 1358 and 1350 B.C. – that is, after Akhenaten's death and before Haremhab's re-establishment of state authority.[3] The goal of

1. [A disordered period some 200 years before the time of Akhenaten, when a Semitic people (the so-called 'Shepherd Kings') ruled Northern Egypt.]

2. If Moses was a high official, this makes it easier to understand the role of leader which he assumed with the Jews; if he was a priest, then it was natural for him to emerge as the founder of a religion. In both these cases he would have been continuing his former profession. A prince of the royal house might easily have been both – a provincial governor and a priest. In the account given by Flavius Josephus (in his *Jewish Antiquities*), who accepts the exposure legend but seems to be in touch with traditions other than the Biblical one, Moses, as an Egyptian general, fought a victorious campaign in Ethiopia. [English translation, 1930, 269 ff.]

3. This would make the Exodus about a century earlier than is supposed by most historians, who put it in the Nineteenth Dynasty under Meranptah [sometimes transliterated 'Meneptah']. Or it may have happened a little later [than is suggested in the text above], for the official [Egyptian] histories seem to have included the interregnum in the reign of Haremhab. [See below, p. 289.]

the migration could only have been the land of Canaan. After the collapse of the Egyptian domination, hordes of warlike Aramaeans had irrupted into that region, conquering and plundering, and had shown in that way where a capable people might win fresh land for themselves. We learn of these warriors from the letters found in 1887 in the ruined city of Amarna. There they are called 'Habiru', and the name was transferred (we do not know how) to the later Jewish invaders – 'Hebrews' – who cannot be intended in the Amarna letters. South of Palestine, too, in Canaan, there lived the tribes which were the nearest relatives of the Jews who were now making their way out of Egypt.

The motives which we have discovered for the Exodus as a whole apply also to the introduction of circumcision. We are familiar with the attitude adopted by people (both nations and individuals) to this primaeval usage, which is scarcely understood any longer. Those who do not practise it look on it as very strange and are a little horrified by it, but those who have adopted circumcision are proud of it. They feel exalted by it, ennobled, as it were, and look down with contempt on the others, whom they regard as unclean. Even to this day a Turk will abuse a Christian as an 'uncircumcised dog'. It may be supposed that Moses, who, being an Egyptian, was himself circumcised, shared this attitude. The Jews with whom he departed from his country were to serve him as a superior substitute for the Egyptians he had left behind. On no account must the Jews be inferior to them. He wished to make them into a 'holy nation', as is expressly stated in the Biblical text,[1] and as a mark of this consecration he introduced among them too the custom which made them at least the equals of the Egyptians. And he could only welcome it if they were to be isolated by such a sign and kept apart from the foreign peoples among whom their wanderings would lead them, just

_____

1. [*Exodus*, xix, 6. The same word is used in this connection elsewhere in the Authorized Version, e.g. *Deuteronomy*, vii, 6. Cf. p. 367 below.]

as the Egyptians themselves had kept apart from all foreigners.[1]

Later on, however, Jewish tradition behaved as though it were put at a disadvantage by the inference we have been drawing. If it were to be admitted that circumcision was an Egyptian custom introduced by Moses, that would be almost as much as to recognize that the religion delivered to them by Moses was an Egyptian one too. There were good reasons for denying that fact, so the truth about circumcision must also be contradicted.

(4)

At this point I expect to be met by an objection to my hypothesis. This placed Moses, an Egyptian, in the Akhenaten period. It derived his decision to take over the Jewish people from the political circumstances in the country at that time, and it recognized the religion that he presented to or imposed on his *protégés* as the Aten religion, which had actually collapsed in Egypt itself. I expect to be told that I have brought forward

1. Herodotus, who visited Egypt about 450 B.C., enumerates in his account of his journey characteristics of the Egyptian people which exhibit an astonishing similarity to traits familiar to us in later Jewry: 'They are altogether more religious in every respect than any other people, and differ from them too in a number of their customs. Thus they practise circumcision, which they were the first to introduce, and on grounds of cleanliness. Further they have a horror of pigs, which is no doubt related to the fact that Seth in the form of a black pig wounded Horus. And lastly and most markedly, they hold cows in the greatest honour, and would never eat or sacrifice them, because this would offend Isis with her cow's horns. For that reason no Egyptian man or woman would ever kiss a Greek or use his knife or his spit or his cauldron or eat the flesh of an otherwise clean ox if it had been cut with a Greek knife ... They look down in narrow-minded pride on other people, who are unclean and are not so close to the gods as they are.' (Erman, 1905, 181.) [This is a summary by Erman of Chapters 36 to 47 of Book II of Herodotus.] – We must not, of course, overlook parallels to this in the life of the Indian people. – And, incidentally, who suggested to the Jewish poet Heine in the nineteenth century A.D. that he should complain of his religion as 'the plague dragged along from the Nile valley, the unhealthy beliefs of Ancient Egypt'? [From a poem on 'The New Jewish Hospital in Hamburg', *Zeitgedichte*, XI.]

this structure of conjectures with too much positiveness, for which there is no basis in the material. This objection is, I think, unjustified. I have already laid stress on the factor of doubt in my introductory remarks; I have, as it were, placed that factor ouside the brackets and I may be allowed to save myself the trouble of repeating it in connection with each item *inside* them.

I may continue the discussion with a few critical remarks of my own. The kernel of my hypothesis – the dependence of Jewish monotheism on the monotheist episode in Egyptian history – has been suspected and mentioned by various writers. I spare myself the trouble of quoting these opinions here, since none of them is able to indicate how this influence can have come into operation. Even though in our view that influence remains linked to the figure of Moses, we ought also to mention some other possibilities in addition to the one we prefer. It must not be supposed that the fall of the official Aten religion brought the monotheist current in Egypt to a complete stop. The priesthood at On, from which it started, survived the catastrophe and may have continued to bring under the sway of its trend of ideas generations after Akhenaten's. Thus the action taken by Moses is still conceivable even if he did not live at the time of Akhenaten and did not fall under his personal influence, if he was only an adherent or perhaps a member of the priesthood of On. This possibility would postpone the date of the Exodus and bring it closer to the date which is usually adopted (in the thirteenth century); but it has nothing else to recommend it. Our insight into the motives of Moses would be lost and the facilitation of the Exodus by the prevailing anarchy in the country would no longer apply. The succeeding kings of the Nineteenth Dynasty established a strong *régime*. It was only during the period immediately after the heretic king's death that there was a convergence of all the conditions, external and internal alike, that were favourable to the Exodus.

The Jews possess a copious literature apart from the Bible, in which the legends and myths are to be found which grew up in the course of centuries round the imposing figure of

their first leader and the founder of their religion, and which
have both illuminated and obscured it. Scattered in this material
there may be fragments of trustworthy tradition for which no
room was found in the Pentateuch. A legend of this sort gives
an engaging account of how the ambition of the man Moses
found expression even in his childhood. Once when Pharaoh
had taken him in his arms and playfully lifted him high in the
air, the little three-year-old boy snatched the crown from the
king's head and put it on his own. This portent alarmed the
king, who did not fail to consult his wise men about it.[1] There
are stories elsewhere of his victorious military actions as an
Egyptian general in Ethiopia, and, in this connection, how he
fled from Egypt because he had reason to be afraid of the envy
of a party at Court or of Pharaoh himself. The Biblical account
itself attributes some features to Moses to which credence may
well be given. It describes him as being of an irascible nature,
flaring up easily, as when, in indignation, he slew the brutal
overseer who was ill-treating a Jewish workman, or when in
his anger at the people's apostasy he broke the Tables of the
Law which he had brought down from the Mount of God
[Sinai; *Exodus*, ii, 11–12; xxxii, 19]; indeed God himself
punished him in the end for an impatient deed, but we are
not told what it was.[2] Since a trait of this kind is not one that
would serve for his glorification, it may perhaps correspond
to a historical truth. Nor can the possibility be excluded that
some of the character traits which the Jews included in their
early picture of their God – describing him as jealous, severe
and ruthless – may have been at bottom derived from a
recollection of Moses; for in fact it was not an invisible God
but the man Moses who brought them out of Egypt.

Another trait attributed to Moses has a special claim to our

1. This anecdote, in a slightly different form, also appears in Josephus.
[*Jewish Antiquities*. English translation, 1930, 265 f.]
2. [If this is a reference to Moses, at the end of his life, not being allowed
to enter the Promised Land (*Deuteronomy*, xxxiv, 4), the explanation was in
fact that he had shown impatience by striking the rock with his rod to draw
water instead of merely speaking to it (*Numbers*, xx, 11–12).]

interest. Moses is said to have been 'slow of speech': he must have suffered from an inhibition or disorder of speech. Consequently, in his supposed dealings with Pharaoh, he needed the support of Aaron, who is called his brother. [*Exodus*, iv, 10 and 14.] This again may be a historical truth and would make a welcome contribution to presenting a lively picture of the great man. But it may also have another and more important significance. It may recall, slightly distorted, the fact that Moses spoke another language and could not communicate with his Semitic neo-Egytians without an interpreter, at all events at the beginning of their relations – a fresh confirmation, then, of the thesis that Moses was an Egyptian.

Now, however, or so it seems, our work has reached a provisional end. For the moment we can draw no further conclusions from our hypothesis that Moses was an Egyptian, whether it has been proved or not. No historian can regard the Biblical account of Moses and the Exodus as anything other than a pious piece of imaginative fiction, which has recast a remote tradition for the benefit of its own tendentious purposes. The original form of that tradition is unknown to us; we should be glad to discover what the distorting purposes were, but we are kept in the dark by our ignorance of the historical events. The fact that our reconstruction leaves no room for a number of show-pieces in the Bible story, such as the ten plagues, the passage of the Red Sea and the solemn law-giving on Mount Sinai – this does not disconcert us. But we cannot treat it as a matter of indifference if we find ourselves in contradiction to the findings of the sober historical researches of the present day.

These modern historians, of whom we may take Eduard Meyer (1906) as a representative, agree with the Bible story on one decisive point. They too are of opinion that the Jewish tribes, which later developed into the people of Israel, took on a new religion at a certain point of time. But in their view this did not take place in Egypt or at the foot of a mountain in the Sinai Peninsula, but in a certain locality known as Meribah-Kadesh, an oasis distinguished by its wealth of springs and wells in the stretch of country south of Palestine, between the eastern exit from the Sinai Peninsula and the western border of Arabia.[1] There they took over the worship of a god Yahweh, probably from the neighbouring Arabian tribe of Midianites. It seems likely that other tribes in the vicinity were also followers of this god.

Yahweh was unquestionably a volcano god. Now, as is well known, Egypt is without volcanoes and the mountains of the Sinai Peninsula have never been volcanic; on the other hand, there are volcanoes which may have been active till recent times along the western border of Arabia. So one of these mountains must have been the Sinai-Horeb which was regarded as the home of Yahweh.[2] In spite of all the revisions to which the Biblical story was subjected, the original picture of the god's character can, according to Eduard Meyer, be reconstructed: he was an uncanny, bloodthirsty demon who went about by night and shunned the light of day.[3]

The mediator between God and the people in the founding of this religion was named Moses. He was the son-in-law of the Midianite priest Jethro, and was keeping his flocks when he received the summons from God. He was also visited by Jethro at Kadesh and given some advice by him. [*Exodus*, iii, 1, and xviii, 2–27.]

Though Eduard Meyer says, it is true, that he never doubted that there was some historical core in the story of the sojourn in Egypt and the catastrophe to the Egyptians,[4] he evidently does not know how to place and what use to make of this fact which he recognizes. The only thing he is prepared to

1. [Its precise position seems uncertain, but it was probably in what is now known as the Negev, on about the same latitude as Petra but some fifty miles further to the West. It is not to be confused with the better-known Kadesh in Syria, to the north of Palestine, which was the scene of a much boasted victory by Ramses II over the Hittites.]

2. At a few places in the Biblical text it is still stated that Yahweh came down from Sinai to Meribah-Kadesh. [E.g. *Numbers*, xx, 6–9. – Sinai and Horeb are usually taken as different names of the same mountain.]

3. Meyer, 1906, 38 and 58.

4. Meyer, 1906, 49.

derive from Egypt is the custom of circumcision. He adds two important indications which go to confirm our previous arguments: first, that Joshua ordered the people to be circumcised in order to 'roll away the reproach [i.e. contempt] of Egypt from off you' [*Joshua*, v, 9] and secondly a quotation from Herodotus saying that 'the Phoenicians (no doubt the Jews) and the Syrians of Palestine themselves admit that they learnt the custom of the Egyptians'.[1] But he has little to say in favour of an Egyptian Moses: 'The Moses we know is the ancestor of the priests of Kadesh – that is, a figure from a genealogical legend, standing in relation to a cult, and not a historical personality. Thus (apart from those who accept tradition root and branch as historical truth) no one who treats him as a historical figure has been able to give any content to him, to represent him as a concrete individual or to point out what he may have done and what his historical work may have been.'[2]

On the other hand, Meyer is never tired of insisting on the relation of Moses to Kadesh and Midian: 'The figure of Moses, which is intimately bound up with Midian and the cult-centres in the desert . . .'[3] and: 'This figure of Moses, then, is inseparably linked with Kadesh (Massah and Meribah[4]) and this is supplemented by his being the son-in-law of the Midianite priest. His link with the Exodus, on the contrary, and the whole story of his youth are entirely secondary and simply the consequence of the interpolation of Moses into a connected and continuous legendary story.'[5] Meyer also points out that the themes included in the story of the youth of Moses were one and all dropped later: 'Moses in Midian is no longer an Egyptian and grandson of Pharaoh, but a shepherd to whom Yahweh revealed himself. In telling of the plagues there is no longer

1. Meyer, 1906, 449. [Quoted from Herodotus, *History*, Book II, Chapter 104.]
2. Meyer, 1906, 451 [footnote].
3. Meyer, 1906, 49.
4. [These seem to be the names of springs at Kadesh. Cf. *Exodus*, xvii, 7.]
5. Meyer, 1906, 72.

any talk of his former connections, though effective use might easily have been made of them, and the command to kill the [new-born] sons of the Israelites [*Exodus*, i, 16 and 22] is completely forgotten. In the Exodus and the destruction of the Egyptians Moses plays no part whatever: he is not even mentioned. The heroic character which the legend of his childhood presupposes is totally absent from the later Moses; he is only the man of God, a miracle-worker equipped by Yahweh with supernatural powers.'[1]

We cannot dispute the impression that this Moses of Kadesh and Midian, to whom tradition could actually attribute the erection of a brazen serpent as a god of healing [*Numbers*, xxi, 9), is someone quite other than the aristocratic Egyptian inferred by us, who presented the people with a religion in which all magic and spells were proscribed in the strictest terms. Our Egyptian Moses is no less different, perhaps, from the Midianite Moses than is the universal god Aten from the demon Yahweh in his home on the Mount of God. And if we have any faith at all in the pronouncements of the recent historians, we shall have to admit that the thread which we have tried to spin from our hypothesis that Moses was an Egyptian has broken for the second time. And this time, as it seems, with no hope of mending.

(5)

Unexpectedly, here once more a way of escape presents itself. Efforts to see in Moses a figure that goes beyond the priest of Kadesh, and to confirm the grandeur with which tradition glorifies him, have not ceased even since Eduard Meyer. (Cf. Gressmann [1913] and others.) Then, in 1922, Ernst Sellin made a discovery which affected our problem decisively. He found in the Prophet Hosea (in the second half of the eighth century B.C.) unmistakable signs of a tradition to the effect that Moses, the founder of their religion, met with a violent end in a rising

1. Meyer, 1906, 47.

of his refractory and stiff-necked people, and that at the same time the religion he had introduced was thrown off. This tradition is not, however, restricted to Hosea; it reappears in most of the later Prophets, and indeed, according to Sellin, became the basis of all the later Messianic expectations. At the end of the Babylonian captivity a hope grew up among the Jewish people that the man who had been so shamefully murdered would return from the dead and would lead his remorseful people, and perhaps not them alone, into the kingdom of lasting bliss. The obvious connection of this with the destiny of the founder of a later religion does not concern us here.

Once again I am not, of course, in a position to judge whether Sellin has interpreted the passages from the Prophets correctly. But if he is right we may attribute historical credibility to the tradition he has recognized, for such things are not readily invented. There is no tangible motive for doing so; but if they have really happened, it is easy to understand that people will be anxious to forget them. We need not accept all the details of the tradition. In Sellin's opinion Shittim, in the country east of the Jordan, is to be regarded as the scene of the attack on Moses. But we shall soon see that that region is not acceptable for our notions.

We will borrow from Sellin his hypothesis that the Egyptian Moses was murdered by the Jews and the religion he had introduced abandoned. This allows us to spin our threads further without contradicting the authentic findings of historical research. But apart from this we shall venture to maintain independence of the authorities and to 'proceed along our own track'. The Exodus from Egypt remains our starting-point. A considerable number of people must have left the country with Moses; a small collection would not have seemed worth while to this ambitious man with his large aims in view. The immigrants had probably been living in Egypt long enough to have grown into quite a large population. But we shall certainly not be going wrong if we assume, with the majority of the authorities, that only a fraction of what was later to be the Jewish people had experienced the events in Egypt. In other words, the tribe that returned from Egypt joined up later, in the stretch of country between Egypt and Canaan, with other kindred tribes, which had been settled there for a considerable time. This union, from which sprang the people of Israel, found expression in the adoption of a new religion, common to all the tribes, the religion of Yahweh — an event which, according to Eduard Meyer [1906, 60 ff.], took place under Midianite influence at Kadesh. Thereafter, the people felt strong enough to undertake their invasion of the land of Canaan. It would not tally with this course of events to suppose that the catastrophe to Moses and his religion occurred in the country east of the Jordan; it must have happened long before the union of the tribes.

There can be no doubt that very different elements came together in the construction of the Jewish people; but what must have made the greatest difference among these tribes was whether they had experienced or not the sojourn in Egypt and what followed it. Having regard to this point, we may say that the nation arose out of a union of two component parts; and it fits in with this that, after a short period of political unity, it split into two pieces — the kingdom of Israel and the kingdom of Judah. History is fond of reinstatements like this, where a later fusion is undone and an earlier separation re-emerges. The most impressive example of this was afforded, as is well known, by the Reformation, which, after an interval of over a thousand years, brought to light once more the frontier between the Germany which had at one time been Roman and the Germany which had remained independent. In the instance of the Jewish people it is not possible to point to such a faithful reproduction of the old state of things; our knowledge of those times is too uncertain to allow us to assert that the settled tribes were once more to be found together in the Northern Kingdom and those who had returned from Egypt in the Southern Kingdom; but here too the later split cannot have been unrelated to the earlier joining up. The former Egyptians were probably fewer in numbers than the others, but showed themselves culturally the stronger. They exercised a more powerful influence on the further evolution of the people, because they brought along with them a tradition which the others lacked.

Perhaps they brought something else with them more tangible than a tradition. One of the greatest enigmas of Jewish prehistory is that of the origin of the Levites. They are traced back to one of the twelve tribes of Israel – that of Levi – but no tradition has ventured to say where that tribe was originally located or what portion of the conquered land of Canaan was allotted to it. They filled the most important priestly offices, but they were distinct from the priests. A Levite is not necessarily a priest; nor is it the name of a caste. Our hypothesis about the figure of Moses suggests an explanation. It is incredible that a great lord, like Moses the Egyptian, should have joined this alien people unaccompanied. He certainly must have brought a retinue with him – his closest followers, his scribes, his domestic servants. This is who the Levites originally were. The tradition which alleges that Moses was a Levite seems to be a clear distortion of the fact: the Levites were the followers of Moses. This solution is supported by the fact which I have already mentioned in my earlier essay that it is only among the Levites that Egyptian names occur later.[1] It is to be presumed that a fair number of these followers of Moses escaped the catastrophe which descended on him himself and the religion he founded. They multiplied in the course of the next generations, became fused with the people they lived among, but remained loyal to their master, preserved his memory and carried out the tradition of his doctrines. At the time of the union with the disciples of Yahweh they formed an influential minority, culturally superior to the rest.

I put it forward as a provisional hypothesis that between the fall of Moses and the establishment of the new religion at

1. [This earlier mention is not to be found. It was no doubt dropped in the course of Freud's revisions of the book. See, however, an Editor's addition to a footnote on p. 252.] My hypothesis fits in well with Yahuda's statements on the the Egyptian influence on early Jewish literature. See Yahuda, 1929.

Kadesh two generations, or perhaps even a century, elapsed. I see no means of deciding whether the Neo-Egyptians (as I should like to call them here) – that is, those who returned from Egypt – met their tribal kinsmen after the latter had already adopted the Yahweh religion or earlier. The second possibility might seem the more probable. But there would be no difference in the outcome. What happened at Kadesh was a compromise, in which the share taken by the tribes of Moses is unmistakable.

Here we may once again call on the evidence afforded by circumcision, which has repeatedly been of help to us, like, as it were, a key-fossil. This custom became obligatory in the Yahweh religion as well and, since it was indissolubly linked with Egypt, its adoption can only have been a concession to the followers of Moses, who – or the Levites among them – would not renounce this mark of their holiness. [Pp. 268–9.] So much of their old religion they wished to rescue, and in return for it they were prepared to accept the new deity and what the priests of Midian told them about it. They may possibly have gained yet other concessions. We have already mentioned that Jewish ritual prescribed certain restrictions on the use of God's name. Instead of 'Yahweh' the word 'Adonai [Lord]' must be spoken. It is tempting to bring this prescription into our context, but that is only a conjecture without any other basis. The prohibition upon a god's name is, as is well known, a taboo of primaeval age. We do not understand why it was revived precisely in the Jewish Law; it is not impossible that this happened under the influence of a fresh motive. There is no need to suppose that the prohibition was carried through consistently; in the construction of theophorous personal names – that is, in compounds – the name of the God Yahweh might be freely used (e.g. Jochanan, Jehu, Joshua). There were, however, special circumstances connected with this name. As we know, critical Biblical research supposes that the Hexateuch has two documentary sources.[1] These are distinguished as J and E, because one of them uses 'Jahve [Yahweh]' as the name

1. [This is elaborated on p. 282 below.]

of God and the other 'Elohim': 'Elohim', to be sure, not 'Adonai'. But we may bear in mind a remark by one of our authorities: 'The different names are a clear indication of two originally different gods.'[1]

We brought up the retention of circumcision as evidence for the fact that the founding of the religion at Kadesh involved a compromise. We can see its nature from the concordant accounts given by J and E, which thus go back on this point to a common source (a documentary or oral tradition). Its leading purpose was to demonstrate the greatness and power of the new god Yahweh. Since the followers of Moses attached so much value to their experience of the Exodus from Egypt, this act of liberation had to be represented as due to Yahweh, and the event was provided with embellishments which gave proof of the terrifying grandeur of the volcano god – such as the pillar of smoke [cloud] which changed at night into a pillar of fire and the storm which laid bare the bed of the sea for a while, so that the pursuers were drowned by the returning waters. [*Exodus*, xiii, 21, and xiv, 21–8.] This account brought the Exodus and the founding of the religion close together, and disavowed the long interval between them. So, too, the law-giving was represented as occurring not at Kadesh but at the foot of the Mount of God, marked by a volcanic eruption. This account, however, did grave injustice to the memory of the man Moses; it was he and not the volcano god who had liberated the people from Egypt. So a compensation was owing to him, and it consisted in the man Moses being transferred to Kadesh or to Sinai-Horeb and put in the place of the Midianite priests. We shall find later that this solution satisfied another imperatively pressing purpose. In this manner a mutual agreement, as it were, was arrived at: Yahweh, who lived on a mountain in Midian, was allowed to extend over into Egypt, and, in exchange for this, the existence and activity of Moses were extended to Kadesh and as far as the country east of the Jordan. Thus he was fused with the figure of the later religious founder, the son-in-law of the Midianite Jethro [p. 274], and

1. Gressmann, 1913, 54.

lent him his name of Moses. Of this second Moses, however, we can give no personal account – so completely was he eclipsed by the first, the Egyptian Moses – unless we pick out the contradictions in the Biblical description of the character of Moses. He is often pictured as domineering, hot-tempered and even violent, yet he is also described as the mildest and most patient of men.[1] These last qualities would evidently have fitted in badly with the Egyptian Moses, who had to deal with his people in such great and difficult matters; they may have belonged to the character of the other Moses, the Midianite. We are, I think, justified in separating the two figures and in assuming that the Egyptian Moses was never at Kadesh and had never heard the name of Yahweh, and that the Midianite Moses had never been in Egypt and knew nothing of Aten. In order to solder the two figures together, tradition or legend had the task of bringing the Egyptian Moses to Midian, and we have seen that more than one explanation of this was current.

(6)

Once again I am prepared to find myself blamed for having presented my reconstruction of the early history of the people of Israel with too great and unjustified certainty. I shall not feel very severely hit by this criticism, since it finds an echo in my own judgement. I know myself that my structure has its weak spots, but it has its strong points too. On the whole my predominant impression is that it is worth while to pursue the work in the direction it has taken.

The Bible narrative that we have before us contains precious and, indeed, invaluable historical data, which, however, have been distorted by the influence of powerful tendentious purposes and embellished by the products of poetic invention. In the course of our efforts so far, we have been able to detect one of these distorting purposes [pp. 246–7]. That discovery points our further path. We must uncover other similar tendentious

1. [See, for instance, *Exodus*, xxxii, 19, and *Numbers*, xii, 3.]

purposes. If we find means of recognizing the distortions produced by those purposes, we shall bring to light fresh fragments of the true state of things lying behind them.

And we will begin by listening to what critical Biblical research is able to tell us about the history of the origin of the Hexateuch, the five books of Moses and the book of Joshua, which alone concern us here.[1] The earliest documentary source is accepted as J (the Yahwistic writer), who in the most recent times has been identified as the priest Ebyatar, a contemporary of King David.[2] Somewhat – it is not known how much – later we come to the so-called Elohistic writer [E], who belonged to the Northern Kingdom.[3] After the collapse of the Northern Kingdom in 722 B.C., a Jewish priest combined portions of J and E and made some additions of his own. His compilation is designated as JE. In the seventh century *Deuteronomy*, the fifth book, was added to this. It is supposed to have been found complete in the Temple. In the period after the destruction of the Temple (586 B.C.), during and after the Exile, the revision known as the 'Priestly Code' was compiled; and in the fifth century the work was given its final revision and since then has not been changed in its essentials.[4]

The history of King David and of his period is most probably the work of a contemporary. It is genuine historical writing,

1. *Encyclopaedia Britannica*, eleventh edition, Vol. III, 1910. Article 'Bible'.

2. See Auerbach (1932).

3. The Yahwistic and Elohistic writings were first distinguished by Astruc in 1753. [Jean Astruc (1684–1766) was a French physician attached to the Court of Louis XV.]

4. It is historically certain that the Jewish type was finally fixed as a result of the reforms of Ezra and Nehemiah in the fifth century before Christ – that is, after the Exile, under the Persian domination which was friendly to the Jews. On our reckoning, some nine hundred years had passed since the emergence of Moses. These reforms took seriously the regulations that aimed at making the entire people holy; their separation from their neighbours was made effective by the prohibition of mixed marriages; the Pentateuch, the true book of the laws, was given its final form and the revision known as the Priestly Code brought to completion. It seems certain, however, that these reforms introduced no fresh tendentious purposes, but took up and strengthened earlier trends.

five hundred years before Herodotus, the 'father of History'. It becomes easier to understand this achievement if, on the lines of our hypothesis, we think of Egyptian influence.[1] A suspicion even arises that the Israelites of that earliest period — that is to say, the scribes of Moses — may have had some share in the invention of the first alphabet.[2] It is, of course, beyond our knowledge to discover how far reports about former times go back to early records or to oral tradition and how long an interval of time there was in individual instances between an event and its recording. The text, however, as we possess it to-day, will tell us enough about its own vicissitudes. Two mutually opposed treatments have left their traces on it. On the one hand it has been subjected to revisions which have falsified it in the sense of their secret aims, have mutilated and amplified it and have even changed it into its reverse; on the other hand a solicitous piety has presided over it and has sought to preserve everything as it was, no matter whether it was consistent or contradicted itself. Thus almost everywhere noticeable gaps, disturbing repetitions and obvious contradictions have come about — indications which reveal things to us which it was not intended to communicate. In its implications the distortion of a text resembles a murder: the difficulty is not in perpetrating the deed, but in getting rid of its traces. We might well lend the word '*Entstellung* [distortion]' the double meaning to which it has a claim but of which to-day it makes no use. It should mean not only 'to change the appearance of something' but also 'to put something in another place, to displace'.[3] Accordingly, in many instances of textual distortion, we may nevertheless count upon finding what has been suppressed and disavowed hidden away somewhere else,

1. Cf. Yahuda, 1929.

2. If they were subject to the prohibition against pictures they would even have had a motive for abandoning the hieroglyphic picture-writing while adapting its written characters to expressing a new language. (Cf. Auerbach, 1932.) [Hieroglyphic writing included both signs depicting objects and signs representing sounds.]

3. ['*Stelle*' means 'a place', and '*ent-*' is a prefix indicating a change of condition.]

though changed and torn from its context. Only it will not always be easy to recognize it.

The distorting purposes which we are anxious to lay hold of must have been at work already on the traditions before any of them were committed to writing. We have already discovered one of them, perhaps the most powerful of all. As we have said, with the setting-up of the new god, Yahweh, at Kadesh, it became necessary to do something to glorify him. It would be more correct to say: it became necessary to fit him in, to make room for him, to wipe out the traces of earlier religions. This seems to have been achieved with complete success as regards the religion of the resident tribes: we hear nothing more of it. With those returning from Egypt it was not such an easy matter; they would not let themselves be deprived of the Exodus, the man Moses or circumcision. It is true that they had been in Egypt, but they had left it, and thenceforward every trace of Egyptian influence was to be disavowed. The man Moses was dealt with by shifting him to Midian and Kadesh, and by fusing him with the priest of Yahweh who founded the religion. Circumcision, the most suspicious indication of dependence on Egypt, had to be retained but no attempts were spared to detach the custom from Egypt – all evidence to the contrary. It is only as a deliberate denial of the betraying fact that we can explain the puzzling and incomprehensibly worded passage in *Exodus* [iv, 24–6], according to which on one occasion Yahweh was angry with Moses because he had neglected circumcision, and his Midianite wife saved his life by quickly carrying out the operation. [Cf. p. 265.] We shall presently come across another invention for making the uncomfortable piece of evidence harmless.

The fact that we find signs of efforts being made to deny explicitly that Yahweh was a new god, alien to the Jews, can scarcely be described as the appearance of a fresh tendentious purpose: it is rather a continuation of the former one. With this end in view the legends of the patriarchs of the people – Abraham, Isaac and Jacob – were introduced. Yahweh asserted that he was already the god of these forefathers; though it is true that he himself had to admit that they had not worshipped him under that name.[1] He does not add, however, what the other name was.

And here was the opportunity for a decisive blow against the Egyptian origin of the custom of circumcision: Yahweh, it was said, had already insisted on it with Abraham and had introduced it as the token of the covenant between him and Abraham. [*Genesis*, xvii, 9–14.] But this was a particularly clumsy invention. As a mark that is to distinguish one person from others and prefer him to them, one would choose something that is not to be found in other people; one would *not* choose something that can be exhibited in the same way by millions of other people. An Israelite who was transplanted to Egypt would have had to acknowledge every Egyptian as a brother in the covenant, a brother in Yahweh. It is impossible that the Israelites who created the text of the Bible can have been ignorant of the fact that circumcision was indigenous in Egypt. The passage in Joshua [v, 9] quoted by Eduard Meyer [see p. 274 above] admits this without question; but for that very reason it had to be disavowed at any price.

We must not expect the mythical structures of religion to pay too much attention to logical coherence. Otherwise popular feeling might have taken justified offence against a deity who made a covenant with their forefathers with mutual obligations and then, for centuries on end, paid no attention to his human partners, till it suddenly occurred to him to manifest himself anew to their descendants. Even more puzzling is the notion of a god's all at once 'choosing' a people, declaring them to be his people and himself to be their god. I believe this is the only instance of its sort in the history of human religions. Ordinarily god and people are indissolubly linked, they are one from the very beginning of things. No doubt we sometimes hear of a people taking on a different god, but never of a god seeking a different people. We may perhaps

1. [Cf. *Exodus*, vi, 3.] This does not make the restrictions upon the use of this new name more intelligible, though it does make them more suspect.

understand this unique event better if we recall the relations between Moses and the Jewish people. Moses had stooped to the Jews, had made them his people: they were his 'chosen people'.[1]

The bringing-in of the patriarchs served yet another purpose. They had lived in Canaan, and their memory was linked with particular localities in that country. It is possible that they were themselves originally Canaanite heroes or local divinities, and were then seized on by the immigrant Israelites for their pre-history. By appealing to the patriarchs they were as it were asserting their indigenous character and defending themselves

1. Yahweh was undoubtedly a volcano god. There was no occasion for the inhabitants of Egypt to worship him. I am certainly not the first person to be struck by the resemblance of the sound of the name 'Yahweh' to the root of the other divine name 'Jupiter (Jove)'. [The letter 'j' in German is pronounced like the English 'y'.] The name 'Jochanan' is compounded with an abbreviation of the Hebrew Yahweh – in the same kind of way as [the German] 'Gotthold [God is gracious]' and the Carthaginian equivalent 'Hannibal'. This name (Jochanan), in the forms 'Johann', 'John', 'Jean', 'Juan', has become the favourite first name in European Christendom. The Italians, in rendering it 'Giovanni' and moreover calling a day of the week 'Giovedi [Thursday]', are bringing to light a resemblance which may possibly mean nothing or possibly a very great deal. At this point, extensive but very uncertain prospects open up before us. It seems that, in those obscure centuries which are scarcely accessible to historical research, the countries round the eastern basin of the Mediterranean were the scene of frequent and violent volcanic eruptions, which must have made the strongest impression on their inhabitants. Evans assumes that the final destruction of the palace of Minos at Knossos too was the consequence of an earthquake. In Crete at that period (as probably in the Aegean world in general) the great mother-goddess was worshipped. The realization that she was not able to protect her house against the assaults of a stronger power may have contributed to her having to give place to a male deity, and, if so, the volcano god had the first claim to take her place. After all, Zeus always remains the 'earth-shaker'. There is little doubt that it was during those obscure ages that the mother-goddesses were replaced by male gods (who may originally perhaps have been sons). The destiny of Pallas Athene, who was no doubt the local form of the mother-goddess, is particularly impressive. She was reduced to being a daughter by the religious revolution, she was robbed of her own mother and, by having virginity imposed on her, was permanently excluded from motherhood. [On the mother-goddesses, see below, pp. 327–8.]

from the odium attaching to an alien conqueror. It was a clever twist to declare that the god Yahweh was only giving them back what their forefathers had once possessed.

In the later contributions to the text of the Bible the intention was put into effect of avoiding the mention of Kadesh. The place at which the religion was founded was fixed once and for all as the Mount of God, Sinai-Horeb. It is not easy to see the motive for this; perhaps people were unwilling to be reminded of the influence of Midian. But all later distortions, especially of the period of the Priestly Code, had another aim in view. There was no longer any need to alter accounts of events in a desired sense – for this had been done long before. But care was taken to shift back commands and institutions of the present day into early times – to base them, as a rule, on the Mosaic law-giving – so as to derive from this their claim to being holy and binding. However much the picture of the past might in this way be falsified, the procedure was not without a certain psychological justification. It reflected the fact that in the course of long ages – between the Exodus from Egypt and the fixing of the text of the Bible under Ezra and Nehemiah some eight hundred years elapsed – the Yahweh religion had had its form changed back into conformity, or even perhaps into identity, with the original religion of Moses.

And this is the essential outcome, the momentous substance, of the history of the Jewish religion.

(7)

Of all the events of early times which later poets, priests and historians undertook to work over, one stood out, the suppression of which was enjoined by the most immediate and best human motives. This was the murder of Moses, the great leader and liberator, which Sellin discovered from hints in the writings of the Prophets. Sellin's hypothesis cannot be called fantastic – it is probable enough. Moses, deriving from the school of Akhenaten, employed no methods other than did the king; he commanded, he forced his faith upon the people.[1] The doctrine of Moses may have been even harsher than that of his master. He had no need to retain the sun-god as a support: the school of On had no significance for his alien people. Moses, like Akhenaten, met with the same fate that awaits all enlightened despots. The Jewish people under Moses were just as little able to tolerate such a highly spiritualized[2] religion and find satisfaction of their needs in what it had to offer as had been the Egyptians of the Eighteenth Dynasty. The same thing happened in both cases: those who had been dominated and kept in want rose and threw off the burden of the religion that had been imposed on them. But while the tame Egyptians waited till fate had removed the sacred figure of their Pharaoh, the savage Semites took fate into their own hands and rid themselves of their tyrant.[3]

Nor can it be maintained that the surviving text of the Bible gives us no warning of such an end to Moses. The account of the 'wandering in the wilderness' [*Numbers*, xiv, 33], which may stand for the period during which Moses ruled, describes a succession of serious revolts against his authority which were also, by Yahweh's command, suppressed with bloody punishment. It is easy to imagine that one such rebellion ended in a way different from what the text suggests. The people's defection from the new religion is also described in the text – only as an episode, it is true: namely in the story of the golden calf. In this, by an ingenious turn, the breaking of the tables of the law (which is to be understood symbolically: 'he has broken the law') is transposed on to Moses himself, and his furious indignation is assigned as its motive. [*Exodus*, xxxii, 19.]

There came a time when people began to regret the murder

1. At that period any other method of influencing them was scarcely possible.

2. ['*Vergeistigte*.' See below, Essay III, Part II (C) and p. 330, footnote.]

3. It is really remarkable how little we hear in the thousands of years of Egyptian history of the violent removal or murder of a Pharaoh. A comparison with Assyrian history, for instance, must increase our surprise at this. It may, of course, be accounted for by the fact that Egyptian history was entirely written to serve official ends.

of Moses and to seek to forget it. This was certainly so at the time of the union of the two portions of the people at Kadesh. But when the Exodus and the foundation of the religion at the oasis [of Kadesh] were brought closer together [p. 280], and Moses was represented as being concerned in the latter instead of the other man [the Midianite priest], not only were the demands of the followers of Moses satisfied but the distressing fact of his violent end was successfully disavowed. In actual fact it is most unlikely that Moses could have taken part in the proceedings at Kadesh even if his life had not been cut short.

We must now make an attempt at elucidating the chronological relations of these events. We have put the Exodus in the period after the end of the Eighteenth Dynasty (1350 B.C.). It may have occurred then or a little later, since the Egyptian chroniclers have included the succeeding years of anarchy in the reign of Haremhab, which brought them to an end and lasted till 1315 B.C. The next (but also the only) fixed point for the chronology is afforded by the stela of [the Pharaoh] Merenptah (1225–15 B.C.), which boasts of his victory over Isiraal (Israel) and the laying waste of her seed (?). The sense to be attached to this inscription is unfortunately doubtful, it is supposed to prove that the Israelite tribes were already at that time settled in Canaan.[1] Eduard Meyer rightly concludes from this stela that Merenptah cannot have been the Pharaoh of the Exodus, as had been lightly assumed previously. The date of the Exodus must have been earlier. The question of who was the Pharaoh of the Exodus seems to me altogether an idle one. There was no Pharaoh of the Exodus, for it occurred during an interregnum. Nor does the discovery of the stela of Merenptah throw any light on the possible date of the union and founding of the religion at Kadesh. All that we can say with certainty is that it was some time between 1350 and 1215 B.C. We suspect that the Exodus comes somewhere very near the beginning of this hundred years and the events at Kadesh not too far away from its end. We should like to claim the greater part of this period for the interval between the two

1. Eduard Meyer, 1906, 222 ff.

occurrences. For we need a comparatively long time for the passions of the returning tribes to have cooled down after the murder of Moses and for the influence of his followers, the Levites, to have become as great as is implied by the compromise at Kadesh. Two generations, sixty years, might about suffice for this, but it is a tight fit. What is inferred from the stela of Merenptah comes too early for us, and since we recognize that in this hypothesis of ours one supposition is only based on another, we must admit that this discussion reveals a weak side of our construction. It is unlucky that everything relating to the settlement of the Jewish people in Canaan is so obscure and confused. Our only resort, perhaps, is to suppose that the name on the 'Israel' stela does not relate to the tribes whose fortunes we are trying to follow and which combined to form the later people of Israel. After all, the name of 'Habiru' (Hebrews) was transferred to these same people in the Amarna period [p. 268].

The union of the tribes into a nation through the adoption of a common religion, whenever it may have taken place, might easily have turned out quite an unimportant happening in world history. The new religion would have been carried away by the current of events, Yahweh would have had to take his place in the procession of departed gods in Flaubert's vision,[1] and all twelve of his tribes would have been 'lost' and not only the ten of them which the Anglo-Saxons have been in search of for so long. The god Yahweh, to whom the Midianite Moses then presented a new people, was probably in no respect a prominent being. A coarse, narrow-minded, local god, violent and bloodthirsty, he had promised his followers to give them 'a land flowing with milk and honey' [*Exodus*, iii, 8] and urged them to exterminate its present inhabitants 'with the edge of the sword' [*Deuteronomy*, xiii, 15]. It is astonishing how much remains, in spite of all the revisions of the Biblical narratives, that allows us to recognize his original nature. It is not even certain that his religion was a genuine monotheism, that it denied the divinity of the deities of other

1. [In *La tentation de Saint Antoine*.]

peoples. It was enough probably that his people regarded their own god as more powerful than any foreign god. If, nevertheless, in the sequel everything took a different course from what such beginnings would have led one to expect, the cause can be found in only one fact. The Egyptian Moses had given to one portion of the people a more highly spiritualized notion of god, the idea of a single deity embracing the whole world, who was not less all-loving than all-powerful, who was averse to all ceremonial and magic and set before men as their highest aim a life in truth and justice. For, however incomplete may be the accounts we have of the ethical side of the Aten religion, it can be no unimportant fact that Akhenaten regularly referred to himself in his inscriptions as 'living in Ma'at' (truth, justice).[1] In the long run it made no difference that the people rejected the teaching of Moses (probably after a short time) and killed him himself. The *tradition* of it remained and its influence achieved (only gradually, it is true, in the course of centuries) what was denied to Moses himself. The god Yahweh had arrived at undeserved honour when, from the time of Kadesh onwards, he was credited with the deed of liberation which had been performed by Moses; but he had to pay heavily for this usurpation. The shadow of the god whose place he had taken became stronger than himself; by the end of the process of evolution, the nature of the forgotten god of Moses had come to light behind his own. No one can doubt that it was only the idea of this other god that enabled the people of Israel to survive all the blows of fate and that kept them alive to our own days.

It is no longer possible to estimate the share taken by the Levites in the final victory of the Mosaic god over Yahweh. They had taken the side of Moses in the past, when the compromise was reached at Kadesh, in a still live memory of the master whose retinue and compatriots they had been. During the centuries since then they had become merged with the

1. His hymns lay stress not only on the god's universality and oneness, but also on his loving care for all creatures; and they encourage joy in nature and enjoyment of its beauty. (Breasted, 1934 [281–302].)

people or with the priesthood, and it had become the main function of the priests to develop and supervise the ritual, and besides this to preserve the holy writ and revise it in accordance with their aims. But was not all sacrifice and all ceremonial at bottom only magic and sorcery, such as had been unconditionally rejected by the old Mosaic teaching? Thereupon there arose from among the midst of the people an unending succession of men who were not linked to Moses in their origin but were enthralled by the great and mighty tradition which had grown up little by little in obscurity: and it was these men, the Prophets, who tirelessly preached the old Mosaic doctrine – that the deity disdained sacrifice and ceremonial and asked only for faith and a life in truth and justice (Ma'at). The efforts of the Prophets had a lasting success; the doctrines with which they re-established the old faith became the permanent content of the Jewish religion. It is honour enough to the Jewish people that they could preserve such a tradition and produce men who gave it a voice – even though the initiative to it came from outside, from a great foreigner.

I should not feel secure in giving this account, if I could not appeal to the judgement of other inquirers with a specialist knowledge who see the significance of Moses for the Jewish religion in the same light as I do, even though they do not recognize his Egyptian origin. Thus, for instance, Sellin (1922, 52) writes: 'Consequently we must picture the true religion of Moses – his belief in the one moral God whom he preaches – as thenceforward necessarily the property of a small circle of the people. We must necessarily not expect to meet with it in the official cult, in the religion of the priests or in the beliefs of the people. We can necessarily only reckon to find an occasional spark emerging, now here and there, from the spiritual torch which he once kindled, to find that his ideas have not entirely perished but have been silently at work here and there upon beliefs and customs, till sooner or later, through the effect of special experiences or of persons specially moved by his spirit, it has broken out more strongly once more and gained influence on wider masses of the population. It is from this point of view that the history of the ancient religion of Israel is necessarily to be regarded. Anyone who sought to construct the Mosaic religion on the lines of the religion we meet with, according to the chronicles, in the life of the people during their first five hundred years in Canaan, would be committing the gravest methodological error.' Volz (1907, 64) speaks even more clearly: it is his belief that 'the exalted work of Moses was understood and carried through to begin with only feebly and scantily, till, in the course of centuries, it penetrated more and more, and at length in the great Prophets it met with like spirits who continued the lonely man's work.'

And here, it seems, I have reached the conclusion of my study, which was directed to the single aim of introducing the figure of an Egyptian Moses into the nexus of Jewish history. Our findings may be thus expressed in the most concise formula. Jewish history is familiar to us for its dualities: *two* groups of people who came together to form the nation, *two* kingdoms into which this nation fell apart, *two* gods' names in the documentary sources of the Bible. To these we add two fresh ones: the foundation of *two* religions – the first repressed by the second but nevertheless later emerging victoriously behind it, and *two* religious founders, who are both called by the same name of Moses and whose personalities we have to distinguish from each other. All of these dualities are the necessary consequences of the first one: the fact that one portion of the people had an experience which must be regarded as traumatic and which the other portion escaped. Beyond this there would be a very great deal to discuss, to explain and to assert. Only thus would an interest in our purely historical study find its true justification. What the real nature of a tradition resides in, and what its special power rests on, how impossible it is to dispute the personal influence upon world-history of individual great men, what sacrilege one commits against the splendid diversity of human life if one recognizes only those motives which arise from material needs, from what sources some ideas (and particularly religious ones) derive their power to subject both men and peoples to their yoke – to study all this in the special case of Jewish history would be an alluring task. To continue my work on such lines as these would be to find a link with the statements I put forward twenty-five years ago in *Totem and Taboo* [1912–13]. But I no longer feel that I have the strength to do so.

III
MOSES, HIS PEOPLE AND MONOTHEIST RELIGION

PART I

PREFATORY NOTE I
([Vienna] before March 1938)

WITH the audacity of one who has little or nothing to lose,
I propose for a second time to break a well-grounded intention
and to add to my two essays on Moses in *Imago*[1] the final
portion which I have held back. I ended the last essay with an
assertion that I knew my strength would not be enough for
this. By that I meant, of course, the weakening of creative
powers which goes along with old age;[2] but I was thinking
of another obstacle as well.

We are living in a specially remarkable period. We find to
our astonishment that progress has allied itself with barbarism.
In Soviet Russia they have set about improving the living
conditions of some hundred millions of people who were held
firmly in subjection. They have been rash enough to withdraw
the 'opium' of religion from them and have been wise enough
to give them a reasonable amount of sexual liberty; but at the
same time they have submitted them to the most cruel coercion
and robbed them of any possibility of freedom of thought.
With similar violence, the Italian people are being trained up

1. [Essays I and II above.]
2. I do not share the opinion of my contemporary Bernard Shaw, that
human beings would only achieve anything good if they could live to be
three hundred years old. A prolongation of life would achieve nothing unless
many other fundamental changes were to be made in the conditions of life.

to orderliness and a sense of duty. We feel it as a relief from an oppressive apprehension when we see in the case of the German people that a relapse into almost prehistoric barbarism can occur as well without being attached to any progressive ideas. In any case, things have so turned out that to-day the conservative democracies have become the guardians of cultural advance and that, strange to say, it is precisely the institution of the Catholic Church which puts up a powerful defence against the spread of this danger to civilization – the Church which has hitherto been the relentless foe to freedom of thought and to advances towards the discovery of the truth!

We are living here in a Catholic country under the protection of that Church, uncertain how long that protection will hold out. But so long as it lasts, we naturally hesitate to do anything that would be bound to arouse the Church's hostility. This is not cowardice, but prudence. The new enemy, to whom we want to avoid being of service, is more dangerous than the old one with whom we have already learnt to come to terms. The psychoanalytic researches which we carry on are in any case viewed with suspicious attention by Catholicism. I will not maintain that this is unjustly so. If our work leads us to a conclusion which reduces religion to a neurosis of humanity and explains its enormous power in the same way as a neurotic compulsion in our individual patients, we may be sure of drawing the resentment of our ruling powers down upon us. Not that I should have anything to say that would be new or that I did not say clearly a quarter of a century ago:[1] but it has been forgotten in the meantime and it could not be without effect if I repeated it to-day and illustrated it from an example which offers a standard for all religious foundations. It would probably lead to our being prohibited from practising psycho-analysis. Such violent methods of suppression are, indeed, by no means alien to the Church; the fact is rather that it feels it as an invasion of its privileges if someone else makes use of those methods. But psychoanalysis, which in the course of my long life has gone everywhere, still possesses no home that

1. [In *Totem and Taboo* (1912–13).]

could be more valuable for it than the city in which it was born and grew up.

I do not only think but I *know* that I shall let myself be deterred by this second obstacle, by the external danger, from publishing the last portion of my study on Moses. I have made yet another attempt to get the difficulty out of the way, by telling myself that my fears are based on an over-estimation of my own personal importance: that it will probably be a matter of complete indifference to the authorities what I choose to write about Moses and the origin of monotheist religions. But I feel uncertain in my judgement of this. It seems to me much more possible that malice and sensationalism will counterbalance any lack of recognition of me in the contemporary world's judgement. So I shall not give this work to the public. But that need not prevent my writing it. Especially as I have written it down already once, two years ago,[1] so that I have only to revise it and attach it to the two essays that have preceded it. It may then be preserved in concealment till some day the time arrives when it may venture without danger into the light, or till someone who has reached the same conclusions and opinions can be told: 'there was someone in darker times who thought the same as you!'

1. [Freud seems in fact to have written it originally *four* years previously, in 1934, and perhaps to have given it a first major revision in 1936. See above, pp. 240–41.]

The quite special difficulties which have weighed on me during my composition of this study relating to the figure of Moses – internal doubts as well as external obstacles – have resulted in this third and concluding essay being introduced by two different prefaces, which contradict each other and indeed cancel each other out. For in the short space of time between the two there has been a fundamental change in the author's circumstances. At the earlier date I was living under the protection of the Catholic Church, and was afraid that the publication of my work would result in the loss of that protection and would conjure up a prohibition upon the work of the adherents and students of psychoanalysis in Austria. Then, suddenly, came the German invasion and Catholicism proved, to use the words of the Bible, 'a broken reed'. In the certainty that I should now be persecuted not only for my line of thought but also for my 'race' – accompanied by many of my friends, I left the city which, from my early childhood, had been my home for seventy-eight years.

I met with the friendliest reception in lovely, free, magnanimous England. Here I now live, a welcome guest; I can breathe a sigh of relief now that the weight has been taken off me and that I am once more able to speak and write – I had almost said 'and think' – as I wish or as I must. I venture to bring the last portion of my work before the public.

There are no external obstacles remaining, or at least none to be frightened of. In the few weeks of my stay here I have received countless greetings from friends who were pleased at my arrival, and from unknown and indeed uninvolved strangers who only wanted to give expression to their satisfaction at my having found freedom and safety here. And in addition there arrived, with a frequency surprising to a

foreigner, communications of another sort, which were concerned with the state of my soul, which pointed out to me
the way of Christ and sought to enlighten me on the future
of Israel. The good people who wrote in this way cannot have
known much about me; but I expect that when this work
about Moses becomes known, in a translation, among my new
compatriots, I shall forfeit enough of the sympathy which a
number of other people as well now feel for me.

As regards *internal* difficulties, a political revolution and a
change of domicile could alter nothing. No less than before,
I feel uncertain in the face of my own work; I lack the consciousness of unity and of belonging together which should exist
between an author and his work. It is not as though there were
an absence of conviction in the correctness of my conclusion.
I acquired that a quarter of a century ago when in 1912 I wrote
my book about *Totem and Taboo*, and it has only grown firmer
since. From that time I have never doubted that religious
phenomena are only to be understood on the pattern of the
individual neurotic symptoms familiar to us – as the return of
long since forgotten, important events in the primaeval history
of the human family – and that they have to thank precisely
this origin for their compulsive character and that, accordingly,
they are effective on human beings by force of the historical
truth[1] of their content. My uncertainty sets in only when I
ask myself whether I have succeeded in proving these theses
in the example which I have chosen here of Jewish monotheism.
To my critical sense this book, which takes its start from the
man Moses, appears like a dancer balancing on the tip of one
toe. If I could not find support in an analytic interpretation of
the exposure myth and could not pass from there to Sellin's
suspicion about the end of Moses, the whole thing would have
had to remain unwritten. In any case, let us now take the plunge.

1. [See below, p. 376 ff.]

A

The Historical Premiss[1]

Here, then, is the historical background of the events which have absorbed our interest. As a result of the conquests of the Eighteenth Dynasty, Egypt became a world-empire. The new imperialism was reflected in the development of the religious ideas, if not of the whole people, at least of its ruling and intellectually active upper stratum. Under the influence of the priests of the sun-god at On (Heliopolis), strengthened perhaps by impulses from Asia, the idea arose of a universal god Aten to whom restriction to a single country and a single people no longer applied. In the young Amenophis IV a Pharaoh came to the throne who had no higher interest than the development of this idea of a god. He promoted the religion of Aten into the state religion, and through him the universal god became the *only* god: everything that was told of other gods was deceit and lies. With magnificent inflexibility he resisted every temptation to magical thought, and he rejected the illusion, so dear to Egyptians in particular, of a life after death. In an astonishing presentiment of later scientific discovery he recognized in the energy of solar radiation the source of all life on earth and worshipped it as the symbol of the power of his god. He boasted of his joy in the creation and of his life in Ma'at (truth and justice).

This is the first and perhaps the clearest case of a monotheist religion in human history; a deeper insight into the historical and psychological determinants of its origin would be of immeasurable value. Care has however been taken that none too much information about the Aten religion should reach us. Already under Akhenaten's feeble successors all that he had

1. I begin with a *résumé* of the findings of my second study on Moses, the purely historical one. Those findings will not be submitted here to any fresh criticism, since they form the premiss to the psychological discussions which start out from them and constantly go back to them.

created collapsed. The vengeance of the priesthood which he had suppressed raged against his memory; the Aten religion was abolished, the capital city of the Pharaoh, who was branded as a criminal, was destroyed and plundered. In about 1350 B.C. the Eighteenth Dynasty came to an end; after a period of anarchy, order was restored by general Haremhab, who reigned till 1315 B.C. Akhenaten's reform seemed to be an episode doomed to be forgotten.

Thus far what is established historically; and now our hypothetical sequel begins. Among those in Akhenaten's *entourage* there was a man who was perhaps called Tuthmosis, like many other people at that time[1] – the name is not of great importance except that its second component must have been '–emose'. He was in a high position and a convinced adherent of the Aten religion, but, in contrast to the meditative king, he was energetic and passionate. For him the death of Akhenaten and the abolition of his religion meant the end of all his expectations. He could remain in Egypt only as an outlaw or as a renegade. Perhaps as governor of the frontier province he had come in contact with a Semitic tribe which had immigrated into it a few generations earlier. Under the necessity of his disappointment and loneliness he turned to these foreigners and with them sought compensation for his losses. He chose them as his people and tried to realize his ideals in them. After he had left Egypt with them, accompanied by his followers, he made them holy by the mark of circumcision, gave them laws and introduced them into the doctrines of the Aten religion, which the Egyptians had just thrown off. The precepts which this man Moses gave to his Jews may have been even harsher than those of his master and teacher Akhenaten, and he may, too, have given up dependence on the sun-god of On, to which Akhenaten had continued to adhere.

We must take the period of the interregnum after 1350 B.C. as the date of the Exodus from Egypt. The interval of time

1. Such as, for instance, the sculptor whose studio was found at Tell el-'Amarna.

which followed, up to the completion of the occupation of the land of Canaan, is particularly inscrutable. Modern historical research has been able to extract two facts from the obscurity which the Biblical narrative has left, or rather created, at this point. The first of these facts, discovered by Ernst Sellin, is that the Jews, who, even by the account in the Bible, were headstrong and unruly towards their law-giver and leader, rose against him one day, killed him and threw off the religion of the Aten which had been imposed on them, just as the Egyptians had thrown it off earlier. The second fact, demonstrated by Eduard Meyer, is that those Jews who had returned from Egypt united later on with closely related tribes in the region between Palestine, the Sinai Peninsula and Arabia, and that there, in a well-watered locality named Kadesh, under the influence of the Arabian Midianites, they took on a new religion, the worship of the volcano god Yahweh. Soon after this they were ready to invade Canaan as conquerors.

The chronological relations of these two events to each other and to the Exodus from Egypt are very uncertain. The closest historical point of reference is provided by a stela of the Pharaoh Merenptah (who reigned till 1215 B.C.) which in the course of a report on campaigns in Syria and Palestine names 'Israel' among the defeated enemy. If we take the date of this stela as a *terminus ad quem*, we are left with about a century (from after 1350 to before 1215 B.C.) for the whole course of events, starting from the Exodus. It is possible, however, that the name 'Israel' did not yet relate to the tribes whose fortunes we are following and that in fact we have a longer interval at our disposal. The settlement in Canaan of what was later the Jewish people was certainly no rapidly completed conquest but took place in waves and over considerable periods of time. If we free ourselves from the limitation imposed by the Merenptah stela, we can all the more easily assign one generation (thirty years) to the period of Moses,[1] and allow at least two generations, but

---

1. This would correspond to the forty years of wandering in the wilderness of the Bible text [*Numbers*, xiv, 33].

probably more, to elapse up to the time of the union at Kadesh.[1] The interval between Kadesh and the irruption into Canaan need only be short. The Jewish tradition, as was shown in the preceding essay [p. 289], had good grounds for shortening the interval between the Exodus and the founding of the religion at Kadesh, while the reverse is in the interest of our account.

All this, however, is still history, an attempt to fill up the gaps in our historical knowledge and in part a repetition of my second essay in Imago [Essay II above]. Our interest follows the fortunes of Moses and of his doctrines, to which the rising of the Jews had only apparently put an end. From the account given by the Yahwist, which was written down in about 1000 B.C. but was certainly based on earlier records, we have discovered that the union and the founding of the religion at Kadesh were accompanied by a compromise in which the two sides are still easily distinguishable. The one partner was only concerned to disavow the novelty and foreign character of the god Yahweh and to increase his claim to the people's devotion; the other partner was anxious not to sacrifice to him precious memories of the liberation from Egypt and of the grand figure of the leader, Moses. The second side succeeded, too, in introducing both the fact and the man into the new account of prehistory, in retaining at least the external mark of the religion of Moses – circumcision – and possibly in establishing certain restrictions on the use of the name of the new god. As we have said, the representatives of these claims were the descendants of the followers of Moses, the Levites, who were separated from his contemporaries and compatriots by only a few generations and were still attached to his memory by a living recollection. The poetically embellished narrative which we attribute to the Yahwist, and to his later rival the Elohist, were like mausoleums beneath which, withdrawn from the knowledge of later generations, the true account of those early things – of the nature of the Mosaic religion and of the violent

1. Thus we should have about 1350 (or 1340)–1320 (or 1310) B.C. for the Moses period; 1260 B.C., or preferably later, for Kadesh; the Merenptah stela before 1215 B.C.

end of the great man – was, as it were, to find its eternal rest. And if we have guessed what happened correctly, there is nothing left about it that is puzzling; but it might very well have signified the final end of the Moses episode in the history of the Jewish people.

The remarkable thing, however, is that that was not the case – that the most powerful effects of the people's experience were to come to light only later and to force their way into reality in the course of many centuries. It is unlikely that Yahweh differed much in character from the gods of the surrounding peoples and tribes. It is true that he struggled with them, just as the peoples themselves fought with one another, but we cannot suppose that it came into the head of a Yahweh-worshipper of those days to deny the existence of the gods of Canaan or Moab or Amalek, and so on, any more than to deny the existence of the peoples who believed in them.

The monotheist idea, which had flared up with Akhenaten, had grown dark once more and was to remain in darkness for a long time to come. Finds in the island of Elephantine, just below the First Cataract of the Nile, have given us the surprising information that a Jewish military colony had been settled there for centuries, in whose temple, alongside of the chief god Yahu, two female deities were worshipped, one of them named Anat-Yahu. These Jews, it is true, were cut off from their mother-country and had not taken part in the religious development there; the Persian government of Egypt (of the fifth century B.C.) conveyed information to them of the new rules of worship issued from Jerusalem.[1] Going back to earlier times, we may say that the god Yahweh certainly bore no resemblance to the Mosaic god. Aten had been a pacifist like his representative on earth – or more properly, his prototype – the Pharaoh Akhenaten, who looked on passively while the world-empire conquered by his ancestors fell to pieces. No doubt Yahweh was better suited to a people who were starting out to occupy new homelands by force. And everything in

1. Auerbach, 2, 1936.

the Mosaic god that deserved admiration was quite beyond the comprehension of the primitive masses.

I have already said – and on that point I have been glad to be able to claim agreement with other writers – that the central fact of the development of the Jewish religion was that in the course of time the god Yahweh lost his own characteristics and grew more and more to resemble the old god of Moses, the Aten. It is true that differences remained to which one would be inclined at a first glance to attribute great importance; but these can easily be explained.

In Egypt Aten had begun to dominate during a fortunate period of established possession, and even when the empire began to totter, his worshippers had been able to turn away from the disturbance and continued to praise and to enjoy his creations. The Jewish people were fated to experience a series of grave trials and painful events; their god became harsh and severe and, as it were, wrapped in gloom. He retained the characteristic of being a universal god, reigning over all countries and peoples, but the fact that his worship had passed over from the Egyptians to the Jews found expression in the additional belief that the Jews were his chosen people whose special obligations would eventually meet with a special reward as well. It may not have been easy for the people to reconcile a belief in being preferred by their omnipotent god with the sad experiences of their unfortunate destiny. But they did not allow themselves to be shaken in their convictions; they increased their own sense of guilt in order to stifle their doubts of God, and it may be that they pointed at last to the 'inscrutable decrees of Providence', as pious people do to this day. If they felt inclined to wonder at his allowing one violent aggressor after another to arise and overthrow and maltreat them – Assyrians, Babylonians, Persians – they could yet recognize his power in the fact that all these evil foes were themselves conquered in turn and that their empires vanished.

In three important respects the later god of the Jews became in the end like the old Mosaic god. The first and decisive point is that he was truly acknowledged as the only god, beside

whom any other god was unthinkable. Akhenaten's monotheism was taken seriously by an entire people; indeed, that
people clung so much to this idea that it became the main
content of their intellectual life[1] and left them no interest for
other things. On this the people and the priesthood who had
become dominant among them were at one. But whereas the
priests exhausted their efforts in erecting the ceremonial for
his worship, they came in opposition to intense currents among
the people which sought to revive two others of the doctrines
of Moses about his god. The voices of the Prophets never tired
of declaring that God despised ceremonial and sacrifice and
required only that people should believe in him and lead a life
in truth and justice. And when they praised the simplicity and
holiness of life in the wilderness they were certainly under the
influence of the Mosaic ideals.

It is time to raise the question of whether there is any need
whatever to call in the influence of Moses as a cause of the
final form taken by the Jewish idea of God, or whether it
would not be enough to assume a spontaneous development
to higher intellectuality[2] during a cultural life extending over
hundreds of years. There are two things to be said about this
possible explanation which would put an end to all our puzzling
conjectures. First, that it explains nothing. In the case of the
Greeks – unquestionably a most highly gifted people – the
same conditions did not lead to monotheism but to a disintegration of their polytheist religion and to the beginning
of philosophical thought. In Egypt, so far as we can understand,
monotheism grew up as a by-product of imperialism: God
was a reflection of the Pharaoh who was the absolute ruler of
a great world-empire. With the Jews, political conditions were
highly unfavourable for the development from the idea of an
exclusive national god to that of a universal ruler of the world.
And where did this tiny and powerless nation find the arrogance

1. ['*Geistesleben.*' Cf. the next footnote.]
2. ['*Geistigkeit.*' See the discussion of the rendering of this word in the
footnote on p. 330 below.]

to declare itself the favourite child of the great Lord? The problem of the origin of monotheism among the Jews would thus remain unsolved, or we should have to be content with the common answer that it is the expression of the peculiar religious genius of that people. Genius is well known to be incomprehensible and irresponsible, and we ought therefore not to bring it up as an explanation till every other solution has failed us.[1]

In addition to this, we come upon the fact that Jewish records and historical writings themselves point us the way, by asserting most definitely – this time without contradicting themselves – that the idea of a single god was brought to the people by Moses. If there is an objection to the trustworthiness of this assurance, it is that the priestly revision of the text we have before us obviously traces far too much back to Moses. Institutions such as the ritual ordinances, which date unmistakably from later times, are given out as Mosaic commandments with the plain intention of lending them authority. This certainly gives us ground for suspicion, but not enough for a rejection. For the deeper motive for an exaggeration of this kind is obvious. The priestly narrative seeks to establish continuity between its contemporary period and the remote Mosaic past; it seeks to disavow precisely what we have described as the most striking fact about Jewish religious history, namely that there is a yawning gap between the law-giving of Moses and the later Jewish religion – a gap which was at first filled by the worship of Yahweh, and was only slowly patched up afterwards. It disputes this course of events by every possible means, though its historical correctness is established beyond any doubt, since, in the particular treatment given to the Biblical text, superabundant evidence has been left to prove it. Here the priestly revision has attempted something similar

1. This same consideration applies, too, to the remarkable case of William Shakespeare. [An allusion to Freud's view that 'Shakespeare' was the pseudonym of Edward de Vere, Earl of Oxford. A letter from Freud arguing in favour of this opinion is included in the third volume of Jones's biography (1957, 487–8).]

to the tendentious distortion which made the new god Yahweh into the god of the Patriarchs [p. 284]. If we take this motive of the Priestly Code into account, we shall find it hard to withhold our belief from the assertion that Moses really did himself give the monotheist idea to the Jews. We should be all the readier to give our assent since we can say where Moses derived this idea from, which the Jewish priests certainly knew no longer.

And here someone might ask what we gain by tracing Jewish to Egyptian monotheism. It merely pushes the problem a little way further back: it tells us nothing more of the genesis of the monotheist idea. The answer is that the question is not one of gain but of investigation. Perhaps we may learn something from it if we discover the real course of events.

B

THE LATENCY PERIOD AND TRADITION

We confess the belief, therefore, that the idea of a single god, as well as the rejection of magically effective ceremonial and the stress upon ethical demands made in his name, were in fact Mosaic doctrines, to which no attention was paid to begin with, but which, after a long interval had elapsed, came into operation and eventually became permanently established. How are we to explain a delayed effect of this kind and where do we meet with a similar phenomenon?

It occurs to us at once that such things are not infrequently to be found in the most various spheres and that they probably come about in a number of ways which are understandable with greater or less ease. Let us take, for instance, the history of a new scientific theory, such as Darwin's theory of evolution. At first it met with embittered rejection and was violently disputed for decades; but it took no longer than a generation for it to be recognized as a great step forward towards truth. Darwin himself achieved the honour of a grave or cenotaph in Westminster Abbey. A case such as that leaves us little to unravel. The new truth awoke emotional resistances; these found expression in arguments by which the evidence in favour of the unpopular theory could be disputed; the struggle of opinions took up a certain length of time; from the first there were adherents and opponents; the number as well as the weight of the former kept on increasing till at last they gained the upper hand; during the whole time of the struggle the subject with which it was concerned was never forgotten. We are scarcely surprised that the whole course of events took a considerable length of time; and we probably do not sufficiently appreciate that what we are concerned with is a process in group psychology.

There is no difficulty in finding an analogy in the mental life of an individual corresponding precisely to this process. Such would be the case if a person learnt something new to him which, on the ground of certain evidence, he ought to recognize as true, but which contradicts some of his wishes and shocks a few convictions that are precious to him. Thereupon he will hesitate, seek for reasons to enable him to throw doubts on this new thing, and for a while will struggle with himself, till finally he admits to himself: 'All the same it *is* so, though it's not easy for me to accept it, though it's distressing to me to have to believe it.' What we learn from this is merely that it takes time for the reasoning activity of the ego to overcome the objections that are maintained by strong affective cathexes. The similarity between this case and the one we are endeavouring to understand is not very great.

The next example we turn to appears to have even less in common with our problem. It may happen that a man who has experienced some frightful accident – a railway collision, for instance – leaves the scene of the event apparently uninjured. In the course of the next few weeks, however, he develops a number of severe psychical and motor symptoms which can only be traced to his shock, the concussion or whatever else it was. He now has a 'traumatic neurosis'. It is a quite unintelligible – that is to say, a new – fact. The time that has passed between the accident and the first appearance of the symptoms is described as the 'incubation period', in a clear allusion to the pathology of infectious diseases. On reflection, it must strike us that, in spite of the fundamental difference between the two cases – the problem of traumatic neurosis and that of Jewish monotheism – there is nevertheless one point of agreement: namely, in the characteristic that might be described as 'latency'. According to our assured hypothesis, in the history of the Jewish religion there was a long period after the defection from the religion of Moses during which no sign was to be detected of the monotheist idea, of the contempt for ceremonial or of the great emphasis on ethics. We are thus prepared for the possibility that the solution of our problem is to be looked for in a particular psychological situation.

We have already repeatedly described what happened at Kadesh when the two portions of what was later to be the Jewish people came together to receive a new religion. In those, on the one hand, who had been in Egypt, memories of the Exodus and of the figure of Moses were still so strong and vivid that they demanded their inclusion in an account of early times. They were grandchildren, perhaps, of people who had known Moses himself, and some of them still felt themselves Egyptians and bore Egyptian names. But they had good motives for repressing the memory of the fate with which their leader and lawgiver had met. The determining purpose of the other portion of the people was to glorify the new god and to dispute his being foreign. Both portions had the same interest in disavowing the fact of their having had an earlier religion and the nature of its content. So it was that the first compromise came about, and it was probably soon recorded in writing. The people who had come from Egypt had brought writing and the desire to write history along with them; but it was to be a long time before historical writing realized that it was pledged to unswerving truthfulness. To begin with it had no scruples about shaping its narratives according to the needs and purposes of the moment, as though it had not yet recognized the concept of falsification. As a result of these circumstances a discrepancy was able to grow up between the written record and the oral transmission of the same material – *tradition*. What had been omitted or changed in the written record might very well have been preserved intact in tradition. Tradition was a supplement but at the same time a contradiction to historical writing. It was less subjected to the influence of distorting purposes and perhaps at some points quite exempt from them, and it might therefore be more truthful than the account that had been recorded in writing. Its trustworthiness, however, suffered from the fact that it was less stable and definite than the written account and exposed to numerous changes and alterations when it was handed on from one generation to another by oral communication. A tradition of such a kind might meet with various sorts of fate. What we should most expect would be that it would be crushed by the written account, would be unable to stand up against it, would become more and more shadowy and would finally pass into oblivion. But it might meet with other fates: one of these would be that the tradition itself would end in a written record, and we shall have to deal with yet others as we proceed.

The phenomenon of latency in the history of the Jewish religion, with which we are dealing, may be explained, then, by the circumstance that the facts and ideas which were intentionally disavowed by what may be called the official historians were in fact never lost. Information about them persisted in traditions which survived among the people. As we are assured by Sellin, indeed, there was actually a tradition about the end of Moses which flatly contradicted the official account and was far nearer the truth. The same, we may assume, also applied to other things which apparently ceased to exist at the same time as Moses – to some of the contents of the Mosaic religion, which had been unacceptable to the majority of his contemporaries.

The remarkable fact with which we are here confronted is, however, that these traditions, instead of becoming weaker with time, became more and more powerful in the course of centuries, forced their way into the later revisions of the official accounts and finally showed themselves strong enough to have a decisive influence on the thoughts and actions of the people. The determinants which made this outcome possible are for the moment, it is true, outside our knowledge.

This fact is so remarkable that we feel justified in looking at it once again. Our problem is comprised in it. The Jewish people had abandoned the Aten religion brought to them by Moses and had turned to the worship of another god who differed little from the Baalim [local gods] of the neighbouring peoples. All the tendentious efforts of later times failed to disguise this shameful fact. But the Mosaic religion had not vanished without leaving a trace; some sort of memory of it had kept alive – a possibly obscured and distorted tradition. And it was this tradition of a great past which continued to operate (from the background, as it were), which gradually acquired more and more power over people's minds and which in the end succeeded in changing the god Yahweh into the Mosaic god and in re-awakening into life the religion of Moses that had been introduced and then abandoned long centuries before. That a tradition thus sunk in oblivion should exercise such a powerful effect on the mental life of a people is an unfamiliar idea to us. We find ourselves here in the field of group psychology, where we do not feel at home. We shall look about for analogies, for facts that are at least of a similar nature, even though in different fields. And facts of that sort are, I believe, to be found.

During the period at which, among the Jews, the return of the religion of Moses was in preparation, the Greek people found themselves in possession of an exceedingly rich store of tribal legends and hero-myths. It is believed that the ninth or eighth century B.C. saw the origin of the two Homeric epics, which drew their material from this circle of legends. With our present psychological insight we could, long before Schliemann and Evans, have raised the question of where it was that the Greeks obtained all the legendary material which was worked over by Homer and the great Attic dramatists in their masterpieces. The answer would have had to be that this people had probably experienced in their prehistory a period of external brilliance and cultural efflorescence which had perished in a historical catastrophe and of which an obscure tradition survived in these legends. The archaeological researches of our days have now confirmed this suspicion, which in the past would certainly have been pronounced too daring. These researches have uncovered the evidences of the impressive Minoan–Mycenaean civilization, which had probably already come to an end on the mainland of Greece before 1250 B.C. There is scarcely a hint at it to be found in the Greek historians of a later age: at most a remark that there was a time when the Cretans exercised command of the sea, and the name of King Minos and of his palace, the Labyrinth. That is all, and beyond it nothing has remained but the traditions which were seized on by the poets.

National epics of other peoples – Germans, Indians, Finns – have come to light as well. It is the business of historians of literature to investigate whether we may assume the same determinants for their origin as with the Greeks. Such an investigation would, I believe, yield a positive result. Here is the determinant which we recognize: a piece of prehistory which, immediately after it, would have been bound to appear rich in content, important, splendid, and always, perhaps, heroic, but which lies so far back, in such remote times, that only an obscure and incomplete tradition informs later generations of it. Surprise has been felt that the epic as an art-form has become extinct in later times. The explanation may be that its determining cause no longer exists. The old material was used up and for all later events historical writing took the place of tradition. The greatest heroic deeds of our days have not been able to inspire an epic, and even Alexander the Great had a right to complain that he would find no Homer.

Long-past ages have a great and often puzzling attraction for men's imagination. Whenever they are dissatisfied with their present surroundings – and this happens often enough – they turn back to the past and hope that they will now be able to prove the truth of the unextinguishable dream of a golden age.[1] They are probably still under the spell of their childhood, which is presented to them by their not impartial memory as a time of uninterrupted bliss.

If all that is left of the past are the incomplete and blurred memories which we call tradition, this offers an artist a peculiar attraction, for in that case he is free to fill in the gaps in memory according to the desires of his imagination and to picture the period which he wishes to reproduce according to his intentions. One might almost say that the vaguer a tradition has become the more serviceable it becomes for a poet. We need not therefore be surprised at the importance of tradition for imaginative writing, and the analogy with the manner in which epics are determined will make us more inclined to accept the strange hypothesis that it was the tradition of Moses which, for the Jews, altered the worship of Yahweh in the direction of the old Mosaic religion. But in other respects the two cases are still too different. On the one hand the outcome is a poem and on the other a religion; and in the latter instance we have assumed that, under the spur of tradition, it was reproduced with a faithfulness for which the instance of the epic can of course offer no counterpart. Accordingly enough of our problem is left over to justify a need for more apposite analogies.

C

The Analogy

The only satisfying analogy to the remarkable course of events that we have found in the history of the Jewish religion lies in an apparently remote field; but it is very complete, and approaches identity. In it we once more come upon the phenomenon of latency, the emergence of unintelligible mani-

---

1. This was the situation on which Macaulay based his *Lays of Ancient Rome*. He put himself in the place of a minstrel who, depressed by the confused party strife of his own day, presented his hearers with the self-sacrifice, the unity and the patriotism of their ancestors.

festations calling for an explanation and an early, and later forgotten, event as a necessary determinant. We also find the characteristic of compulsion, which forces itself on the mind along with an overpowering of logical thought – a feature which did not come into account, for instance, in the genesis of the epic.

This analogy is met with in psychopathology, in the genesis of human neuroses – in a field, that is to say, belonging to the psychology of individuals, while religious phenomena have of course to be reckoned as part of group psychology. We shall see that this analogy is not so surprising as might at first be thought – indeed that it is more like a postulate.

We give the name of *traumas* to those impressions, experienced early and later forgotten, to which we attach such great importance in the aetiology of the neuroses. We may leave on one side the question of whether the aetiology of the neuroses in general may be regarded as traumatic. The obvious objection to this is that it is not possible in every case to discover a manifest trauma in the neurotic subject's earliest history. We must often resign ourselves to saying that all we have before us is an unusual, abnormal reaction to experiences and demands which affect everyone, but as worked over and dealt with by other people in another manner which may be called normal. When we have nothing else at our disposal for explaining a neurosis but hereditary and constitutional dispositions, we are naturally tempted to say that it was not acquired but developed.

But in this connection two points must be stressed. Firstly, the genesis of a neurosis invariably goes back to very early impressions in childhood.[1] Secondly, it is true that there are cases which are distinguished as being 'traumatic' because their effects go back unmistakably to one or more powerful impressions in these early times – impressions which have escaped being dealt with normally, so that one is inclined to judge that

1. This therefore makes it nonsensical to say that one is practising psychoanalysis if one excludes from examination and consideration precisely these earliest periods – as happens in some quarters. [An allusion to the theories and methods of C. G. Jung.]

if they had not occurred the neurosis would not have come about either. It would be enough for our purposes if we were obliged to restrict the analogy we are in search of to these traumatic cases. But the gap between the two groups [of cases] appears not to be unbridgeable. It is quite possible to unite the two aetiological determinants under a single conception; it is merely a question of how one defines 'traumatic'. If we may assume that the experience acquires its traumatic character only as a result of a quantitative factor – that is to say, that in every case it is an excess in demand that is responsible for an experience evoking unusual pathological reactions – then we can easily arrive at the expedient of saying that something acts as a trauma in the case of one constitution but in the case of another would have no such effect. In this way we reach the concept of a sliding 'complemental series' as it is called,[1] in which two factors converge in fulfilling an aetiological requirement. A less of one factor is balanced by a more of the other; as a rule both factors operate together and it is only at the two ends of the series that there can be any question of a simple motive being at work. After mentioning this, we can disregard the distinction between traumatic and non-traumatic aetiologies as irrelevant to the analogy we are in search of.

In spite of a risk of repetition, it will perhaps be as well to bring together here the facts which comprise the analogy that is significant for us. They are as follows. Our researches have shown that what we call the phenomena (symptoms) of a neurosis are the result of certain experiences and impressions which for that very reason we regard as aetiological traumas. We now have two tasks before us: to discover (1) the common characteristics of these experiences and (2) those of neurotic symptoms, and in doing so we need not avoid drawing a somewhat schematic picture.

(1) (a) All these traumas occur in early childhood up to about the fifth year. Impressions from the time at which a child is beginning to talk stand out as being of particular

1. [See Lecture 22 in the *Introductory Lectures* (1916–17), *P.F.L.*, **1**, 392.]

interest; the periods between the ages of two and four seem to be the most important; it cannot be determined with certainty how long after birth this period of receptivity begins. (b) The experiences in question are as a rule totally forgotten, they are not accessible to memory and fall within the period of infantile amnesia, which is usually broken into by a few separate mnemic residues, what are known as 'screen memories'.[1] (c) They relate to impressions of a sexual and aggressive nature, and no doubt also to early injuries to the ego (narcissistic mortifications). In this connection it should be remarked that such young children make no sharp distinction between sexual and aggressive acts, as they do later. (Cf. the misunderstanding of the sexual act in a sadistic sense.[2]) The predominance of the sexual factor is, of course, most striking and calls for theoretical consideration.

These three points – the very early appearance of these experiences (during the first five years of life), the fact of their being forgotten and their sexual-aggressive content – are closely interconnected. The traumas are either experiences on the subject's own body or sense perceptions, mostly of something seen and heard – that is, experiences or impressions. The interconnection of these three points is established by a theory, a product of the work of analysis which alone can bring about a knowledge of the forgotten experiences, or, to put it more vividly but also more incorrectly, bring them back to memory. The theory is that, in contrast to popular opinion, the sexual life of human beings (or what corresponds to it later on) exhibits an early efflorescence which comes to an end at about the fifth year and is followed by what is known as the period of latency (till puberty) in which there is no further development of sexuality and indeed what has been attained undergoes a retrogression. This theory is confirmed by the anatomical investigation of the growth of the internal genitalia; it leads us to suppose that the human race is descended from a species of animal which reached sexual maturity in five years and

1. [See Lecture 13 in the *Introductory Lectures* (1916–17), *P.F.L.*, **1**, 237.]
2. 'The Sexual Theories of Children' (1908*c*), *P.F.L.*, **7**, 198–200.

rouses a suspicion that the postponement of sexual life and its diphasic onset [in two waves] are intimately connected with the history of hominization.[1] Human beings appear to be the only animal organisms with a latency period and sexual retardation of this kind. Investigations on the primates (which, so far as I know, are not available) would be indispensable for testing this theory. It cannot be a matter of indifference psychologically that the period of infantile amnesia coincides with this early period of sexuality. It may be that this state of things provides the true determinant for the possibility of neurosis, which is in a sense a human prerogative and from this point of view appears as a vestige – a 'survival'[2] – of primaeval times like certain portions of our bodily anatomy.

(2) Two points must be stressed in regard to the common characteristics or peculiarities of neurotic phenomena: (a) The effects of traumas are of two kinds, positive and negative. The former are attempts to bring the trauma into operation once again – that is, to remember the forgotten experience or, better still, to make it real, to experience a repetition of it anew, or, even if it was only an early emotional relationship, to revive it in an analogous relationship with someone else. We summarize these efforts under the name of 'fixations' to the trauma and as a 'compulsion to repeat'. They may be taken up into what passes as a normal ego and, as permanent trends in it, may lend it unalterable character-traits, although, or rather precisely because, their true basis and historical origin are forgotten. Thus a man who has spent his childhood in an excessive and to-day forgotten attachment to his mother, may spend his whole life looking for a wife on whom he can make himself dependent and by whom he can arrange to be nourished and supported. A girl who was made the object of a sexual seduction in her early childhood may direct her later sexual life so as constantly to provoke similar attacks. It may easily be guessed that from such discoveries about the problem of

1. ['*Menschwerdung*', 'the process of becoming human'.]
2. [In English in the original.]

neurosis we can penetrate to an understanding of the formation of character in general.

The negative reactions follow the opposite aim: that nothing of the forgotten traumas shall be remembered and nothing repeated. We can summarize them as 'defensive reactions'. Their principal expression are what are called 'avoidances', which may be intensified into 'inhibitions' and 'phobias'. These negative reactions too make the most powerful contributions to the stamping of character. Fundamentally they are just as much fixations to the trauma as their opposites, except that they are fixations with a contrary purpose. The symptoms of neurosis in the narrower sense are compromises in which both the trends proceeding from traumas come together, so that the share, now of one and now of the other tendency, finds preponderant expression in them. This opposition between the reactions sets up conflicts which in the ordinary course of events can reach no conclusion.

(b) All these phenomena, the symptoms as well as the restrictions on the ego and the stable character-changes, have a *compulsive* quality: that is to say that they have great psychical intensity and at the same time exhibit a far-reaching independence of the organization of the other mental processes, which are adjusted to the demands of the real external world and obey the laws of logical thinking. They [the pathological phenomena] are insufficiently or not at all influenced by external reality, pay no attention to it or to its psychical representatives, so that they may easily come into active opposition to both of them. They are, one might say, a State within a State, an inaccessible party, with which co-operation is impossible, but which may succeed in overcoming what is known as the normal party and forcing it into its service. If this happens, it implies a domination by an internal psychical reality over the reality of the external world and the path to a psychosis lies open.[1] Even if things do not go so far, the practical importance of this situation can scarcely be over-estimated. The inhibition upon the life of those who are

1. [Cf. the Editor's footnote on p. 379 below.]

dominated by a neurosis and their incapacity for living constitute a most important factor in a human society and we may recognize in their condition a direct expression of their fixation to an early portion of their past.

And now let us inquire about latency, which, in view of the analogy, is bound to interest us especially. A trauma in childhood may be followed immediately by a neurotic outbreak, an infantile neurosis, with an abundance of efforts at defence, and accompanied by the formation of symptoms. This neurosis may last a considerable time and cause marked disturbances, but it may also run a latent course and be overlooked. As a rule defence retains the upper hand in it; in any case alterations of the ego,[1] comparable to scars, are left behind. It is only rarely that an infantile neurosis continues without interruption into an adult one. Far more often it is succeeded by a period of apparently undisturbed development – a course of things which is supported or made possible by the intervention of the physiological period of latency. Not until later does the change take place with which the definitive neurosis becomes manifest as a belated effect of the trauma. This occurs either at the irruption of puberty or some while later. In the former case it happens because the instincts, intensified by physical maturation, are able now to take up the struggle again in which they were at first defeated by the defence. In the latter case it happens because the reactions and alterations of the ego brought about by the defence now prove a hindrance in dealing with the new tasks of life, so that severe conflicts come about between the demands of the real external world and the ego, which seeks to maintain the organization which

1. [The relations between alteration of the ego, anticathexis and reaction-formation were first explained in *Inhibitions, Symptoms and Anxiety* (1926*d*), P.F.L., **10**, 317–19 and 322–4. The *therapeutic* alteration of the ego (not considered here) is regarded in Freud's later writings as the undoing of those alterations of the ego that have taken place as a result of defence mechanisms. Cf. Section V of 'Analysis Terminable and Interminable' (1937*c*) and Chapter VI of *Outline of Psycho-Analysis* (1940*a*).]

it has painstakingly achieved in its defensive struggle. The phenomenon of a latency of the neurosis between the first reactions to the trauma and the later outbreak of the illness must be regarded as typical. This latter illness may also be looked upon as an attempt at cure – as an effort once more to reconcile with the rest those portions of the ego that have been split off by the influence of the trauma and to unite them into a powerful whole *vis-à-vis* the external world. An attempt of this kind seldom succeeds, however, unless the work of analysis comes to its help, and even then not always; it ends often enough in a complete devastation or fragmentation of the ego or in its being overwhelmed by the portion which was early split off and which is dominated by the trauma.

In order to convince the reader, it would be necessary to give detailed reports of the life histories of numerous neurotics. But in view of the diffuseness and difficulty of the topic, this would completely destroy the character of the present work. It would turn into a monograph on the theory of the neuroses and even so would probably only have an effect on that minority of readers who have chosen the study and practice of psychoanalysis as their life-work. Since I am addressing myself here to a wider audience, I can only beg the reader to grant a certain provisional credence to the abridged account I have given above; and this must be accompanied by an admission on my part that the implications to which I am now leading him need only be accepted if the theories on which they are based turn out to be correct.

Nevertheless, I can attempt to tell the story of a single case which exhibits with special clarity some of the characteristics of a neurosis which I have mentioned. We must not expect, of course, that a single case will show everything and we need not feel disappointed if its subject-matter is far removed from the topic for which we are seeking an analogy.

A little boy, who, as is so often the case in middle-class families, shared his parents' bedroom during the first years of his life, had repeated, and indeed regular, opportunities of observing sexual acts between his parents – of seeing some things and hearing still more – at an age when he had scarcely learnt to speak. In his later neurosis, which broke out immediately after his first spontaneous emission, the earliest and most troublesome symptom was a disturbance of sleep. He was extraordinarily sensitive to noises at night and, once he was woken up, was unable to go to sleep again. This disturbance of sleep was a true compromise-symptom. On the one hand it was an expression of his defence against the things he had experienced at night, and on the other an attempt to re-establish the waking state in which he was able to listen to those impressions.

The child was aroused prematurely by observations of this kind to an aggressive masculinity and began to excite his little penis with his hand and to attempt various sexual attacks on his mother, thus identifying himself with his father, in whose place he was putting himself. This went on until at last his mother forbade him to touch his penis and further threatened that she would tell his father, who would punish him by taking his sinful organ away. This threat of castration had an extraordinarily powerful traumatic effect on the boy. He gave up his sexual activity and altered his character. Instead of identifying himself with his father, he was afraid of him, adopted a passive attitude to him and, by occasional naughti- nesses, provoked him into administering corporal punishment; this had a sexual meaning for him, so that he was thus able to identify himself with his ill-treated mother. He clung to his mother herself more and more anxiously, as though he could not do without her love for a single moment, since he saw in it a protection against the danger of castration which threatened him from his father. In this modification of the Oedipus complex he passed his latency period, which was free from any marked disturbances. He became an exemplary boy and was quite successful at school.

So far we have followed the immediate effect of the trauma and have confirmed the fact of latency.

The arrival of puberty brought with it the manifest neurosis and disclosed its second main symptom – sexual impotence. He had forfeited the sensitivity of his penis, did not attempt to touch it, did not venture to approach a woman for sexual purposes. His sexual activity remained limited to psychical masturbation accompanied by sadistic-masochistic phantasies in which it was not hard to recognize off-shoots of his early observations of intercourse between his parents. The wave of intensified masculinity which puberty brought along with it was employed in furious hatred of his father and insubordination to him. This extreme relation to his father, reckless to the pitch of self-destruction, was responsible as well for his failure in life and his conflicts with the external world. He must be a failure in his profession because his father had forced him into it. Nor did he make any friends and he was never on good terms with his superiors.

When, burdened by these symptoms and incapacities, he at last, after his father's death, had found a wife, there emerged in him, as though they were the core of his being, character-traits which made contact with him a hard task for those about him. He developed a completely egoistic, despotic, and brutal personality, which clearly felt a need to suppress and insult other people. It was a faithful copy of his father as he had formed a picture of him in his memory: that is to say, a revival of the identification with his father which in the past he had taken on as a little boy from sexual motives. In this part of the story we recognize the *return* of the repressed, which (along with the immediate effects of the trauma and the phenomenon of latency) we have described as among the essential features of a neurosis.

D

APPLICATION

Early trauma – defence – latency – outbreak of neurotic illness – partial return of the repressed. Such is the formula which we have laid down for the development of a neurosis. The reader is now invited to take the step of supposing that something occurred in the life of the human species similar to what occurs in the life of individuals: of supposing, that is, that here too events occurred of a sexually aggressive nature, which left behind them permanent consequences but were for the most part fended off and forgotten, and which after a long latency came into effect and created phenomena similar to symptoms in their structure and purpose.

We believe that we can guess these events and we propose to show that their symptom-like consequences are the phenomena of religion. Since the emergence of the idea of evolution no longer leaves room for doubt that the human race has a prehistory, and since this is unknown – that is, forgotten – a conclusion of this kind almost carries the weight of a postulate. When we learn that in both cases the operative and forgotten traumas relate to life in the human family, we can greet this as a highly welcome, unforeseen bonus which has not been called for by our discussions up to this point.

I put forward these assertions as much as a quarter of a century ago in my *Totem and Taboo* (1912–13) and I need only repeat them here. My construction starts out from a statement of Darwin's [1871, **2**, 362 f.] and takes in a hypothesis of Atkinson's [1903, 220 f.]. It asserts that in primaeval times primitive man lived in small hordes,[1] each under the domination of a powerful male. No date can be assigned to this, nor has it been synchronized with the geological epochs known to us: it is probable that these human creatures had not advanced far in the development of speech. An essential part of the construction is the hypothesis that the events I am about to describe occurred to all primitive men – that is, to all our ancestors. The story is told in an enormously condensed form, as though it had happened on a single occasion, while in fact it covered thousands of years and was repeated countless times during that long period. The strong male was lord and father of the entire horde and unrestricted in his power, which he

---

1. [Freud always used this term in the sense of a small and more or less organized group. See *Totem and Taboo*, p. 185 and *n*. 3.]

exercised with violence. All the females were his property – wives and daughters of his own horde and some, perhaps, robbed from other hordes. The lot of his sons was a hard one: if they roused their father's jealousy they were killed or castrated or driven out. Their only resource was to collect together in small communities, to get themselves wives by robbery, and, when one or other of them could succeed in it, to raise themselves into a position similar to their father's in the primal horde. For natural reasons, youngest sons occupied an exceptional position. They were protected by their mother's love, and were able to take advantage of their father's increasing age and succeed him on his death. We seem to detect echoes in legends and fairy tales both of the expulsion of elder sons and of the favouring of youngest sons.

The first decisive step towards a change in this sort of 'social' organization seems to have been that the expelled brothers, living in a community, united to overpower their father and, as was the custom in those days, devoured him raw. There is no need to balk at this cannibalism; it continued far into later times. The essential point, however, is that we attribute the same emotional attitudes to these primitive men that we are able to establish by analytic investigation in the primitives of the present day – in our children. We suppose, that is, that they not only hated and feared their father but also honoured him as a model, and that each of them wished to take his place in reality. We can, if so, understand the cannibalistic act as an attempt to ensure identification with him by incorporating a piece of him.

It must be supposed that after the parricide a considerable time elapsed during which the brothers disputed with one another for their father's heritage, which each of them wanted for himself alone. A realization of the dangers and uselessness of these struggles, a recollection of the act of liberation which they had accomplished together, and the emotional ties with one another which had arisen during the period of their expulsion, led at last to an agreement among them, a sort of social contract. The first form of a social organization came about with a *renunciation of instinct*,[1] a recognition of mutual *obligations*, the introduction of definite *institutions*, pronounced inviolable (holy) – that is to say, the beginnings of morality and justice. Each individual renounced his ideal of acquiring his father's position for himself and of possessing his mother and sisters. Thus the *taboo on incest* and the injunction to *exogamy* came about. A fair amount of the absolute power liberated by the removal of the father passed over to the women; there came a period of *matriarchy*. Recollection of their father persisted at this period of the 'fraternal alliance'. A powerful animal – at first, perhaps, always one that was feared as well – was chosen as a substitute for the father. A choice of this kind may seem strange, but the gulf which men established later between themselves and animals did not exist for primitive peoples; nor does it exist for our children, whose animal phobias we have been able to understand as fear of their father. In relation to the totem animal the original dichotomy in the emotional relation to the father (ambivalence) was wholly retained. On the one hand the totem was regarded as the clan's blood ancestor and protective spirit, who must be worshipped and protected, and on the other hand a festival was appointed at which the same fate was prepared for him that the primal father had met with. He was killed and devoured by all the tribesmen in common. (The totem meal, according to Robertson Smith [1894].) This great festival was in fact a triumphant celebration of the combined sons' victory over their father.

What is the place of religion in this connection? I think we are completely justified in regarding totemism, with its worship of a father-substitute, with its ambivalence as shown by the totem meal, with its institution of memorial festivals and of prohibitions whose infringement was punished by death – we are justified, I say, in regarding totemism as the first form in which religion was manifested in human history and in confirming the fact of its having been linked from the first with social regulations and moral obligations. Here we can only

1. [This is the subject of Section D of Part II, p. 363 ff. below.]

give the most summary survey of the further developments of religion. They no doubt proceeded in parallel with the cultural advances of the human race and with the changes in the structure of human communities.

The first step away from totemism was the humanizing of the being who was worshipped. In place of the animals, human gods appear, whose derivation from the totem is not concealed. The god is still represented either in the form of an animal or at least with an animal's face, or the totem becomes the god's favourite companion, inseparable from him, or legend tells us that the god slew this precise animal, which was after all only a preliminary stage of himself. At a point in this evolution which is not easily determined great mother-goddesses appeared, probably even before the male gods, and afterwards persisted for a long time beside them. In the meantime a great social revolution had occurred. Matriarchy was succeeded by the re-establishment of a patriarchal order. The new fathers, it is true, never achieved the omnipotence of the primal father; there were many of them, who lived together in associations larger than the horde had been. They were obliged to be on good terms with one another, and remained under the limitation of social ordinances. It is likely that the mother-goddesses originated at the time of the curtailment of the matriarchy, as a compensation for the slight upon the mothers. The male deities appear first as sons beside the great mothers and only later clearly assume the features of father-figures. These male gods of polytheism reflect the conditions during the patriarchal age. They are numerous, mutally restrictive, and are occasionally subordinated to a superior high god. The next step, however, leads us to the theme with which we are here concerned – to the return of a single father-god of unlimited dominion.[1]

1. [The greater part of the material in this account is discussed at greater length in Essay IV of *Totem and Taboo* (1912–13), p. 159 ff. above, though there is rather more discussion here than anywhere else of the mother-goddesses. (On this last point, cf. the footnote on p. 286 above. See also some remarks in Chapter XII of *Group Psychology* (1921c), *P.F.L.*, **12**.) The general subject is taken up again in Part II (D), p. 366 ff. below.]

It must be admitted that this historical survey has gaps in it and is uncertain at some points. But anyone who is inclined to pronounce our construction of primaeval history purely imaginary would be gravely under-estimating the wealth and evidential value of the material contained in it. Large portions of the past, which have been linked together here into a whole, are historically attested: totemism and the male confederacies, for instance. Other portions have survived in excellent replicas. Thus authorities have often been struck by the faithful way in which the sense and content of the old totem meal is repeated in the rite of the Christian Communion, in which the believer incorporates the blood and flesh of his god in symbolic form. Numerous relics of the forgotten primaeval age have survived in popular legends and fairy tales, and the analytic study of the mental life of children has provided an unexpected wealth of material for filling the gaps in our knowledge of the earliest times. As contributions to our understanding of the son's relation to the father which is of such great importance, I need only bring forward animal phobias, the fear, which strikes us as so strange, of being eaten by the father, and the enormous intensity of the dread of being castrated. There is nothing wholly fabricated in our construction, nothing which could not be supported on solid foundations.

If our account of primaeval history is accepted as on the whole worthy of belief, two sorts of elements will be recognized in religious doctrines and rituals: on the one hand fixations to the ancient history of the family and survivals of it, and on the other hand revivals of the past and returns, after long intervals, of what has been forgotten. It is this last portion which, hitherto overlooked and therefore not understood, is to be demonstrated here in at least one impressive instance.

It is worth specially stressing the fact that each portion which returns from oblivion asserts itself with peculiar force, exercises an incomparably powerful influence on people in the mass, and raises an irresistible claim to truth against which logical objections remain powerless: a kind of *'credo quia absurdum*.[1] This remarkable feature can only be understood on the pattern of the delusions of psychotics. We have long understood that a portion of forgotten truth lies hidden in delusional ideas, that when this returns it has to put up with distortions and misunderstandings, and that the compulsive conviction which attaches to the delusion arises from this core of truth and spreads out on to the errors that wrap it round. We must grant an ingredient such as this of what may be called *historical* truth to the dogmas of religion as well, which, it is true, bear the character of psychotic symptoms but which, as group phenomena, escape the curse of isolation.[2]

No other portion of the history of religion has become so clear to us as the introduction of monotheism into Judaism and its continuation in Christianity – if we leave on one side the development which we can trace no less uninterruptedly, from the animal totem to the human god with his regular companions. (Each of the four Christian evangelists still has his own favourite animal.) If we provisionally accept the world-empire of the Pharaohs as the determining cause of the emergence of the monotheist idea, we see that that idea, released from its native soil and transferred to another people was, after a long period of latency, taken hold of by them, preserved by them as a precious possession and, in turn, itself kept them alive by giving them pride in being a chosen people: it was the religion of their primal father to which were attached their hope of reward, of distinction and finally of world-dominion. This last wishful phantasy, long abandoned by the Jewish people, still survives among that people's enemies in a belief in a conspiracy by the 'Elders of Zion'. We reserve for discussion in later pages how the special peculiarities of the monotheist religion borrowed from Egypt affected the Jewish people and how it was bound to leave a permanent imprint on their character through its rejection of magic and mysticism, its

1. ['I believe because it is absurd.' Attributed to Tertullian. This was discussed by Freud in Chapter V of *The Future of an Illusion* (1927c), *P.F.L.*, **12**. See also p. 365 below.]
2. [See p. 376 ff. below.]

invitation to advances in intellectuality[1] and its encouragement
of sublimations; how the people, enraptured by the possession
of the truth, overwhelmed by the consciousness of being
chosen, came to have a high opinion of what is intellectual
and to lay stress on what is moral; and how their melancholy
destinies and their disappointments in reality served only to
intensify all these trends. For the moment we will follow their
development in another direction.

The re-establishment of the primal father in his historic rights
was a great step forward but it could not be the end. The
other portions of the prehistoric tragedy insisted on being
recognized. It is not easy to discern what set this process in
motion. It appears as though a growing sense of guilt had
taken hold of the Jewish people, or perhaps of the whole
civilized world of the time, as a precursor to the return of the
repressed material. Till at last one of these Jewish people found,
in justifying a politico-religious agitator, the occasion for
detaching a new – the Christian – religion from Judaism. Paul,
a Roman Jew from Tarsus, seized upon this sense of guilt and
traced it back correctly to its original source. He called this
the 'original sin'; it was a crime against God and could only
be atoned for by death. With the original sin death came into
the world. In fact this crime deserving death had been the
murder of the primal father who was later deified. But the
murder was not remembered: instead of it there was a phantasy
of its atonement, and for that reason this phantasy could be
hailed as a message of redemption (*evangelium*). A son of God
had allowed himself to be killed without guilt and had thus
taken on himself the guilt of all men. It had to be a son, since

---

1. [The Advance in Intellectuality' is the title of Section C of Part II of
this essay (p. 358 below). The German word here translated 'intellectuality'
is '*Geistigkeit*' and its rendering raises much difficulty. The obvious alternative
would be 'spirituality', but in English this arouses some very different
associations. The best plan, perhaps, is to examine Freud's own account of
the concept in the Section just referred to and to form one's conclusions on
that.]

it had been the murder of a father. It is probable that traditions from oriental and Greek mysteries had had an influence on the phantasy of redemption. What was essential in it seems to have been Paul's own contribution. In the most proper sense he was a man of an innately religious disposition: the dark traces of the past lurked in his mind, ready to break through into its more conscious regions.

That the redeemer had sacrificed himself without guilt was evidently a tendentious distortion, which offered difficulties to logical understanding. For how could someone guiltless of the act of murder take on himself the guilt of the murderers by allowing himself to be killed? In the historical reality there was no such contradiction. The 'redeemer' could be none other than the most guilty person, the ringleader of the company of brothers who had overpowered their father. We must in my judgement leave it undecided whether there was such a chief rebel and ringleader. That is possible; but we must also bear in mind that each one of the company of brothers certainly had a wish to commit the deed by himself alone and so to create an exceptional position for himself and to find a substitute for his identification with the father which was having to be given up and which was becoming merged in the community. If there was no such ringleader, then Christ was the heir to a wishful phantasy which remained unfulfilled; if there was one, then he was his successor and his reincarnation. But no matter whether what we have here is a phantasy or the return of a forgotten reality, in any case the origin of the concept of a hero is to be found at this point – the hero who always rebels against his father and kills him in some shape or other.[1] Here too is the true basis for the 'tragic guilt' of the hero of drama, which is otherwise hard to explain. It can scarcely be doubted that the hero and chorus in Greek drama represent the same rebellious hero and company of brothers; and it is not without

1. Ernest Jones has pointed out that the god Mithras, who kills the bull, might represent this ringleader boasting of his deed. It is well known for how long the worship of Mithras struggled with the young Christianity for the final victory.

significance that in the Middle Ages what the theatre started with afresh was the representation of the story of the Passion.

We have already said that the Christian ceremony of Holy Communion, in which the believer incorporates the Saviour's blood and flesh, repeats the content of the old totem meal – no doubt only in its affectionate meaning, expressive of veneration, and not in its aggressive meaning. The ambivalence that dominates the relation to the father was clearly shown, however, in the final outcome of the religious novelty. Ostensibly aimed at propitiating the father god, it ended in his being dethroned and got rid of. Judaism had been a religion of the father; Christianity became a religion of the son. The old God the Father fell back behind Christ; Christ, the Son, took his place, just as every son had hoped to do in primaeval times. Paul, who carried Judaism on, also destroyed it. No doubt he owed his success in the first instance to the fact that, through the idea of the redeemer, he exorcized humanity's sense of guilt; but he owed it as well to the circumstance that he abandoned the 'chosen' character of his people and its visible mark – circumcision – so that the new religion could be a universal one, embracing all men. Though a part may have been played in Paul's taking this step by his personal desire for revenge for the rejection of his innovation in Jewish circles, yet it also restored a feature of the old Aten religion – it removed a restriction which that religion had acquired when it was handed over to a new vehicle, the Jewish people.

In some respects the new religion meant a cultural regression as compared with the older, Jewish one, as regularly happens when a new mass of people, of a lower level, break their way in or are given admission. The Christian religion did not maintain the high level in things of the mind to which Judaism had soared. It was no longer strictly monotheist, it took over numerous symbolic rituals from surrounding peoples, it re-established the great mother-goddess and found room to introduce many of the divine figures of polytheism only lightly veiled, though in subordinate positions. Above all, it did not, like the Aten religion and the Mosaic one which followed it, exclude the entry of superstitious, magical and mystical elements, which were to prove a severe inhibition upon the intellectual development of the next two thousand years.

The triumph of Christianity was a fresh victory for the priests of Amun over Akhenaten's god after an interval of fifteen hundred years and on a wider stage. And yet in the history of religion – that is, as regards the return of the repressed – Christianity was an advance and from that time on the Jewish religion was to some extent a fossil.

It would be worth while to understand how it was that the monotheist idea made such a deep impression precisely on the Jewish people and that they were able to maintain it so tenaciously. It is possible, I think, to find an answer. Fate had brought the great deed and misdeed of primaeval days, the killing of the father, closer to the Jewish people by causing them to repeat it on the person of Moses, an outstanding father-figure. It was a case of 'acting out' instead of remembering, as happens so often with neurotics during the work of analysis. To the suggestion that they should remember, which was made to them by the doctrine of Moses, they reacted, however, by disavowing their action; they remained halted at the recognition of the great father and thus blocked their access to the point from which Paul was later to start his continuation of the primal history. It is scarcely a matter of indifference or of chance that the violent killing of another great man became the starting-point of Paul's new religious creation as well. This was a man whom a small number of adherents in Judaea regarded as the Son of God and as the Messiah who had been announced, and to whom, too, a part of the childhood story invented for Moses was later carried over [p. 251], but of whom in fact we know scarcely more with certainty than of Moses – whether he was really the great teacher portrayed by the Gospels or whether, rather, it was not the fact and circumstances of his death which were decisive for the importance which his figure acquired. Paul, who became his apostle, had not known him himself.

The killing of Moses by his Jewish people, recognized by

333

Sellin from traces of it in tradition (and also, strange to say, accepted by the young Goethe without any evidence[1]) thus becomes an indispensable part of our construction, an important link between the forgotten event of primaeval times and its later emergence in the form of the monotheist religions.[2] It is plausible to conjecture that remorse for the murder of Moses provided the stimulus for the wishful phantasy of the Messiah, who was to return and lead his people to redemption and the promised world-dominion. If Moses was this first Messiah, Christ became his substitute and successor, and Paul could exclaim to the peoples with some historical justification: 'Look! the Messiah has really come: he has been murdered before your eyes!' Then, too, there is a piece of historical truth in Christ's resurrection, for he was the resurrected Moses and behind him the returned primal father of the primitive horde, transfigured and, as the son, put in the place of the father.[3]

The poor Jewish people, who with their habitual stubbornness continued to disavow the father's murder, atoned heavily for it in the course of time. They were constantly met with the reproach 'You killed our God!' And this reproach is true, if it is correctly translated. If it is brought into relation with the history of religions, it runs: 'You will not *admit* that you murdered God (the primal picture of God, the primal father, and his later reincarnations).' There should be an addition declaring: 'We did the same thing, to be sure, but we have *admitted* it and since then we have been absolved.' Not all the reproaches with which anti-semitism persecutes the descendants of the Jewish people can appeal to a similar justification. A phenomenon of such intensity and permanence as the people's hatred of the Jews must of course have more than

1. 'Israel in der Wüste' ['Israel in the Wilderness']. In the Weimar Edition, **7**, 170.

2. On this subject see Frazer's well-known discussions in Part III of *The Golden Bough* (*The Dying God*). [Frazer, 1911c.]

3. [In *Gesammelte Werke*, **16**, 196, the words 'the resurrected Moses and behind him' are omitted from this sentence.]

one ground. It is possible to find a whole number of grounds, some of them clearly derived from reality, which call for no interpretation, and others, lying deeper and derived from hidden sources, which might be regarded as the specific reasons. Of the former, the reproach of being aliens is perhaps the weakest, since in many places dominated by anti-semitism to-day the Jews were among the oldest portions of the population or had even been there before the present inhabitants. This applies, for instance, to the city of Cologne, to which the Jews came with the Romans, before it was occupied by the Germans.[1] Other grounds for hating the Jews are stronger – thus, the circumstances that they live for the most part as minorities among other peoples, for the communal feeling of groups requires, in order to complete it, hostility towards some extraneous minority, and the numerical weakness of this excluded minority encourages its suppression. There are, however, two other characteristics of the Jews which are quite unforgivable. First is the fact that in some respects they are different from their 'host' nations. They are not fundamentally different, for they are not Asiatics of a foreign race, as their enemies maintain, but composed for the most part of remnants of the Mediterranean peoples and heirs of the Mediterranean civilization. But they are none the less different, often in an indefinable way different, especially from the Nordic peoples, and the intolerance of groups is often, strangely enough, exhibited more strongly against small differences than against fundamental ones.[2] The other point has a still greater effect: namely, that they defy all oppression, that the most cruel persecutions have not succeeded in exterminating them, and, indeed, that on the contrary they show a capacity for holding their own in commercial life and, where they are admitted, for making valuable contributions to every form of cultural activity.

1. [In his *Autobiographical Study* (1925*d*), Freud mentions a tradition that his father's family were settled for a long time at Cologne (*P.F.L.*, **15**).]

2. [Cf. 'the narcissism of minor differences' in Chapter V of *Civilization and its Discontents* (1930*a*), *P.F.L.*, **12**, where anti-semitism is also discussed.]

The deeper motives for hatred of the Jews are rooted in the remotest past ages; they operate from the unconscious of the peoples, and I am prepared to find that at first they will not seem credible. I venture to assert that jealousy of the people which declared itself the first-born, favourite child of God the Father, has not yet been surmounted among other peoples even to-day: it is as though they had thought there was truth in the claim. Further, among the customs by which the Jews made themselves separate, that of circumcision has made a disagreeable, uncanny impression, which is to be explained, no doubt, by its recalling the dreaded castration and along with it a portion of the primaeval past which is gladly forgotten. And finally, as the latest motive in this series, we must not forget that all those peoples who excel to-day in their hatred of Jews became Christians only in late historic times, often driven to it by bloody coercion. It might be said that they are all 'misbaptized'. They have been left, under a thin veneer of Christianity, what their ancestors were, who worshipped a barbarous polytheism. They have not got over a grudge against the new religion which was imposed on them; but they have displaced the grudge on to the source from which Christianity reached them. The fact that the Gospels tell a story which is set among Jews, and in fact deals only with Jews, has made this displacement easy for them. Their hatred of Jews is at bottom a hatred of Christians, and we need not be surprised that in the German National Socialist revolution this intimate relation between the two monotheist religions find such a clear expression in the hostile treatment of both of them.[1]

1. [Freud seems to have first mentioned the unconscious root of anti-semitism in the castration complex and circumcision in his 'Little Hans' case history (1909*b*), *P.F.L.*, **8**, 198 *n.* 2. He repeated the point in a footnote added in 1919 to Chapter III of his Leonardo study (1910*c*), ibid., **14**. A reference to anti-semitism in *Civilization and its Discontents* has been given in the previous footnote. The present discussion, however, is much more elaborate than any of these.]

E

Difficulties

Perhaps by what I have said I have succeeded in establishing the analogy between neurotic processes and religious events and in thus indicating the unsuspected origin of the latter. In this transference from individual to group psychology two difficulties arise, differing in their nature and importance, to which we must now turn.

The first of these is that we have here dealt with only a single instance from the copious phenomenology of religions and have thrown no light on any others. I must regretfully admit that I am unable to give more than this one example and that my expert knowledge is insufficient to complete the inquiry. From my limited information I may perhaps add that the case of the founding of the Mohammedan religion seems to me like an abbreviated repetition of the Jewish one, of which it emerged as an imitation. It appears, indeed, that the Prophet intended originally to accept Judaism completely for himself and his people. The recapture of the single great primal father brought the Arabs an extraordinary exaltation of their self-confidence, which led to great worldly successes but exhausted itself in them. Allah showed himself far more grateful to his chosen people than Yahweh did to his. But the internal development of the new religion soon came to a stop, perhaps because it lacked the depth which had been caused in the Jewish case by the murder of the founder of their religion. The apparently rationalistic religions of the East are in their core ancestor-worship and so come to a halt, too, at an early stage of the reconstruction of the past. If it is true that in primitive peoples of to-day the recognition of a supreme being is the only content of their religion, we can only regard this as an atrophy of religious development and bring it into relation with the countless cases of rudimentary neuroses which are to be observed in the other field. Why it is that in the one case just as in the other things have gone no further, our knowledge is in both cases insufficient to tell us. We can only attribute the responsibility to the individual endowment of these peoples, the direction taken by their activity and their general social condition. Moreover, it is a good rule in the work of analysis to be content to explain what is actually before one and not to seek to explain what has *not* happened.

The second difficulty about this transference to group psychology is far more important, because it poses a fresh problem of a fundamental nature. It raises the question in what form the operative tradition in the life of peoples is present – a question which does not occur with individuals, since there it is solved by the existence in the unconscious of memory-traces of the past. Let us return to our historical example. We have attributed the compromise at Kadesh to the survival of a powerful tradition among those who had returned from Egypt. This case involves no problem. According to our theory, a tradition of this kind was based on conscious memories of oral communications which people then living had received from their ancestors only two or three generations back who had themselves been participants and eye-witnesses of the events in question. But can we believe the same thing of the later centuries – that the tradition still had its basis in a knowledge normally handed on from grandfather to grandchild? It is no longer possible to say, as it was in the earlier case, who the people were who preserved this knowledge and handed it on by word of mouth. According to Sellin the tradition of the murder of Moses was always in the possession of priestly circles till eventually it found expression in writing which alone enabled Sellin to discover it. But it can only have been known to a few people; it was not public property. And is that enough to explain its effect? Is it possible to attribute to knowledge held like this by a few people the power to produce such a lasting emotion in the masses when it came to their notice? It seems, rather, as though there must have been something present in the ignorant masses, too, which was in some way akin to the knowledge of the few and went half way to meet it when it was uttered.

A decision is made still more difficult when we turn to the analogous case in primaeval times. It is quite certain that

in the course of thousands of years the fact was forgotten
that there had been a primal father with the characteristics
we know and what his fate had been; nor can we suppose
that there was any oral tradition of it, as we can in the case
of Moses. In what sense, then, does a tradition come in question
at all? In what form can it have been present?

In order to make it easier for readers who do not desire
or are not prepared to plunge into a complicated psychological
state of affairs, I will anticipate the outcome of the investigation
that is to follow. In my opinion there is an almost complete
conformity in this respect between the individual and the group:
in the group too an impression of the past is retained in unconscious memory-traces.

In the case of the individual we believe we can see clearly.
The memory-trace of his early experience has been preserved
in him, but in a special psychological condition. The individual
may be said to have known it always, just as one knows about
the repressed. Here we have formed ideas, which can be confirmed without difficulty through analysis, of how something
can be forgotten and how it can then reappear after a while.
What is forgotten is not extinguished but only 'repressed';
its memory-traces are present in all their freshness, but isolated
by 'anticathexes'. They cannot enter into communication with
other intellectual processes; they are unconscious – inaccessible
to consciousness. It may also be that certain portions of the
repressed, having evaded the process [of repression], remain
accessible to memory and occasionally emerge into consciousness; but even so they are isolated, like foreign bodies out
of connection with the rest. It may be so, but it need not
be so; repression may also be complete, and it is with that
alternative that we shall deal in what follows.

The repressed retains its upward urge, its effort to force
its way to consciousness. It achieves its aim under three conditions: (1) if the strength of the anticathexis is diminished by
pathological processes which overtake the other part [of the
mind], what we call the ego, or by a different distribution

of the cathectic energies in that ego, as happens regularly in the state of sleep; (2) if the instinctual elements attaching to the repressed receive a special reinforcement (of which the best example is the processes during puberty); and (3) if at any time in recent experience impressions or experiences occur which resemble the repressed so closely that they are able to awaken it. In the last case the recent experience is reinforced by the latent energy of the repressed, and the repressed comes into operation behind the recent experience and with its help. In none of these three alternatives does what has hitherto been repressed enter consciousness smoothly and unaltered; it must always put up with distortions which testify to the influence of the resistance (not entirely overcome) arising from the anti-cathexis, or to the modifying influence of the recent experience or to both.

The difference between whether a psychical process is conscious or unconscious has served us as a criterion and a means of finding our bearings. The repressed is unconscious. Now it would simplify things agreeably if this sentence admitted of reversal — if, that is, the difference between the qualities of conscious (*Cs.*) and unconscious (*Ucs.*) coincided with the distinction between 'belonging to the ego' and 'repressed'.[1] The fact of there being isolated and unconscious things like this in our mental life would be sufficiently novel and important. But in reality the position is more complicated. It is true that everything repressed is unconscious, but it is not true that everything belonging to the ego is conscious. We notice that consciousness is a transient quality which attaches to a psychical process only in passing. For our purposes therefore we must replace 'conscious' by 'capable of being conscious' and we call this quality 'preconscious' (*Pcs.*). We then say,

1. [It may be remarked that these abbreviations make their final appearance here after a long interval, having hardly been used since the structural account of the mind was established some fifteen years earlier in *The Ego and the Id* (1923*b*), *P.F.L.*, **11**, 342 ff. It is a curious fact that in the present work they are used, quite contrary to Freud's normal practice, in a 'descriptive' sense.]

more correctly, that the ego is mainly preconscious (virtually conscious) but that portions of the ego are unconscious.

The establishment of this latter fact shows us that the qualities on which we have hitherto relied are insufficient to give us our bearings in the obscurity of mental life. We must introduce another distinction which is no longer qualitative but *topographical* and – what gives it special value – at the same time *genetic*. We now distinguish in our mental life (which we regard as an apparatus compounded of several agencies, districts or provinces) one region which we call the *ego* proper and another which we name the *id*. The id is the older of the two; the ego has developed out of it, like a cortical layer, through the influence of the external world. It is in the id that all our primary instincts are at work, all the processes in the id take place unconsciously. The ego, as we have already said, coincides with the region of the preconscious; it includes portions which normally remain unconscious. The course of events in the id, and their mutual interaction, are governed by quite other laws than those prevailing in the ego. It is in fact the discovery of these differences that has led to our new view and justifies it.

The *repressed* is to be counted as belonging to the id and is subject to the same mechanisms; it is distinguished from it only in respect to its genesis. The differentiation is accomplished in the earliest period of life, while the ego is developing out of the id. At that time a portion of the contents of the id is taken into the ego and raised to the preconscious state; another portion is not affected by this translation and remains behind in the id as the unconscious proper. In the further course of the formation of the ego, however, certain psychical impressions and processes in the ego are excluded [i.e. expelled] from it by a defensive process; the characteristic of being preconscious is withdrawn from them, so that they are once more reduced to being component portions of the id. Here then is the 'repressed' in the id. So far as intercourse between the two mental provinces is concerned, we therefore assume that, on the one hand, unconscious processes in the id are raised to the level of the preconscious and incorporated into the ego, and that, on the other hand, preconscious material in the ego can follow the opposite path and be put back into the id. The fact that later on a special region – that of the 'super-ego' – is separated off in the ego lies outside our present interest.[1]

All of this may appear to be far from simple.[2] But when one has grown reconciled to this unusual spatial view of the mental apparatus, it can present no particular difficulties to the imagination. I will add the further comment that the psychical topography that I have developed here has nothing to do with the anatomy of the brain, and actually only touches it at one point.[3] What is unsatisfactory in this picture – and I am aware of it as clearly as anyone – is due to our complete ignorance of the *dynamic* nature of the mental processes. We tell ourselves that what distinguishes a conscious idea from a preconscious one, and the latter from an unconscious one, can only be a modification, or perhaps a different distribution, of psychical energy. We talk of cathexes and hypercathexes, but beyond this we are without any knowledge on the subject or even any starting-point for a serviceable working hypothesis. Of the phenomenon of consciousness we can at least say that it was originally attached to perception. All sensations which originate from the perception of painful, tactile, auditory or visual stimuli are what are most readily conscious. Thought-processes, and whatever may be analogous to them in the id, are in themselves unconscious and obtain access to conscious-ness by becoming linked to the mnemic residues of visual and auditory perceptions along the path of the function of

1. [Some discussion of the super-ego will however be found below (p. 364).]

2. [A fuller account is given in Lecture 31 of the *New Introductory Lectures* (1933*a*), *P.F.L.*, **2**, 88 ff.]

3. [This single point – as Freud explains in parallel accounts in *Beyond the Pleasure Principle* (1920*g*), *P.F.L.*, **11**, 295, and *The Ego and the Id* (1923*b*), ibid., **11**, 357 – lies in the perceptual system, which is regarded as cortical both in anatomy and in Freud's metapsychology.]

speech.[1] In animals, which lack speech, these conditions must be of a simpler kind.

The impressions of early traumas, from which we started out, are either not translated into the preconscious or are quickly put back by repression into the id condition. Their mnemic residues are in that case unconscious and operate from the id. We believe we can easily follow their further vicissitudes so long as it is a question of what has been experienced by the subject himself. But a fresh complication arises when we become aware of the probability that what may be operative in an individual's psychical life may include not only what he has experienced himself but also things that were innately present in him at his birth, elements with a phylogenetic origin – an *archaic heritage*. The questions then arise of what this consists in, what it contains and what is the evidence for it.

The immediate and most certain answer is that it consists in certain [innate] dispositions such as are characteristic of all living organisms: in the capacity and tendency, that is, to enter particular lines of development and to react in a particular manner to certain excitations, impressions and stimuli. Since experience shows that there are distinctions in this respect between individuals of the human species, the archaic heritage must include these distinctions; they represent what we recognize as the *constitutional* factor in the individual. Now, since all human beings, at all events in their early days, have approximately the same experiences, they react to them, too, in a similar manner; a doubt was therefore able to arise whether we should not include these reactions, along with their individual distinctions, in the archaic heritage. This doubt should be put on one side: our knowledge of the archaic heritage is not enlarged by the fact of this similarity.

Nevertheless, analytic research has brought us a few results which give us cause for thought. There is, in the first place, the universality of symbolism in language. The symbolic

1. [For a technical discussion of this, see Part VII of 'The Unconscious' (1915e), *P.F.L.*, **11**, 206 ff.]

343

representation of one object by another – the same thing applies to actions – is familiar to all our children and comes to them, as it were, as a matter of course. We cannot show in regard to them how they have learnt it and must admit that in many cases learning it is impossible. It is a question of an original knowledge which adults afterwards forget. It is true that an adult makes use of the same symbols in his dreams, but he does not understand them unless an analyst interprets them to him, and even then he is reluctant to believe the translation. If he makes use of one of the very common figures of speech in which this symbolism is recorded, he is obliged to admit that its true sense has completely escaped him. Moreover, symbolism disregards differences of language; investigations would probably show that it is ubiquitous – the same for all peoples. Here, then, we seem to have an assured instance of an archaic heritage dating from the period at which language developed. But another explanation might still be attempted. It might be said that we are dealing with thought-connections between ideas – connections which had been established during the historical development of speech and which have to be repeated now every time the development of speech has to be gone through in an individual. It would thus be a case of the inheritance of an intellectual disposition similar to the ordinary inheritance of an instinctual disposition – and once again it would be no contribution to our problem.

The work of analysis has, however, brought something else to light which exceeds in its importance what we have so far considered. When we study the reactions to early traumas, we are quite often surprised to find that they are not strictly limited to what the subject himself has really experienced but diverge from it in a way which fits in much better with the model of a phylogenetic event and, in general, can only be explained by such an influence. The behaviour of neurotic children towards their parents in the Oedipus and castration complex abounds in such reactions, which seem unjustified in the individual case and only become intelligible phylogenetically – by their connection with the experience of earlier generations.

It would be well worth while to place this material, which I am able to appeal to here, before the public in a collected form. Its evidential value seems to me strong enough for me to venture on a further step and to posit the assertion that the archaic heritage of human beings comprises not only dispositions but also subject-matter – memory-traces of the experience of earlier generations. In this way the compass as well as the importance of the archaic heritage would be significantly extended.

On further reflection I must admit that I have behaved for a long time as though the inheritance of memory-traces of the experience of our ancestors, independently of direct communication and of the influence of education by the setting of an example, were established beyond question. When I spoke of the survival of a tradition among a people or of the formation of a people's character, I had mostly in mind an inherited tradition of this kind and not one transmitted by communication. Or at least I made no distinction between the two and was not clearly aware of my audacity in neglecting to do so. My position, no doubt, is made more difficult by the present attitude of biological science, which refuses to hear of the inheritance of acquired characters by succeeding generations. I must, however, in all modesty confess that nevertheless I cannot do without this factor in biological evolution. The same thing is not in question, indeed, in the two cases: in the one it is a matter of acquired characters which are hard to grasp, in the other of memory-traces of external events – something tangible, as it were. But it may well be that at bottom we cannot imagine one without the other.

If we assume the survival of these memory-traces in the archaic heritage, we have bridged the gulf between individual and group psychology: we can deal with peoples as we do with an individual neurotic. Granted that at the time we have no stronger evidence for the presence of memory-traces in the archaic heritage than the residual phenomena of the work of analysis which call for a phylogenetic derivation, yet this evidence seems to us strong enough to postulate that such is the fact. If it is not so, we shall not advance a step further along the path we entered on, either in analysis or in group psychology. The audacity cannot be avoided.

And by this assumption we are effecting something else. We are diminishing the gulf which earlier periods of human arrogance had torn too wide apart between mankind and the animals. If any explanation is to be found of what are called the instincts[1] of animals, which allow them to behave from the first in a new situation in life as though it were an old and familiar one – if any explanation at all is to be found of this instinctive life of animals, it can only be that they bring the experiences of their species with them into their own new existence – that is, that they have preserved memories of what was experienced by their ancestors. The position in the human animal would not at bottom be different. His own archaic heritage corresponds to the instincts of animals even though it is different in its compass and contents.

After this discussion I have no hesitation in declaring that men have always known (in this special way) that they once possessed a primal father and killed him.

Two further questions must now be answered. First, under what conditions does a memory of this kind enter the archaic heritage? And, secondly, in what circumstances can it become active – that is, can it advance to consciousness from its unconscious state in the id, even though in an altered and distorted shape? The answer to the first question is easy to formulate: the memory enters the archaic heritage if the event was important enough, or repeated often enough, or both. In the case of parricide both conditions are fulfilled. On the second question there is this to be said. A whole number of influences may be concerned, not all of which are necessarily known. A spontaneous development is also conceivable, on the analogy of what happens in some neuroses. What is certainly of decisive importance, however, is the awakening of the forgotten memory-trace by a recent real repetition of the event. The

1. [Here and in the remainder of this paragraph the German word is 'Instinkt' and not 'Trieb'. Similarly on p. 382 below.]

murder of Moses was a repetition of this kind and, later, the supposed judicial murder of Christ: so that these events come into the foreground as causes. It seems as though the genesis of monotheism could not do without these occurrences. We are reminded of the poet's words:

> Was unsterblich im Gesang soll leben,
> Muss im Leben untergehn.[1]

And lastly a remark which brings up a psychological argument. A tradition that was based only on communication could not lead to the compulsive character that attaches to religious phenomena. It would be listened to, judged, and perhaps dismissed, like any other piece of information from outside; it would never attain the privilege of being liberated from the constraint of logical thought. It must have undergone the fate of being repressed, the condition of lingering in the unconscious, before it is able to display such powerful effects on its return, to bring the masses under its spell, as we have seen with astonishment and hitherto without comprehension in the case of religious tradition. And this consideration weighs heavily in favour of our believing that things really happened in the way we have tried to picture them or at least in some similar way.[2]

1. [Literally: 'What is to live immortal in song must perish in life.'] Schiller, 'Die Götter Griechenlands'.
2. [The discussion of the 'archaic heritage' in this section is by far the longest in Freud's writings. The question of the relative parts played in mental life by heredity and experience was, of course, a repeated topic for discussion from the earliest times. But this particular point of the possibility of the inheritance of actual ancestral experiences had appeared relatively late in Freud's writings. The problem of the transmission of ancestral experiences was necessarily raised in *Totem and Taboo* (1912–13). 'What are the ways and means', Freud asks there, 'employed by one generation in order to hand on its mental states to the next one?' (p. 221 above). His reply in this passage is non-committal, though he seems to suggest that the process can be accounted for by conscious and unconscious communication from one generation to another. But it is not difficult to see that even then he had other ideas at the back of his mind. Indeed, the possibility of the inheritance of an 'archaic constitution as an atavistic vestige' is explicitly

mentioned there in connection with ambivalence (p. 123 above). It seems probable that these ideas were precipitated (like so much else) in connection with the 'Wolf Man' analysis and particularly with the topic of 'primal phantasies'. This analysis was actually in progress while Freud was writing *Totem and Taboo* and his first draft of the case history was written in 1914. The possibility of a 'phylogenetic heritage' had, however, also arisen in connection with symbolism. This question was discussed somewhat allusively in Lecture 10 of the *Introductory Lectures* (1916–17), *P.F.L.*, **1**, 199–201, and more explicitly in Lecture 13, ibid., 235. The first definite reference to the inheritance of primal phantasies seems to have been in Lecture 23 of the *Introductory Lectures*, ibid., 418, but it was further developed in one of the passages added after this to the 'Wolf Man' case history (1918*b*), *P.F.L.*, **9**, 337 f. The actual term '*archaische Erbschaft*' seems to appear for the first time in 1919 – in a paragraph added in that year to Chapter VII (B) of *The Interpretation of Dreams* (1900*a*), ibid., **4**, 700, and in 'A Child is Being Beaten' (1919*e*), ibid., **10**, 180. Thereafter the concept and term appear frequently, though only in Chapter III of *The Ego and the Id* (1923*b*), *P.F.L.*, **11**, 376–8, is the subject discussed at any length. – The whole question of Freud's views on the inheritance of acquired characters is discussed in Jones's biography of Freud (1957), Volume 3, Chapter X.

PART II

The part of this study which follows cannot be given to the public without extensive explanations and apologies. For it is nothing other than a faithful (and often word-for-word) repetition of the first part [of the third Essay], abbreviated in some of its critical inquiries and augmented by additions relating to the problem of how the special character of the Jewish people arose. I am aware that a method of exposition such as this is no less inexpedient than it is inartistic. I myself deplore it unreservedly. Why have I not avoided it? The answer to that is not hard for me to find, but it is not easy to confess. I found myself unable to wipe out the traces of the history of the work's origin, which was in any case unusual.

Actually it has been written twice: for the first time a few years ago in Vienna, where I did not think it would be possible to publish it. I determined to give it up; but it tormented me like an unlaid ghost, and I found a way out by making two pieces of it independent and publishing them in our periodical *Imago*: the psychoanalytic starting-point of the whole thing 'Moses an Egyptian' [Essay I], and the historical construction erected on this 'If Moses was an Egyptian ...' [Essay II]. The remainder, which included what was really open to objection and dangerous – the application [of these findings] to the genesis of monotheism and the view of religion in general – I held back, as I thought, for ever. Then, in March 1938, came the unexpected German invasion, which forced me to leave my home but also freed me from my anxiety lest my publication might conjure up a prohibition of psychoanalysis in a place where it was still tolerated. I had scarcely arrived in England before I found the temptation irresistible to make the knowledge I had held back accessible to the world, and I began to revise the third part of my study to fit it on to the two parts that had already been published. This naturally involved a partial rearrangement of the material. I did not succeed, however, in including the whole of this material in my second version; on the other hand I could not make up my mind to give up the earlier versions entirely. And so it has come about that I have adopted the expedient of attaching a whole piece of the first presentation to the second unchanged which has brought with it the disadvantage of involving extensive repetition.

I might, however, console myself with the reflection that the things I am treating are in any case so new and so important, apart from how far my account of them is correct, that it can be no misfortune if the public is obliged to read the same thing about them twice over. There are things which should be said more than once and which cannot be said often enough. But the reader must decide of his own free will whether to linger over the subject or to come back to it. He must not be surreptitiously led into having the same thing put before him twice in one book. It is a piece of clumsiness for which the author must take the blame. Unluckily an author's creative power does not always obey his will: the work proceeds as it can, and often presents itself to the author as something independent or even alien.

A

THE PEOPLE OF ISRAEL

If we are clear in our mind that a procedure like ours of accepting what seems to us serviceable in the material presented to us and of rejecting what does not suit us and of putting the different pieces together in accordance with psychological probability – if we are clear that a technique of this kind can give no certainty that we shall arrive at the truth, then it may justly be asked why we are undertaking this work at all. The answer is an appeal to the work's outcome. If we greatly tone down the strictness of the requirements made upon a historico-psychological investigation, it will perhaps be possible to throw light on problems which have always seemed to deserve attention and which recent events have forced upon our observation anew. As we know, of all the peoples who lived round the basin of the Mediterranean in antiquity, the Jewish people is almost the only one which still exists in name and also in substance. It has met misfortunes and ill-treatment with an unexampled capacity for resistance; it has developed special character-traits and incidentally has earned the hearty dislike of every other people. We should be glad to understand more of the source of this viability of the Jews and of how their characteristics are connected with their history.

We may start from a character-trait of the Jews which dominates their relation to others. There is no doubt that they have a particularly high opinion of themselves, that they regard themselves as more distinguished, of higher standing, as superior to other peoples – from whom they are also distinguished by many of their customs.[1] At the same time they are inspired

1. The aspersion, so common in antiquity, that the Jews were 'lepers' (cf. Manetho [*History of Egypt*, English translation, 1940, 119 ff.]) no doubt has the sense of a projection: 'they keep as much apart from us as though we were lepers'. [Manetho (*c* 300 B.C.), an Egyptian high priest, wrote his *History* in Greek from older Egyptian sources. Only fragments of it survive.]

by a peculiar confidence in life, such as is derived from the secret ownership of some precious possession, a kind of optimism: pious people would call it trust in God.

We know the reason for this behaviour and what their secret treasure is. They really regard themselves as God's chosen people, they believe that they stand especially close to him; and this makes them proud and confident. Trustworthy reports tell us that they behaved in Hellenistic times just as they do to-day, so that the complete Jew was already there; and the Greeks, among whom and alongside of whom they lived, reacted to the Jewish characteristics in the same way as their 'hosts' do to-day. It might be thought that they reacted as though they too believed in the superiority which the people of Israel claimed for themselves. If one is the declared favourite of the dreaded father, one need not be surprised at the jealousy of one's brothers and sisters, and the Jewish legend of Joseph and his brethren shows very well where this jealousy can lead. The course of world-history seemed to justify the presumption of the Jews, since, when later on it pleased God to send mankind a Messiah and redeemer, he once again chose him from the Jewish people. The other peoples might have had occasion then to say to themselves: 'Indeed, they were right, they *are* God's chosen people.' But instead of this, what happened was that redemption by Jesus Christ only intensified their hatred of the Jews, while the Jews themselves gained no advantage from this second act of favouritism, since they did not recognize the redeemer.

On the basis of our earlier discussions, we may now assert that it was the man Moses who imprinted this trait – significant for all time – upon the Jewish people. He raised their self-esteem by assuring them that they were God's chosen people, he enjoined them to holiness [p. 367] and pledged them to be apart from others. Not that other peoples were lacking in self-esteem. Just as to-day, so in those days each nation thought itself better than any other. But the self-esteem of the Jews was given a religious anchorage by Moses: it became a part of their religious faith. Owing to their especially intimate relation to their God they acquired a share in his grandeur. And since we know that behind the God who had chosen the Jews and freed them from Egypt stands the figure of Moses, who had done precisely that, ostensibly at God's command, we venture to declare that it was this one man Moses who created the Jews. It is to him that this people owes its tenacity of life but also much of the hostility it has experienced and still experiences.

B

THE GREAT MAN

How is it possible for a single man to evolve such extraordinary effectiveness that he can form a people out of random individuals and families, can stamp them with their definitive character and determine their fate for thousands of years? Is not a hypothesis such as this a relapse into the mode of thought which led to myths of a creator and to the worship of heroes, into times in which the writing of history was nothing more than a report of the deeds and destinies of single individuals, of rulers or conquerors? The modern tendency is rather towards tracing back the events of human history to more concealed, general and impersonal factors, to the compelling influence of economic conditions, to alterations in food habits, to advances in the use of materials and tools, to migrations brought about by increases in population and climatic changes. Individuals have no other part to play in this than as exponents or representatives of group trends, which are bound to find expression and do so in these particular individuals largely by chance.

These are prefectly justifiable lines of approach, but they give us occasion for drawing attention to an important discrepancy between the attitude taken up by our organ of thought and the arrangement of things in the world, which are supposed to be grasped by means of our thought. It is enough for our need to discover causes (which, to be sure, is imperative) if each event has *one* demonstrable cause. But in the reality lying outside us that is scarcely the case; on the contrary, each event seems to be overdetermined and proves to be the effect of several convergent causes. Frightened by the immense complication of events, our investigations take the side of one correlation as against another and set up contradictions which do not exist but have only arisen owing to a rupture of more comprehensive relations.[1] Accordingly, if the investigation of a particular case demonstrates to us the transcendent influence of a single personality, our conscience need not reproach us with having by this hypothesis flown in the face of the doctrine of the importance of the general and impersonal factors. There is room in principle for both. In the case of the genesis of monotheism, however, we can point to no external factor other than the one we have already mentioned – that this development was linked with the establishment of closer relations between different nations and with the building up of a great empire.

Thus we reserve a place for 'great men' in the chain, or rather the network, of causes. But it may not, perhaps, be quite useless to inquire under what conditions we confer this title of honour. We shall be surprised to find that it is never quite easy to answer this question. A first formulation – 'we do so if a man possesses to a specially high degree qualities that we value greatly' – clearly misses the mark in every respect. Beauty, for instance, and muscular strength, however enviable they may be, constitute no claim to 'greatness'. It would seem, then, that the qualities have to be mental ones – psychical and intellectual distinctions. As regards these, we are held up by the consideration that nevertheless we should not un-hesitatingly describe someone as a great man simply because

1. I protest, however, against being misunderstood to say that the world is so complicated that any assertion one may make is bound to hit upon a piece of truth somewhere. No. Our thought has upheld its liberty to discover dependent relations and connections to which there is nothing corresponding in reality; and it clearly sets a very high value on this gift, since it makes such copious use of it both inside and outside of science.

he was extraordinarily efficient in some particular sphere. We should certainly not do so in the case of a chess master or of a virtuoso on a musical instrument; but not very easily, either, in the case of a distinguished artist or scientist. In such cases we should naturally speak of him as a great poet, painter, mathematician or physicist, or as a pioneer in the field of this or that activity; but we refrain from pronouncing him a great man. If we unhesitatingly declare that, for instance, Goethe and Leonardo da Vinci and Beethoven were great men, we must be led to it by something other than admiration for their splendid creations. If precisely such examples as these did not stand in the way, the idea would probably occur to us that the name of a 'great man' is preferably reserved for men of action – conquerors, generals, rulers – and is in recognition of the greatness of their achievement, the force of the effects to which they gave rise. But this too is unsatisfactory and is entirely contradicted by our condemnation of so many worthless figures whose effects upon their contemporary world and upon posterity can nevertheless not be disputed. Nor shall we be able to choose success as a sign of greatness, when we reflect on the majority of great men who instead of achieving success have perished in misfortune.

For the moment, then, we are inclined to decide that it is not worth while to look for a connotation of the concept of a 'great man' that is unambiguously determined. It seems to be only a loosely used and somewhat arbitrarily conferred recognition of an over-large development of certain human qualities, with some approximation to the original literal sense of 'greatness'. We must recollect, too, that we are not so much interested in the essence of great men as in the question of the means by which they affect their fellow-men. We will, however, keep this inquiry as short as possible, since it threatens to lead us far away from our goal.

Let us, therefore, take it for granted that a great man influences his fellow-men in two ways: by his personality and by the idea which he puts forward. That idea may stress some ancient wishful image of the masses, or it may point out a new wishful aim to them, or it may cast its spell over them in some other way. Occasionally – and this is undoubtedly the more primary case – the personality works by itself and the idea plays a quite trivial part. Not for a moment are we in the dark as to why a great man ever becomes important. We know that in the mass of mankind there is a powerful need for an authority who can be admired, before whom one bows down, by whom one is ruled and perhaps even ill-treated. We have learnt from the psychology of individual men what the origin is of this need of the masses. It is a longing for the father felt by everyone from his childhood onwards, for the same father whom the hero of legend boasts he has overcome. And now it may begin to dawn on us that all the characteristics with which we equipped the great man are paternal characteristics, and that the essence of great men for which we vainly searched lies in this conformity. The decisiveness of thought, the strength of will, the energy of action are part of the picture of a father – but above all the autonomy and independence of the great man, his divine unconcern which may grow into ruthlessness. One must admire him, one may trust him, but one cannot avoid being afraid of him too. We should have been led to realize this from the word itself: who but the father can have been the 'great man' in childhood?[1]

There is no doubt that it was a mighty prototype of a father which, in the person of Moses, stooped to the poor Jewish bondsmen to assure them that they were his dear children. And no less overwhelming must have been the effect upon them of the idea of an only, eternal, almighty God, to whom they were not too mean for him to make a covenant with them and who promised to care for them if they remained loyal to his worship. It was probably not easy for them to distinguish the image of the man Moses from that of his God; and their feeling was right in this, for Moses may have introduced traits of his own personality into the character of his God – such as his wrathful temper and his relentlessness. And

1. [In German '*der grosse Mann*' means not only 'the great man' but 'the tall man' or 'the big man'.]

if, this being so, they killed their great man one day, they were only repeating a misdeed which in ancient times had been committed, as prescribed by law, against the Divine King and which, as we know, went back to a still more ancient prototype.[1]

If on the one hand we thus see the figure of the great man grown to divine proportions, yet on the other hand we must recall that the father too was once a child. The great religious idea for which the man Moses stood was, on our view, not his own property: he had taken it over from King Akhenaten. And he, whose greatness as the founder of a religion is unequivocally established, may perhaps have been following hints which had reached him – from near or distant parts of Asia – through the medium of his mother[2] or by other paths.

We cannot follow the chain of events further, but if we have rightly recognized these first steps, the monotheist idea returned like a boomerang to the land of its origin. Thus it seems unfruitful to try to fix the credit due to an individual in connection with a new idea. It is clear that many have shared in its development and made contributions to it. And, again, it would obviously be unjust to break off the chain of causes at Moses and to neglect what was effected by those who succeeded him and carried on his ideas, the Jewish Prophets. The seed of monotheism failed to ripen in Egypt. The same thing might have happened in Israel after the people had thrown off the burdensome and exacting religion. But there constantly arose from the Jewish people men who revived the fading tradition, who renewed the admonitions and demands made by Moses, and who did not rest till what was lost had been established once again. In the course of constant efforts over centuries, and finally owing to two great reforms, one before and one after the Babylonian exile, the transformation was accomplished of the popular god Yahweh into the God whose worship had been forced upon the Jews by Moses.

1. Cf. Frazer, loc. cit. [See p. 334 n. 2.]

2. [The theory held at one time, that Akhenaten's mother, Queen Tiye, was of foreign origin, has been abandoned in view of the discovery of her parents' tomb at Thebes.]

And evidence of the presence of a peculiar psychical aptitude in the masses who had become the Jewish people is revealed by the fact that they were able to produce so many individuals prepared to take on the burdens of the religion of Moses in return for the reward of being the chosen people and perhaps for some other prizes of a similar degree.

C

THE ADVANCE IN INTELLECTUALITY [1]

In order to bring about lasting psychical results in a people, it is clearly not enough to *assure* them that they have been chosen by the deity. The fact must also be *proved* to them in some way if they are to believe it and to draw consequences from the belief. In the religion of Moses the Exodus from Egypt served as the proof; God, or Moses in his name, was never tired of appealing to this evidence of favour. The feast of the Passover was introduced in order to maintain the memory of that event, or, rather, an old-established feast was injected with the contents of that memory. Nevertheless, it was only a memory: the Exodus belonged to a hazy past. In the present, signs of God's favour were decidedly scanty; the people's history pointed rather to his *dis*favour. Primitive peoples used to depose their gods or even to castigate them, if they failed to do their duty in securing them victory, happiness and comfort. In all periods kings have been treated in no way differently from gods; an ancient identity is thus revealed: an origin from a common root. Thus, modern peoples, too, are in the habit of expelling their kings if the glory of their reign is spoilt by defeats and the corresponding losses in territory and money. Why the people of Israel, however, clung more

1. [This section, as has been mentioned in the Editor's Note, p. 239, appeared first separately in the *Internationale Zeitschrift für Psychoanalyse und Imago*, **24** (1939), 6–9. Two variants from the final version are noted below. For a discussion of the English rendering of the title see the footnote on p. 330 above.]

and more submissively to their God the worse they were treated by him – that is a problem which for the moment we must leave on one side.

It may encourage us to inquire whether the religion of Moses brought the people nothing else besides an enhancement of their self-esteem owing to their consciousness of having been chosen. And indeed another factor can easily be found. That religion also brought the Jews a far grander conception of God, or, as we might put it more modestly, the conception of a grander God. Anyone who believed in this God had some kind of share in his greatness, might feel exalted himself. For an unbeliever this is not entirely self-evident; but we may perhaps make it easier to understand if we point to the sense of superiority felt by a Briton in a foreign country which has been made insecure owing to an insurrection – a feeling that is completely absent in a citizen of any small continental state. For the Briton counts on the fact that his Government[1] will send along a warship if a hair of his head is hurt, and that the rebels understand that very well – whereas the small state possesses no warship at all. Thus, pride in the greatness of the British Empire[2] has a root as well in the consciousness of the greater security – the protection – enjoyed by the individual Briton. This may resemble the conception of a grand God. And, since one can scarcely claim to assist God in the administration of the world, the pride in God's greatness fuses with the pride in being chosen by him.

Among the precepts of the Moses religion there is one that is of greater importance than appears to begin with. This is the prohibition against making an image of God – the compulsion to worship a God whom one cannot see. [Cf. p. 264 above.] In this, I suspect, Moses was outdoing the strictness of the Aten religion. Perhaps he merely wanted to be consistent: his God would in that case have neither a name nor a countenance. Perhaps it was a fresh measure against

1. [In English in the original.]
2. [Also in English.]

magical abuses.[1] But if this prohibition were accepted, it must have a profound effect. For it meant that a sensory perception was given second place to what may be called an abstract idea – a triumph of intellectuality over sensuality or, strictly speaking, an instinctual renunciation, with all its necessary psychological consequences.

This may not seem obvious at first sight, and before it can carry conviction we must recall other processes of the same character in the development of human civilization. The earliest of these and perhaps the most important is merged in the obscurity of primaeval ages. Its astonishing effects compel us to assert its occurrence. In our children, in adults who are neurotic, as well as in primitive peoples, we meet with the mental phenomenon which we describe as a belief in the 'omnipotence of thoughts'. In our judgement this lies in an over-estimation of the influence which our mental (in this case, intellectual) acts can exercise in altering the external world. At bottom, all magic, the precursor of our technology, rests on this premiss. All the magic of words, too, has its place here, and the conviction of the power which is bound up with the knowledge and pronouncing of a name. The 'omnipotence of thoughts' was, we suppose, an expression of the pride of mankind in the development of speech, which resulted in such an extraordinary advancement of intellectual activities. The new realm of intellectuality was opened up, in which ideas, memories and inferences became decisive in contrast to the lower psychical activity which had direct perceptions by the sense-organs as its content. This was unquestionably one of the most important stages on the path to hominization [p. 318 n. 1].

We can far more easily grasp another process of a later date. Under the influence of external factors into which we need not enter here and which are also in part insufficiently known, it came about that the matriarchal social order was succeeded by the patriarchal one – which, of course, involved a revolution in the juridical conditions that had so far prevailed. An echo

1. [Cf. a remark on this in *Totem and Taboo* (1912–13), p. 137 n. 1.]

of this revolution seems still to be audible in the *Oresteia* of Aeschylus.[1] But this turning from the mother to the father points in addition to a victory of intellectuality over sensuality – that is, an advance in civilization, since maternity is proved by the evidence of the senses while paternity is a hypothesis, based on an inference and a premiss. Taking sides in this way with a thought-process in preference to a sense perception has proved to be a momentous step.

At some point between the two events that I have mentioned[2] there was another which shows the most affinity to what we are investigating in the history of religion. Human beings found themselves obliged in general to recognize 'intellectual [*geistige*]' forces – forces, that is, which cannot be grasped by the senses (particularly by the sight) but which none the less produce undoubted and indeed extremely powerful effects. If we may rely upon the evidence of language, it was movement of the air that provided the prototype of intellectuality [*Geistigkeit*], for intellect [*Geist*] derives its name from a breath of wind – '*animus*', '*spiritus*',[3] and the Hebrew '*ruach* (breath)'. This too led to the discovery of the mind [*Seele* (soul)]] as that of the intellectual [*geistigen*] principle in individual human beings. Observation found the movement of air once again in men's breathing, which ceases when they die. To this day a dying man 'breathes out his spirit [*Seele*]'. Now, however, the world of spirits [*Geisterreich*] lay open to men. They were prepared to attribute the soul [*Seele*] which they had discovered in themselves to everything in Nature. The whole world was animate [*beseelt*]; and science, which came so much later, had plenty to do in divesting part of the world

1. [The theme of this trilogy is the murder of Agamemnon by his wife Clytemnestra, the vengeance taken on her by their son Orestes, his pursuit by the Furies and his trial and acquittal by the Court of the Areopagus in Athens.]

2. [Between the development of speech and the end of the matriarchy.]

3. [In the original version of this section (see p. 358 n.) the Greek word '*ἄνεμος* (anemos, wind)' appears here as well.]

of its soul once more; indeed it has not completed that task even to-day.[1]

The Mosaic prohibition elevated God to a higher degree of intellectuality, and the way was opened to further alterations in the idea of God which we have still to describe. But we may first consider another effect of the prohibition. All such advances in intellectuality have as their consequence that the individual's self-esteem is increased, that he is made proud – so that he feels superior to other people who have remained under the spell of sensuality. Moses, as we know, conveyed to the Jews an exalted sense of being a chosen people. The dematerialization of God brought a fresh and valuable contribution to their secret treasure. The Jews retained their inclination to intellectual interests. The nation's political misfortune taught it to value at its true worth the one possession that remained to it – its literature. Immediately after the destruction of the Temple in Jerusalem by Titus, the Rabbi Jochanan ben Zakkai asked permission to open the first Torah school in Jabneh.[2] From that time on, the Holy Writ and intellectual concern with it were what held the scattered people together.

This much is generally known and accepted. All I have wanted to do is to add that this characteristic development of the Jewish nature was introduced by the Mosaic prohibition against worshipping God in a visible form.

The pre-eminence given to intellectual labours throughout some two thousand years in the life of the Jewish people has, of course, had its effect. It has helped to check the brutality and the tendency to violence which are apt to appear where the development of muscular strength is the popular ideal. Harmony in the cultivation of intellectual and physical activity, such as was achieved by the Greek people, was denied to the

1. [It will have been seen that this last paragraph is untranslatable. '*Geist*' means not only 'intellect' but 'spirit' and 'soul'. '*Seele*' means 'soul', 'spirit' and 'mind'.]

2. [He is reputed to have escaped from Jerusalem in a coffin, and to have obtained leave from the Roman general to start a college for instruction in the Law (*Torah*) at a town near the sea to the west of Jerusalem (A.D. 70).]

Jews. In this dichotomy their decision was at least in favour of the worthier alternative.[1]

D

RENUNCIATION OF INSTINCT

It is not obvious and not immediately understandable why an advance in intellectuality, a set-back to sensuality, should raise the self-regard both of an individual and of a people. It seems to presuppose the existence of a definite standard of value and of some other person or agency which maintains it. For an explanation let us turn to an analogous case in individual psychology which we have come to understand.

If the id in a human being gives rise to an instinctual demand of an erotic or aggressive nature, the simplest and most natural thing is that the ego, which has the apparatus of thought and the muscular apparatus at its disposal, should satisfy the demand by an action. This satisfaction of the instinct is felt by the ego as pleasure, just as its non-satisfaction would undoubtedly have become a source of unpleasure. Now a case may arise in which the ego abstains from satisfying the instinct in view of external obstacles – namely, if it perceives that the action in question would provoke a serious danger to the ego. An abstention from satisfaction of this kind, the renunciation of an instinct on account of an external hindrance – or, as we say, in obedience to the reality principle – is not pleasurable in any event. The renunciation of the instinct would lead to a lasting tension owing to unpleasure, if it were not possible to reduce the strength of the instinct itself by displacements of energy. Instinctual renunciation can, however, also be imposed for other reasons, which we correctly describe as *internal*. In the course of an individual's development a portion of the inhibiting forces in the external world are internalized and an agency is constructed in the ego which confronts the rest of the ego in

1. [In the original version (see p. 358 *n*.): 'the alternative that was more significant culturally'.]

an observing, criticizing and prohibiting sense. We call this new agency the *super-ego*. Thenceforward the ego, before putting to work the instinctual satisfactions demanded by the id, has to take into account not merely the dangers of the external world but also the objections of the super-ego, and it will have all the more grounds for abstaining from satisfying the instinct. But whereas instinctual renunciation, when it is for external reasons, is *only* unpleasurable, when it is for internal reasons, in obedience to the super-ego, it has a different economic effect. In addition to the inevitable unpleasurable consequences it also brings the ego a yield of pleasure – a substitutive satisfaction, as it were. The ego feels elevated; it is proud of the instinctual renunciation, as though it were a valuable achievement. We believe we can understand the mechanism of this yield of pleasure. The super-ego is the successor and representative of the individual's parents (and educators) who had supervised his actions in the first period of his life; it carries on their functions almost unchanged. It keeps the ego in a permanent state of dependence and exercises a constant pressure on it. Just as in childhood, the ego is apprehensive about risking the love of its supreme master; it feels his approval as liberation and satisfaction and his reproaches as pangs of conscience. When the ego has brought the super-ego the sacrifice of an instinctual renunciation, it expects to be rewarded by receiving more love from it. The consciousness of deserving this love is felt by it as pride. At the time when the authority had not yet been internalized as a super-ego, there could be the same relation between the threat of loss of love and the claims of instinct: there was a feeling of security and satisfaction when one had achieved an instinctual renunciation out of love for one's parents. But this happy feeling could only assume the peculiar narcissistic character of pride after the authority had itself become a portion of the ego.

What help does this explanation of the satisfaction arising from instinctual renunciation give us towards understanding the processes that we want to study – the elevation of self-regard when there are advances in intellectuality? Very little, it seems.

The circumstances are quite different. There is no question of any instinctual renunciation and there is no second person or agency for whose sake the sacrifice is made. We shall soon feel doubts about this last assertion. It can be said that the great man is precisely the authority for whose sake the achievement is carried out; and, since the great man himself operates by virtue of his similarity to the father, there is no need to feel surprise if in group psychology the role of the super-ego falls to him. So that this would apply too to the man Moses in relation to the Jewish people. As regards the other point, however, no proper analogy can be established. An advance in intellectuality consists in deciding against direct sense-perception in favour of what are known as the higher intellectual processes – that is, memories, reflections and inferences. It consists, for instance, in deciding that paternity is more important than maternity, although it cannot, like the latter, be established by the evidence of the senses, and that for that reason the child should bear his father's name and be his heir. Or it declares that our God is the greatest and mightiest, although he is invisible like a gale of wind or like the soul. The rejection of a sexual or aggressive instinctual demand seems to be something quite different from this. Moreover, in the case of some advances in intellectuality – for instance, in the case of the victory of patriarchy – we cannot point to the authority which lays down the standard which is to be regarded as higher. It cannot in this case be the father, since he is only elevated into being an authority by the advance itself. Thus we are faced by the phenomenon that in the course of the development of humanity sensuality is gradually overpowered by intellectuality and that men feel proud and exalted by every such advance. But we are unable to say why this should be so. It further happens later on that intellectuality itself is overpowered by the very puzzling emotional phenomenon of faith. Here we have the celebrated 'credo quia absurdum',[1] and, once more, anyone who has succeeded in this regards it as a supreme achievement. Perhaps the common element in all these psychological situations is

1. [See footnote, p. 329 above.]

something else. Perhaps men simply pronounce that what is more difficult is higher, and their pride is merely their narcissism augmented by the consciousness of a difficulty overcome.

These are certainly not very fruitful considerations, and it might be thought that they have nothing at all to do with our inquiry as to what has determined the character of the Jewish people. That would only be to our advantage; but a certain connection with our problem is betrayed nevertheless by a fact which will concern us still more later on. The religion which began with the prohibition against making an image of God develops more and more in the course of centuries into a religion of instinctual renunciations. It is not that it would demand sexual *abstinence*; it is content with a marked restriction of sexual freedom. God, however, becomes entirely removed from sexuality and elevated into the ideal of ethical perfection. But ethics is a limitation of instinct. The Prophets are never tired of asseverating that God requires nothing other from his people than a just and virtuous conduct of life – that is, abstention from every instinctual satisfaction which is still condemned as vicious by our morality to-day as well. And even the demand for belief in him seems to take a second place in comparison with the seriousness of these ethical requirements. In this way instinctual renunciation seems to play a prominent part in the religion, even if it did not stand out in it from the first.

This is the place, however, for an interpolation, in order to avoid a misunderstanding. Even though it may seem that instinctual renunciation and the ethics founded on it do not form part of the essential content of religion, yet genetically they are most intimately connected with it. Totemism,[1] which is the earliest form of a religion which we recognize, carries with it, as indispensable constituents of its system, a number of commands and prohibitions which have no other significance, of course, than as instinctual renunciations: the worship of the totem, which includes a prohibition against injuring or killing it, exogamy – that is, renunciation of the

1. [Cf. above, p. 326 ff.]

passionately desired mothers and sisters in the horde – the granting of equal rights to all the members of the fraternal alliance – that is, restricting the inclination to violent rivalry among them. In these regulations are to be seen the first beginnings of a moral and social order. It does not escape us that two different motives are at work here. The first two prohibitions operate on the side of the father who has been got rid of: they carry on his will, as it were. The third command – the granting of equal rights to the allied brothers – disregards the father's will; it is justified by an appeal to the necessity for permanently maintaining the new order which succeeded the father's removal. Otherwise a relapse into the earlier state would have become inevitable. It is here that social commands diverge from the others which, as we might say, are derived directly from religious connections.

The essential part of this course of events is repeated in the abbreviated development of the human individual. Here, too, it is the authority of the child's parents – essentially, that of his autocratic father, threatening him with his power to punish – which calls on him for a renunciation of instinct and which decides for him what is to be allowed and what forbidden. Later on, when society and the super-ego have taken the parents' place, what in the child was called 'well-behaved' or 'naughty' is described as 'good' and 'evil' or 'virtuous' and 'vicious'. But it is still always the same thing – instinctual renunciation under the pressure of the authority which replaces and prolongs the father.

A further depth is added to these discoveries when we examine the remarkable concept of holiness. What is it really that seems to us 'holy' in preference to other things that we value highly and recognize as important?[1] On the one hand, the connection of holiness or sacredness with what is religious

1. [The word *'heilig'*, here translated either 'sacred' or 'holy', was discussed by Freud somewhat differently in his paper on 'civilized' sexual morality (1908*d*), *P.F.L.*, **12**, 39. The word *'heilig'* appears also, as applied to persons in the sense of 'saintly', in *Civilization and its Discontents* (1930*a*), ibid., **12**, 318, where the wider aspects of the topic are also considered.]

is unmistakable. It is insisted upon emphatically: everything religious is sacred, it is the very core of sacredness. On the other hand, our judgement is disturbed by the numerous attempts to apply the characteristic of sacredness to so many other things – people, institutions, functions – which have little to do with religion. These efforts serve obvious tendentious purposes. Let us start from the prohibitive character which is so firmly attached to sacredness. What is sacred is obviously something that may not be touched. A sacred prohibition has a very strong emotional tone but has in fact no rational basis. For why, for instance, should incest with a daughter or sister be such a specially serious crime – so much worse than any other sexual intercourse?[1] If we ask for a rational basis we shall certainly be told that all our feelings rebel against it. But that only means that people regard the prohibition as self-evident and that they know of no basis for it.

It is easy enough to show the futility of such an explanation. What is represented as insulting our most sacred feelings was a universal custom – we might call it a usage made holy – among the ruling families of the Ancient Egyptians and of other early peoples. It was taken as a matter of course that a Pharaoh should take his sister as his first and principal wife; and the later successors of the Pharaohs, the Greek Ptolemies, did not hesitate to follow that model. We are compelled, rather, to a realization that incest – in this instance between a brother and sister – was a privilege which was withheld from common mortals and reserved to kings as representatives of the gods, just as similarly, no objection was taken to incestuous relations of this kind in the world of Greek and Germanic legend. It may be suspected that the scrupulous insistence upon equality of birth among our aristocracy is a relic of this ancient privilege and it can be established that, as a result of the inbreeding practised over so many generations in the highest social strata, Europe is ruled to-day by members of a single family and a second one.

1. [The 'horror of incest' is the subject of the first Essay in *Totem and Taboo* (1912–13), p. 53 ff. above.]

Evidence of incest among gods, kings and heroes helps us as well to deal with another attempt, which seeks to explain the horror of incest biologically and to trace it to an obscure knowledge of the damage done by inbreeding. It is not even certain, however, that there *is* any danger of damage from inbreeding – let alone that primitive peoples can have recognized it and reacted against it. The uncertainty in defining the permitted and forbidden degrees of kinship argues just as little in favour of the hypothesis that a 'natural feeling' is the ultimate basis of the horror of incest.

Our construction of prehistory forces us to another explanation. The command in favour of exogamy, of which the horror of incest is the negative expression, was a product of the will of the father and carried this will on after he had been removed. Hence come the strength of its emotional tone and the impossibility of finding a rational basis for it – that is, its sacredness. We confidently expect that an investigation of all the other cases of a sacred prohibition would lead to the same conclusion as in that of the horror of incest: that what is sacred was originally nothing other than the prolongation of the will of the primal father. This would also throw light on the hitherto incomprehensible ambivalence of the words which express the concept of sacredness. It is the ambivalence which in general dominates the relation to the father. [The Latin] *'sacer'* means not only 'sacred', 'consecrated', but also something that we can only translate as 'infamous', 'detestable' (e.g. *'auri sacra fames'*).[1] But the father's will was not only something which one might not touch, which one had to hold in high respect, but also something one trembled before, because it demanded a painful instinctual renunciation. When we hear that Moses made his people holy [p. 268] by introducing the custom of circumcision we now understand the deep meaning of that assertion. Circumcision is the symbolic substitute for the castration which the primal father once inflicted upon his sons in the plenitude of his absolute power, and whoever accepted that symbol was

1. ['Execrable hunger for gold.' Virgil, *Aeneid*, VI, 816. Cf. 'The Antithetical Meaning of Primal Words' (1910*e*).]

showing by it that he was prepared to submit to the father's will, even if it imposed the most painful sacrifice on him.

Going back to ethics, we may say in conclusion that a part of its precepts are justified rationally by the necessity for delimiting the rights of society as against the individual, the rights of the individual as against society and those of individuals as against one another. But what seems to us so grandiose about ethics, so mysterious and, in a mystical fashion, so self-evident, owes these characteristics to its connection with religion, its origin from the will of the father.

E

WHAT IS TRUE IN RELIGION

How enviable, to those of us who are poor in faith, do those inquirers seem who are convinced of the existence of a Supreme Being! To that great Spirit the world offers no problems, for he himself created all its institutions. How comprehensive, how exhaustive and how definitive are the doctrines of believers compared with the laborious, paltry and fragmentary attempts at explanation which are the most we are able to achieve! The divine Spirit, which is itself the ideal of ethical perfection, has planted in men the knowledge of that ideal and, at the same time, the urge to assimilate their own nature to it. They perceive directly what is higher and nobler and what is lower and more base. Their affective life is regulated in accordance with their distance from the ideal at any moment. When they approach to it – at their perihelion, as it were – they are brought high satisfaction; when, at their aphelion, they have become remote from it, the punishment is severe unpleasure. All of this is laid down so simply and so unshakably. We can only regret that certain experiences in life and observations in the world make it impossible for us to accept the premiss of the existence of such a Supreme Being. As though the world had not riddles enough, we are set the new problem of understanding how these other people have been able to acquire their belief in the

Divine Being and whence that belief obtained its immense power, which overwhelms 'reason and science'.[1]

Let us return to the more modest problem which has occupied us hitherto. We wanted to explain the origin of the special character of the Jewish people, a character which is probably what has made their survival to the present day possible. We found that the man Moses impressed this character on them by giving them a religion which increased their self-esteem so much that they thought themselves superior to all other peoples. Thereafter they survived by keeping apart from others. Mixtures of blood interfered little with this, since what held them together was an ideal factor, the possession in common of certain intellectual and emotional wealth. The religion of Moses led to this result because (1) it allowed the people to take a share in the grandeur of a new idea of God, (2) it asserted that this people had been chosen by this great God and were destined to receive evidences of his special favour and (3) it forced upon the people an advance in intellectuality which, important enough in itself, opened the way, in addition, to the appreciation of intellectual work and to further renunciations of instinct.

This is what we have arrived at. And, though we do not wish to take back any of it, we cannot hide from ourselves that it is somehow or other unsatisfying. The cause does not, so to speak, match the effect; the fact that we want to explain seems to be of a different order of magnitude from everything by which we explain it. May it be that all the investigations we have so far made have not uncovered the whole of the motivation but only a certain superficial layer, and that behind it another very important factor awaits discovery? In view of the extraordinary complexity of all causation in life and history, something of the sort was to be expected.

Access to this deeper motivation would seem to be given at a particular point in the previous discussions. The religion of Moses did not produce its effects immediately but in a

1. [An allusion to an ironical remark by Mephistopheles in *Faust*, Part I, Scene 4.]

remarkably indirect manner. This does not mean to say simply that it did not work at once, that it took long periods of time, hundreds of years, to deploy its full effect, for that is self-evident when it is a question of the imprinting of a people's character. But the restriction relates to a fact which we have derived from the history of the Jewish religion or, if you like, have introduced into it. We have said that after a certain time the Jewish people rejected the religion of Moses once more – whether they did so completely or retained some of its precepts we cannot guess. If we suppose that in the long period of the seizure of Canaan and the struggle with the peoples inhabiting it the Yahweh religion did not differ essentially from the worship of the other Baalim [p. 312], we shall be on historical ground in spite of all the later tendentious efforts to throw a veil over this shaming state of things.

The religion of Moses, however, had not disappeared without leaving a trace. A kind of memory of it had survived, obscured and distorted, supported, perhaps, among individual members of the priestly caste by ancient records. And it was this tradition of a great past which continued to work in the background, as it were, which gradually gained more and more power over men's minds, and which finally succeeded in transforming the god Yahweh into the god of Moses and in calling back to life the religion of Moses which had been established and then abandoned long centuries earlier.

In a previous portion of this study [Sections C, D and E of Part I, p. 314 ff.] we have considered what assumption seems inevitable if we are to find such an achievement of tradition comprehensible.

F

THE RETURN OF THE REPRESSED

There are a quantity of similar processes among those which the analytic investigation of mental life has taught us to know. Some of them are described as pathological, others are counted among the diversity of normal events. But that matters little, since the boundaries between the two [the pathological and the normal] are not sharply drawn, their mechanisms are to a large extent the same, and it is of far more importance whether the alterations in question take place in the ego itself or whether they confront it as alien to it – in which case they are known as symptoms.

From the mass of material I shall first bring forward some cases which relate to the development of character. Take, for instance, the girl who has reached a state of the most decided opposition to her mother. She has cultivated all those characteristics which she has seen that her mother lacked, and has avoided everything that reminded her of her mother. We may supplement this by saying that in her early years, like every female child, she adopted an identification with her mother and that she is now rebelling against this energetically. But when this girl marries and herself becomes a wife and a mother, we need not be surprised to find that she begins to grow more and more like the mother to whom she was so antagonistic, till finally the identification with her which she surmounted is unmistakably re-established. The same thing happens too with boys; and even the great Goethe, who in the period of his genius certainly looked down upon his unbending and pedantic father, in his old age developed traits which formed a part of his father's character. The outcome can become even more striking when the contrast between the two personalities is sharper. A young man whose fate it was to grow up beside a worthless father, began by developing, in defiance of him, into a capable, trustworthy and honourable person. In the prime of life his character was reversed, and thenceforward he behaved as though he had taken this same father as a model. In order not to miss the connection with our theme, we must keep in mind the fact that at the beginning of such a course of events there is always an identification with the father in early child-hood. This is afterwards repudiated, and even overcompensated, but in the end establishes itself once more.

It has long since become common knowledge that the

experiences of a person's first five years exercise a determining effect on his life, which nothing later can withstand. Much that deserves knowing might be said about the way in which these early impressions maintain themselves against any influences in more mature periods of life – but it would not be relevant here. It may, however, be less well known that the strongest compulsive influence arises from impressions which impinge upon a child at a time when we would have to regard his psychical apparatus as not yet completely receptive. The fact itself cannot be doubted; but it is so puzzling that we may make it more comprehensible by comparing it with a photographic exposure which can be developed after any interval of time and transformed into a picture. I am nevertheless glad to point out that this uncomfortable discovery of ours has been anticipated by an imaginative writer, with the boldness that is permitted to poets. E. T. A. Hoffmann used to trace back the wealth of figures that put themselves at his disposal for his creative writings to the changing images and impressions which he had experienced during a journey of some weeks in a post-chaise while he was still an infant at his mother's breast. What children have experienced at the age of two and have not understood, need never be remembered by them except in dreams; they may only come to know of it through psychoanalytic treatment. But at some later time it will break into their life with obsessional impulses, it will govern their actions, it will decide their sympathies and antipathies and will quite often determine their choice of a love-object, for which it is so frequently impossible to find a rational basis. The two points at which these facts touch upon our problem cannot be mistaken.

First, there is the remoteness of the period concerned,[1] which

1. Here, too, a poet may speak. In order to explain his attachment, he imagines: 'Ach, du warst in abgelebten Zeiten meine Schwester oder meine Frau.' [Literally: 'Ah, you were, in a past life, my sister or my wife.' From a poem dedicated by Goethe to Charlotte von Stein: 'Warum gabst du uns die tiefen Blicke.']

is recognized here as the truly determining factor – in the special state of the memory, for instance, which in the case of these childhood experiences we classify as 'unconscious'. We expect to find an analogy in this with the state which we are seeking to attribute to tradition in the mental life of the people. It was not easy, to be sure, to introduce the idea of the unconscious into group psychology.

Regular contributions [secondly] are made to the phenomena we are in search of by the mechanisms which lead to the formation of neuroses. Here again the determining events occur in early childhood times, but here the stress is not upon the *time* but upon the process by which the event is met, the reaction to it. We can describe it schematically thus. As a result of the experience, an instinctual demand arises which calls for satisfaction. The ego refuses that satisfaction, either because it is paralysed by the magnitude of the demand or because it recognizes it as a danger. The former of these grounds is the more primary one; both of them amount to the avoidance of a situation of danger.[1] The ego fends off the danger by the process of repression. The instinctual impulse is in some way inhibited, its precipitating cause, with its attendant perceptions and ideas, is forgotten. This, however, is not the end of the process: the instinct has either retained its forces, or collects them again, or it is reawakened by some new precipitating cause. Thereupon it renews its demand, and, since the path to normal satisfaction remains closed to it by what we may call the scar of repression, somewhere, at a weak spot, it opens another path for itself to what is known as a substitutive satisfaction, which comes to light as a symptom, without the acquiescence of the ego, but also without its understanding. All the phenomena of the formation of symptoms may justly be described as the 'return of the repressed'.[2] Their distinguishing characteristic, however,

1. [For 'situations of danger' see *Inhibitions, Symptoms and Anxiety* (1926*d*), *P.F.L.*, **10**, 324 ff.]

2. [The term, as well as the concept, go back to the period of Freud's very early writings on psychoanalysis, between 1890 and 1900.]

is the far-reaching distortion to which the returning material has been subjected as compared with the original. It will perhaps be thought that this last group of facts has carried us too far away from the similarity with tradition. But we ought not to regret it if it has brought us close to the problems of the renunciation of instinct.

G

HISTORICAL TRUTH

We have undertaken all these psychological diversions in order to make it more credible to us that the religion of Moses only carried through its effect on the Jewish people as a tradition. It is likely that we have not achieved more than a certain degree of probability. Let us suppose, however, that we have succeeded in completely proving it. Even so the impression would remain that we have merely satisfied the *qualitative* factor of what was demanded, but not the quantitative one as well. There is an element of grandeur about everything to do with the origin of a religion, certainly including the Jewish one, and this is not matched by the explanations we have hitherto given. Some other factor must be involved to which there is little that is analogous and nothing that is of the same kind, something unique and something of the same order of magnitude as what has come out of it, as religion itself. [Cf. p. 371 above.]

Let us try to approach the subject from the opposite direction. We understand how a primitive man is in need of a god as creator of the universe, as chief of his clan, as personal protector. This god takes his position behind the dead fathers [of the clan], about whom tradition still has something to say. A man of later days, of our own day, behaves in the same way. He, too, remains childish and in need of protection, even when he is grown up; he thinks he cannot do without support from his god. That much is undisputed. But it is less easy to understand why there may only be a *single* god, why precisely the

376

advance from henotheism[1] to monotheism acquires an over-whelming significance. No doubt it is true, as we have explained [pp. 352 and 371], that the believer has a share in the greatness of his god; and the greater the god the more reliable is the protection which he can offer. But a god's power does not necessarily presuppose that he is the only one. Many peoples regarded it only as a glorification of their chief god if he ruled over other deities who were inferior to him, and they did not think it diminished his greatness if there were other gods besides him. No doubt, if this god became a universal one and had all countries and peoples as his concern, it meant a sacrifice of intimacy, too. It was as though one were sharing one's god with the foreigners and one had to make up for this by the proviso that one was preferred by him. We can make the further point that the idea of a single god means in itself an advance in intellectuality, but it is impossible to rate this point so highly.

Pious believers, however, know how to fill this obvious gap in motivation adequately. They say that the idea of a single god produced such an overwhelming effect on men because it is a portion of the eternal *truth* which, long concealed, came to light at last and was then bound to carry everyone along with it. We must admit that a factor of this kind is at last some-thing that matches the magnitude both of the subject and of its effect.

We too would like to accept this solution. But we are brought up by a doubt. The pious argument rests on an optimistic and idealistic premiss. It has not been possible to demonstrate in other connections that the human intellect has a particularly fine flair for the truth or that the human mind shows any special inclination for recognizing the truth. We have rather found, on the contrary, that our intellect very easily

1. [The word has not been very clearly defined. It is used to mean the belief of a community in one particular god of its own, and also to mean the belief in the dominance of one particular god over a hierarchy of other gods. In neither case does the belief imply that the god in question is the *only* god.]

goes astray without any warning, and that nothing is more easily believed by us than what, without reference to the truth, comes to meet our wishful illusions. We must for that reason add a reservation to our agreement. We too believe that the pious solution contains the truth – but the *historical* truth and not the *material* truth. And we assume the right to correct a certain distortion to which this truth has been subjected on its return. That is to say, we do not believe that there is a single great god to-day, but that in primaeval times there was a single person who was bound to appear huge at that time and who afterwards returned in men's memory elevated to divinity.

We had assumed that the religion of Moses was to begin with rejected and half-forgotten and afterwards broke through as a tradition. We are now assuming that this process was being repeated then for the second time. When Moses brought the people the idea of a single god, it was not a novelty but signified the revival of an experience in the primaeval ages of the human family which had long vanished from men's conscious memory. But it had been so important and had produced or paved the way for such deeply penetrating changes in men's life that we cannot avoid believing that it had left behind it in the human mind some permanent traces, which can be compared to a tradition.

We have learnt from the psychoanalysis of individuals that their earliest impressions, received at a time when the child was scarcely yet capable of speaking, produce at some time or another effects of a compulsive character without themselves being consciously remembered. We believe we have a right to make the same assumption about the earliest experiences of the whole of humanity. One of these effects would be the emergence of the idea of a single great god – an idea which must be recognized as a completely justified memory, though, it is true, one that has been distorted. An idea such as this has a compulsive character: it *must* be believed. To the extent to which it is distorted, it may be described as a *delusion*; in so far as it brings a return of the past, it must be called the *truth*. Psychiatric delusions, too, contain a small fragment of truth and the patient's conviction extends over from this truth on to its delusional wrappings.[1]

What follows, from here to the end, is a slightly modified repetition of the discussions in Part I [of the present (third) essay].

In 1912 I attempted in my *Totem and Taboo*, to reconstruct the ancient situation from which these consequences followed. In doing so, I made use of some theoretical ideas put forward by Darwin, Atkinson and particularly by Robertson Smith, and combined them with the findings and indications derived from psychoanalysis. From Darwin I borrowed the hypothesis that human beings originally lived in small hordes, each of which was under the despotic rule of an older male who appropriated all the females and castigated or disposed of the younger males, including his sons. From Atkinson I took, in continuation of this account, the idea that this patriarchal system ended in a rebellion by the sons, who banded together against their father, overcame him and devoured him in common. Basing myself on Robertson Smith's totem theory, I assumed that subsequently the father-horde gave place to the totemic

1. [The notion contained in this last sentence was expressed by Freud in very similar terms in the first edition of *The Psychopathology of Everyday Life* (1901*b*), *P.F.L.*, **5**, 318 and *n*. 2, as well as in *Gradiva* (1907*a*). The matter was investigated more deeply in Section B of 'Some Neurotic Mechanisms in Jealousy, Paranoia and Homosexuality' (1922*b*), ibid., **10**, 199 ff.; but the general idea can be followed much further back to passages in the Fliess correspondence dating from 24 January 1897 and 1 January 1896 (Freud, 1950*a*, Letter 57 and Draft K). The related distinction drawn in this section between 'historical' and 'material' truth is of much more recent origin. The idea appears towards the end of *Totem and Taboo* (1912–13), p. 224 ff. above; there may be a hint of it in *The Future of an Illusion* (1927*c*), *P.F.L.*, **12**, and there is a more definite allusion to it in connection with myths in the paper on the acquisition of fire (1932*a*), p. 233 ff. above. But the first explicit reference is in the 'Postscript' (1935*a*) to the *Autobiographical Study*. The subject has already been touched upon above (pp. 299 and 329). – For a reference to a possibly analogous distinction between psychical and external reality, see p. 319 above.]

brother-clan. In order to be able to live in peace with one another, the victorious brothers renounced the women on whose account they had, after all, killed their father, and instituted exogamy. The power of fathers was broken and the families were organized as a matriarchy. The ambivalent emotional attitude of the sons to their father remained in force during the whole of later development. A particular animal was set up in the father's place as a totem. It was regarded as ancestor and protective spirit and might not be injured or killed. But once a year the whole male community came together to a ceremonial meal at which the totem animal (worshipped at all other times) was torn to pieces and devoured in common. No one might absent himself from this meal: it was the ceremonial repetition of the killing of the father, with which social order, moral laws and religion had taken their start. The conformity between Robertson Smith's totem meal and the Christian Lord's Supper had struck a number of writers before me. [See above, pp. 217 and 325–8.]

To this day I hold firmly to this construction. I have repeatedly met with violent reproaches for not having altered my opinions in later editions of my book in spite of the fact that more recent ethnologists have unanimously rejected Robertson Smith's hypotheses and have in part brought forward other, totally divergent theories. I may say in reply that these ostensible advances are well known to me. But I have not been convinced either of the correctness of these innovations or of Robertson Smith's errors. A denial is not a refutation, an innovation is not necessarily an advance. Above all, however, I am not an ethnologist but a psychoanalyst. I had a right to take out of ethnological literature what I might need for the work of analysis. The writings of Robertson Smith – a man of genius – have given me valuable points of contact with the psychological material of analysis and indications for its employment. I have never found myself on common ground with his opponents.

H

The Historical Development

I cannot here repeat the contents of *Totem and Taboo* in greater detail. But I must undertake to fill up the long stretch between that hypothetical primaeval period and the victory of monotheism in historical times. After the institution of the combination of brother-clan, matriarchy, exogamy and totemism, a development began which must be described as a slow 'return of the repressed'. Here I am not using the term 'the repressed' in its proper sense. What is in question is something in a people's life which is past, lost to view, superseded and which we venture to compare with what is repressed in the mental life of an individual. We cannot at first sight say in what form this past existed during the time of its eclipse. It is not easy for us to carry over the concepts of individual psychology into group psychology; and I do not think we gain anything by introducing the concept of a 'collective' unconscious. The content of the unconscious, indeed, is in any case a collective, universal property of mankind. For the moment, then, we will make shift with the use of analogies. The processes in the life of peoples which we are studying here are very similar to those familiar to us in psychopathology, but nevertheless not quite the same. We must finally make up our minds to adopt the hypothesis that the psychical precipitates of the primaeval period became inherited property which, in each fresh generation, called not for acquisition but only for awakening. In this we have in mind the example of what is certainly the 'innate' symbolism which derives from the period of the development of speech, which is familiar to all children without their being instructed, and which is the same among all peoples despite their different languages. What we may perhaps still lack in certainty here is made good by other products of psycho-analytic research. We find that in a number of important relations our children react, not in a manner corresponding to their own experience, but instinctively, like the animals, in a manner that is only explicable as phylogenetic acquisition.[1]

The return of the repressed took place slowly and certainly not spontaneously but under the influence of all the changes in conditions of life which fill the history of human civilization. I cannot give a survey here of these determinants nor more than a fragmentary enumeration of the stages of this return. The father once more became the head of the family, but was not by any means so absolute as the father of the primal horde had been. The totem animal was replaced by a god in a series of transitions which are still very plain. To begin with, the god in human form still bore an animal's head; later he turned himself by preference into that particular animal, and afterwards it became sacred to him and was his favourite attendant; or he killed the animal and himself bore its name as an epithet. Between the totem animal and the god, the hero emerged, often as a preliminary step towards deification. The idea of a supreme deity seems to have started early, at first only in a shadowy manner without intruding into men's daily interests. As tribes and peoples came together into larger unities, the gods too organized themselves into families and into hierarchies. One of them was often elevated into being supreme lord over gods and men. After this, the further step was hesitatingly taken of paying respect to only one god, and finally the decision was taken of giving all power to a single god and of tolerating no other gods beside him. Only thus was it that the supremacy of the father of the primal horde was re-established and that the emotions relating to him could be repeated.

The first effect of meeting the being who had so long been missed and longed for was overwhelming and was like the traditional description of the law-giving from Mount Sinai. Admiration, awe and thankfulness for having found grace in his eyes – the religion of Moses knew none but these positive feelings towards the father-god. The conviction of his irresisti-

1. [What Freud has in mind here are no doubt chiefly the 'primal phantasies'. See the Editor's footnote on the 'archaic heritage' (p. 347 above). The word translated here 'instinctively' is *'instinktmässig'*. Cf. p. 346 above.]

bility, the submission to his will, could not have been more unquestioning in the helpless and intimidated son of the father of the horde – indeed those feelings only become fully intelligible when they are transposed into the primitive and infantile setting. A child's emotional impulses are intensely and inexhaustibly deep to a degree quite other than those of an adult; only religious ecstasy can bring them back. A rapture of devotion to God was thus the first reaction to the return of the great father.

The direction to be taken by this father-religion was in this way laid down for all time. Yet this did not bring its develop-ment to an end. Ambivalence is a part of the essence of the relation to the father: in the course of time the hostility too could not fail to stir, which had once driven the sons into killing their admired and dreaded father. There was no place in the framework of the religion of Moses for a direct expression of the murderous hatred of the father. All that could come to light was a mighty reaction against it – a sense of guilt on account of that hostility, a bad conscience for having sinned against God and for not ceasing to sin. This sense of guilt, which was uninterruptedly kept awake by the Prophets, and which soon formed an essential part of the religious system, had yet another superficial motivation, which neatly disguised its true origin. Things were going badly for the people; the hopes resting on the favour of God failed in fulfilment; it was not easy to maintain the illusion, loved above all else, of being God's chosen people. If they wished to avoid renouncing that happi-ness, a sense of guilt on account of their own sinfulness offered a welcome means of exculpating God: they deserved no better than to be punished by him since they had not obeyed his commandments. And, driven by the need to satisfy this sense of guilt, which was insatiable and came from sources so much deeper, they must make those commandments grow ever stricter, more meticulous and even more trivial. In a fresh rapture of moral asceticism they imposed more and more new instinctual renunciations on themselves and in that way reached – in doctrine and precept, at least – ethical heights which had remained inaccessible to the other peoples of antiquity. Many Jews regard this attainment of ethical heights as the second main characteristic and the second great achievement of their religion. The way in which it was connected with the first one – the idea of a single god – should be plain from our remarks. These ethical ideas cannot, however, disavow their origin from the sense of guilt felt on account of a suppressed hostility to God. They possess the characteristic – uncompleted and incapable of completion – of obsessional neurotic reaction-formations; we can guess, too, that they serve the secret purposes of punishment.

The further development takes us beyond Judaism. The remainder of what returned from the tragic drama of the primal father was no longer reconcilable in any way with the religion of Moses. The sense of guilt of those days was very far from being any longer restricted to the Jewish people; it had caught hold of all the Mediterranean peoples as a dull *malaise*, a premonition of calamity for which no one could suggest a reason. Historians of our day speak of an ageing of ancient civilization, but I suspect that they have only grasped accidental and contributory causes of this depressed mood of the peoples. The elucidation of this situation of depression sprang from Jewry. Irrespectively of all the approximations and preparations in the surrounding world, it was after all a Jewish man, Saul of Tarsus (who, as a Roman citizen, called himself Paul), in whose spirit the realization first emerged: 'the reason we are so unhappy is that we have killed God the father.' And it is entirely understandable that he could only grasp this piece of truth in the delusional disguise of the glad tidings: 'we are freed from all guilt since one of us has sacrificed his life to absolve us.' In this formula the killing of God was of course not mentioned, but a crime that had to be atoned by the sacrifice of a victim could only have been a murder. And the inter-mediate step between the delusion and the historical truth was provided by the assurance that the victim of the sacrifice had been God's son. With the strength which it derived from the source of historical truth, this new faith overthrew every obstacle. The blissful sense of being chosen was replaced by the liberating sense of redemption. But the fact of the parricide, in returning to the memory of mankind, had to overcome greater resistances than the other fact, which had constituted the subject-matter of monotheism;[1] it was also obliged to submit to a more powerful distortion. The unnameable crime was replaced by the hypothesis of what must be described as a shadowy 'original sin'.

Original sin and redemption by the sacrifice of a victim became the foundation stones of the new religion founded by Paul. It must remain uncertain whether there was a ringleader and instigator to the murder among the band of brothers who rebelled against the primal father, or whether such a figure was created later by the imagination of creative artists in order to turn themselves into heroes, and was then introduced into the tradition. After the Christian doctrine had burst the frame-work of Judaism, it took up components from many other sources, renounced a number of characteristics of pure mono-theism and adapted itself in many details to the rituals of the other Mediterranean peoples. It was as though Egypt was taking vengeance once more on the heirs of Akhenaten. It is worth noticing how the new religion dealt with the ancient ambivalence in the relation to the father. Its main content was, it is true, reconciliation with God the Father, atonement for the crime committed against him; but the other side of the emotional relation showed itself in the fact that the son, who had taken the atonement on himself, became a god himself beside the father and, actually, in place of the father. Christianity, having arisen out of a father-religion, became a son-religion. It has not escaped the fate of having to get rid of the father.

Only a portion of the Jewish people accepted the new doctrine. Those who refused are still called Jews to-day. Owing to this cleavage, they have become even more sharply divided from other peoples than before. They were obliged to hear the new religious community (which, besides Jews, included

1. [Namely, the fact of the existence of the primal father.]

Egyptians, Greeks, Syrians, Romans and eventually Germans) reproach them with having murdered God. In full, this reproach would run as follows: 'They will not accept it as true that they murdered God, whereas we admit it and have been cleansed of that guilt.' It is easy therefore to see how much truth lies behind this reproach. A special inquiry would be called for to discover why it has been impossible for the Jews to join in this forward step which was implied, in spite of all its distortions, by the admission of having murdered God. In a certain sense they have in that way taken a tragic load of guilt on themselves; they have been made to pay heavy penance for it.

Our investigation may perhaps have thrown a little light on the question of how the Jewish people have acquired the characteristics which distinguish them. Less light has been thrown on the problem of how it is that they have been able to retain their individuality till the present day. But exhaustive answers to such riddles cannot in fairness be either demanded or expected. A contribution, to be judged in view of the limitations which I mentioned at the start [p. 351], is all that I can offer.

BIBLIOGRAPHY
AND AUTHOR INDEX

Titles of books and periodicals are in italics, titles of papers are in inverted commas. Abbreviations are in accordance with the *World List of Scientific Periodicals* (London, 1963–5). Further abbreviations used in this volume will be found in the List at the end of this bibliography. Numerals in bold type refer to volumes, ordinary numerals refer to pages. The figures in round brackets at the end of each entry indicate the page or pages of this volume on which the work in question is mentioned.

In the case of the Freud entries, only English translations are given. The initial dates are those of the German, or other, original publications. (The date of writing is added in square brackets where it differs from the latter.) The letters attached to the dates of publication are in accordance with the corresponding entries in the complete bibliography of Freud's writings included in Volume 24 of the *Standard Edition*. Details of the original publication, including the original German (or other) title, are given in the editorial introduction to each work included in the *Pelican Freud Library*.

For non-technical authors, and for technical authors where no specific work is mentioned, see the General Index.

ABRAHAM, K. (1911) 'Über die determinierende Kraft des Namens', *Zentbl. Psychoanal.*, **2**, 133. (112)
[*Trans.*: 'On the Determining Power of Names', *Clinical Papers and Essays on Psycho-Analysis*, London and New York, 1955, Part I: Clinical Papers, IV.]
(1914) 'Über Einschränkungen und Umwandlungen der Schaulust bei den Psychoneurotikern', *Jb. Psychoanal.*, **6**, 25. (188)
[*Trans.*: 'Restrictions and Transformations of Scoptophilia in Psycho-Neurotics', *Selected Papers*, London, 1927; New York, 1953, Chap. IX.]
(1965) With FREUD, S. *See* FREUD, S. (1965a)

ADLER, A. (1910) 'Der psychische Hermaphroditismus im Leben und in der Neurose', *Fortschr. Med.*, **28**, 486. (148)

ANDREAS-SALOMÉ, L., and FREUD, S. (1966) *See* FREUD, S. (1966*a*)

ATKINSON, J. J. (1903) *Primal Law*, London. Included in A. Lang, *Social Origins*, London. (185, 186, 203, 324)

AUERBACH, E. (1932, 1936) *Wüste und Gelobtes Land* (2 vols.), Berlin. (282, 283, 304)

BACHOFEN, J. J. (1861) *Das Mutterrecht*, Stuttgart. (206)

BASTIAN, A. (1874–5) *Die deutsche Expedition an der Loango-Küste* (2 vols.), Jena. (100, 102)

BATCHELOR, J. (1901) *The Ainu and their Folk-Lore*, London. (137)

BLEULER, E. (1910) 'Vortrag über Ambivalenz' (Berne), Report in *Zentbl. Psychoanal.*, **1**, 266. (83)

BLUMENTRITT, F. (1891) 'Über die Eingeborenen der Insel Palawan', *Globus*, **59**, 181. (109)

BOAS, F. (1888) 'The Central Eskimo', *Sixth Ann. Rep. Bur. Amer. Ethn.*, 399. (114)
    (1890) 'Second General Report on the Indians of British Columbia', *Report of Sixtieth Meeting of the British Association*, 562. (108)

BREASTED, J. H. (1906) *A History of Egypt*, London. (244, 258)
    (1934) *The Dawn of Conscience*, London. (244, 245, 258, 260, 261, 262, 291)

BREUER, J., and FREUD, S. (1893) *See* FREUD, S. (1893*a*)
    (1895) *See* FREUD, S. (1895*d*)

BROWN, W. (1845) *New Zealand and its Aborigines*, London. (97)

BUSCHAN, G. (ed.) (1922–6) *Illustrierte Völkerkunde* (2 vols. in 3), Stuttgart. (229)

Cambridge Ancient History (1924) (ed. J. B. Bury, S. A. Cook and F. E. Adcock), Vol. II, *The Egyptian and Hittite Empires to 1000 B.C.*, Cambridge. (Historical Egyptian Chapters by J. H. Breasted.) (258)

CAMERON, A. L. P. (1885) 'Notes on Some Tribes of New South Wales', *J. anthrop. Inst.*, **14**, 344. (57)

CODRINGTON, R. H. (1891) *The Melanesians*, Oxford. (63, 65, 140)

CRAWLEY, E. (1902) *The Mystic Rose, A Study of Primitive Marriage*, London. (166, 167)

DARWIN, C. (1871) *The Descent of Man* (2 vols.), London. (186, 324)
    (1875) *The Variation of Animals and Plants under Domestication* (2 vols.), 2nd ed., London. (1st ed., 1868.) (184)

DOBRIZHOFFER, M. (1784) *Historia de Abiponibus* (3 vols.), Vienna. (111)

DORSEY, J. O. (1884) 'An Account of the War Customs of the Osages', *Amer. Nat.*, **18**, 113. (92)

DURKHEIM, E. (1898) 'La prohibition de l'inceste et ses origines', *Année sociolog.*, **1**, 1. (176, 180, 184)

　(1902) 'Sur le totémisme', *Année sociolog.*, **5**, 82. (176, 180)

　(1905) 'Sur l'organisation matrimoniale des sociétés australiennes', *Année sociolog.*, **8**, 118. (176, 180)

　(1912) *Les formes élémentaires de la vie religieuse: Le système totémique en Australie*, Paris. (172)

EDER, M. D. (1913) 'Augenträume', *Int. Z. ärztl. Psychoanal.*, **1**, 157. (190)

ELLIS, HAVELOCK (1914) *Studies in the Psychology of Sex*, Vol. IV: *Sexual Selection in Man*, Philadelphia. (182)

ELLIS, W. (1832–6) *Polynesian Researches*, 2nd ed. (4 vols.), London. (108)

Encyclopaedia Britannica (1910–11) 11th ed., Cambridge. (72, 134, 282)

ERLENMEYER, E. H. (1932) 'Notiz zur Freudschen Hypothese über die Zähmung des Feuers', *Imago*, **18**, 5. (229)

　[*Trans.*: 'Note on Freud's Hypothesis Regarding the Taming of Fire', *Int. J. Psycho-Analysis*, **13** (1932), 411.]

ERMAN, A. (1905) *Die Ägyptische Religion*, Berlin. (260, 269)

FERENCZI, S. (1913*a*) 'Ein kleiner Hahnemann', *Int. Z. ärztl. Psychoanal.*, **1**, 240. (190, 191, 215)

　[*Trans.*: 'A Little Chanticleer', *First Contributions to Psycho-Analysis*, London, 1952, Chap. IX.]

　(1913*b*) 'Zur Augensymbolik', *Int. Z. ärztl. Psychoanal.*, **1**, 161. (190)

　[*Trans.*: 'On Eye Symbolism', *First Contributions to Psycho-Analysis*, London, 1952, Chap. X (ii).]

FISON, L. (1885) 'The Nanga', *J. anthrop. Inst.*, **14**, 14. (63)

FISON, L., and HOWITT, A. W. (1880) *Kamilaroi and Kurnai*, Melbourne. (66, 170)

FRASER, J. (1892) *The Aborigines of New South Wales*, Sydney. (114)

FRAZER, J. G. (1910) *Totemism and Exogamy* (4 vols.), London. (53, 57, 63 ff., 161 ff., 166 ff., 173 ff., 176 ff., 180 ff., 184, 185, 192, 200)

　(1911*a*) *The Magic Art* (2 vols.) (*The Golden Bough*, 3rd ed., Part I), London. (97, 106, 136 ff., 140 ff., 211, 213, 232)

FRAZER, J. G. (*cont.*)

(1911*b*) *Taboo and the Perils of the Soul* (*The Golden Bough*, 3rd ed., Part II), London. (81, 90 f., 93 ff., 97–111, 113, 141, 156, 158)

(1911*c*) *The Dying God* (*The Golden Bough*, 3rd ed., Part III), London. (334)

(1912) *Spirits of the Corn and of the Wild* (2 vols.) (*The Golden Bough*, 3rd ed., Part V), London. (200, 212)

(1914) *Adonis, Attis, Osiris*, 3rd ed. (2 vols.) (*The Golden Bough*, 3rd ed., Part IV), London. (92)

FREUD, M. (1957) *Glory Reflected*, London. (21)

FREUD, S. (1891*b*) *On Aphasia*, London and New York, 1953. (14, 24)

(1893*a*) With BREUER, J., 'On the Psychical Mechanism of Hysterical Phenomena: Preliminary Communication', in *Studies on Hysteria*, Standard Ed., **2**, 3; *P.F.L.*, **3**, 53. (25, 34)

(1895*b* [1894]) 'On the Grounds for Detaching a Particular Syndrome from Neurasthenia under the Description "Anxiety Neurosis"', *Standard Ed.*, **3**, 87; *P.F.L.*, **10**, 31. (31, 34)

(1895*d*) With BREUER, J., *Studies on Hysteria*, London, 1956; *Standard Ed.*, **2**; *P.F.L.*, **3**. (25)

(1900*a*) *The Interpretation of Dreams*, London and New York, 1955; *Standard Ed.*, **4–5**; *P.F.L.*, **4**. (8, 21, 25, 39, 46, 118, 121, 213, 228, 233, 247, 249, 348)

(1901*b*) *The Psychopathology of Everyday Life*, Standard Ed., **6**; *P.F.L.*, **5**. (21, 25, 379)

(1905*c*) *Jokes and their Relation to the Unconscious*, London, 1960; *Standard Ed.*, **8**; *P.F.L.*, **6**. (112)

(1905*d*) *Three Essays on the Theory of Sexuality*, London, 1962; *Standard Ed.*, **7**, 125; *P.F.L.*, **7**, 31. (25, 70, 146, 228)

(1905*e* [1901]) 'Fragment of an Analysis of a Case of Hysteria', *Standard Ed.*, **7**, 3; *P.F.L.*, **8**, 29. (227, 228)

(1906*a* [1905]) 'My Views on the Part Played by Sexuality in the Aetiology of the Neuroses', *Standard Ed.*, **7**, 271; *P.F.L.*, **10**, 71. (34)

(1907*a*) *Delusions and Dreams in Jensen's 'Gradiva'*, Standard Ed., **9**, 3; *P.F.L.*, **14**. (379)

(1907*b*) 'Obsessive Actions and Religious Practices', *Standard Ed.*, **9**, 116; *P.F.L.*, **13**, 27. (231)

(1908*b*) 'Character and Anal Erotism', *Standard Ed.*, **9**, 169; *P.F.L.*, **7**, 205. (29, 228)

(1908c) 'On the Sexual Theories of Children', *Standard Ed.*, **9**, 207; *P.F.L.*, **7**, 183. (235, 317)

(1908d) '"Civilized" Sexual Morality and Modern Nervous Illness', *Standard Ed.*, **9**, 179; *P.F.L.*, **12**, 27. (41, 46)

(1909a [1908]) 'Some General Remarks on Hysterical Attacks', *Standard Ed.*, **9**, 229; *P.F.L.*, **10**, 95. (228)

(1909b) 'Analysis of a Phobia in a Five-Year-Old Boy', *Standard Ed.*, **10**, 3; *P.F.L.*, **8**, 165. (25, 189, 190, 205, 336)

(1909c) 'Family Romances', *Standard Ed.*, **9**, 237; *P.F.L.*, **7**, 217. (249)

(1909d) 'Notes upon a Case of Obsessional Neurosis', *Standard Ed.*, **10**, 155; *P.F.L.*, **9**, 31. (28, 40, 131, 143, 145, 149, 158)

(1910a [1909]) *Five Lectures on Psycho-Analysis, Standard Ed.*, **11**, 3; in *Two Short Accounts of Psycho-Analysis*, Penguin Books, Harmondsworth, 1962. (16, 25)

(1910c) *Leonardo da Vinci and a Memory of his Childhood, Standard Ed.*, **11**, 59; *P.F.L.*, **14**. (336)

(1910e) 'The Antithetical Meaning of Primal Words', *Standard Ed.*, **11**, 155. (123, 369)

(1911b) 'Formulations on the Two Principles of Mental Functioning', *Standard Ed.*, **12**, 215; *P.F.L.*, **11**, 29. (141, 144)

(1911c [1910]) 'Psycho-Analytic Notes on an Autobiographical Account of a Case of Paranoia (Dementia Paranoides)', *Standard Ed.*, **12**, 3; *P.F.L.*, **9**, 129. (25, 150)

(1912g) 'A Note on the Unconscious in Psycho-Analysis', *Standard Ed.*, **12**, 257; *P.F.L.*, **11**, 45. (152)

(1912–13) *Totem and Taboo*, London, 1950; New York, 1952; *Standard Ed.*, **13**, 1; *P.F.L.*, **13**, 43. (25, 28, 294, 296, 299, 324, 327, 347, 348, 360, 368, 379, 381)

(1913i) 'The Disposition to Obsessional Neurosis', *Standard Ed.*, **12**, 313; *P.F.L.*, **10**, 129. (29)

(1914c) 'On Narcissism: An Introduction', *Standard Ed.*, **14**, 69; *P.F.L.*, **11**, 59. (147)

(1914d) 'On the History of the Psycho-Analytic Movement', *Standard Ed.*, **14**, 3; *P.F.L.*, **15**. (25)

(1915b) 'Thoughts for the Times on War and Death', *Standard Ed.*, **14**, 275; *P.F.L.*, **12**, 57. (131)

(1915e) 'The Unconscious', *Standard Ed.*, **14**, 161; *P.F.L.*, **11**, 159. (38, 343)

(1916–17 [1915–17]) *Introductory Lectures on Psycho-Analysis*, New

FREUD, S. (*cont.*)

York, 1966; London, 1971; *Standard Ed.*, **15–16**; *P.F.L.*, **1**. (8, 26, 29, 36, 316, 317, 348)

(1917*c*) 'On Transformations of Instinct as Exemplified in Anal Erotism', *Standard Ed.*, **17**, 127; *P.F.L.*, **7**, 293. (29)

(1918*a* [1917]) 'The Taboo of Virginity', *Standard Ed.*, **11**, 193; *P.F.L.*, **7**, 261. (131)

(1918*b* [1914]) 'From the History of an Infantile Neurosis', *Standard Ed.*, **17**, 3; *P.F.L.*, **9**, 225. (26, 29, 227, 348)

(1919*e*) 'A Child is Being Beaten', *Standard Ed.*, **17**, 177; *P.F.L.*, **10**, 159. (348)

(1919*h*) 'The "Uncanny" ', *Standard Ed.*, **17**, 219; *P.F.L.*, **14**. (144)

(1920*g*) *Beyond the Pleasure Principle*, London, 1961; *Standard Ed.*, **18**, 7; *P.F.L.*, **11**, 269. (26, 342)

(1921*c*) *Group Psychology and the Analysis of the Ego*, London and New York, 1959; *Standard Ed.*, **18**, 69; *P.F.L.*, **12**, 91. (26, 131, 224, 241, 327)

(1922*b* [1921]) 'Some Neurotic Mechanisms in Jealousy, Paranoia and Homosexuality', *Standard Ed.*, **18**, 223; *P.F.L.*, **10**, 195. (379)

(1923*b*) *The Ego and the Id*, London and New York, 1962; *Standard Ed.*, **19**, 3; *P.F.L.*, **11**, 339. (26, 37, 340, 342, 348)

(1924*c*) 'The Economic Problem of Masochism', *Standard Ed.*, **19**, 157; *P.F.L.*, **11**, 409. (37)

(1924*d*) 'The Dissolution of the Oedipus Complex', *Standard Ed.*, **19**, 173; *P.F.L.*, **7**, 313. (228)

(1925*d* [1924]) *An Autobiographical Study*, *Standard Ed.*, **20**, 3; *P.F.L.*, **15**. (12, 335)

(1925*j*) 'Some Psychical Consequences of the Anatomical Distinction Between the Sexes', *Standard Ed.*, **19**, 243; *P.F.L.*, **7**, 323. (228)

(1926*d* [1925]) *Inhibitions, Symptoms and Anxiety*, London, 1960; *Standard Ed.*, **20**, 77; *P.F.L.*, **10**, 227. (26, 29, 126, 320, 375)

(1927*a*) 'Postscript to *The Question of Lay Analysis*', *Standard Ed.*, **20**, 251; *P.F.L.*, **15**. (12)

(1927*c*) *The Future of an Illusion*, London, 1962; *Standard Ed.*, **21**, 3; *P.F.L.*, **12**, 179. (26, 224, 329, 379)

(1930*a* [1929]) *Civilization and its Discontents*, New York, 1961; London, 1963; *Standard Ed.*, **21**, 59; *P.F.L.*, **12**, 243. (26, 37, 46, 126, 228, 229, 232, 335, 336)

(1932a) 'The Acquisition and Control of Fire', *Standard Ed.*, **22**, 185; *P.F.L.*, **13**, 225. (379)

(1933a [1932]) *New Introductory Lectures on Psycho-Analysis*, New York, 1966; London, 1971; *Standard Ed.*, **22**; *P.F.L.*, **2**. (8, 126, 228, 342)

(1935a) Postscript (1935) to *An Autobiographical Study*, new edition, London and New York; *Standard Ed.*, **20**, 71; *P.F.L.*, **15**. (12, 379)

(1937c) 'Analysis Terminable and Interminable', *Standard Ed.*, **23**, 211. (320)

(1939a [1934–8]) *Moses and Monotheism*, *Standard Ed.*, **23**, 3; *P.F.L.*, **13**, 237. (26, 224, 233)

(1940a [1938]) *An Outline of Psycho-Analysis*, New York, 1968; London, 1969; *Standard Ed.*, **23**, 141; *P.F.L.*, **15**. (26, 241, 320)

(1950a [1887–1902]) *The Origins of Psycho-Analysis*, London and New York, 1954. (Partly, including 'A Project for a Scientific Psychology', in *Standard Ed.*, **1**, 175.) (15, 23, 24, 25, 46, 228, 379)

(1960a) *Letters 1873–1939* (ed. E. L. Freud) (trans. T. and J. Stern), New York, 1960; London, 1961. (23, 240)

(1963a [1909–39]) *Psycho-Analysis and Faith. The Letters of Sigmund Freud and Oskar Pfister* (ed. H. Meng and E. L. Freud) (trans. E. Mosbacher), London and New York, 1963. (23)

(1965a [1907–26]) *A Psycho-Analytic Dialogue. The Letters of Sigmund Freud and Karl Abraham* (ed. H. C. Abraham and E. L. Freud) (trans. B. Marsh and H. C. Abraham), London and New York, 1965. (23)

(1966a [1912–36]) *Sigmund Freud and Lou Andreas-Salomé: Letters* (ed. E. Pfeiffer) (trans. W. and E. Robson-Scott), London and New York, 1972. (23)

(1968a [1927–39]) *The Letters of Sigmund Freud and Arnold Zweig* (ed. E. L. Freud) (trans. W. and E. Robson-Scott), London and New York, 1970. (23)

(1970a [1919–35]) *Sigmund Freud as a Consultant. Recollections of a Pioneer in Psychoanalysis* (Letters from Freud to Edoardo Weiss, including a Memoir and Commentaries by Weiss, with Foreword and Introduction by M. Grotjahn), New York, 1970. (23)

(1974a [1906–23]) *The Freud/Jung Letters* (ed. W. McGuire) (trans.

FREUD, S. (*cont.*)

R. Manheim and R. F. C. Hull), London and Princeton, N.J., 1974. (23)

GARDINER, SIR A. (1927) *Egyptian Grammar*, London. (2nd ed., 1950; 3rd ed., 1957.) (242)

GILLEN, F. J., and SPENCER, B. *See* SPENCER, B., and GILLEN, F. J.

GOLDENWEISER, A. (1910) 'Totemism, an Analytical Study', *J. Amer. Folk-Lore*, **23**, 179. (168)

GRAMBERG, J. S. G. (1872) 'Eene maand in de binnenlanden van Timor', *Verh. batavia Genoot.*, **36**, 161. (91)

GRESSMANN, H. (1913) *Mose und seine Zeit: ein Kommentar zu den Mose-Sagen*, Göttingen. (275, 280)

GUIS, LE PÈRE J. (1902) 'Les Canaques', *Missions Catholiques*, **34**, 208. (109)

HADDON, A. C. (1902) 'Presidential Address to the Anthropological Section', *Report of the Seventy-Second Meeting of the British Association*, 738. (173, 174)

HAEBERLIN, P. (1912) 'Sexualgespenster', *Sexualprobleme*, **8**, 96. (122)

HERLITZ, G., and KIRSCHNER, B. (eds.) (1930) *Jüdisches Lexikon*, **4**, Berlin. (244)

HERODOTUS *History*. (265, 269, 274)

[*Trans.* by A. D. Godley, Vol. I (Loeb Classical Library), London and New York, 1921.]

HOWITT, A. W. (1904) *The Native Tribes of South-East Australia*, London. (181)

HOWITT, A. W., and FISON, L. *See* FISON, L., and HOWITT, A. W.

HUBERT, H., and MAUSS, M. (1899) 'Essai sur la nature et la fonction du sacrifice', *Année sociolog.*, **2**, 29. (201)

(1904) 'Esquisse d'une théorie générale de la magie', *Année sociolog.*, **7**, 1. (135)

JEVONS, F. B. (1902) *An Introduction to the History of Religion*, 2nd ed., London. (1st ed., 1896.) (197)

JONES, E. (1953) *Sigmund Freud: Life and Work*, Vol. 1, London and New York. (23)

(1955) *Sigmund Freud: Life and Work*, Vol. 2, London and New York. (23, 47)

(1957) *Sigmund Freud: Life and Work*, Vol. 3, London and New York. (Page references are to the English edition.) (23, 227, 240, 307, 348)

JOSEPHUS, FLAVIUS *Antiquitates Judaicae.* (271)
[*Trans.: Ancient History of the Jews* (trans. W. Whiston), London, 1874; in *Josephus,* Vol. IV, Loeb Classical Library (trans. H. St J. Thackeray), London and New York, 1930.]

JOUSTRA, M. (1902) 'Het leven, de zeden en gewoonten der Bataks', *Meded. ned. Zend.,* **46**, 385. (64)

JUNG, C. G. (1906, 1909) *Diagnostische Assoziationsstudien* (2 vols.), Leipzig. (112)
[*Trans.: Studies in Word-Association,* London, 1918; New York, 1919.]

(1911–12) 'Wandlungen und Symbole der Libido', *Jb. psychoanalyt. psychopath. Forsch.,* **3**, 120, and **4**, 162; in book form, Leipzig and Vienna, 1912. (49, 208, 213)
[*Trans.: Psychology of the Unconscious,* New York, 1916; London, 1917.]

(1913) 'Versuch einer Darstellung der psychoanalytischen Theorie', *Jb. psychoanalyt. psychopath. Forsch.,* **5**, 307; in book form, Leipzig and Vienna, 1913. (49)
[*Trans.: The Theory of Psycho-Analysis,* New York, 1915.]

(1974) With FREUD, S. *See* FREUD, S. (1974*a*)

JUNOD, H. A. (1898) *Les Ba-Ronga,* Neuchâtel. (64)

KAEMPFER, E. (1727) *The History of Japan* (2 vols.), London. (100)

KEANE, A. H. (1899) *Man, Past and Present,* Cambridge. (169)

KIRSCHNER, B., and HERLITZ, G. *See* HERLITZ, G., and KIRSCHNER, B.

KLEINPAUL, R. (1898) *Die Lebendigen und die Toten in Volksglauben, Religion und Sage,* Leipzig. (114)

KRAFFT-EBING, R. VON (1867) *Beiträge zur Erkennung und richtigen forensischen Beurteilung krankhafter Gemütszustände für Ärzte, Richter und Verteidiger,* Erlangen. (31)

LABBÉ, P. (1903) *Un bagne russe, l'île de Sakhaline,* Paris. (138)

LAMBERT, LE PÈRE (1900) *Mœurs et superstitions des Néo-Calédoniens,* Nouméa. (63)

LANG, A. (1903) *Social Origins,* London. (169, 171, 176)
(1905) *The Secret of the Totem,* London. (55, 168, 169 ff., 176, 178, 180, 186, 187)
(1910–11) 'Totemism', *Encyclopaedia Britannica,* 11th ed., **27**, 79. (62)
(1911) 'Lord Avebury on Marriage, Totemism, and Religion', *Folk-Lore,* **22**, 402. (187)

LESLIE, D. (1875) *Among the Zulus and Amatongas*, 2nd ed., Edinburgh. (67)

LORENZ, E. (1931) 'Chaos und Ritus', *Imago*, **17**, 433. (229)

LOW, H. (1848) *Sarawak*, London. (192)

LÖWENFELD, L. (1904) *Die psychischen Zwangserscheinungen*, Wiesbaden. (31)

LOZANO, P. (1733) *Descripción corográfica del Gran Chaco Gualamba*, Cordova. (111)

LUBBOCK, J. (LORD AVEBURY) (1870) *The Origin of Civilisation*, London. (66, 170)

MCLENNAN, J. F. (1865) *Primitive Marriage*, Edinburgh. (Reprinted in same author's *Studies in Ancient History*, London, 1876.) (169, 181)

(1869–70) 'The Worship of Animals and Plants', *Fortnightly Rev.*, N.S., **6**, 407 and 562; N.S., **7**, 194. (Reprinted in same author's *Studies in Ancient History: Second Series*, London, 1896.) (169)

MANETHO *The History of Egypt*. (351)
[*Trans.*: In *Manetho*, Loeb Classical Library (trans. W. G. Waddell), London and Cambridge, Mass., 1940.]

MANN, T. (1929) 'Die Stellung Freuds in der modernen Geistesgeschichte', *Psychoanal. Beweg.*, **1**, 3. (47)
[*Trans.*: 'Freud's Position in the History of Modern Culture', *Psychoanal. Rev.*, **28** (1941), 92.]

MAORI, A PAKEHA [F. E. MANING] (1884) *Old New Zealand*, new ed., London. (97)

MARETT, R. R. (1900) 'Pre-Animistic Religion', *Folk-Lore*, **11**, 162. (148, 150)

MARILLIER, L. (1898) 'La place du totémisme dans l'évolution religieuse', *Rev. Hist. Relig.*, **37**, 204. (201)

MARINER, W. (1818) *An Account of the Natives of the Tonga Islands*, 2nd ed. (2 vols.), London. (1st ed., 1817.) (108)

MAUSS, M., and HUBERT, H. *See* HUBERT, H., and MAUSS, M.

MAX-MÜLLER, F. (1897) *Contributions to the Science of Mythology* (2 vols.), London. (169)

MEYER, E. (1905) 'Die Mosesagen und die Lewiten', *S.B. Akad. Wiss. Berl.* (Phil.-Hist. Kl.), **31**, 640. (252)

(1906) *Die Israeliten und ihre Nachbarstämme*, Halle. (250, 252, 272 ff., 277, 289)

MORGAN, L. H. (1877) *Ancient Society*, London. (59, 181)

MOUSTIER, M., and ZWEIFEL, J. *See* ZWEIFEL, J., and MOUSTIER, M.

MÜLLER, S. (1857) *Reizen en Onderzoekingen in den Indischen Archipel*, Amsterdam. (93)

PARKINSON, R. (1907) *Dreissig Jahre in der Südsee*, Stuttgart. (63)

PAULITSCHKE, P. (1893–6) *Ethnographie Nordost-Afrikas* (2 vols.), Berlin. (91)

PECKEL, P. G. (1908) 'Die Verwandtschaftsnamen des mittleren Neumecklenburg', *Anthropos*, **3**, 456. (63)

PFISTER, O., and FREUD, S. (1963) *See* FREUD, S. (1963*a*)

PIKLER, J., and SOMLÓ, F. (1900) *Der Ursprung des Totemismus*, Berlin. (169)

RANK, O. (1907) *Der Künstler. Ansätze zu einer Sexualpsychologie*, Leipzig and Vienna. (70)
[*Trans.: Art and the Artist: Creative Urge and Personality Development*, New York, 1932.]
(1909) *Der Mythus von der Geburt des Helden*, Leipzig and Vienna. (246, 250)
[*Trans.: The Myth of the Birth of the Hero*, New York, 1914.]
(1912) *Das Inzestmotiv in Dichtung und Sage*, Leipzig and Vienna. (70)
(1913) 'Eine noch nicht beschriebene Form des Ödipus-Traumes', *Int. Z. ärztl. Psychoanal.*, **I**, 151. (190)

REINACH, S. (1905–12) *Cultes, mythes et religions* (4 vols.), Paris. (135, 149, 160, 172, 216, 218)

REITLER, R. (1913) 'Zur Augensymbolik', *Int. Z. ärztl. Psychoanal.*, **I**, 159. (190)

RIBBE, C. (1903) *Zwei Jahre unter den Kannibalen der Salomo-Inseln*, Dresden. (65)

RIVERS, W. H. R. (1909) 'Totemism in Polynesia and Melanesia', *J. R. anthrop. Inst.*, **39**, 156. (177)

ROSE, H. J. (1928) *A Handbook of Greek Mythology*, London. (231)

ROTH, H. LING (1896) *The Natives of Sarawak and British North Borneo* (2 vols.), London. (138)

SCHAEFFER, A. (1930) 'Der Mensch und das Feuer', *Psychoanal. Beweg.*, **2**, 201. (229)

SCHREBER, D. P. (1903) *Denkwürdigkeiten eines Nervenkranken*, Leipzig. (150)
[*Trans.: Memoirs of My Nervous Illness* (trans. I. Macalpine and R. A. Hunter), London, 1955.]

SELLIN, E. (1922) *Mose und seine Bedeutung für die israelitisch-jüdische Religionsgeschichte*, Leipzig. (292)

SILBERER, H. (1909) 'Bericht über eine Methode, gewisse symbolische Halluzinations-Erscheinungen hervorzurufen und zu beobachten', *Jb. psychoanalyt. psychopath. Forsch.*, **1**, 513. (213)

SMITH, LINDON (1956) *Tombs, Temples and Ancient Art*, Oklahoma. (242)

SMITH, W. ROBERTSON (1894) *Lectures on the Religion of the Semites*, new [2nd] ed., London. (1st ed., 1889.) (193 ff., 201, 204, 209, 213, 326)

SOLOWEITSCHIK, M. (1930) Contribution to *Jüdisches Lexikon* (ed. Herlitz and Kirschner), Berlin, **4** (1), 303. (244)

SOMLÓ, F., and PIKLER, J. *See* PIKLER, J., and SOMLÓ, F.

SPENCER, B., and GILLEN, F. J. (1899) *The Native Tribes of Central Australia*, London. (60, 173)

SPENCER, H. (1870) 'The Origin of Animal Worship', *Fortnightly Rev.*, N.S., **7**, 535. (152, 170)

(1893) *The Principles of Sociology*, 3rd ed., Vol. I, London. (134, 170)

STEKEL, W. (1911) 'Die Verpflichtung des Namens', *Z. Psychother. med. Psychol.*, **3**, 110. (112)

STORFER, A. J. (1911) *Zur Sonderstellung des Vatermordes*, Leipzig and Vienna. (62)

TAYLOR, R. (1870) *Te Ika a Maui*, 2nd ed., London. (1st ed., 1855.) (81, 97, 114)

TEIT, J. A. (1900) *The Thompson Indians of British Columbia* (*Jessup North Pacific Expedition*, Vol. 1), New York. (109)

THOMAS, N. W. (1910–11a) 'Magic', *Encyclopaedia Britannica*, 11th ed., **17**, 304. (141)

(1910–11b) 'Taboo', *Encyclopaedia Britannica*, 11th ed., **26**, 337. (72)

TYLOR, E. B. (1889) 'A Method of Investigating the Development of Institutions', *J. anthrop. Inst.*, **18**, 245. (66)

(1891) *Primitive Culture*, 3rd ed. (2 vols.), London. (1st ed., 1871.) (132, 134, 136)

VOLZ, P. (1907) *Mose: ein Beitrag zur Untersuchung über die Ursprünge der Israelitischen Religion*, Tübingen. (293)

WEIGALL, A. (1922) *The Life and Times of Akhnaton*, new and revised ed., London. (1st ed., 1910.) (262)

WEISS, E., and FREUD, S. (1970) *See* FREUD, S. (1970a)

WESTERMARCK, E. (1901) *The History of Human Marriage*, 3rd ed., London. (1st ed., 1891.) (59)

(1906–8) *The Origin and Development of Moral Ideas* (2 vols.), London. (114, 115 ff., 182)

WILKEN, G. A. (1884) 'Het animisme bij de volken van den Indischen Archipel', *Ind. Gids*, **6** (Part I), 925. (138, 178)

WULFF, M. [M. WOOLF] (1912) 'Beiträge zur infantilen Sexualität', *Zentbl. Psychoanal.*, **2**, 6. (188)

WUNDT, W. (1906) *Völkerpsychologie*, Vol. 2, Part II: *Mythus und Religion*, Leipzig. (56, 71, 76 ff., 114, 121, 133 ff., 150)

(1912) *Elemente der Völkerpsychologie*, Leipzig. (159, 165, 179) [*Trans.: Elements of Folk Psychology*, New York and London, 1916.]

YAHUDA, A. S. (1929) *Die Sprache des Pentateuch in ihren Beziehungen zum Ägyptischen*, Berlin. (278, 283)

ZWEIFEL, J., and MOUSTIER, M. (1880) *Voyage aux sources du Niger*, Marseilles. (104)

ZWEIG, A., and FREUD, S. (1968) *See* FREUD, S. (1968*a*)

LIST OF ABBREVIATIONS

Gesammelte Schriften	=	Freud, *Gesammelte Schriften* (12 vols.), Vienna, 1924–34.
Gesammelte Werke	=	Freud, *Gesammelte Werke* (18 vols.), Vols. 1–17 London, 1940–52, Vol. 18 Frankfurt am Main, 1968. From 1960 the whole edition published by S. Fischer Verlag, Frankfurt am Main.
S.K.S.N.	=	Freud, *Sammlung kleiner Schriften zur Neurosenlehre* (5 vols.), Vienna, 1906–22.
Almanach 1933	=	*Almanach der Psychoanalyse 1933*, Internationaler Psychoanalytischer Verlag, Vienna, 1932.
Collected Papers	=	Freud, *Collected Papers* (5 vols.), London, 1924–50.
Standard Edition	=	*The Standard Edition of the Complete Psychological Works of Sigmund Freud* (24 vols.), Hogarth Press and The Institute of Psycho-Analysis, London, 1953–74.
P.F.L.	=	*Pelican Freud Library* (15 vols.), Penguin Books, Harmondsworth, from 1973.

GENERAL INDEX

This index includes the names of non-technical authors. It also includes the names of technical authors where no reference is made in the text to specific works. For reference to specific technical works, the Bibliography should be consulted.

MORE ABOUT PENGUINS, PELICANS, PEREGRINES AND PUFFINS

For further information about books available from Penguins please write to Dept EP, Penguin Books Ltd, Harmondsworth, Middlesex UB7 0DA.

In the U.S.A.: For a complete list of books available from Penguins in the United States write to Dept DG, Penguin Books, 299 Murray Hill Parkway, East Rutherford, New Jersey 07073.

In Canada: For a complete list of books available from Penguins in Canada write to Penguin Books Canada Limited, 2801 John Street, Markham, Ontario L3R 1B4.

In Australia: For a complete list of books available from Penguins in Australia write to the Marketing Department, Penguin Books Australia Ltd, P.O. Box 257, Ringwood, Victoria 3134.

In New Zealand: For a complete list of books available from Penguins in New Zealand write to the Marketing Department, Penguin Books (N.Z.) Ltd, Private Bag, Takapuna, Auckland 9.

In India: For a complete list of books available from Penguins in India write to Penguin Overseas Ltd, 706 Eros Apartments, 56 Nehru Place, New Delhi 110019.